HOLLYWOOD RENAISSANCE

Like many of our greatest writers in the last century, American film directors from the late 1930s to the early 1960s instigated a renaissance of original artistic works that helped reinvigorate and renew American culture. During a time of unprecedented danger from antidemocratic forces both abroad and at home, the most imaginative and creative films of these directors – John Ford, Frank Capra, Howard Hawks, Fred Zinnemann, Elia Kazan, George Stevens – articulated issues, themes, and realities at the core of the American experience.

In this provocative and original book, Sam Girgus offers a fresh look at films such as *The Searchers, Mr. Smith Goes to Washington, It's a Wonderful Life, High Noon,* and *On the Waterfront,* and shows how they are part of the cultural and historical debate that examines, structures, and questions what modern America means to its people, the world, and history.

Sam B. Girgus is Professor of English at Vanderbilt University. He has written or edited several books on American culture, literature, film, and thought, including *The Films of Woody Allen* (Cambridge, 1993), *Desire and the Political Unconscious in American Literature, The New Covenant: Jewish Writers and the American Idea,* and *The American Self: Myth, Ideology, and Popular Culture.*

HOLLYWOOD RENAISSANCE
THE CINEMA OF DEMOCRACY IN THE ERA
OF FORD, CAPRA, AND KAZAN

SAM B. GIRGUS

CAMBRIDGE
UNIVERSITY PRESS

PUBLISHED BY THE PRESS SYNDICATE OF THE UNIVERSITY OF CAMBRIDGE
The Pitt Building, Trumpington Street, Cambridge CB2 1RP, United Kingdom

CAMBRIDGE UNIVERSITY PRESS
The Edinburgh Building, Cambridge CB2 1RU, United Kingdom   http://www.cup.cam.ac.uk
40 West 20th Street, New York, NY 10011-4211, USA   http://www.cup.org
10 Stamford Road, Oakleigh, Melbourne 3166, Australia

© Sam B. Girgus 1998

First published 1998

Printed in the United States of America

Typeset in Sabon and Gill Sans [MG]

Library of Congress Cataloging-in-Publication Data
Girgus, Sam B., 1941–
    Hollywood Renaissance : the cinema of democracy in the era of Ford, Capra,
and Kazan / Sam B. Girgus.
        p.   cm.
    ISBN 0-521-62388-X (hb.) – ISBN 0-521-62552-1 (pbk.)
        1. Motion pictures – United States – History.   2. Motion picture producers and
directors – United States – Production and direction.   I. Title.
PN1993.5.U6G497   1998
791.43´0233´092273 – dc21   97–47090
                                                                                                              CIP

A catalog record for this book is available from the British Library

ISBN 0 521 62388 X hardback
ISBN 0 521 62552 1 paperback

To Arielle Gianni
Katya and Jeff
Meighan and Ali
Jennifer
and Scottie

CONTENTS

ILLUSTRATIONS

ACKNOWLEDGMENTS

They say it generally takes over a year and usually more than a hundred people to make a movie. It has taken many more people over many more years to help make this book even given its relatively moderate length.

Ideas and insights that were generated in and around my film classes at Vanderbilt University pervade this book. Given the close relationship between this book and those classes, I would like to emphasize the individual contribution of each of the students in those classes to this volume. Teaching and working with them has been a genuine privilege and pleasure. A special dedication to this book belongs to all of them for their participation in classes on America on film, desire and film, modernism and film. Although I cannot mention them all, I can name many who worked over the past six to seven years individually and in groups on special projects and problems related to the book. I list them according to their work, projects, year, and class, and I apologize in advance to any individuals that advancing age and incipient dotage have caused me to miss: Lori Flanagan, April Foscue, Kate Fullinwider, Chad Gervich, Brook Armand Rabinowitz, Abigail Smith, Dru Warner, Anthony Wilson. Dana Blanton, Scott Evans, Britt Farwick, Laura Garten, Will Geist, Julia Gleize, Kelly Haun, Teryn Luciani, Chris Neary, Nicholas Nicholas, Beach von Oesen, Susan Quest, Amanda Restifo, Kristi Boernhoeft Sands, Alexis Saunders. Jessica Allen, Lauren Petty Banta, Alison Barnes, John Bryan, Amanda Dake, Aimee DeSantis, Chris Gallagher, Brian Given, Aimee Gould, Lloyd Griffin, Suzie Grossman, Whitney Haas, Cakki Hogan, Shayna Davis Humphrey, Hilton Keith, Amy Kelly, Eileen Kennelly, Gina Licari, Taylor Mayes, Paige Sudderth Polishook, Lee Ruddick, Christa Sutphin, Lyndsay Wyngarden, Greg Xethalis, Jennifer Youngquist. Margie Berger, Chris Coffey, Keith Hayasaka, Doug Hilfiker, Peter Kaiser, Jim Kim, Andy Levinson, Lisa Siefker-Long, Tamsen Love, Hieu Nguyen, Liz Peeples, Matt Rowland, Monika Schramm, Lucy Roberts Smiles, James Stammer, Josephine Van Devender, Jan Zamojski. Nicole Alvino, Glen Carter, Amanda Costanzo, China Curtiss, Melanie Dayani, Courtney Dorn, John Gilmore, Jen Giordano, Alyson Goldman, Rowena Harbour,

Eric Johnson, Erik Kornfield, Jackie Leitzes, Doreen Linnemann, Oliver Luckett, Bailey Lynch, Katie McCall, Sean Malleus, "D. J." Meehan, Brook Reed, Rebecca Schmidt, Stacey Sward, Anastasia Telesetsky, Tracy Tosh, Charlotte Walker, Amanda White. The efforts of these students on various projects related to the book, as well as the involvement of their fellow students, have given this work special meaning to me. Without the commitment of all these students to class and to film studies, *Hollywood Renaissance* might never have been written at all.

Although such students seem to keep getting better and stronger, some things never change. So after so many years, I once again must thank some people who are very special to me for their continued support and encouragement. Joel Jones, Sacvan Bercovitch, and John Cawelti read all or parts of the manuscript. Their friendship and encouragement over the years on this and other endeavors have proven invaluable to me. Moreover, they each embody models and styles of scholarship and pedagogy that I still strive to emulate. Melinda Barlow and Scott Simmon were quite brilliant and constructive in their suggestions for ways to improve the book's argument and structure. Robert Mack's suggestions and recommendations concerning an important portion of the manucript were of critical significance to my progress. The commitment of Ann Cook Calhoun and Cecelia Tichi as well as Vereen Bell, Paul Elledge, and E. F. Infante to broadening our studies to include film and culture studies provided vital and meaningful encouragement to me. Aline Baehler and Thadious Davis helped me to rethink some basic concepts related to the volume. Colleagues in the Department of English continue to cultivate an environment for exciting intellectual and scholarly exchange. I would like to express my appreciation to Emerson Brown, Leonard Nathanson, Michael Kreyling, Teresa Goddu, Mark Schoenfield, Mark Wollaeger, Tony Earley, Dennis Kezar, and Jay Clayton. I especially wish to thank our great friend John Halperin for his insistence that, in spite of so much evidence to the contrary, it really is "a wonderful life."

Of all the other colleagues, associates, and friends who remain great sources of ideas and support, I especially would like to mention Emory Elliott, Ray Carney, Cristina Giorcelli, Tom Gregor, Volney Gay, Sam McSeveney, Ham and Arlette Hill, Mary Bess Whidden, Angela Boone, Peter White, Ed Hotaling, Bill and Susie Jones, Brian and Judy Jones, Gene and Susan Wright, Martha Matzke, Julie Jones, Jane Ritter, John Bomhoff, Derah Meyers, Gerry Calhoun, Carole and Keith Hagan, Camille Holt, Cathy, Charlie, and Madeline Simons, John and Martha Bomboy, Alix Schijman, Kaaren Allen, Linda and Pat Anderson, Harry and Marilyn Carey, Wendy Goldstein and Delbert McClinton, Cindy Hay and Bill Nagel. Continuing our old class discussions as special friends are Eddie O'Neil, Bob Johnstone, J. Delayney Barber, Phil Burnham, Michele Conte, Magda Zaborowska,

Zsuzsa Manness, Karen Stenard, Mike Snell, Boozer Downs, Ginia McPhearson, Cathy Mosteller, Sally Greene, Melissa Perkins, Cindy Lyle, Trey Harwell. On the road, great help was provided by Arthur and Gracie Forman, Steve Elwell, Steve Millhollon, Kim and Clay Walker, Paige Anderson, and Christopher and Carola Chataway.

I once again feel compelled to offer a kind of academic kaddish by attempting to honor the memory of my late teacher George Arms of the University of New Mexico. During many years as his student and colleague, I am not sure if we ever once discussed a film; different things mattered then. However, without his methodological model of rigor and discipline, sensitive critical analysis, and assiduous and economical writing, it would have been impossible for me to venture into new fields and areas for my teaching, research, and publication.

The enthusiastic endorsement of this project by my original editor at Cambridge University Press, Beatrice Rehl, was crucial to its development and completion. Her support and encouragement after reading my early work on the book was a great source of reassurance to me. I also wish to thank Anne Sanow at Cambridge, who assumed editorial responsibility for the project. Her creative intelligence, energy and commitment, and personal involvement gave the production phase of the book the feeling of genuine editorial partnership. Stephen Grimm was particularly patient, professional, and invariably personable, especially during the initial stages of production, while the expertise and professionalism of Michael Gnat, the copy/production editor, once again proved invaluable in completing the project.

In addition, Mary Corliss of the Film Stills Archive of the Museum of Modern Art in New York was quite helpful in locating illustrations. Special thanks also goes to the staff of the Department of English at Vanderbilt, beginning especially with Janis May and including Paul Burch, Sara Corbitt, Carolyn Levinson, and Dori Mikus. I also wish to thank the staff of the Learning Resource Center at Vanderbilt for their continued help and support, including Penny Peirce, Jaime Adams, Valerie Frierson, and Carol Beverley.

Finally, of course, I wish to recognize the help that my family has given me in completing this book. Much of this volume has been written, revised, and rewritten in the homes of my daughters and their families over various summers and holidays. During those times on the road, I repeatedly enlisted tactical and strategic support in the form of computers, printing, copying, video equipment, research, reading, space, and time from: Katya, Jeff, and Arielle Gianni Arrington; Meg and Ali Vafa, with important input from Danny, Negi, and Emily "Kimberly" Fowler; and Jennifer, the only real *cinéphile* in the group. (My mother continued to ask if I ever would write a book that anybody she knows would want to read.) I also wish to express my appreciation to Aida Scot-Smith and Audrey and Harris Shapiro, Ellen and Gene

Winter, Joan Girgus, Bryan Girgus. As always, my greatest thanks and appreciation go to Scottie, the eternal optimist, whose vision of Hollywood happy endings comes true every time she looks upon or ponders our children and their wonderful families.

John Halperin was right after all.

CHAPTER 1

ETHNICS AND ROUGHNECKS: THE MAKING OF THE HOLLYWOOD RENAISSANCE

From our distant perspective at the end of the twentieth century, the outcome of events from the Great Depression through the Second World War to the origins of the Cold War all seems inevitable and predestined: the midcentury triumph over fascism and totalitarianism in Europe and Asia; the dissolution of extremist parties of hatred and animosity on the left and right within our own country during and after the depression; the emergence in America of a liberal state blending welfare paternalism with corporate and entrepreneurial capitalism; the unprecedented growth of a prosperous and comfortable middle class; the strengthening of individual and group rights after a tumultuous if exhilarating civil rights movement; and the eruption of marginalized groups and minorities into the mainstream of American democracy.

To F. O. Matthiessen in the late 1930s, however, the times seemed precarious indeed. Democracy appeared to be more endangered from forces both within and without than at any period since the Civil War. Matthiessen saw before him American values and institutions challenged by an ever-widening array of enemies and forces. Overseas the threat of totalitarianism grew ever closer and increasingly menacing, while at home the continuing depredations of unemployment, inequality, and injustice cultivated movements and causes of incipient fascism and communism. To Matthiessen, therefore, the future seemed filled with uncertainty.

In response to these times of trouble, Matthiessen turned to a strange place, a place that at first would seem to be without much relevance to such economic, social, and political turmoil: He turned to the past and to American literature to define his times and structure a vision for the future. Specifically, he examined a five-year period of our national and literary history that he called a renaissance because it marked America's "coming to its first maturity and affirming its rightful heritage in the whole expanse of art and culture."[1] He noted that "the half-decade of 1850–55 saw the appearance" of Ralph Waldo Emerson's *Representative Men,* Nathaniel Hawthorne's *The Scarlet Letter* and *The House of the Seven Gables,* Herman Melville's *Moby-Dick* and *Pierre,* Henry David Thoreau's *Walden,* and Walt Whitman's

Leaves of Grass. Matthiessen says, "You might search all the rest of American literature without being able to collect a group of books equal to these in imaginative vitality" (vii).

Our own study will focus on another American Renaissance – a renaissance in film that began even while Matthiessen, in his prime, was still at work on his classic study. The later renaissance relates to the first as part of a process within history of the continuing renewal of American culture. The leaders of the second renaissance were also great artists but in the relatively new world of film. In contrast to the writers of the nineteenth century, the directors who led and defined what I call the Hollywood Renaissance, as well as the directors who were related to it, tended not to be of Anglo-Saxon origin. The Hollywood directors were instead ethnics or roughnecks – or both. Not only did John Ford, Frank Capra, Elia Kazan, Fred Zinnemann, William Wyler, and Billy Wilder have ethnic roots, most of this group also were immigrants to America. Others – like John Huston, Howard Hawks, George Stevens, and William Wellman – were vagabonds and roughnecks. While Matthiessen discerned a renewal of the culture of democracy in the American writers of the mid-nineteenth century, the Hollywood directors of Matthiessen's time were creating in their art their own renaissance of the values and institutions of democracy. The cultural and ideological continuities and differences between these two movements of renewal are significant. Therefore, before examining the importance of the Hollywood Renaissance, it will be useful to consider why and how Matthiessen saw those nineteenth-century writers to be of such special relevance to America during his lifetime. Matthiessen's analysis and interpretation of these authors provide a model for understanding the significance of the Hollywood directors. Moreover, his articulation of the relationship between literature and culture informs our understanding of the connection between film and culture in the mid-twentieth century.

According to Matthiessen, "The one common denominator of my five writers, uniting even Hawthorne and Whitman, was their devotion to the possibilities of democracy" (ix). Of these authors, Matthiessen continues:

> Emerson, Hawthorne, Thoreau, Whitman, and Melville all wrote for democracy in a double sense. They felt that it was incumbent upon their generation to give fulfilment to the potentialities freed by the Revolution, to provide a culture commensurate with America's political opportunity. Their tones were somewhat optimistic, sometimes blatantly, even dangerously expansive, sometimes disillusioned, even despairing, but what emerges from the total pattern of their achievement – if we will make the effort to repossess it – is literature for our democracy. (xv)

Matthiessen, of course, speaks here of democracy in the broadest terms. He suggests a healing of the fissure between the individual and society, the real and the ideal – an ideal that would by today's standards of equality and justice no doubt seem less than totally inclusive.

Nevertheless, for Matthiessen the authors of the American Renaissance address questions of literature and culture, politics and society, that are transhistorical and relevant to all periods and peoples in the American experience, including the marginalized and disadvantaged in his era and in our own. The American Renaissance authors articulated their response to these tensions of democracy in a way that structured the thought and consciousness of their own and succeeding generations. In shaping a "literature for democracy" and envisioning "the possibilities of democracy," the five writers established a frame, according to Matthiessen, based on the past but designed to anticipate future change and innovation. In a sense, Matthiessen fulfills the sensibility and work of the American Renaissance authors through his process and method of analysis. In his scholarly and critical project, he synthesizes the symbolism and autonomy of literature, as espoused by the New Critics, with the historical and social consciousness of what became the interdisciplinary American studies movement.[2]

The search by Matthiessen for a source for a renaissance of democratic values in his own times relates to developments generally outside of his critical purview – in Hollywood. The ideology nurtured in *American Renaissance* as Matthiessen deliberated over his book from the perspective of places like Cambridge, Massachusetts, Kittery, Maine, and Santa Fe, New Mexico, occurred also in Hollywood, California. As Matthiessen labored on *American Renaissance*, a cinema for democracy was emerging both to represent and to transform American culture. This new renaissance in film matches the vigor, imagination, and creativity of the American Renaissance writers in focusing on "the possibilities of democracy." Indeed, the simultaneity of this movement in Hollywood and of Matthiessen's scholarly enterprise attests to the validity of his vision. This parallel movement occurring in Harvard and Hollywood meets a key test suggested by one of the century's greatest philosophers of democracy, John Dewey. Working in the same historic moment and cultural context as Matthiessen, Dewey says: "The struggle for democracy has to be maintained on as many fronts as culture has aspects: political, economic, international, educational, scientific and artistic, religious."[3] Significantly, Dewey's words appear in *Freedom and Culture* in 1939, the year of the release of several major films by directors at the heart of Hollywood's own renaissance of American democratic values: Frank Capra's *Mr. Smith Goes to Washington* and John Ford's *Stagecoach, Young Mr. Lincoln*, and *Drums along the Mohawk*.

Along with Capra and Ford, other directors in this historic Hollywood Renaissance to be considered in this study include Howard Hawks, Elia Kazan, Fred Zinnemann, and George Stevens. They led and helped define the

Hollywood Renaissance because their films so immediately and directly concern vital continuities and transformations of American culture. In the work of these directors, artistic excellence matches cultural consciousness. As in the case of the writers of the American Renaissance, for these directors questions of aesthetics inexorably connect to the ever-expanding discourse about the meaning of America. Their best films achieve the depth and breadth, intensity, and complexity of serious art; at the same time, these films engage and interrogate the values and beliefs of the American idea and sustain and transform the narrative heart of the myth of America.

These directors do more than simply reflect American life and society in their films. Rather, the major films of Capra, Ford, Hawks, Kazan, Stevens, and Zinnemann become part of the drama of the ideology and myth of America. In their classic films, the renaissance directors transform the very terms of belief itself. Jefferson Smith, Bedford Falls and George Bailey, the Ringo Kid, Liberty Valance and the "searchers," Marshal Kane and *High Noon*, the "male war bride," *The Big Sky* and *Red River*, Terry Malloy, *Gentleman's Agreement*, *Shane*, *Giant*, and *A Place in the Sun* – these are not just titles of films or names of characters but ideas, issues, and images that are now themselves symbols and problems to be discussed and analyzed as part of our historical national consciousness. Through their films, these directors contribute to the continuing construction of the American ideology of sanctuary as well as the American myth of rebirth. They promulgate the idea of America as an unprecedented experience in human history, a land of unlimited opportunity and a culture of freedom for all peoples throughout the world.

Moreover, the artistry of the classic works of these directors functions to support their ideological position of democratic debate and dialogue. The directors establish an ideology of aesthetic form that entails structured innovation and coherent invention. This aesthetic ideology works with the elaboration in the classic films of the American idea and myth. As Matthiessen writes: "An artist's use of language is the most sensitive index to cultural history, since a man can articulate only what he is, and what he has been made by the society of which he is a willing or an unwilling part" (xv). Today, it would no doubt be said, Matthiessen's argument is qualified by the "sexism" inherent in his choice of words.

Nevertheless, Matthiessen's emphasis upon the relationship between language and culture applies to the work of the Hollywood Renaissance directors. Through their individual cinematic languages, these filmmakers create an aesthetic field and force to deepen, expand, and intensify democratic discourse. In fact, in recent years several film scholars and critics have come to question the received conventional view that all classic Hollywood films purposely make the camera and director invisible so as to create an illusion of total realism. According to the conventional position, such effacement of camera and director suggests a transparent presentation of reality that seduces and mesmerizes the spectator into passively accepting the hegemonic ideological position of ruling elites. Even radical scholars no longer accept this conventional critical wisdom. As Stephen Heath observes,

> It is too readily assumed that the operation – the determination, the effect, the pleasure – of classical cinema lies in the attempt at an invisibility of process, the intended transparency of a kind of absolute "realism" from which all signs of production have been effaced. The actual case is much more complex and subtle, and much more telling. Classical cinema does not efface the signs of production, it contains them . . . .[4]

The aesthetic ideology and practice of the renaissance directors confirm this case for the complexity of classic Hollywood cinema.

Still, comparing the iconic writers of the American Renaissance to Hollywood directors may seem odd. How can writers celebrated – even during our age of political correctness – for extraordinary depth, complexity, and ambiguity be compared to a generation of directors who helped institute classic Hollywood cinema, a medium repeatedly accused of conceding to the lowest common denominator in public taste and intelligence in order to attract the widest possible audience?

To begin, we probably should note that the significance of these filmmakers to American culture as a whole, let alone to the history of international and American film, probably still deserves greater recognition. Some of these directors were not only taken for granted during their years of unprecedented production, but were also often subsequently forgotten or denigrated as tastes and styles changed. They produced so much so quickly, and are so strongly identified with both the positive and the negative aspects of Hollywood, that we can better appreciate their significance as artists through a perspective that considers their overall achievements in the context of their times and surroundings.

In addition, as already suggested, we have learned much about film since the pioneering work of classic Hollywood directors. Several decades of critical theory and the serious study of film have transformed both the understanding of film as an art form and medium as well as the awareness of just how much this Hollywood generation accomplished. Interestingly, French critics, directors, and writers in *Cahiers du cinéma* were among the first to revolutionize the understanding of film as a unique art to be distinguished from other art forms. Thus, in the 1950s and 1960s such *cinéphiles* as Jean Cocteau, François Truffaut, and Jean-Luc Godard promulgated a critical theory of film as a thoroughly new and original artistic medium entailing multiple channels of expression, a heterogeneous or hybrid art of diverse elements

– visual image, speech, sound, music, writing. These semiotic channels or modes of expression often contradict as well as complement each other. The insights of these *cinéphiles* dramatically advanced critical awareness of the complex nature of film.

Moreover, the most influential criticism of the *Cahiers* writers tended to focus on the classic Hollywood tradition. While the *cinéphiles* judged the Hollywood of their own time as fading, they often celebrated and extolled the virtues of the earlier generation of American directors. They challenged the familiar characterizations, as already noted, of Hollywood as fostering an artistically demeaning and mindless popular culture. To these partisans of cinema, such attacks against classic Hollywood cinema belie the complexity of the cinematic form the classic directors helped to invent and construct. As Jim Hillier notes:

> The general tone of despondency at much of the output of Hollywood had already marked the 1963 *Cahiers* editorial discussion "Questions about American Cinema." The tone here is symptomatic, as the former critical "young Turks" of the 1950s, most of them now *nouvelle vague* film-makers and perhaps somewhat "old guard" critics . . . recognize that American cinema is no longer what it was. . . . The crisis in attitudes toward American cinema was exacerbated, and partly caused, by the situation of American cinema at this time. In the late 1950s and early 1960s a number of major Hollywood directors, and ones much admired by *Cahiers*, were reaching or maintaining a certain peak. . . .[5]

These Hollywood directors in their renaissance circumvent a dichotomy that concerned Matthiessen from the beginning of his critical conception of the *American Renaissance* – namely, the split he so presciently appreciates between the special value of complex art versus the sociology of popular and mass culture. Although advocating a literature for the entire society and all the people, Matthiessen steadfastly maintains that the best literature speaks for the whole age and encompasses the entire culture in ways beyond the means of the popular and mediocre. Noting the extraordinary success and popularity of such works as T. S. Arthur's *Ten Nights in a Barroom and What I Saw There*, Susan Warner's *The Wide, Wide World*, and Maria Cummins's *The Lamplighter*, Matthiessen realizes that "[s]uch material still offers a fertile field for the sociologist and for the historian of our taste" (xi). With all of their artistic genius and their passion for the subject of America, Emerson and Thoreau, Hawthorne and Melville, and Whitman could only dream of reaching the vast numbers of readers of these best-selling authors. Appreciating the importance of these popular writers in helping to create and then to capture the culture's first modern mass audience of readers, Matthiessen nevertheless remains recalcitrant in distinguishing between such popular works as barometers or indexes of moods and trends as opposed to serious art that deeply engages the full complexity of experience and culture:

But I agree with Thoreau, "Read the best books first, or you may not have a chance to read them at all." And during the century that has ensued, the successive generations of common readers, who make the decisions, would seem finally to have agreed that the authors of the pre-Civil War era who bulk largest in stature are the five who are my subject. (xi)

However, the very nature of Hollywood film both as an art form and as a corporate industry tempers Matthiessen's elitist impulse, an aesthetic and cultural standard that remains controversial today. Though the *auteur* Hollywood directors compare to Matthiessen's authors in their individualistic impulse toward artistic excellence, film necessarily becomes a collective endeavor involving the participation of innumerable experts in distinct fields of production ranging from cinematography to sound, music, design, and costuming. Also, as Hollywood directors, they by definition create movies with popular appeal. They integrate the elitism of serious art with the interests of mass audiences, thereby accomplishing in film what so many innovative artists achieve in music, literature, and the other visual arts.

In *American Renaissance*, Matthiessen identifies "recurrent themes" and "types of interrelation" (xiv) that organize his writers into a collective flowering. This pattern of connections helps to structure his book. Many of Matthiessen's themes and interrelations – the individual and society, the nature of good and evil, the unity of art and the people – resonate in a modern guise in the Hollywood Renaissance, such as reconsidering the role of gender and sexuality in constructing selfhood and rethinking the relationship of culture and society to values and beliefs.

The Hollywood Renaissance can be marked from 1939, the year of *Gone with the Wind*, a film that represents the triumph of the classic Hollywood studio system during its period of greatest power and influence. However, as already noted, 1939 also includes classics of Capra and Ford that are key to the dialogue and debate over the meaning of America. The films of these directors can readily be placed in the context of the writings and arguments of some of our most influential democratic thinkers. The renaissance extends to 1966, also a convenient year, reflecting the view of the *Cahiers* critics of the decline of Hollywood cinema as well as the deepening mire of Vietnam and the steadily accelerating revolutions involving women, sexuality, race, and youth. The differences between the major films of 1966, the last year of the renaissance, and those of 1967 indicate the depth and extent of the break from the cultural and cinematic traditions of classic Hollywood film.[6] The films of 1966 include *A Man for All Seasons* and *Who's Afraid of Virginia Woolf?*, two movies based on tightly structured and well-conceived plays. The next year offered *The Graduate* and *Bonnie and Clyde*, films that radically challenged many Hollywood conventions of casting, theme, and presentation to reconsider sexuality, violence, and family in America. *In the Heat of the Night* and *Guess Who's Coming to Dinner* also appeared in

1967, reflecting extreme changes in attitudes toward race relations in the country.

The directors of the Hollywood Renaissance were, like their predecessors in the American Renaissance, all white men; yet this apparent continuity of male domination deflects attention from crucial differences between the men of these different artistic movements and historic periods.

The diverse origins of the Hollywood directors, as already noted, stand in sharp contrast to the Anglo-Saxon heritage of the American Renaissance writers. Ford was the thirteenth and youngest child of Irish immigrants surnamed Feeney; his lifelong fascination with the Irish in so many of his movies, as well as in his personal relationships and interests, contradicts Gary Wills's recent assertion that "much of John Ford's Irishness was sham."[7] Capra was born Francesco Capra in Palermo, Sicily; the Greek Kazan was born Elia Kazanjoglou in Turkish Constantinople; Fred Zinnemann was born in Vienna. As directors with ethnic origins, their lives and backgrounds were consistent with the immigrant and ethnic foundations of Hollywood itself. The industry, of course, was built by people with names like Goldwyn, Skouras, Lasky, Cohn, Mayer.[8] Other directors with similar backgrounds whose work reflects the Hollyood Renaissance include William Wyler of Mulhouse, Alsace, and Billy Wilder of Vienna.[9]

In contrast, George Stevens was born into an acting family in Oakland, California. The vagaries of theatrical life were part of his earliest childhood days. Howard Hawks, born in Indiana, studied at Philips–Exeter Academy and went on to Cornell University, where he studied mechanical engineering. A professional car and airplane racer from the age of sixteen, he served as a pilot in the First World War and subsequently worked in a factory designing and flying airplanes before deciding to go into films in Hollywood. Other directors who relate to the Hollywood Renaissance and had similar roughneck backgrounds include John Huston, who came from a theatrical family and lived a dramatic life filled with boxing, horse racing, and many marriages and relationships. Also, William Wellman, a World War I hero with the French Lafayette Escadrille, achieved fame as a brawling director of extraordinary independence and integrity.

The heterogeneous backgrounds and unconventional beginnings of these renaissance-era directors reflect some of the country's major transformations since the days of the American Renaissance. In addition to differences based on ethnicity and social origins, others regarding gender and masculinity also dramatically distinguish these Hollywood directors from Matthiessen's authors. Indeed, Matthiessen uses the masculine gender in a borrowed quotation from Whitman to characterize and define the ideal American during the American Renaissance. Whitman proclaims the originality of the American hero as the "man in the open air" (626), and envisions the American male as an autonomous Adamic hero on the fringe of history and society. Living on the boundaries of civilization, this mythic hero functions as an example of individual behavior and collective belief. All of the white Anglo-Saxon males in Matthiessen's study help develop the myth of this hero. The dangers such superindividualism present to democracy – especially in an age of rampant totalitarianism – did not escape Matthiessen's notice. He recognized an incipient connection between Emerson and Whitman's belief in "the individual as his own Messiah" and the abuse of Nietzsche's "doctrine of the Superman" when vented by "Hitler's megalomania" (546).

The profound male tendentiousness of the American Renaissance authors manifests itself in the knowledge that, with some notable exceptions, including Hawthorne's *The Scarlet Letter* and Melville's neurotic *Pierre*, these writers proffer a world devoid of women. In stark contrast, women pervade the films of the Hollywood Renaissance directors. Indeed, women often define and structure masculinity in these films. Moreover, the varieties of masculinity in these films consistently challenge ideological stereotypes of male hegemony. Often, these representations of masculinity actually refreshingly reconsider gender relations in America. In many of these films, the melding of masculinity and American character suggests a multiplicity of masculinities and ideologies as opposed to a unitary and monolithic model of masculinity, gender, and culture.

The revision of masculinity in the Hollywood Renaissance transforms Matthiessen's concept of the individual in the American Renaissance. The representations of masculinity in these films often suggest the emergence of a pattern of fluid subjectivities in which gender constitutes a problem for investigation and a category of negotiation and discussion rather than an absolute imperative. In Matthiessen's day, discussion focused on classic individualism in a political context of modernism. The recent interest in subjectivity as the construction of gender in a cultural and linguistic context reflects the work in the past several decades of various schools of literary and film criticism – feminist, psychoanalytic, and semiotic. Examples of such fluid subjectivities in the films of the Hollywood Renaissance abound: the complexity of the Jimmy Stewart characters in both *Mr. Smith Goes to Washington* and *It's a Wonderful Life*; the multiplicities of masculinity and the various roles of women in *From Here to Eternity*; the complexity of gender positions and roles in *I Was a Male War Bride* or *Red River*; the blending of questions of democratic ideology, sexuality, and gender in *A Place in the Sun* and *Giant*; the conflicted relationship between masculinity and American identity and character in *On the Waterfront* and *High Noon*.

As in the case of their attitudes toward gender and sexuality, the Hollywood directors also differ to a degree with the American Renaissance writers in their understanding of the relationship of art and reality. Matthiessen emphasizes the faith placed by his writers in Coleridge's romantic notion of the unity of the word and thing. However, the directors' diverse cultural experiences and the heterogeneity of the cinematic form tend to attenuate the directors' belief in the unity of symbolism. As part of the modernistic movement and sensibility, these filmmakers see reality as somewhat fragmented and divergent. Their use of the multiple dimensions and channels of film feeds this impulse for diversity.

Significantly, the appreciation of the Hollywood directors for diversity and multiplicity in culture and art does not immunize them from the same kind of charges of privilege and exclusion that have been mounted against Matthiessen and the American Renaissance writers during the past two decades. For many years now, Matthiessen has been attacked by leading scholars in literary and culture studies for privileging a small elite of white men in his theory of the American Renaissance. Many careers and reputations have been developed by defining positions of opposition to Matthiessen based on gender, race, and ideology. He has been challenged for failing to appreciate the power of women and sentimentality in shaping nineteenth-century American culture, for undervaluing the centrality of slavery and racism in American consciousness, for allowing his liberal sensibilities to vitiate his more radical proclivities in assessing the destructiveness to the American character and psyche of capitalistic exploitation and imperialism.[10] In essence, such critics emphasize the "Other Renaissance" of women writers, of slave narratives and experiences, of Native American accounts of white genocide, and of working-class resistance and responses to economic inequality and control.

Also important has been a challenge to the continuity and coherence of American culture and history that Matthiessen envisioned from the Puritans and the revolutionary generation to his own times. To scholars and critics who see themselves as giving voice and new life to the multiple versions of the "Other Renaissance," American history and culture should be studied from the perspectives of the marginalized and oppressed. This diversity of perspectives renders American history and culture more discontinuous and fragmented than so-called consensus critics and historians appreciated. To advocates of the "Other Renaissance" approach, Matthiessen's portrayal constitutes a critical and historical justification of mainstream domination. As Sacvan Bercovitch explains, "the reason for the current ferment in American literary studies" concerns the belief that the "assumptions behind that vision" of continuity, inclusion, and identity "no longer account for the evidence":

> We have come to feel that the context they provide conceals as much as it reveals. To use an old-fashioned phrase, the paradigm has become inoperative. What we have instead is a Babel of contending approaches, argued with a ferocity reminiscent of the sectarian polemics that erupted in the early days of the Reformation. . . .[11]

Of course, the challenge to Matthiessen also implies opposition to other critics and historians who shared his sense of American culture and character as a coherent unity and identity comprising various divergent parts and factions. Matthiessen's contemporaries and successors in intellectual history who held this view include Gunnar Myrdal, Daniel Boorstin, and Max Lerner, among many others.

The ideas of such thinkers approximated notions about America that were expressed throughout the culture, including in Hollywood Renaissance films. Thus, Myrdal in *An American Dilemma* sees the American experience as energized and structured by an intrinsic tension between an "ethos" and "creed" of the "high and uncompromising ideals" of democracy as opposed to a "reality" of "wrongs."[12] For Myrdal the unending pursuit to fulfill the ideals of the creed constitutes the American system's genius for adaptation, change, and the incorporation of new groups. The belief in the promise of the democratic achievement of the creed's ideals accounts for the extraordinary persuasiveness of the American ideology to gain the loyalty of all peoples as opposed to the failure of coercive totalitarian ideologies. Myrdal therefore calls the American ideology a "dynamic creed" that grows as it organizes change. "But taking the broad historical view, the American Creed has triumphed. It has given the main direction to change in this country" (7). The ideology achieves hegemony by managing to be both liberal and conservative at the same time, to both change and preserve the society through its openness to others. "The American Creed, just because it is a living reality in a developing democracy, is not a fixed and clear-cut dogma. It is still growing" (23).

Myrdal typifies his generation of consensus scholars and critics in seeing in the ideology of America the convergence of national ideals and minority interests. Indeed for Myrdal, the ideology of the national creed and ethos becomes the primary vehicle for minority access to rights and advancement as well as the intellectual structure for change. The pervasiveness of the creed in American thought and action guarantees concern for minorities and fuels continuing reform and growth. Accordingly, Myrdal parallels the contrast between ideals and realities, on the one hand, to the tension between struggling minorities and entrenched groups on the other. He argues that the ideology of the American Creed perfectly suits the needs of what he calls "the others" because the survival of the system rests upon its ability to incorporate outsiders. Such inclusion involves the definition of the creed itself. Although the creed protects insiders, it lives by including the outsiders.

Some recent historians and thinkers update challenges to Myrdal's paradigm as too idealistic and optimistic, especially in regard to expectations concerning white leadership in overcoming racism. As James T. Patterson says, "White racial prejudice and structural discrimination proved to have great staying power":

With the advantage of hindsight it is clear that *An American Dilemma* had its limitations as analysis. Myrdal and his collaborators were first of all too affirmative, too optimistic about the potential of the "American Creed."[13]

However, in their monumental, multilayered analysis of race in America today, Stephan and Abigail Thernstrom modernize Myrdal's investigation and remind us that even at the time of its publication, *An American Dilemma* was challenged for being too optimistic as well for being as too negative about the prospects for meaningful change for blacks in America. Though Richard Wright saw Myrdal as promulgating an indispensable argument for improving the condition of African Americans, Ralph Ellison at the start of his career attacked Myrdal. To Ellison, Myrdal represented the black as a permanent victim who remains forever dependent upon the goodness of whites to achieve progress. The response to *An American Dilemma* therefore helped to initiate the modern debate over seeing racial equality and justice in dichotomous terms of minority action versus passive victimization. As the Thernstroms note, for Wright and Thurgood Marshall, *An American Dilemma* provided the "proof of damage" done to blacks by whites, whereas for a few others like Ellison, Myrdal's work "robbed blacks of all dignity" by making them appear totally reactive."[14]

From these different perspectives of both critics and admirers of *An American Dilemma,* the focus of Myrdal's work in the 1940s upon what was then termed the "Negro problem" demonstrates his perspicacious understanding of race as the test of the American Creed's validity and continuity. Thus in his history of modern America, Patterson quotes a reference by Kenneth Clark, the famous psychologist and advocate of black identity and power, to the "American Dilemma" that indicates the perdurability of Myrdal's theory of the ideal and real as an explanation for the continuing process of reform and change in America. Clark wrote: "The new American Dilemma is power. . . . Ideals alone . . . do not bring justice. Ideals, combined with necessity, may."[15]

Clark's notion of power does not conflict with Myrdal's model for reform. For Myrdal, the ideal of the creed provides a foundation, mechanism, and impetus for change. The ideal not only focuses change, it also motivates and energizes:

> The "Old Americans," all those who have thoroughly come to identify themselves with the nation – which are many more than the Sons and Daughters of the Revolution – adhere to the Creed as the faith of their ancestors. The others – the Negroes, the new immigrants, the Jews, and other disadvantaged and unpopular groups – could not possibly have invented a system of political ideals which better corresponded to their interests. So, by the logic of the unique American history, it has developed that the rich and secure, out of pride and conservatism, and the poor and insecure, out of dire need, have come to profess the identical social ideals. (13)

Myrdal's hopes at the end of World War II for the power and persuasiveness of the American Creed to structure the argument for change in America seem justified by some of the most recent and comprehensive studies of the relations between whites and African Americans. Although they differ markedly in their attitudes toward affirmative action and other instruments for change and justice, both the Thernstroms and Orlando Patterson, the brilliant Harvard sociologist and historian of freedom and race, agree that much has improved since Myrdal's time. Under the heading of "the good news," the Thernstroms detail an array of facts that suggest significant improvement for African Americans in terms of income, jobs, education, power, and influence. Patterson similarly argues,

> As we have seen, there is undoubtedly much to complain about. But on balance, there can be no doubt that the record of the past half century, especially the past thirty years, has been one of progress, in some cases considerable progress. The positive progress made toward social, political, and cultural inclusion has been phenomenal, reflected in the impressive growth of the middle class and the not insignificant penetration of the nation's upper class by Afro-Americans.[16]

For Myrdal this success of the creed and its importance to the world community make the creed a kind of national civic religion. He sees the unity of insiders and outsiders as a "spiritual convergence" (13), and he describes the tension between ideals and reality as a struggle for the American spirit: "America is continuously struggling for its soul" (4).

For Daniel Boorstin, the origins of this merger of the religious and the civic with national identity go back to the Puritan settlement of New England. Boorstin maintains that "The New England Way" became "an earlier version" of "the modern notion of the American Way of Life."[17] The Puritan forces behind this evolution from the settlement of Massachusetts Bay to a national culture of democracy involve "the sermon as an American institution," especially election-day sermons. The ritual of the sermon also helped institutionalize the symbolism of New England's mission as a "city upon a hill," meaning its role as a beacon, a sanctuary, and an asylum to the world's peoples. The Puritans, Boorstin asserts, were "community-building" in America as opposed to merely colonizing.[18]

More recently, Myrdal's notion of an American democratic creed of inclusion and growth and Boorstin's argument of the Puritan origins of the American way achieve synthesis and contemporaneity in Bercovitch's theory of an American ideology of consensus, a consensus historically structured by the Puritan sermon in the rhetorical form of the prophetic Hebrew jeremiad. Bercovitch advances Myrdal and Boorstin and their generation of thinkers through his amalgamation of creed, jeremiad, and consensus. He argues that in the American ideology the oppositional and adversarial merges with the culturally representative. The culture nurtures its most radical dissenters. By making radical dissent the American way and by defining opposition as the basis for consensus, the American ideology achieves an hegemony unmatched by other national ideologies. He maintains that the American ideology "undertakes above all, as a condition of its nurture, to absorb the spirit of protest for social ends" and "has accomplished this most effectively through its rhetoric of dissent" (367):

> In this view, America's classic texts represent the stategies of a triumphant liberal hegemony. Far from subverting the status quo, their diagnostic and prophetic modes attest to the capacities of the dominant culture to absorb alternative forms, to the point of making basic change seem virtually unthinkable, except as apocalypse. (367)

Accordingly, protest in the form of the moral extremes of the jeremiad becomes the rhetorical strategy to control change.

> The point here is not that these classic writers had no quarrel with America, but that they seem to have had nothing but that to quarrel about. Having adopted the culture's controlling metaphor – "America" as synonym for human possibility – and having made this tenet of consensus the ground of radical dissent, they redefined radicalism as an affirmation of cultural values. For the metaphor, thus universalized, does not transcend ideology. It portrays the American ideology, as all ideologies yearn to be portrayed, in the transcendent colors of utopia. (367)

Thus, Matthiessen, according to Bercovitch, correctly appreciated the power of "antebellum literary renaissance" figures as different as Emerson and Whitman to make "chastising the nation" a form of seeing "the American future as utopia, and utopia, by extension, as the American *Way*" (367). For Bercovitch, "what Matthiessen termed the one common denominator of his classic texts lies in the possibilities of democracy as these have been shaped into strategies of consensus" (368).

> Hence the representative, *American* radicalism of this classic literature: it was the aesthetic flowering of an ideology adopted from the start precisely for its ability to transmute radicalism of all kinds, from religious protest to revolutionary war, into varieties of ideological consensus. And since this approach implies a fundamental challenge both to the old consensus and to large parts of the current dissensus, I want to add once more . . . that the argument I have just outlined does not in any sense diminish the aesthetic power of the texts themselves. (368)

Furthermore, for Bercovitch the model of consensus and "dissensus" even incorporates the "recent trend toward multi-culturalism. Or rather, the latest re-trend toward pluralism, for the ideal of heterogeneity (in its many forms) is integral to the American symbology, and a continuing pattern of American scholarship" (372–3). Developing Myrdal's theme of "cacophony" as opposed to "harmony" in the American creed (3), Bercovitch in the "Music of

America" speaks of "heterogeneity" as "a function of hegemony" in the American ideology (14).

The line of interpretation from Myrdal to Bercovitch, the hermeneutics of America as sacred text made real in the national history of expansive consensus, literally involves not only the consideration of American history and culture in its entirety but also the special academic and intellectual history of critical theory in recent decades. Bercovitch's effort to bring together all of these elements – historical, literary, cultural, critical, theoretical, from Matthiessen to the "Other Renaissance" critics, from the New Critics to the leaders of American studies, from classic European studies of ideology to recent innovations of critical theory – has been heroic.

Moreover, for our study of the Hollywood Renaissance, Bercovitch's work helps position our directors at the intersection of several forces. Their efforts at cultural renewal and artistic excellence place them in a vital American democratic tradition of cultural and aesthetic criticism but also align them against voices of institutionalized Otherness and endowed and supported adversarial opposition. The jeremiad tradition of renewal and consensus distinguishes them from those who in the choice between different versions of the jeremiad echo, "I prefer not."[19]

The ideology of consensus as articulated by Myrdal, Boorstin, Dewey, Matthiessen, Max Lerner, and Bercovitch, among so many others, helps mediate between this generation of directors and our own. In these directors, we can see what Donald E. Pease, in a very different context and for very different purposes, calls the "Other Scene" of Bercovitch's tradition of the "American Jeremiad" as well as additional "scenes" of "cultural persuasion."[20] Scenes in some 1939 renaissance films illustrate how the other scene of the American jeremiad and various scenes of cultural persuasion exemplify the ideology of consensus in major Hollywood productions.

Accordingly, at the conclusion of Ford's *Drums along the Mohawk*, the victorious American revolutionaries pause to admire their new flag as it is raised in triumph over their fort. Henry Fonda, Claudette Colbert, and Ward Bond, among others, are properly respectful. However, shots of an African-American slave woman and a Native-American scout are especially compelling. The woman in the center of the frame looks up in awe with just the slightest suggestion of uncertainty on her face. The Native American salutes in a classic representation of the Noble Savage as the ally of white America. Both shots and frames remind one of Roland Barthes's famous study in *Mythologies*: "[A] young Negro in a French uniform is saluting, with his eyes uplifted, probably fixed on a fold of the tricolour." Barthes, of course, uses this image on the cover of *Paris-Match* to demonstrate the relationship of signification to ideology and the internalization of oppression. To Barthes, the image signifies the dominant culture's wish to convince that France is a great Empire, that all her sons, without any colour discrimination, faithfully serve under her flag, and that there is no better answer to the detractors of an alleged colonialism than the zeal shown by this Negro in serving his so-called oppressors.[21]

In *Drums along the Mohawk,* however, the irony of presenting a slave woman and an Indian saluting the new American flag is countered by the cultural awareness of other scenes in society and in film, including this film, of ideological persuasion based upon the American Creed and ideal of inclusion. Such visual images of persuasion represent a collective memory that culturally and cinematically overlap with the negative meanings of the images of the slave woman and Indian. The images of ideological persuasion convey the promise and responsibility that are proposed in the philosophies of democracy by Matthiessen, Boorstin, Myrdal, and Lerner. Both the jeremiad of ideological consensus and the equally powerful signs of failure and oppression reside in the visual images of *Drums along the Mohawk.*

The montage in Capra's *Mr. Smith Goes to Washington* of Jimmy Stewart – the grown-up boy ranger – touring Washington, D.C., provides a powerful representation of a prolonged scene of ideological consensus. The montage works on two levels combining both myth and history. A sequence of shots of monuments, historic sites, and documents in combination with the patriotic music of the sound track forms a mythic narrative of American culture and character. The mythic narrative propels Stewart into the history of his living moment in Washington. Lighting, setting, and nondiegetic music dramatize the role of the Lincoln Monument as a temple of democracy. The architectural design as constructed and shot conveys strength; the balance of lighting and shadow and the tension between constricted spaces and solid Lincolnesque pillars suggest both security and mystery. The patriotic montage achieves an ideological and emotional climax with the appearance of a young boy reading Lincoln's words aloud to an elderly man whose profile clearly indicates his Jewishness. In addition, a humble black man appears to look up reverentially to the figure of Lincoln. The montage thereby functions as a powerful visualization of the ideology of consensus. It presents the myth of America as what Lincoln himself called "the last best hope of earth" for precisely the kind of people gathered at the statue memorializing the assassinated president.[22] The montage illustrates the power of the creed of America and the historic process of inclusion, continuity, and renewal to generate an emotional sense of commitment, community, and belonging.

Similarly, in a later montage of idealistic young boys putting out a special edition of their newspaper to help Mr. Smith/Stewart in his battle with the forces of corruption, an African-American boy enters from the bottom of the screen to the center of the frame. The visual surprise of the sudden splinter-

ing of the scene by the insertion of this boy disrupts the visual and social order only to expand and reorganize it into a new coherence with greater meaning and significance. The boy's entry becomes a signifying moment of the
process of disruption and expansion that characterizes the jeremiad of democracy and the ideology of consensus. Such scenes also serve to inform and
enlighten the scenes of the slave and the Native American in the Ford film.

These scenes also suggest the immanent presence of still another scene of
belief and persuasion in the minds and work of the renaissance directors to
which we already have alluded. This scene involves the ideology of universalism and of ethnic diversity – namely, the belief in the composite character of
the American people. At least since Hector St. John de Crèvecoeur's assertion
at the end of the eighteenth century of a "new American" composed of all the
races and peoples of the world, the notion of America as a universal nation
has made our national experience unique in human history.[23] Thus, Ben J.
Wattenberg has proposed in his published study and on public television that
the ideology of universalism not only engenders the fundamental originality
of the American idea but also constitutes the country's greatest resource for
the strengthening and renewal of democracy as we enter a new century:

> For five hundred years, America has been the biggest story in the world, page one
> above the fold. That story isn't over. . . . The United States of America, in more
> ways than one, is becoming the first universal nation. We are universalizing at
> home; Americans now come from everywhere. And the American way of life – for
> good and for ill, although mostly for good – is the pervasive, persuasive, universal
> model for activity all over the world.[24]

To Wattenberg and other advocates of universalism, the history of this ideology provides the best means for understanding and dealing with the ever-
growing numbers of peoples from Asia and Central and South America who
are even today changing the faces and colors of American identity.

In recent years, however, some have challenged the continued validity of
this ideology of universalism. Although such contemporary critics as Bercovitch and Henry Louis Gates, Jr., insist on what could be termed a "liberal
multiculturalism" that merely modernizes historic American pluralism, arguments for forms of multiculturalism based on fragmentation and separation
persist.[25] Of course, for the directors in the Hollywood Renaissance, the ideology of universalism formed the center of the American idea. So many of
them had lived the experience themselves.

The efforts of the Hollywood Renaissance directors to balance the aesthetics of cinematic modernism with the demands of popular taste are comparable to their attempts to present the paradox of bringing together a nation of
rugged individualists from all over the world into a working democracy. The
directors were contemporaries of the great modernists in art and literature,

and the enthusiasm of these filmmakers for cultivating the complex heterogeneity of the cinematic text reflects this modernistic impulse toward diversity. They also were fascinated by the heterogeneity of American culture and character as a living text for their films. Their work strives to meet this great variety of demands: modernist aesthetics and sensibilities, mass audiences and tastes, corporate and capitalistic expectations, the representation of the heterogeneity of America in the context of a common culture and history. They sensed the need to nurture and celebrate difference and diversity in ways that would strengthen the whole. For them, such unity through difference and diversity seemed the right and plausible way to face the dilemmas of the present and the uncertainties of the future. Their successes and failures in achieving these goals constitute a renaissance of art and culture comparable to earlier moments of such renewal in our history. To a considerable degree, the work of this generation also anticipates future change by preparing the way for the innovation and creative diversity of what Diane Jacobs has called a "period of cinematic 'rebirth'" in the 1970s with such directors as Martin Scorsese, John Cassavetes, Francis Ford Coppola, Robert Altman, Woody Allen, and Paul Mazursky.[26]

Accordingly, the reconsideration of the relationship between reality and vision in art, culture, and politics by the earlier generation of Ford, Capra, Hawks, Zinnemann, Kazan, and Stevens also can be important in informing our efforts to understand and shape our own times. Perhaps in looking back to this relatively recent past, we can reestablish our connections to an even more distant period of renewal that so powerfully influenced Matthiessen's generation. The consciousness of a culture of renewal and of a history of one generation's power to awaken and motivate another can help us locate the resources for renewal today. What more appropriate artistic medium than film and what more talented and persuasive group of directors and works than those in the Hollywood Renaissance for a revisioning of the past? Their combined aesthetic and cultural achievement and their willful reconstruction of history and culture proffer the opportunity once again for another generation's engagement in the dialogue between scenes of alienation and scenes of persuasion. These directors invite – even demand – our active participation and entry into the living, historic montage, the negotiations and mediations that engender our understandings of the present and the past and assert our authority over our individual and cultural future.

CHAPTER 2

A CINEMA FOR DEMOCRACY: JOHN FORD AND THE CRISIS OF MODERNITY, MYTH, AND MEANING

Structure, Style, Ideology

Over years and generations, a critical and popular consensus has deemed John Ford the quintessential American director. He occupies a special status as both an American artist and an American consciousness. In Ford, it is argued, the complexity and originality of the aesthetic imagination matches the depth, range, and intensity of his social and cultural imagination. Art, ideology, and culture cohere in the Ford canon to engender a representation and reconstruction of American culture in ways that are usually associated with major works of literature and art. The extent and quality of his aesthetic and cultural achievements make Ford a seminal force behind a movement that I have termed the Hollywood Renaissance of cinema and democracy that flowered during the middle decades of this century. In his work as a director and his influence as a cultural force, Ford's contribution toward establishing a democratic aesthetic of film compares to the efforts a century earlier of our most celebrated authors.

Accordingly, John Ford plays a crucial role in the genesis and history of the Hollywood Renaissance. He looms like a patriarchal presence over this movement. Of all the powerful men who pioneered in the creative and industrial flowering of film in Hollywood, no one exercised greater leadership or influence than Ford. John Wayne even dubbed him "Pappy," an epithet of affection and admiration that insinuates Ford's parental and originating authority as a director and Hollywood force. Soon after Ford's death, Wayne said: "Pappy was a painter with a camera, a rock of strength for his friends and acquaintances. Many will miss him; I most of all."[1]

However, the nickname also domesticates and mitigates a less benign aspect of Ford's character and persona. As Gary Wills so well documents in his recent study of the "idea" of John Wayne, Ford could be "sadistic" in his bullying insistence upon exerting absolute control over a set and extracting exactly the performances he desired.[2] Ford developed a reputation for toughness and brutality that could arouse dread and anxiety among colleagues and actors. As Peter Bogdanovich noted, "Ford's work, like his personality, is filled with ambiguities."³

The avatar of classic Hollywood cinema and the system that produced it, he also attained the strongest and most authentic admiration from the most modernistic and avant-garde of European directors as well as other students of film as a serious art form. A legend in his own time, he participated actively and brilliantly in the invention of himself. "My name's John Ford. I am a director of Westerns," he said in a statement that brazenly blends both self-effacement and self-promotion.⁴

The circumstances surrounding that famous introduction of himself also suggest much about Ford. It was delivered in 1950 at an emergency meeting of the Screen Directors Guild during which Ford opposed Cecil B. DeMille's promotion of a loyalty oath to help drive alleged communists out of Hollywood. By resisting blacklists and McCarthyism, Ford, who proudly served in the Navy during the Second World War and loved to flaunt his uniform, legitimately earned his credentials as a liberal hero without sacrificing or even moderating his aggressive proclivity toward cantankerous independence. He once said, "I'm a liberal Democrat. Mostly, I'm a rebel" (Gallagher 342). According to Wills, "John Ford always considered himself a radical" (161). In Ford's case, the term radical really connotes more about his personality and independence than his politics.

The investment by both filmmakers and critics in Ford's elevation to cultural icon and artistic prophet entails some degree of self-service and self-promotion. Such elevation necessarily promotes film itself as an art form, a cultural institution, a major industry, and an important commodity. Ford's triumph as a director and artist becomes a victory for others in all aspects of the field.

In his biographical and critical study, Ronald L. Davis succinctly demonstrates what has become the conventional veneration by critics and the public of John Ford:

> Ford remains the most honored director in Hollywood history, having won six Academy Awards and four New York Film Critics Awards for his work. He was the recipient of the American Film Institute's first Life Achievement Award and continues to be a cult figure among movie enthusiasts around the world, revered by professionals as Hollywood's film poet.

Davis goes on to note that during a career of more than half a century, "Ford made 136 pictures" of which only 54 were westerns. He emphasizes that none of the Academy Awards went for the westerns but were awarded instead to films that "reflect Ford's versatility and dimension as a cinematic artist" – *The Informer* (1935), *The Grapes of Wrath* (1940), *How Green Was My Valley* (1941), and *The Quiet Man* (1952).⁵

Figure 1. John Ford: The quintessential American director and a leading force behind the Hollywood Renaissance (The Museum of Modern Art / Film Stills Archive).

Several specific factors help explain the amazing longevity of Ford's reputation. These include his prolificacy in directing so many films from 1917 to
1966, ranging from the westerns to melodramas, social and historical dramas, and documentaries; the widely ackowledged artistry and genius of his
direction; exemplary professionalism; his charismatic personality and leadership. Equally important, his films invariably represent classic American
themes in ways that merge his work intimately with American consciousness.
These American themes usually provide the foundation for the narrative
structure of Ford's films, so that the films achieve a meaning beyond their
own presentation without losing the familiarity, immediacy, and efficiency
of popular formulas. Representative themes are the individual and society;
violence versus the law; the frontier as a vast stage for exciting drama and a
source of American values and character; domesticity as both refuge and prison; the masculinization of bravery and independence; women as complex
mixtures of saint and sinner, mother and lover, stolid strength and thought-

ful tenderness; the richness of ethnic roots and life-styles; the importance of loyalty, character, and self-reliance as ultimate values.

Ford's most popular and influential films brilliantly represent such typical American values and conflicts in concrete ways that achieve permanence in our cultural consciousness. In movie after movie, Ford instantiates classic ideological and mythic themes, making them into tangible cinematic moments and indelible visual images. Examples of such instantiation abound. In *My Darling Clementine* (1946), Ford's black-and-white dramatization of the gunfight at the O.K. Corral in Tombstone, Arizona, the director transforms a generally formulaic text into stark visual representations of abstract ideas. One scene epitomizes what obtains for the entire film: Wyatt Earp's (Henry Fonda) attempt to balance himself on a tipped-back chair. This scene resonates with meaning beyond mere comic awkwardness because of the way the entire film has been cast, shot, and visually organized.[6] Ford's established pattern before the chair incident, visually representing conflict and tension through a powerful rhythm and organization of shots, anticipates the meaning of Fonda's balancing act. The scene visually and dramatically develops and intensifies all that preceded it; Fonda's teetering in the chair compresses the film's tensions involving the individual and the community, the repressed desires of the main characters, and the difficulties of life on the frontier. The ability to achieve such significance from such simplicity characterizes Ford's genius as a director.

At the same time, Ford's work cannot be reduced to mere illustrations of broad general abstractions or reflections of popular values. He is no simple cartoonist of cultural and psychological complexities. His work extends beyond fundamental qualities and strengths of direction to another level of creative and cultural achievement. Scores of Hollywood directors emulate his work. They deal with the same kinds of cinematic and cultural codes and conventions in westerns, dramas, and historical or documentary narratives. Ford's special directing style also has been imitated by innumerable filmmakers. These directors learn from Ford's careful balance of exterior landscapes and interior spaces, his perfectly timed organization of long shots with a dazzling variety of close-ups and medium shots, his brilliantly framed and staged long takes that present a beautifully composed mise-en-scène to develop and complicate editing and narrative structure; yet few have matched Ford's artistic success. He still stands out and dominates as a distinctive artist with an original genius. He achieves a special status through his unique blending of aesthetic power and cultural authority.

Ford's strength and creative force stem in large part from the relationship he establishes between the aesthetics of the cinematic text and the contexts of American culture and character. His unique aesthetics of film – meaning his established style as a director and his method of making and structuring a

Figure 2. John Ford: Aesthetic achievement and cultural consciousness (The Museum of Modern Art / Film Stills Archive).

film – invariably relate to his conception of American culture and his vision of America's place in the world and history. Artistic imagination melds with cultural and social imagination to create popular works of aesthetic and cultural complexity. The films that dominate critical and even popular attention function on several layers and open various dimensions of meaning that belie their apparent simplicity as mass-audience entertainment.

Ford, of course, notoriously disdained any intellectualizations about or sophisticated interpretations of his work, and denied any preconceived aesthetic ambitions or cultural notions about his films. Nevertheless, I think Ford's great films establish a democratic aesthetic of film; in other words, they incite the creative imagination and the critical intelligence of his audience. He relates the techniques, structures, and style of his original aesthetics of filmmaking to the freedom, openness, and energy of democratic culture. As demonstrated in many of his works, Ford's film practice involves thought, imagination, critical engagement; that these elements are key to his aesthetic is a stark contrast to the manipulation and sensationalism often associated by some with classic Hollywood genres. Ford's artistry and ideology clash even more aggressively with the fascist film aesthetic of superheroes, party propaganda, absolute power, totalitarian thought, blood politics, and racial purity emerging during the same era in Nazi Germany via Leni Riefenstahl.

A progenitor of a democratic aesthetic that helps define the Hollywood Renaissance, Ford deserves greater recognition as to how his work relates historically to other movements in America of art and democracy. His aesthetic compares, in terms of cinema, to what mid-nineteenth-century American Renaissance authors achieved in their writing. From these authors he assumes the mantle of leadership and representation through rebellion and radical individualism, inheriting from them the role of the rebel outsider, the adversarial figure who represents the culture in opposition to and criticism of that culture. Like these writers, as opposed to simply reflecting popular beliefs or promulgating hegemonic values, Ford institutes a dialogue about American democracy and culture. He creates a cinema for the people that includes a democratic aesthetic of discussion and debate. The complex hybrid cinematic text and heterogeneous cinematic form structure this discourse while the diverse semiotic channels of image, sound, music, writing, dialogue engage each other in democratic self-examination and criticism.

As in the works of the American Renaissance, in Ford renewal and consensus are gained through conflict, "dissensus," and dialogue. For Ford, growth comes from making and sustaining an oppositional stance and taking an adversarial position against established centers of power, stultifying institutions, and conventional systems of belief and behavior. He shares an attraction with Hawthorne and Melville to the dark side of the imagination and the power of negative thinking. Like them, he grows by challenging easy answers and insisting upon examining experience in all of its dimensions. An American consciousness, his imagination extends beyond geographical boundaries. Like Hawthorne and Melville, Ford feels compelled to face the evil in man and society and to proclaim his sovereignty over his own vision and art. As Herman Melville wrote: "There is the grand truth about Nathaniel Hawthorne. He says NO! in thunder; but the Devil himself cannot make him say *yes*. For all men who say *yes*, lie."[7] The same could be said of Ford.

Ford's work, beside being part of traditions of American democracy, incorporates a modernistic sensibility. Ford began making films during the second decade of the century, when modernism in thought and art was in ascendancy in Europe and America. Film itself, as Leo Braudy notes, emerged concomitantly with the dominance of the modernist movement.[8] Although certainly not an academic student of such movements and philosophies, Ford evidences a modernistic sensibility and consciousness throughout the broad body of his work. In his greatest films, representations and conceptions of time, history, perspective, and narrative reflect the epistemology and psychology of modernism. Ford's films also demonstrate a keen awareness of irrationality, moral incertitude, skepticism, and the epistemological variance between experience and mind. This modernistic sensibility helps structure his art as well as his understanding and representation of American culture.

The Myth and Ideology of America: The Modernity of *The Searchers*

One film of John Ford's mature phase of direction best dramatizes the fulfillment of his democratic aesthetic and modernistic sensibility in the context of the Hollywood Renaissance. *The Searchers* (1956) marks the culmination of the Ford canon and encapsulates his artistic genius. As Joseph McBride and Michael Wilmington note, "The film is not in fact an aberration, but a crystallization of all the fears, obsessions and contradictions which had been boiling up under the surface of Ford's work since his return from World War II."[9] *The Searchers* illustrates a process of aesthetic, ideological, and cultural maturation that parallels his own personal and psychological growth, development, and ultimate decline. The veneration of Ford as a director of artistic genius and as a source of cultural authority in America also culminates with *The Searchers*, extending to commentary and criticism about the film by later generations of critics, professionals, writers, and filmgoers.

As a cultural artifact and construction, *The Searchers* compares in significance in the mid-twentieth century to the great literary expressions of the American Renaissance a century earlier. The film becomes an artistic reconstruction of America. It does not merely reflect American society; nor is it a realistic documentary of America at midcentury. In the critical terminology of modern film scholars, *The Searchers,* rather than simply mirroring or opening a window upon America, demonstrates the complexity of film as a modern art form.[10] *The Searchers* becomes a representation of American culture that both presents and transforms it. It revivifies the classic western genre into a relevant force in modern American consciousness. This Ford western operates on many different levels and through many dimensions; and it fulfills all of them, melding different strains together into a single cinematic form to present the confusion of contemporary life and culture and to delineate the historic, cultural, and psychological complexities of the contemporary moral and intellectual condition.

Two articles separated by more than a dozen years reflect the perdurability of Ford's influence for widely different directors and audiences. The inspiration for each article is a new film that takes *The Searchers* as a model.

In the first, from 1979, Stuart Byron writes that prominent film critics Andrew Sarris and Pauline Kael see *The Searchers* as a direct influence upon a new film, *Hardcore* with George C. Scott, about a moralistic father's violent search for his lost daughter in the pornographic film culture of San Francisco. Byron notes that the film's director, Paul Schrader, freely and repeatedly acknowledged this influence, and argues that "references to *The Searchers* have appeared in so many recent movies" as to create a "*Searchers* cult" of extraordinary proportions. Cleverly citing Hemingway's famous claim that "All modern American literature comes from one book by Mark Twain called *Huckleberry Finn*," he adds, "I think that in the same broad sense it can be said that all recent American cinema derives from John Ford's *The Searchers*." Byron then documents his claim that "You could construct half the syllabus for a course on contemporary American cinema just from films that, consciously or not, have been influenced by *The Searchers*." In addition to Schrader and *Hardcore,* Byron lists the following directors and films as making *The Searchers* "the Super-Cult Movie of the New Hollywood": John Milius, *Dillinger* (1973), *The Wind and the Lion* (1975), and *Big Wednesday* (1978); Martin Scorsese, *Mean Streets* (1973) and *Taxi Driver* (1976); Steven Spielberg, *Close Encounters of the Third Kind* (1977); Robert Aldrich, *Ulzana's Raid* (1972); George Lucas, *Star Wars* (1977); Michael Cimino, *The Deer Hunter* (1978). Several of these directors passionately profess their debt to *The Searchers*. Scorsese says, "The dialogue is like poetry! And the changes of expression are so subtle, so magnificent! I see it once or twice a year." Similarly, Milius declares the film "The best American movie – and its protagonist, Ethan Edwards, is the one classic character in films."[11]

The second article about the influence of Ford and *The Searchers* upon contemporary cinema appeared in 1993 in *Rolling Stone,* a magazine whose readership is not usually associated with Ford's generation. In this piece, Peter Travers proposes important thematic connections between *The Searchers* and Mario Van Peebles's *Posse,* a new black cowboy film. Travers notes, "Coincidentally, *Posse* opens the same week as a revival of the 1956 classic, *The Searchers,* an attack on racism that some mistook for a typical John Wayne horse opera." His admiration for and celebration of Ford at least matches Byron's enthusiasm in the earlier article. Travers calls *The Searchers* "the best and most emotionally devastating western ever crafted." "It's up there in movie-great heaven with *Citizen Kane, Vertigo, 2001: A Space Odyssey, Raging Bull* and a handful of other groundbreakers."[12]

Both articles comment on the surface simplicity of the film, a crowded story with many major and minor characters, which was adapted from a novel by Alan LeMay with a screenplay by Frank S. Nugent. In the story, Ethan Edwards, a former Confederate soldier played by John Wayne, returns somewhat mysteriously three years after the war's end to the Texas ranch of his brother, Aaron (Walter Coy). The movie suggests multiple tensions between the brothers about the war, about Ethan's absence since the war's end, and about his commitment to farming, but mostly about lingering romantic feelings between Ethan and his sister-in-law, Martha (Dorothy Jordan). There are three children, including ten-year-old Debbie, played by Lana Wood; Natalie Wood plays a grown-up Debbie later in the film. The cast includes an older sister, Lucy (Pippa Scott), who is being courted by Brad Jorgensen (Harry Carey, Jr.), the son of neighboring ranchers from Sweden: Lars Jorgensen, played by the veteran Ford character actor John Qualen (the Muley figure in *The Grapes of Wrath*) and Mrs. Jorgensen (Olive Carey). There is also an adopted nephew, Martin Pawley (Jeffrey Hunter), who is grown, part Cherokee, and indebted to Ethan for finding and saving him after his family was massacred by Indians. Ethan belittles this generous and heroic act as purely coincidental to his being there at the right moment: "It just happened to be me. You don't need to make more of it." His comment thus not only reflects his strong-man code of self-effacement but also reveals his mixed feelings about saving the life of someone with Indian blood.

Other important characters include Old Mose Harper (Hank Worden), a sort of holy fool whose bizarre mutterings provide an ironic commentary upon events; Laurie Jorgensen (Vera Miles), Martin's fiancée, whose romantic frustrations are meant to add comedy to the film; and a Texas Ranger and frontier judge and minister, Captain Samuel Johnson Clayton (Ward Bond), whose combination of several official roles and duties in the community dramatizes the mixture of violence and piety on the frontier and in American culture. After Comanches attack the ranch, rape and kill Martha, kill Aaron and his boy, and capture the girls, the narrative thrust of the film concerns Ethan's and Martin's seven-year search for the girls (with Laurie anxiously awaiting Martin's return). However, the search becomes profoundly complicated by the obsessions, drives, and racism that motivate Ethan. The search becomes a vehicle for a drama of serious psychological and cultural ambiguities.

"*The Searchers*! God, what a story!" wrote Kirk Douglas to Ford;[13] yet the story alone cannot completely explain the film's enormous impact. More than its epic narrative quality must be understood and studied to account for the resonance and importance of *The Searchers* for so many over so many years. Even the combination of this story with the film's compelling Technicolor cinematography, its brilliant cast, and Ford's own inspired direction does not suffice to explain the special place *The Searchers* has attained in the American imagination.

Much of the film's special strength comes from its fusion of multiple layers of cultural and artistic meaning as well as its coherent interconnection and organization of several modes of cinematic expression. At its basic structural level, *The Searchers* brings together two of America's most fundamental narrative and rhetorical structures: Its form, as Richard Slotkin notes, derives directly from the classic Indian captivity narrative;[14] the film also perpetuates the Puritan jeremiad.

The Indian captivity narrative, of course, originates in colonial New England in the seventeenth century. Its form was established with the first accounts of those Puritans who were attacked, captured, forced to go into the wilderness with their Native American captors, and ultimately were released back into the Puritan communities to write about the experience. The Puritan accounts tended to dramatize the captivity experience as a journey of trial during captivity and a time of ultimate redemption upon returning into the white community. To be sure, the journeys also became allegories of the psychological state of the captives, measuring the moral strength and endurance of their characters, as well as metaphors for their overall religious condition and experience. According to Slotkin, captivity narratives established "the first coherent myth-literature developed in America for American audiences," and Lee Clark Mitchell asserts that "the captivity narrative established initial conventions for depicting threats of violation that have continued ever since."[15] Slotkin says these narratives dominated the publication of stories of the frontier between 1680 and 1716. They became, as he says, sermon-narratives.[16]

In America, as Sacvan Bercovitch has shown, the form of the jeremiad, as derived from the Puritans' readings of Jewish Scripture and the prophets, provided the basic structure for the Puritan sermon.[17] Whereas Indian markers and signs revealed the paths through the forests, the jeremiad provided the map for Puritans interpreting the signs of the religious meaning of their entire experience in the New World, including, of course, Indian captivity. The jeremiad tended to organize experience in terms of moral extremes and radical alternatives. On the one hand, the Puritans sought redemption and renewal in this New England community of saints; on the other, they used what Harry S. Stout terms a "rhetoric of failure" as a means to energize the drive for reform.[18] The implications of this failure terrified the devout. To the serious Puritan, failure to keep God's New Covenant would condemn these new chosen people to the hatred of future generations for missing the opportunity to achieve spiritual regeneration on Earth. As John Williams, a Puritan minister and the author of one of the major captivity narratives and jeremiads, proclaimed: "You have the World, as it were, to begin again" (Demos 59). This tension between redemption and corruption dramatizes the moral imperative and psychological desperation of what became known as the New England Way. The jeremiad psychology and ideology inform both John Winthrop's founding sermon in 1630 aboard the *Arbella* and Samuel Danforth's election-day excoriation in 1670 of the new generation for its moral lassitude. Interestingly, the amalgamation of captivity narrative and jeremiad seems an obvious outgrowth of the Puritans' view of the moral significance of the journey to America. The trial depicted in the Indian captivity narrative maintains the original religious dimension and moral challenge of the pilgrimage to the New World.

The continuity from the Puritans' pilgrimage to Ford's *The Searchers* confirms that, from the beginning, Americans were searchers. Though the image applies initially to Native American hunters, then to Spanish conquistadors searching for gold, it holds just as well for the first Puritan settlers in New England. In the famous words of Danforth's 1670 election sermon, that first generation came on an "errand into the wilderness" in search of a New Jerusalem.[19] Many in this founding generation believed they could build what their leader Winthrop in 1630 termed "a city upon a hill" that would be a beacon and example to the world. However, the physical journey to the site of that city soon proved to be an external manifestation of deeper spiritual, psychological, religious, and cultural journeys. It became an extension of individual and communal pilgrimage.

Moreover, the nature of the journey as defined by the jeremiad also influenced the Puritans' perception of its destination and object. The moral extremes of perennial promise and inevitable failure ultimately made the journey's end unattainable. The sense of an unreachable resolution turns the landscape of the journey itself into a nightmare and condemns the pilgrim to an eternal search.

The existential and moral situation of the Puritan prefigures the journey of John Wayne's Ethan Edwards in *The Searchers*. In fact, Wayne in this film anticipates his concerns about the character he dubs "Pilgrim" (played by Jimmy Stewart) in the later film *The Man Who Shot Liberty Valance*. The religious, indeed the puritanical, nature of Ethan's role and journey in *The Searchers* has been emphasized by others. Describing Ethan as the exemplary "Fordian hero," Tag Gallagher characterizes these heroes in this way: "They must purify the world: right a wrong, restore honor, purge disease, avenge crime, purify law, uphold ideals" (336).

This understanding of the Fordian hero helps to explain how Ethan as a fighter for the Confederacy still qualifies as a Puritan sensibility and consciousness. Gallagher's insight into the moral psychology of the Puritan impulse to purify relates directly to Ethan as rebel. Ethan's connection to the Confederacy works symbolically, dramatizing his foundational independence and isolation, the purity, so to speak, of his individualism. His status as a Puritan and rebel signals his identity as self-determined and beyond the reach of any community that would define and hold him – even one that esteems him as its most charismatic and representative leader. Ethan clearly occupies the ambivalent position of the loner leader, who ironically represents his society through his estrangement from it. Although his brother serves as the head of the family and the captain (Bond) holds several important positions, no one surpasses Ethan in terms of personal authority and earned respect. Undoubtedly, much of Ethan's power derives from Wayne, who dominates his scenes and frames, and whose commanding physical appearance and overwhelming presence exaggerate his estimable leadership skills and expertise as a soldier and frontier fighter. However, Ethan also conveys an aura of self-assured independence that influences the reaction to his physical appearance. Much of his strength comes from this very sense of independence. So thoroughly autonomous and self-reliant, he embodies these celebrated values of the American frontier. At the same time, his resistance to authority and his refusal to adhere to others' standards both empower him and turn him into an alien among his own people. He designates his own conscience as the ultimate judge of right and wrong for others as well as himself. He remains a Puritan consciousness on a lonely journey. As Gallagher writes, "Fordian heroes are lonely; isolation and self-exclusion are the prices they pay. . . . All are obsessed with duty, all become 'priests,' take vows equivalent to chastity, give up everything for their task" (336–7). Ethan, of course, functions as precisely this kind of complex and ambiguous figure in *The Searchers*.

In addition, being a Confederate veteran helps to make Ethan a modern figure, bridging him between the Puritan past and concerns of more recent history. In the first place, his association with the Confederacy institutionalizes the racism that grips his psyche, as evidenced in his reaction to Martin Pawley at their meeting with the family at the dinner table early in the film. Sitting at the opposite end of the same side of the dinner table, Wayne glares at Martin while cutting into his food: "A fellow could mistake you for a half-breed." Ford cuts from Ethan sitting at the corner with Martha, his sister-in-law, to the other end of the table, where the questioning glances of brother Aaron, Martin, and Lucy isolate Ethan in his paranoia and prejudice. Martin apologetically explains that he is only an eighth Cherokee; the rest is Welsh and English. When Martin softly thanks Lucy for serving him, Ethan's glare turns to palpable anger with the realization that the young man truly has become part of the family. Wayne sugars his coffee, freshly refilled by Martha, and looks twice at Martin, disapproval clearly visible on his face.

Other key elements of Ethan's individualistic, Puritan character gain significance through their association with the Confederacy. When Captain Clayton arrives with Mose to swear in a posse to try to investigate the loss of Jorgensen's cattle, Ethan's past becomes a problem. His independence and rebelliousness suddenly assume a quality of lawlessness, perhaps even a taint of untrustworthiness. "Are you wanted for a crime?" the captain asks, reopening suspicions about the source of Ethan's money, his activities during and after the war, and his overall attitude toward the law and society. Similarly, his romanticism, self-reliance, and penchant for lost causes quickly evolve into a rationalization for violence. He mocks the captain for surrendering at the end of the war, declaring that he doesn't "believe in surrender," that he still has his "saber," and has refused to turn it into a "plowshare." His fierce sense of loyalty and commitment now seem rigid and extreme as he berates the captain by asserting that a man needs to swear his oath to only one cause.

The captain's epithet for Ethan, "the prodigal brother," thus dramatizes the moral and social complexity of Ethan as a modern lost pilgrim. He remains a pilgrim on a mission, an independent soul, but one who carries burdens of racism, violence, and hatred with him. He has become not just the pilgrim avenger, the knight on a holy mission, but also the modern alien and outsider who exists at times and in ways with no structure to his loyalties and identities – a character prefigured in Melville's heroes of alienation, Wellingborough Redburn and Captain Ahab, as also noted by Greil Marcus and more recently by Wills (271).[20] As Ford told Bogdanovich:

> It's the tragedy of a loner. He's the man who who came back from the Civil War, probably went over into Mexico, became a bandit, probably fought for Juarez or Maximilian – probably Maximilian because of the medal. He was just a plain loner – could never really be a part of the family.[21]

With this array of cultural and psychological complexities and contradictions, it should be helpful to ground Ethan and *The Searchers* to a concrete historical character and moment. Ethan's situation and story in many ways hauntingly resemble the case of John Williams, the venerated Puritan minister of Deerfield, Massachusetts, who described his captivity in *The Redeemed Captive Returning to Zion*. In 1704, a force of French troops and their Indian allies – Canadian Abenakis, Hurons, and Mohawk Iroquois – massacred the town, and captured Williams, a prisoner prized because of his eminence as a minister, along with his wife, Eunice Mather Williams, and their five children. During the forced march they underwent extraordinary hardships, the worst being the hatchet killing of Mrs. Williams by an Indian. Other captives also suffered abuse and death at the hands of the warriors. The terror and brutality of the attack on Deerfield and the Williams household compare to the scenes of the attack on the ranch in *The Searchers*.

However, the plight of one of the youngest children, also named Eunice, makes *The Redeemed Captive Returning to Zion* especially relevant to *The Searchers*. Upon the return of the minister and his other children after nearly three years of captivity, Eunice remains behind, held by Indians like Debbie in *The Searchers*. She is adopted by the Mohawks who, as John Williams was told and reports in his sermon, "would as soon part with their hearts" as with this child (Demos 84). Eunice eventually seems to prefer the Indians to the family of her birth. Demos even boldly suggests a greater love for Eunice among the Indians and away from the austerity of her father's house and the restrictions of the Puritans. Ultimately, she decides on her own to spend her life among the Indians. She marries an Indian, raises a family with him, and converts to the Catholicism of the French. She becomes, as John Demos says, "the unredeemed captive" in stark contrast to her minister father, "the redeemed captive." Eunice's acquiescence to this new alien way amazes, embarrasses, and humiliates her English family and the Puritan community. Demos notes that probably less than two years after her arrival in the Indian village of Kahnawake, Eunice no longer can speak English (Demos 146). For Demos, the intensity of Eunice's desire to be with her Indian lover makes their union and marriage "a love-match, it seems" (Demos 105). He emphasizes that although she received an Indian name soon after coming to the village, at some point she takes on a second Indian name, Gannenstenhawi, meaning "she brings in corn," a sign perhaps of her genuine involvement and participation in the Indian society (Demos 159). Her allegiance to the Indians inflames her Puritan family and the community, provoking their repeated efforts for more than three decades to have her return to the fold; these all fail.

Both the "redeemed" and "unredeemed" captives speak to us again through Ethan Edwards in *The Searchers*. The Puritan narrative informs the more recent story and enlightens us about its importance. It tells us more, perhaps, about Ethan and his world than he could tell on his own. Although the two stories differ in many respects, important similarities make Williams's narrative and sermonic form a construction that discourses with and helps define *The Searchers*. As the archetypal Indian captivity narrative, *The Redeemed Captive* not only establishes the narrative pattern of events, it also articulates the philosophical and psychological dimensions of the efforts to find redemption on both journeys.

For both the Puritans and the Texans, responses to the Indian attack and the subsequent captivity achieve special intensity as they relate to the girls who are the objects of a search. As Mitchell says of the captivity narrative: "That narrative's central image was the prospect of danger as often to women as to men, with the implication that violation of the female body placed colonial culture metonymically under attack."[22] The girls' plight exacerbates the dilemmas and tensions associated with Indian warfare and captivity. The girls concretize Puritan abstractions about race, religion, God, cultural superiority, and the meaning of survival; their situation becomes a focal point for the tensions the Puritans felt in America. As McBride and Wilmington say, "Miscegenation, next to war itself, is probably the most dramatic form of collision between two cultures, and by exploring a community's reaction to it, Ford is testing its degree of internal tension."[23] The accommodation of the girls to captivity challenges the alleged cultural superiority of the white people, including the moral superiority of white men. The girls prefer – or, in Debbie's case, at least accept – a culture they are supposed to disdain. Eunice Williams rejects efforts throughout her extended captivity to return her to the Puritans; Debbie initially also rejects Martin's heroic efforts to rescue her. She tells Martin when he finally comes for her, "I used to pray to you. Come and get me. Take me home! You didn't come!" She then adds, "These are my people," emphasizing her split identity and genuine attachment to her captors, especially the Comanche Chief Scar (Henry Brandon). In contrast to Eunice, however, Debbie ultimately succumbs to appeals to return home.

The casting of Henry Brandon, born Henry Kleinbach, as Chief Scar provides insight into more than the innate racism and prejudice of Hollywood film during this period. His role also signifies how acting and casting contribute to and complicate levels of meaning in a film. Brandon's dark features and facial structure suggest ethnic European origins but also blatantly advertise a non-Indian identity. Because of his features, he often was cast in unconventional roles. Anthony Quinn, who is of Mexican and Irish descent, similarly was cast as an Indian in Cecil B. DeMille's *The Plainsman* (1937). Such use of both Quinn and Brandon, along with so many other character actors, demonstrates Hollywood's long history of denying major roles to people of color. In *The Searchers,* however, casting Brandon as Scar updates the film's psychological linkage of race and sexuality. By brazenly denying any Indian identity in the actor playing an Indian chief, the film replicates the racism and fears within the society of the commingling of white women, in this instance actress Natalie Wood, with men of color. The production and casting of *The Searchers* thereby repeats and reinforces the film's racist theme. Thus while Ethan blames the victimized white women for their forced association with Indian men, the film itself protects Wood from such a connection – a more subtle racist act and position.

In *The Searchers,* denying the Indian chief his identity as an Indian relates to the Texans' dehumanization of the white women captives for their sexuality. Thus, latent sexual tensions in Williams's story/sermon *The Redeemed Captive* become manifest in *The Searchers* in Ethan's violent hatred of Debbie and the other captive women. When Ethan and Martin search for Debbie among white women who have been driven mad by their captivity, a man says, "It's hard to believe they're white." Ethan responds, "They ain't white anymore. They're Comanche." The camera then zooms onto Ethan's face, with all its dark and terrible hatred. This shot anticipates the murderous violence of Ethan's reaction to Debbie and her relationship to Chief Scar, a warrior whose name suggests the internal psychic wound of Ethan's Ahab-like madness. Ethan hammers at Martin, who wants to save Debbie because of their family relationship, "No kin. She's been with a buck." Upon hearing later that Debbie is still alive, Ethan says, "Living with Comanches ain't being alive." Of course, Ethan's ultimate act of total hatred occurs in his failed attempt to shoot Debbie when they first find her among the Indians. Only Pawley's interference and a wound Ethan suffers during an Indian attack enable Debbie to flee from her white rescuers. Moreover, the sexual aspect of Ethan's tensions toward Debbie helps explain his earlier discomfort in his brother's house. The proximity of the sister-in-law arouses illicit desires and conflicts that must be denied.

In addition, the frontier in the narrative and film generates cultural tensions and ambiguities that are endemic in the culture as a whole. In both the film and the narrative, the frontier is not just a place but a frame of mind and a way of belief. It intensifies living conditions and dangers and imposes stark choices with limited options. As Demos says, "The 'frontier' connection seems to hold a particular and lasting resonance for John Williams. His sermon explicitly joins 'armies *and* frontiers'. . . ." (Demos 75). On the frontier, Williams and his family and Ethan and his people are in a constant state of war in their individual and social struggles for survival and redemption. An amazing moment in *The Searchers* dramatizes the moral, philosophical, and psychological consequences of this state of war on the frontier. When Ethan and the Texans, including Martin, Jorgensen and his son, Captain Clayton, and Old Mose, go off to investigate Jorgensen's loss of cattle, they find them all dead and realize that the Indians have fooled and lured the men from their ranches and families. As usual, only Ethan has anticipated this development. He declares the Indians are on a "murder raid" and that the real danger exists for either the Jorgensen family or his own, two ranches left relatively defenseless by the absence of the men as much as forty miles away in the case of the Edwards ranch. Jorgensen immediately panics in a thoroughly convincing and moving way. "Momma! Laurie! Oh, please God, please no!" Jorgensen cries, a sense of genuine terror resonating in his voice. In effect, his prayer for his family constitutes a wish for the destruction of the other family – a horrible and impossible choice made inevitable and understandable by circumstances on the frontier.

Equally moving, without any excessive gesture or cry of his own, Wayne's face in an amazing shot reveals his recognition of his failure to protect his family from the horror of the massacre because of his readiness to follow the good-hearted but incompetent captain to chase after the cattle. The shadow of guilt and grief weighs heavily over him. Such guilt as well as signs of pain, weakness, and vulnerability all find expression on Wayne's face and body. In such moments, Wayne's acting and physical presence surpass the visual cliché of unrestrained and simpleminded masculinity often associated with him. In contrast, Captain Clayton, the typical political figure, ignorantly muddles through the catastrophe of his own making, largely unconcerned about his guilt and responsibility as the leader for events.

The melding of images of fighting, frontier, and family in the Puritan imagination affirm that in both the narrative and film men remain the central consciousness. Although the pursuit of captured young girls or women provides the objective and focus for the narrative and film, both are ultimately about the men; the salvation of the men assumes primary importance, even over the rescue of the captured women. Demos notes, "The most featured character is, unsurprisingly, John Williams himself. And the theme, in virtually every case, is some sort of contest: typically, Williams versus one or another (or several) of his 'Romish' adversaries" (Demos 70). For Williams and other Puritans, the sense of perpetual embattlement and conflict over ultimate issues encourages a culture of violence. Self-obsession becomes the rule for such minds, which forever are weighing the likelihood of salvation according to the outcome of endless moral engagements and contests. Such self-absorption under these conditions often distorts reality, limits options, and invites violence. Guilt over violence in turn both signals and perpetuates moral insecurity.

Thus, the violent reaction of the white communities in both the Puritan narrative and the film to frontier life and dangers further subverts claims of white moral superiority. Certainly, Ethan personifies a hatred and violence that often exceeds the violence of his Indian enemies. Even in *The Redeemed Captive,* the Puritans rejoice in the violent punishment inflicted upon the Indians, an action they prefer to see as divine retribution for the wrongs committed against peaceful whites by savage heathens. Close readings of Williams's text and actions and the film problematize the Puritans' belief in their moral superiority.

The psychological and cultural tensions and anxieties embedded in Williams's text erupt in the violence of a later generation. His son Samuel becomes the kind of soldier-saint that typifies the Puritan's relationship to the moral ambiguities of the frontier. As John Demos recounts:

> In April, a force of 30 men left Deerfield to "scout" for Indians in the upper Connecticut Valley; Samuel Williams, John's eldest son now grown to manhood, was its "lieutenant." After days of fruitless "tracking," a small group of Indians was surprised in canoes "on ye water": by "firing briskly on them . . . we did kill 9." Among the dead, wrote Samuel's brother Stephen some while later, was "my old master Wottanommon." (Did Stephen feel gratified by this? Or perhaps a twinge of regret? He gives us no hint.) For Wottanommon's scalp (and the others) scout-members received 30 [pounds] compensation from the colony's General Court. (Demos 96)

Interestingly, Demos's discussion of Samuel's fight parenthetically raises the kinds of moral questions at the heart of the religious dimension of the captivity narrative and the Puritan experience. Demos emphasizes the Puritans' own recognition of these moral issues. They understand the danger of exchanging what they deem as their moral superiority for what they consider to be the savagery of the Indians. They know the risk behind assuming the necessity of the evils of violence and domination. They fear losing their moral identity and their civilization through the violent actions that are adopted by them to protect and sustain the New England Way.

In his military success and violence, Williams's son resembles the archetypal figure of Captain Benjamin Church, the Puritan Indian fighter who captured and killed King Philip in the first great Indian war in New England. Interestingly for the Williams saga, Church also led the Puritan forces in their retaliatory war against the French and Indians for the massacre at Deerfield that resulted in the captivity of the Williams family. Demos reports:

> But the massacre evoked a broader spectrum of response than shame and religious soul-searching. There was grief: "Poor Deerfield beset by French & Indians . . . and almost depopulated," commented a diarist in the Masschusetts countryside. There was anxiety for the future, especially of the captives: their plight, wrote [Samuel] Sewall, "would make a hard heart bleed." There was fury: thus the venerable "Indian fighter" Benjamin Church excoriated "the French and Indian enemy" for "many cruelties . . . particularly the horrid action at Deerfield this last winter, in killing . . . and scalping, without giving any notice at all, or opportunity to ask quarter." There was thirst for vengeance: Church himself would soon be commissioned to lead a retaliatory expedition against the Indians of Maine and the French in Nova Scotia – and the Massachusetts General Court raised the bounty for Indian scalps from 10 [pounds] to 40 and then to 100 within a scant few months. (Demos 41–2)

The search for Debbie by Ethan Edwards and Martin Pawley through the Western desert revivifies all these concerns and elements of the Puritan narrative. The Puritan captivity narrative and jeremiad frame and contextualize the psyche and moral mission of the men on the search, and the society they represent. The sermon-narrative indicates that the journey in *The Searchers* has an extensive history with roots in the origins of the settlement of the nation and the founding of the country.

At the same time, the modernistic consciousness of *The Searchers* also helps to account for its power and permanence in the American imagination. Indeed, its modernistic sensibility actually disrupts the genre of the western, transforming the basic story into a metaphor of modern abandonment and alienation. Ford institutes a multiple transformation that makes the western a form for our times and life. Though Ford's western incorporates the basic narrative of captivity and the rhetorical structure of the jeremiad, it does so in ways that revivify those classic structures through the modernism of its cinematic aesthetics and cultural consciousness. The modernism of Ford's direction and imagination prevents the western genre from being merely an exercise in nostalgia for revisiting the lost values and ideals of a romanticized American past. In sum, *The Searchers* revolutionizes the classic genre, narrative, and moral argument by casting them in a modern guise to make them part of an American tradition of cultural discourse and reform.

The ironic treatment of religion in *The Searchers* helps modernize this captivity narrative, transforming it into a story of modern man's moral and spiritual dilemma. Biblical names, allusions, and metaphors appear throughout, as they had in *The Grapes of Wrath,* Ford's 1940 film of the John Steinbeck novel. Whereas the religious dimension of *The Grapes of Wrath* contributes structure, depth, and direction, *The Searchers* ridicules and satirizes institutionalized forms of religious belief, activity, and speech. In this film, Moses becomes Mose, a blithering fool without wisdom or vision, whose words trivialize and diminish religious sensibility. He chants that cattle are Kiowas when they were slaughtered by warring renegade Comanches, thanks God for "the blessings we are about to receive" in anticipation of a murderous Indian attack, and proudly proclaims his baptism in a race to the river to escape howling and pursuing Indians. Neither Mose nor Aaron, Ethan's rather inept brother who is killed by Scar's party during the Indian raid, are part of the extended seven-year search through the desert. In addition, in *The Searchers* the representative of official religion, Captain Clayton, also happens to be a military officer. Meanwhile the main figure of the story, Ethan, continues a quest that has become primarily his own personal campaign of blood vengeance, racial hatred, and death.

The deprecation and trivialization of religion and its representatives in *The Searchers* would seem to subvert and contradict Ethan's role as a pilgrim. In fact, however, it works as a counterpoint to the journey, adding depth to Ethan's quest as the epitomization of the search for belief and faith in the modern age. As an allegory for the putative moral mission of American culture in the world, Ethan's search for a form of redemption gains substance and moral complexity through the film's ironic treatment of religion. Ethan remains a pilgrim in a Godless world. In a secular universe, the search for the "city on a hill" becomes the search for a civil society of democratic consensus; the nature of Ethan's journey, however, complicates and vexes his relationship to that consensus. Ethan, the Confederate rebel and outsider, operates as an emissary of death on a special mission in the service of his private vision of the right and proper social order. The lawlesssness of his mission of vengeance and death threatens society. In his quest to purify and reform according to his own values, Ethan stands as a moral extremist ready to sacrifice and destroy in order to save.

The challenge of the film, therefore, involves converting Ethan and altering his mission without trivializing the significance of his meaning for American culture. Ford immediately poses that challenge to Ethan through the character of Martin Pawley. Martin's insistence on joining Ethan on the search dramatically subverts Ethan's wish to form a nation of one without any responsibility to anyone outside of himself. Martin's presence turns the pilgrimage into a social experience that becomes part of the film's overall process of humanizing Ethan. His participation begins Ford's effort to reconsider the situation of America as a democracy of continued relevance to its own people and for the world during a period of increasing activism by minorities and people of color. Can America still work and hold together or will it be destroyed by various forces – an internal avenging superego of miserable feelings and hurts as represented by Ethan, or an alienated and abused minority like the Indians? Ford's personal agony over such questions can be felt throughout this film, and Wayne's own intuitive appreciation of the stakes for human history in the future of the American idea also motivates his performance into a triumph of cinematic acting. From the beginning, Ethan has felt threatened, defeated, eager to destroy the perceived enemy of his world and beliefs. How can he achieve a compromise between the past and the needs for the future without destroying everything that hangs in the balance – past ideals, future generations, lasting values, new hopes?

The Searchers, thus, profoundly gets to the core conflict of American democracy, a society that exists by always transforming itself while remaining a coherent and unified historical continuity. *The Searchers* projects the culture's history of anxiety and change in waves of thought and feeling on Wayne's face and person, exactly as John Ford envisioned it all when he put them there.[24]

The crisis of religious belief in the film highlights the transformation of Ethan's pilgrimage into a modernistic tale of loss and abandonment. He becomes a tormented pilgrim wandering in the Western wilderness for a total of seven years. With hatred for Debbie as his motivation and the service of death as his cause, the perverted logic of the journey demands avoiding its completion. Fulfilling his death wish for Debbie would be an act so thoroughly reprehensible as to amount to a form of suicide for himself, a sort of double execution that would forever separate him from his own family and, indeed, the human family.

Ethan, therefore, must evade the very death he seeks and must silence his dark ideology of final endings; so the journey serves as its own justification, a kind of self-exile for eternal wandering. Its object becomes the journey itself and the avoidance of confronting the implications of the dreaded end. The pilgrim now wanders in a wilderness no longer created by God as a test of religious faith but in a nightmare landscape of nihilism and disbelief of man's own making. The pilgrim's impulse remains and continues to define Ethan: He still wishes to purify and cleanse and save the world, but the purposes and rationale of the cause fade. His wish for death conflicts with his wish for a reason to escape death, so he becomes a kind of existential hero in the manner of Kierkegaard: living as a moving ghost, seeking death to kill the death in him and his world, appearing as a figure of terror, like the Ancient Mariner, to those around him. Ethan epitomizes modern man in his search for a vision of values and beliefs to give life direction and his world meaning.

Interestingly, Ford proposes a Native American, a dead Comanche warrior, to symbolize best the modernistic condition and situation that Ethan comes to represent – a fascinating ideological choice in its suggestion of the common bond of all people in feeling the despair of disbelief and the condition of alienation in contemporary life. In the first stages of the search for the captured Edwards sisters, the Texas posse comes across the warrior's grave. The men uncover the shallow grave, and Ethan, while still on his horse, fires two shots at the corpse to take out his eyes. In disgust, the Captain/Reverend Clayton asks Ethan "what good" this act of mutilation accomplished. Ethan bellows: "By what you preach, none. But what that Comanche believes – ain't got no eyes, can't enter the spirit land. Has to wander forever between the winds. You get it, reverend." Of course, Ethan doesn't "get" that he really has just described his own life and destiny of wandering over a nightmare landscape that denies "the spirit" and the value and meaning of life. As though to confirm that Ethan creates his own future and sentences himself to a fate of self-inflicted abandonment and misery, he then barks at Martin Pawley: "Come on, blanket head." He himself gives the order to proceed on this nightmare journey, his cruel, racist language powerfully exhibiting his own blindness that condemns him to futile wandering. Without vision, Ethan cannot perceive or conceive of any truth that will save him and others, so he must search blindly until finally gaining the ability to see and create a society and life far different than what he previously has envisioned. Later in the film, Ford pursues this use of Indians to symbolize the nomadic condition of wandering without clear direction or apparent spiritual guidance. Ethan describes what appears to be the erratic, meaningless, and confused movements of the Indians. He identifies this band as "Noyeke" Comanches and explains their behavior: "Man says he's goin' one place, means to go t'other. Roundabout."[25]

Ethan's understanding in these instances of the Comanche's beliefs and behavior strongly suggests his own modern situation of displacement and homelessness. The Comanches already are displaced aliens in their own lands and territory. Ethan also shares with this enemy a kind of spiritual barrenness and psychic alienation that many white American writers saw as the developing condition of American culture after the Civil War. Tony Tanner talks about several largely neglected Mark Twain stories as particularly representative of the modern American mind. Of these, two especially anticipate the sense of loss and despair of *The Searchers:* In "An Adventure in Remote Seas," the crew of a lost ship finds a remote island and destroys the life on it in an allegorical repetition of the discovery of America. In "The Great Dark" a man, interestingly enough also named Edwards, dreams of sailing across a drop of water that he had been examining under his microscope. The drop becomes a sea, but the means for navigation do not exist without stars, light, and charts. As grotesque monsters emerge and attack, the nightmare becomes increasingly frightening; the story obviously works as a dark metaphor for the spiritual and intellectual life of America. These stories of the "unrelenting vision of life as chaos," as Tanner says, certainly typify Ford's sense in *The Searchers* of a nightmare journey through a world without a meaningful end or purpose.[26]

Caught in such a journey without a visible or comprehensible end in sight, Ethan's consciousness centers on the moment. He becomes a true modernist in focusing on the immediate instant even as he spends his days on his endless search for Debbie. His refrain throughout the film, "That'll be the day," expounds a kind of modernist creed as reconfigured by a pilgrim's sensibility. The mixture of defiance, irony, and skepticism in the mood and voice behind Ethan's "That'll be the day" emphatically denies the possibility that some future day will define the present; there is only the moment and his own existential relationship to it to determine reality and heroic action. At the same time, the repetition of the phrase throughout the film creates the expectation of Judgment Day and the possibility of redemption, the desire for more than the failed experience of the moment to give that moment meaning. The framing of the expectation in terms of its continuous negation still keeps open the potential for final meaning. Psychologically and ideologically, he requires a belief in the potential for some kind of culminative act to justify and explain his experience. The psychology of the film thereby retains a basic Puritan teleological view of history but one that challenges Ethan's powers of imagination and articulation.

The absence for Ethan of a clearly discernible or acceptable ending to his journey seriously influences his experience of it, depriving him of an abiding sense of direction other than his own need to keep moving. For Ethan, the paradox of the moment and modernity also means that he loses the felt experience of the moment. He undergoes what Leo Charney terms, in his interpretation of Martin Heidegger and Walter Benjamin, "this evacuation of the present." Developing Heidegger's phrase for modernity, "falling into lostness," Charney writes: "With modernity came the awareness that people were always already alienated from the time in which they were living." The vacuum of belief and faith emphasizes the dilemma of the lost present in which thought and emotion can never occupy the same segment of time. According to Charney, "We can acknowledge the moment's occurrence only after the moment in which it seemed to occur. The cognition of the moment and the sensation of the moment can never inhabit the same moment." Charney then pursues this important problem of modernism's emphasis on the impossibility of the moment except as a construction after the fact. "The present, really, cannot occur, since the mind can recognize the present only after it is no longer present; the present can be acknowledged only once it has become past. We can never be present in a present."[27]

This absence of the felt present as well as a known future describes the nightmare of Ethan's journey in *The Searchers,* a journey that reenacts the wandering of the Indians either "between the winds" or in a "Roundabout," getting nowhere. In fact, during most of the seven years covered in *The Searchers,* Ethan and Martin are lost to the spectator, as though existing in a distant universe with a different order of time and space. Thus, the lack of traditional narrative structure in the film conforms to the film's theme of loss and abandonment. For the searchers, the journey becomes destructured, episodic events without an inherently connecting beginning or an end.

The modernism of *The Searchers* starkly contrasts with the classic narrative organization of Ford's earlier great film, *Stagecoach* (1939). *Stagecoach* typifies classic narrative structure with a three-phased organization of events starting with the departure from Tonto, to the actual journey, and the arrival in Lordsburg (Gallagher 148). The wonderful multiplicity of meanings in *Stagecoach* derives from Ford's direction, which makes the simple story into a complex interaction of characters and themes. In contrast, *The Searchers* could serve as a case study for the modernist sensibility of contemporary narrative and belief. *The Searchers* illustrates what Hayden White describes as the "modernist" resistance to "the temptation" to demonstrate "how one's end may be contained in one's beginning." This denial of the rigid coherence of beginnings and ends in *The Searchers* qualifies the film as an example of what White terms "anti-narrative non-stories produced by literary modernism."[28]

The chaos of the journey in *The Searchers* gets so profound that at one point Ford interjects an ordered commentary into the situation in the form of a letter from Martin to Laurie that Laurie reads aloud. However, the letter only emphasizes the inevitable failure of the attempt to impose classic narrative organization on a disorderly universe. Rather than making Ethan's and Martin's journey understandable and coherent, the humorous treatment of both the letter and the circumstances of its reading undermines Martin's correspondence as a source of narrative authority. Laurie's reading of the letter before her father, mother, and Charlie McCorry (Ken Curtis) – who has delivered it with the intention of courting her – turns to farce. The father's inflation of the importance of the arrival and reading of the letter contributes to the farce. He becomes ridiculous by turning the event into a kind of formal ritual, putting on his spectacles just to listen to Laurie read. The ludicrous nature of the letter's contents – Martin's account of how he married an Indian woman without realizing it – mocks the possibility of providing coherence and explanation to events. The way Martin informs Laurie, his prospective bride, of this Indian marriage and the way she learns of it by reading the news aloud make the whole event a joke. The description of the cruel abuse of the Indian woman in the story, Look (Beulah Archuletta), by both Martin and Ethan further demeans and belittles everyone involved in the episode, including those who learn about it all from the letter. The extreme miscommunication between Martin and Laurie emphasizes in a compressed form the film's theme of the difficulty of providing order to the universe. The letter as a commentary on events compares in silliness to the chaos of the actual journey and reinforces the loss of direction and place for Ethan and Martin. In its own way, the letter makes a strong case for the modernist view of antinarrative, nonstory that does not pretend to empirical certitude in depicting reality. The only certain truth in Martin's missive seems to be totally unintended by him: He is a complete idiot in matters concerning women and love.

Moreover, as developed by Ford, the Western setting sustains the modernistic theme of the film. Most of the outdoor scenes for *The Searchers* were shot in Monument Valley in Utah and Arizona, favorite locations for Ford along with Colorado and New Mexico. Ford uses this boundless landscape of desert, mesas, and ancient rock formations as a great, untamed dramatic stage to conceptually and visually reinforce the drama of the moral quest and emotional despair being played out on it. The physical geography externalizes Ethan's inner mental state of psychological desperation and moral turmoil. In *The Searchers*, the geography and landscape of the West become a vast mise-en-scène of modernistic displacement and abandonment.

In addition to representing the mental and moral condition of modernism through its vision of the West, Ford's film also develops the enormous magnificence of the landscape into a visual metaphor for the modernistic concept of displaced time and space. Ethan and Pawley's endless search in an endless wilderness dramatizes these forces of time and space as being distorted and transformed, as they are in modern art, literature, and thought. This physical environment and geography visually portray the breakdown of narrative order and meaning. The landscape defies the conventional notion of beginnings, middles, and ends. Unstructured space supplants temporal order.

The sense of the West as an environment of displaced time and space that exceeds human authority and rationality manifests itself in Jorgensen's sorrowful comment to Ethan when Ethan returns home at one point without having found Debbie. "Oh, Ethan," he sighs, "this country." He looks off into the distance with the vacant stare of a sailor lost at sea. A little later, he exclaims that Ethan was not responsible for the death of his son, Brad, or for the search for Debbie and Lucy: "It's this country that killed my boy." Consuming all who attempt to transgress it, this endless frontier graphically illustrates the inner loss and despair that for some characterize modernism's destructive force.

However, this landscape provides a hospitable setting for the reinvention of Ethan, the classic American hero. As the scene of modernistic displacement, Ford's Monument Valley offers the soil for modernizing the American Puritan. Ethan and the landscape in all its multiple meanings become contiguous. Partly through the power of this environment, which works as an active force on the film's structure and meaning, *The Searchers'* modernism recontextualizes and resignifies Ethan's role, making him an agent in representing the paradox of narrativity and the moment. This modernism transforms his mythic role as the American Puritan and Westerner into a relevant modernistic heroism of great potential significance.

In revisioning and recasting Ethan into a hero of modernistic displacement, Ford and Wayne go to the core of the American experience and transform it. Ethan, the great Indian fighter, embodies a tradition that goes back at least to Benjamin Church in King Philip's War, through Daniel Boone and James Fenimore Cooper's *Leatherstocking Tales,* of the frontiersman-soldier who survives by becoming part of the frontier environment and the native culture.[29] Like Church in his classic council with Annawon, the great Indian advisor to the slaughtered King Philip, the white leader in his triumph becomes part of the very culture he would subdue and destroy. Marginalized in his existence between two cultures, white and Indian, civilized and tribal, he advances white, Puritan values, rhetoric, and rituals with a gun. Ethan Edwards embodies this figure of white culture and violence, especially as articulated in D. H. Lawrence's famous description of Cooper's classic *Leatherstocking* American hero, Natty Bumppo: "a saint with a gun." Lawrence's description of Cooper's hero as rendered in *The Deerslayer* could serve verbatim for Ford's and Wayne's Ethan Edwards: "A man who turns his back on white society. A man who keeps his moral integrity hard and intact. An isolate, almost selfless, stoic, enduring man, who lives by death, by killing, but who is pure white." Lawrence concludes with a general characterization of the American that has lasted for about eight decades: "The essential American soul is hard, isolate, stoic, and a killer. It has never yet melted."[30]

The political and cultural implications of this congeries of myths and symbols induced F. O. Matthiessen to articulate in *American Renaissance* a clear and systematic alternative theory of American literature as a source for the survival and maintenance of democracy. Matthiessen felt the need for such a theory partly because he so fully recognized the dangers to democracy that were present, if inchoate, in some of the ideas of the American Renaissance writers. Thus, Matthiessen foresaw the incipient fascism of Walt Whitman's version of the American Adam, the prototype of the classic American hero. Matthiessen notes with alarm how Whitman "annihilates all valid distinctions between the actual and the ideal" in order to transfer religious "supremacy to himself."

> This religious assurance, unleashed from all control in dogma or creed, must be called no less than terrifying in the lengths to which it was to go in proclaiming the individual as his own Messiah. For this tendency, so mildly innocent in Emerson, so confused and bombastic in Whitman, was to result in the hardness of Nietzsche, in the violence of those characters of Dostoyevsky's who have have been uprooted from all tradition and find no law but themselves, in such demonic nihilism as that of Kirilov in *The Possessed*.[31]

For Matthiessen, of course, such religious fervor formed a direct and immediate line to fascist political thought and action: "When the doctrine of the Superman was again transformed, or rather, brutally distorted, the voice of Hitler's megalomania was to be heard sounding through it."[32]

The fascistic potentials in both myth and modernism converge in the figure of Ethan Edwards. He personifies the pilgrim's messianic fanaticism and zeal in combination with the violence of modernistic rootlessness and displacement. Fulfilling the deadly potential of both of these impulses, Wayne becomes a Prince of Darkness. A performance made possible to a considerable extent by Ford's ingenious direction, Wayne's achievement represents a remarkable collaboration between the actor and director that originated in *Stagecoach*. Ford as a director could sometimes act like a god himself, and in regard to Wayne he probably could make a reasonable case for his divinity. He helped transform Wayne from an impressive cowboy actor in rather mundane features to a figure of true cinematic and cultural importance. After demonstrating wonderful humanity and refreshing openness in *Stagecoach*, years later in *The Searchers* Wayne nearly attains superhuman proportions as a powerfully complex and disturbed figure. The shots of him as a kind of Dark Angel of death achieve a new dimension for him and Ford of the cinematic representation of a conflicted hero hovering on an existential abyss of nihilism and abandonment. One shot of him early in the film that we already have discussed deserves mention again as the visual and dramatic epitomization of Wayne's new stature as a dark, menacing, and alienated hero. After finding Jorgensen's slaughtered cattle, Ethan, realizing that the Comanches have lured the men away from their ranches, foresees the destruction of his family. He stares from behind his horse and saddle as Pawley races off to the ranch forty miles away, disregarding Ethan's warning that the horses need rest and grain to make the return trip. In close-up with his head above his

Figure 3. The dark vision of John Wayne in *The Searchers* (Warner / C. V. Whitney: The Museum of Modern Art / Film Stills Archive).

horse and saddle, the shot of Wayne's anguished face dramatizes many layers of meaning. Fear, foreboding, grief, and horror all play out across his frozen stare and burning eyes. The intensity of the outward look matches the sense of inner guilt and dread over his failure to protect his family.

Other examples of the dark brilliance of Wayne's performance and Ford's direction abound, including Wayne's panic and flight on horseback after finding Lucy's mutilated body in a hidden canyon. The depth of his emotion and pain over what he saw of her in the canyon are dramatically conveyed when Wayne has to tell Brad Jorgensen (Harry Carey, Jr.), Lucy's fiancé, what he saw and did with Lucy's body, after Brad mistakenly thinks he spotted the captured Lucy with some Indians. Ethan says, "What you saw wasn't Lucy. . . . What you saw was a buck wearing Lucy's dress. I found Lucy back in the canyon . . . wrapped her in my coat, buried her with my own hands, thought it best to keep it from you." Although Wayne ostensibly speaks to Brad and Pawley, his facial expression and body language dramatize that he also addresses some inner region of his own tormented soul and psyche. His face and voice resonate with the hidden reality of the horror that his words can only suggest. The cadences and rhythm of his speech, which have been ridiculed and mimicked for years, in this instance defy imitation. When Brad cannot comprehend the terrible truth of how Lucy died, Wayne explodes: "What do you want me to do, draw you a picture? Spell it out? Don't ever ask me! As long as you live, don't ever ask me!"

Another shot worth mentioning again for provocatively exemplifying the contending forces in Ethan of violent danger, racism, heroism, depth of feeling, and visceral fascism involves the shadow and darkness on Wayne's face that accentuate his anger and insidious intent as he casts a final venomous look of malice upon the mad white women who have been rescued by the cavalry. Yet another example of such cinematic success by Wayne and Ford concerns the development of Wayne's discovery of his massacred family. First, in a brilliant and poignant exterior shot, he overlooks the smoldering house from atop a hill. Then, as shot by Ford from inside the house, the viewer can only imagine the horror that Ethan sees based upon the pain and rage Wayne evinces. It also should be noted that Ford continually positions Wayne in exquisite frames and shots in which Wayne embodies everything romantic and exciting about the West, beginning with the opening, when Martha observes him in the distance riding home, to the two-shots of Ethan and Pawley on horseback. Interior shots are also composed to maintain the power of Wayne's presence. As Wills suggests, the combination of Wayne's powers as an actor – body, movement, language, voice, poise – presents him as "indomitable" (17). In *The Searchers,* Wayne becomes exactly the kind of superman of potential evil that Matthiessen dreads and that Ford himself also certainly abhors – partly, no doubt, because of his own psychological and personal attraction to such unqualified power and charisma.

Thus, Wayne's portrayal of Ethan Edwards and Ford's direction in *The Searchers* establish a thread to a fascistic aesthetics that has been so problematic in cinema since at least the 1920s. For example, Thomas Elsaesser notes the concern of some over an "inherently fascist" cinema and "the legacy of Nazi aesthetics." He asks, "In the age of the blockbuster, who does not recognize the seductive appeal of creating a substitute world, of treating power as a work of art, in short of the *eros* and *thanatos* of objectification?"[33] More specifically, Miriam Hansen discusses modernism and fascism in film in a way that relates to the significance of Ethan Edwards in *The Searchers.* She notes how one form of modernity moves toward fascism through the development of "the timelessness of a new megamyth: monumental nature, the heroic body, the re-armored mass ornament – in short the Nazi modernism exemplified by Leni Riefenstahl."[34] Certainly, Edwards represents an American "megamyth" that endangers democracy and challenges Ford's democratic aesthetics.

For Matthiessen, the humanity and democratic spirit in Whitman mitigates the potential for fascism in his work and thought. What Matthiessen
terms "the strength of Whitman's democratic faith," as well as the poet's
"qualities" of "sympathy, solidarity," also characterize Ford's genius.[35] In
The Searchers, Pawley operates as Ford's agent of social equality, becoming
one of the strongest forces behind the democratization of Ethan. He serves
as a democratic Ishmael to counter the madness of Ethan's Ahab. Martin becomes the egalitarian everyman ultimately capable of great deeds, including
his insistence upon joining Ethan in the first place because, as he tells the frustrated Laurie, he sees in Ethan "a man who can go crazy wild" and therefore
must be controlled in order to protect Debbie at the end of the search. Significantly, Martin not only finally saves Debbie both from the Indians and from
the raid of the Texas Rangers, he also kills Scar, leaving the Indian's scalp for
Ethan – acts that signify his developing maturity and strength as well as the
possible weakening of Ethan's abilities.

Pawley's strength as a character lends credibility to his role as a mediator
between the two cultures of the Native Americans and the whites. As a so-
called "half-breed" who evokes the film's first signs of Ethan's racism, Martin occupies the classic Indian role in the myth of the white man's supportive Indian partner. The roots of this relationship again go back to Benjamin
Church and Annawon and also proceed through Chingachgook, the Mo-
hican chief in Cooper's *Leatherstocking Tales*, to Tonto and The Lone Ranger, and even to more contemporary buddy stories and films. Martin's role
throughout *The Searchers* represents the growing consciousness of race in
America in the 1950s. Thus, Wills notes that "Wayne's character has been influenced by Marty, by a man he has come to respect despite his Indian blood.
This is already a partial redemption" (259). Moreover, Martin's relationship
with Ethan displaces the central racial issue of the era concerning the civil
rights movement and the crisis of African-American and white relations.
Pawley indicates the beginnings of a sea change in attitudes toward race and
ethnicity. His role suggests Ford's growing sense of the difficulty and inevitability behind the challenge to transform the national consensus to include
people of color.

Along with Pawley's influence, modernism itself as a cultural and formal
ideology helps develop Ethan's character. The modernistic nature of film contributes to Ford's democratic aesthetic. Just as Whitman's experiment with
language serves the democratic spirit that Matthiessen so staunchly avers, so
also Ford's commitment to a modernistic consciousness in film reinforces his
democratic cinematic aesthetic. Like Whitman, Ford takes the liberal path
in the modernist fork in the road. In *The Searchers*, as in Ford's other great
films, the ideology of form sustains a democratic cultural and political ideology. The connection in *The Searchers* concerning the ideology of form,

democracy, and modernism rests on the linkage we discussed earlier that Charney maintains between the "cinematic conception of space and time" and "the evacuation of the present in modernity."[36] In other words, film as an art form of moving representational images highlights the dichotomy of the break between consciousness and emotion in the experience of the moment. The very form and nature of film compare to modernistic sensibility in presenting disruption and displacement as characterizing life and experience. This modernistic moment of lost meaning engenders a sense of displacement; but the displaced moment also entails a potential for freedom, by emphasizing the existential challenge to the individual to create one's identity and relationship to experience rather than to assume a given continuity of truth and meaning. Although, in using this terminology of the moment, Charney elaborates upon the philosophical insights into film by the French director and thinker of the twenties Jean Epstein, the critical connection between film and modernism applies with equal validity to Ford's practice and work. Accordingly, Ford's modernistic displacement of time and space in *The Searchers* disrupts and displaces Ethan's character in a manner that enables his transformation into a democratic hero. Ethan's dislocation ultimately overcomes his impulse for destruction and leads to his growth. Thus Ford's modernism makes Wayne into a democratic hero without sacrificing the aesthetic integrity of the film to ideological demands. In Ethan's case, the displacement and dislocation of modernism as represented by the seven-year search finally lead to some degree of acceptance of love, mourning, and his own vulnerability.

Until the end of the film, two expressions of a frontier code of strength and combativeness help explain the journey. At one point, when Pawley and Ethan lose the trail of the Comanches in the snow, Pawley says, "Well, why don't you say it. We're beat and you know it." Wayne's gritty response summarizes his blind determination: "Nope. . . . There's such a thing as a critter'll just keep coming on. So we'll find 'em in the end. I promise you. Just as sure as the turning of the earth." Later, when they report to the Jorgensens on the failures and losses of their search to that point, Lars Jorgensen complains woefully, but Mrs. Jorgensen (Olive Carey) responds with a kind of homegrown existentialism that articulates an ideology of pioneer survival on the frontier: "Just happens we be Texicans. Just so happens, Texicans is nothing but a human man. Way out on a limb. This year and next. And maybe 'til a hundred more."

However, to achieve some degree of resolution on an individual as well as a cultural and historical level, Ethan must go beyond such an ideology of energy and survival. He must find a way to come home, to locate the means within himself to return to his community[37] – a reengagement that ultimately requires a reawakening of his capacity to love and to care about others. In *The Searchers,* love, home, and reengagement with the human community demand Ethan's reconciliation with women and the female body. From the beginning of the film, Ford establishes an opposition between Ethan, forever the phallic horseman, as the perennial outsider and woman as the ultimate insider. He maintains this tension between the masculine outdoors and the smothering security of feminine interior spaces. *The Searchers'* marvelous opening shot and sequence, as noted above, suggest these tensions and oppositions. In the shadowed darkness of the door and narrow entrance of the Edwards house on the frontier, we look out past the woman in the doorway and into the blazing light of the open spaces of the West. That woman, Martha Edwards, intuits a distant rider's identity as though she has never stopped waiting for him. The significance of these exciting and vivid images becomes readily apparent. While the exterior landscape suggests freedom, opportunity, and adventure, the environment also implies danger. The interior space suggests security, the womb, and rebirth, but it also connotes death, tomb, and the inner tensions of maximum security. Gallagher summarizes these symbolic sexual and psychological relationships:

> When, in *The Searchers'* first shot, Martha opens her door from blackness to the bright world outside, the equation of home with blackness suggests (as is subsequently confirmed) that within the doorway dwells our innerness, heart and womb, our vulnerability, even our unconscious. On this occasion Martha is opening herself to Ethan – the imagery accounts for the sequence's extraordinary emotional power – but the necessity to protect, to seal off our interiority from the world outside, from other people, produces psychic isolation, the consummate sin from which stems all the lack of empathy we noted in the letter scene, and all the intolerance, racism, opportunism, obsessive hate, and insanity of *The Searchers'* world. (Gallagher 334)

Gallagher succinctly develops the sexual tension at the center of these relationships. "Martha and her home seem the prime desires of Ethan's interiority. But they are also the prime frustrations: Ethan is left outside alone at night as Aaron takes Martha indoors to bed" (Gallagher 334). He further notes how Ethan avoids doors as a sign of sexual entry that he also must resist, especially regarding his brother's wife.

In the context of the entire film, these opening images of sexuality, desire, and loss require further elucidation. We need to emphasize that the interior shot does not refer only to the woman but concerns Ethan's psyche as well. Moreover, as the story evolves, it becomes clearer that the forces of sexuality and desire identified by Gallagher work in *The Searchers* in a way that Freud analyzed as the relationship involving mourning, melancholia, and identification. From the opening scene, through the journey and search, to the conclusion, the film's external events serve as a metaphor and a visualization of the internal workings of mourning and melancholia in Ethan's character. We remember, of course, that Ethan returns to the ranch in a disconsolate and alienated mood. He is consumed by aggressions and hostilities stemming in large part from his unfulfilled and illicit desire for his brother's wife, Martha, feelings that she obviously reciprocates. The intensity of these feelings becomes blatant when we see Martha fetishize Ethan's rebel coat. Having offered to put the coat away, Martha, as noted by several critics, later caresses it by herself in a manner that clearly makes Captain Clayton uncomfortable as he notices her actions from another room. He is uncomfortable enough to linger in the room as Ethan and Martha say good-bye to each other. Although he gives the couple some privacy by not looking directly at them, his physical presence, the frown on his face, and the agitated swirling of his coffee cup all indicate a profound concern about the potential danger in this prohibited intimacy between Ethan and Martha. In this one scene, Bond rather than Wayne dominates the frame as the Captain/Reverend occupies the center of the frame and faces the camera, the very personification of the paternal and social prohibition against violating the taboo that keeps Ethan and Martha apart.

In Freudian terms, Ethan's bitterness and anger in these opening scenes dramatize the "melancholic displays" of "an extraordinary diminution in his self-regard, an impoverishment of his ego on a grand scale."[38] In a manner consistent with Freud's theory, Ethan's shattered self-image and self-regard rest on an inflated sense of his ego as well as an excessive investment in the importance of his own conscience. Rather than "evincing" the "humility and submissiveness" of the truly crushed, Ethan as a melancholic, demonstrates feelings of being "slighted" and "treated with great injustice" (*M&M* 248). Ethan's belief in his own moral independence and superiority, his insistence on going it alone, his refusal to accept surrender or defeat all suggest such a high sense of his own worth as to anticipate an equally radical reaction to failure and rejection. Ethan, therefore, sees the failure of his love for Martha as a failure of his own identity. Narcissism displaces his love that has been withdrawn from her and internalized in himself. Such narcissism becomes self-punishment as a way of indirectly and unconsciously attacking not only himself but also Martha, the lost love object.

As in mourning, in melancholia ambivalence over the object of one's love can involve a pathological mental state. In contrast to mourning, in which the love object literally disappears, in melancholia the continued presence of the object necessitates an emphasis upon ambivalence about the mixture of love and hatred toward the loved one and oneself. According to Freud, "In melancholia the relation to the object is no simple one; it is complicated by the conflict due to ambivalence" (*M&M* 256). He says, "The loss of a love-object is an excellent opportunity for the ambivalence in love-relationships to make itself effective and come into the open" (*M&M* 250–1). Describing how such ambivalence leads to various forms of aggression, Freud adds that the allegedly aggrieved individual often assumes "the circuitous path of self-punishment, in taking revenge on the original object and in tormenting their loved one through their illness, having resorted to it in order to avoid the need to express their hostility to him openly" (*M&M* 251). Ethan's absence from the family for several years after the war, his bitter attitude about paying his own way upon his return, his overall sense of abandonment indicate a hidden need to punish himself in order also to punish Martha for being with his brother. The nature of such feelings in Ethan remains repressed but reveals itself through all forms of pathological language and behavior. As Freud writes,

> If the love for the object – a love which cannot be given up though the object itself is given up – takes refuge in narcissistic identification, then the hate comes into operation on this substitutive object, abusing it, debasing it, making it suffer and deriving sadistic satisfaction from its suffering. (*M&M* 251)

This "self-tormenting in melancholia" (*M&M* 251) describes Ethan's penchant for suffering on his search, a journey that becomes an exercise in alternating sadism and self-punishment. Although sadistic hatred becomes especially manifest in his attitude toward Native Americans, in fact Ethan evinces extreme hostility toward most people in the film. Similarly, in *The Man Who Shot Liberty Valance* (1962), the character played by Wayne, Tom Doniphon, exhibits a mental state and behavior comparable to Ethan's condition when he drunkenly sets his house on fire and stays inside it as a means of punishing the woman who has left him. By immolating himself and destroying the house that was meant for him and the woman, Wayne will make her pay for her betrayal. Woody Strode (Pompey), the great black actor, plays Wayne's sidekick who saves him from the fire, and Vera Miles – Laurie in *The Searchers* – plays the girl who leaves Wayne for James Stewart, once again portraying a character caught in frustrated and conflicted gender roles and love relationships.

In *The Searchers*, horrible deaths exacerbate the pathology of Ethan's mental state. The massacre of his family, the captivity of the girls, and the need for the search itself ulcerate what Freud terms the "open wound" of his obsessive melancholia (*M&M* 253). Events dictate the awful marriage in Ethan's mind of melancholia and mourning. The "work of mourning," in which the ego heals and adjusts to its loss so that "the ego becomes free and uninhibited again" (*M&M* 245), cannot occur because of the melancholia that preceded the catastrophe. Guilt, aggression, and pain retard this "internal work" of mourning (*M&M* 245). As frontier leader and hero, Ethan blames himself for the family's awful fate. He failed them, but his own ambivalence fuels and compounds his terrible guilt. At one level, the death of Martha and her husband and the destruction of the family represent a wish fulfillment for Ethan. At the same time, this death further shatters his ego in the sense of affirming his total failure to live up to his ideal vision of himself and his values of conscience; both ego ideal and superego condemn him. For Ethan, what Freud calls "the economics of pain" in this situation literally becomes psychologically unbearable. Since the implications of these losses must be "withdrawn from consciousness" for Ethan, "reality testing" (*M&M* 245, 244), in the form of seriously and accurately analyzing his situation, proves impossible.

This psychic situation helps account for the way Ethan transfers his hatred to the one individual he should love the most, Debbie, who is so utterly dependent upon him and so completely the victim of circumstances beyond her control. Ethan's psychology helps explain the depth of his racist death wish for Debbie: He transfers his feelings toward himself and Martha onto the girl. Debbie functions as part of his own ego and identity, the part he has repressed in his ambivalent feelings toward Martha and his self-hatred. She must die as a surrogate for her mother; she must die to stifle Ethan's own guilt. She also deserves death as the living remnant of the person who destroyed Ethan's sense of himself by rejecting him. In the sick part of Ethan's mind, Debbie's crime that justifies killing her derives not just from the fact that she has lived with an Indian, as he claims, but that she represents all of Ethan's failures as the kind of man he envisions himself to be.

Instead of undergoing the curative work of mourning through the operations of his own psyche, Ethan fetishizes his search, displacing onto his hideous mission of murder the hidden, perverted force of his deep denial of weakness, vulnerability, and guilt. The fringed rifle sheath Ethan carries with him throughout the search serves as the visible fetish that signifies the journey's secret purpose of denial. As a symbolization of denial, guilt, misplaced aggression, and vulnerability, the fringed sheath compares to Scar's lance of scalps, a totemistic representation of fulfilled and realized basic violence.

It deserves repeated emphasis that all of these conflicted emotions, values, and ideas come alive in the film because of the collaboration between Ford and Wayne. As directed by Ford, Wayne powerfully represents the seething mixture of so many divergent impulses that we have been discussing. Wayne also manages to make the film's resolution of all of these dilemmas realistic.

At the same time, Wayne's acting and Ford's direction succeed partly because the film's major elements – narrative, ideology, psychology – cohere so well as to make Ethan's partial healing and resolution of his conflicts credible. First, time accounts for some of the changes that occur. Freud says that "in mourning time is needed for the command of reality-testing to be carried out in detail, and that when this work has been accomplished the ego will have succeeded in freeing its libido from the lost object" (*M&M* 252). The extended period of the search helps Ethan learn to do the work of mourning. So much time also allows for Ethan's developing relationship with Pawley to nurture the process of psychic healing. Time and Pawley's influence lend credibility to changes in Ethan's character. The most important changes occur after Ethan has been wounded while trying to shoot Debbie. Leaving Debbie, Ethan and Martin flee to a cave, a recuperative symbol of the feminine, where they remain while Martin nurses the older man by draining the "poison" from the wound inflicted upon him by an Indian arrow. However, Pawley also works on the poison in Ethan's mind and soul. Failing to kill Debbie, suffering a life-threatening wound that tests his readiness to die, and finding himself dependent upon Martin develop Ethan's character. His precarious situation makes him more receptive to Martin's humanizing influence. As a sign of such healing, Ethan "bequeaths" all his possessions to Martin, an indication of his grudging recognition of their family connection. Significantly, however, Martin rejects the offer in anguish over Ethan's continued hatred of Debbie, as though realizing that that hatred also reveals Ethan's deeper feelings toward him. This helps explain the emotional if momentary intensity of Martin's death wish for Ethan.

Given the depth and intensity of Ethan's repressed mourning and pervasive melancholia, Ford still needed to go beyond narrative developments to dramatize a convincing healing process for Ethan's psychic wounds. The symbolism of the cave sustains the psychoanalytical perspective for explaining the beginnings of Ethan's psychic and spiritual renewal. The cave symbolically mediates and mitigates the compulsive tensions and ambivalences in Ethan's mind; it serves, as Peter Lehman suggests, as a climactic womb image that originates for Ethan with the opening shot from the interior of the Edwards household.[39] The psychology and symbolism of that opening shot repeats itself in the shot from within the darkness of the cave, in which Pawley nurses the wounded Ethan. Pawley here displaces the feminine that Ethan has resisted. Ethan's recuperation within the cave marks a step toward resolving his fear of the feminine and love as symbolized by another earlier interior shot of his reaction to the horrifying sight of his massacred family. That sight fulfills all of his fears and guilt concerning sexuality, love, emotional vulnerability, and the feminine. In a sense, the whole search has been a way for Ethan to avoid returning to that sight in the hateful part of his sick psyche.

Ethan and Debbie rejoin each other only after the Indians have gone full circle, "Roundabout," and have returned to the general location of the original frontier so that Clayton and his Rangers once again can pursue them, this time successfully. With Debbie running away on foot and Ethan on horseback, he has her completely in his power to live or die. Ethan gets away from the protective Pawley and chases her down. In the film's most famous scene, instead of killing Debbie, Ethan picks her up, swings her, and says: "Let's go home, Debbie." In finally facing and accepting her, he also at last can accept himself.

Of course, he still fails to make it completely home. Ethan rides back to the ranch with Debbie cradled against his body, but he cannot enter the interior spaces of the house. The shot from within the doorway repeats the film's opening shot. Wayne stands by the door and executes some choreographed footwork as the various people go home in their different ways. Wayne, his great body by the doorway, walks off alone, still the loner at war with himself. The healing time of the cave fades into memory and dream.

For Ford, of course, Ethan and his type, as played by Wayne in so many films, remain not only relevant but indispensable. Politically and culturally, Ethan still represents steadfast masculine strength, power, and aggression that constitute essentials for the survival of any society, including a democracy. In this regard, Ethan again compares to Tom Doniphon in *The Man Who Shot Liberty Valance*, one of Ford's other "masterpieces" (Gallagher 384). In *Liberty Valance*, Wayne as the tough and independent fighter seems expendable in a new civilized West as compared to Ransom Stoddard, the tenderfoot "Pilgrim" played by James Stewart, who becomes a senator and a hero, wins the girl Hallie (Vera Miles), and achieves great fame through the apparently mistaken general belief that he brought law and order to the West by killing Liberty Valance (Lee Marvin), a dreaded bully and gunfighter. When Stewart and Miles return to the town for Wayne's funeral, we learn in an extended flashback that Wayne once admitted to Stewart that in the crucial shootout involving the notorious Liberty Valance, it was Wayne and not the Pilgrim who killed Valance. Realizing this, Stewart has been living a lie. When he leaves the town and a train conductor repeats the common belief of the people that "Nothing is too good for the man who shot Liberty Valance," the words are cruelly ironic. Earlier, when Stewart tells the whole story to the new editor of the paper, the editor decides not to print it. In the film's most famous line, the editor says, "When the legend becomes fact, print the legend." The idea, of course, is absurd. Ford himself exposes the legend and supposedly reveals the truth to the movie audience, so he contradicts and disobeys the editor's message. Obviously, Ford makes a subtler point that goes back to Doniphon telling Stoddard the alleged truth as to what really happened. In fact, we only get Doniphon's version of the story. We see the shootout again, this time from Doniphon's perspective as opposed to Stoddard's. In reality, we only have Doniphon's word for what happened. He has many reasons to lie, including self-promotion and vanity in light of his wounded pride over losing Hallie to Ransom Stoddard as well as his diminished status in the town. More charitably, kindness toward his old friend Ransom also could have inspired Doniphon to assume the responsibility for the killing so as to alleviate the Pilgrim's guilty conscience, thereby enabling Stoddard to proceed with his political career while also inflating his own sense of heroics.

For Ford, therefore, the truth for everyday life as in art becomes a human construction demanding a multiplicity of efforts and perspectives. Empirical fact and imaginative legend constitute two parts of the same quest for an understanding of experience; they work together and depend upon each other. Similarly, Ford's great films, such as *The Searchers* and *The Man Who Shot Liberty Valance,* synthesize popular culture and serious art. These films have the simplicity of popular films for mass audiences but also structure complex levels of meaning. His democratic aesthetic incorporates the mass of people who are part of democracy without losing the vitality and originality of art to renew culture. Moreover, this pragmatic conception of truth and art also manifests itself in Ford's overall view of democracy. In a world of violence and hatred, both Ethan Edwards and Tom Doniphon are indispensable to the survival of life, freedom, and democracy. Thus, in *Liberty Valance,* Ford questions Doniphon's violence but also ridicules Ransom Stoddard's self-righteousness.

In these two films, Ford also begins to question the authenticity of a democratic consensus that perpetuates injustice and inequality for people of color. Both *The Searchers* and *Liberty Valance* exhibit Ford's fresh sensitivity regarding people of color and the movement toward renewing cultural consensus for minorities. In his treatment of Pawley in *The Searchers* and of Pompey (Woody Strode) in *Liberty Valance,* Ford emotionally stands on the threshold of the society's great change over race without ever quite making it conceptually across to an understanding of the new egalitarianism of the post-Kennedy years. As Lehman says, "*The Searchers* deals centrally with racism, and its main character is a racist. This does not mean, however, that the film should be simply characterized as racist. Much of the film critiques racism. . . ."[40] As Lehman suggests, Ford saw the need for social, political, and cultural change but could not quite envision its reality. Both films, therefore, dramatize the ambivalence and tension of the society as a whole at this time on this issues of racism and equality.

The Searchers stands as Ford's greatest single example of a cinema for democracy and of the practice of a democratic aesthetic. In this film, Ethan achieves a form of redemption that constitutes a renewal for American democracy as well: Although he remains the stoic outcast and isolated individual, he nevertheless returns home with a sense of his connection to others and a renewed faith in the human community.

Equally important, in bringing Debbie home, the film not only proffers her redemption but also enables us to envision the redemption at last of that original captive, Eunice Williams. *The Searchers* serves as Ford's act of regeneration and redemption for American history and culture; it demonstrates his desire to expand and deepen the American consensus and mission to the world. *The Searchers* weaves family and home into a metaphor for American culture for all peoples. Just as Whitman proclaimed, love and identity must form the heart and soul of the American ideology and community.

CHAPTER 3

GENDER AND AMERICAN CHARACTER: FRANK CAPRA

Ford and Capra

John Ford's personal pilgrimage of faith and belief as represented in *The Searchers* was not an unusual quest for someone of his era and place. He had considerable company. Most of the directors in what I call the Hollywood Renaissance were involved in similar searches in their work and in their lives. During this era of great transition and turmoil, these directors as a group sought to rediscover and represent American values and beliefs. The result of their efforts was an extraordinary flowering of cinematic and cultural creativity. In this group of directors, the journey of Frank Capra seems especially remarkable considering his impoverished origins in Sicily. Given such humble beginnings, his subsequent fame and achievements are the material of the American myth of success. Looking back to his childhood journey of immigration – crossing the ocean in steerage, traversing the country by train in filthy underclothes to struggling relatives in California – Capra could claim truly to have lived the American dream of triumph over great difficulties and challenges. Although he recalled these events with a powerful awareness of his misery and loneliness at the time – "I hated America" – he never underestimated their importance in transforming his life. As biographer Joseph McBride writes:

> The immensity of the ocean, the boy would later say, "drove everything else out of my head."
>
> The ocean crossing was a rebirth for Francesco Capra. America would write his story afresh. It was the first and most radical of the character transformations he would undergo in his lifetime, and he admitted, "It scared the hell out of me."
>
> His memory of the ship crossing always remained extraordinarily vivid, so much so that he would speak of it often in the present tense, as if for the rest of his life he was, in some profound sense, always on that ship, always in the process of becoming an American.[1]

Figure 4. Frank Capra: Success, failure, and renewal in America (The Museum of Modern Art / Film Stills Archive).

With such a personal history, it seems especially appropriate that Capra's mature achievement as a director constitutes a study and example of a cinema for democracy.

At the peak of his career, Capra's importance and impact as a director in Hollywood probably should be compared only to Ford's. Even after a period of unfortunate neglect, Capra today is remembered, again like Ford, for the influence of his creative genius and social vision on his own and later generations of filmmakers and viewers. As Richard T. Jameson says,

> Frank Capra was, with John Ford, the most esteemed American director in the decade preceding and partly including World War II: the first man to win three Academy Awards as Best Director – for *It Happened One Night* (1934), *Mr. Deeds Goes to Town* ('36), and *You Can't Take It with You* ('38). . . .[2]

In addition to being honored and studied for his artistic genius and success as a director, Capra's reputation continues as the avatar of the democratic impulse in cinema. Thus, Wes D. Gehring states that Capra actually defined a special film genre form, "the populist film comedy":

> The archetype author of the populist film comedy is director Frank Capra. At its most basic, this genre celebrates the common man, the inherent goodness of the people and the leaders that spring from the people, and the importance of traditional values, which start with the family. Capra's classic populist works are the trilogy *Mr. Deeds Goes to Town* (1936), *Mr. Smith Goes to Washington* (1939), and *Meet John Doe* (1941). After World War II he made the genre more palatable to a disillusioned public by adding fantasy in *It's a Wonderful Life* (1946).[3]

Ford himself also saw Capra's work and career as a representation of American values and ideals. He called Capra "an inspiration to those who believe in the American Dream."[4]

Ford's casting and style of directing James Stewart in *The Man Who Shot Liberty Valance* indicate an artistic debt to Capra and demonstrate significant continuity between them and their work. Ford's way of presenting and developing Stewart as Ransom Stoddard, the so-called "Pilgrim" in *Liberty Valance*, immediately and impressively indicates the importance of Capra to Ford. Stewart, of course, gave signature performances as Jefferson Smith in *Mr. Smith Goes to Washington* and George Bailey in *It's a Wonderful Life*. He was as important to Capra as Wayne was to Ford: Stewart's triumphs in these classic Capra films were as crucial in making Capra a supremely successful director as were Wayne's roles in helping to make Ford a Hollywood institution and a living legend. Although Capra's production and success drastically declined in the 1950s, Ford directed some of his most critically acclaimed films during the decades after the war even in the face of his deteriorating health, aggravated alcoholism, and growing sense of personal and professional alienation. Thus, Stewart's role in *Liberty Valance* as conceived by Ford suggests an awareness of Capra's continued relevance to film at a time when Capra's star seemed somewhat dimmed.

Ford's use of Stewart in *Liberty Valance* implies a form of intertextual collaboration between the two directors. Ford, in effect, incorporates the earlier work of Capra and Stewart within the layered texts of his own film, establishing an imagistic archeology of multiple meanings for *The Man Who Shot Liberty Valance*. As directed by Ford, Stewart's role involves more than simply transferring certain visual images and exterior presentations from one director's work to another. Ford makes Stewart's Capra roles part of the visual and ideological texts of *Liberty Valance*. The complex set of values, conflicts, and meanings associated with Stewart, especially in his portrayal of Smith in *Mr. Smith Goes to Washington,* becomes embedded in his role of

Stoddard in *Liberty Valance*. Stewart's history with Capra and his continuity as an actor and image are part of the narrative, psychological, and ideological structures of the Ford film.

From the perspective of Stewart's role, *Liberty Valance* becomes "Ransom Stoddard Goes to Shinbone." In his performance in *Liberty Valance*, Stewart returns to his Capra past, only as an older man, just as Ransom Stoddard returns with Hallie (Vera Miles) to the Western city of Shinbone in the opening scenes of the film for Tom Doniphon's (Wayne) funeral only to find himself meditating upon the meaning of his own life. Upon arriving in town, Stewart soon tells the story of his relationship to Doniphon to a group of townspeople, including the local newspaper editor, all of whom apparently never even heard of the dead man Ransom hopes to honor with his presence. In an extended flashback, Stewart relates the story of his past in Shinbone, one that began before he even arrived: a young lawyer who had been robbed and whipped unconscious by Liberty Valance (Lee Marvin) in a stagecoach holdup on the road to the town. In the *Liberty Valance* flashback, Stewart remains the "Boy Ranger" of *Mr. Smith Goes to Washington,* still the lost idealist with a powerful proclivity for using self-punishment to arouse and cultivate the sympathy and support of others, especially women. Throughout the film, Stewart's facial expressions, look, body language all repeat actions and patterns from the earlier Capra film. This repetition includes his reactions to the bullying of both Liberty and Tom, when he invariably gets beaten and brutalized after various insulting incidents. Also, his intimate intensity with Hallie as she nurses his wounds after the shootout with Liberty echoes Saunders's (Jean Arthur) climactic mothering of Jefferson Smith at the Lincoln Memorial in *Mr. Smith*. Stewart's physical performance of Ransom Stoddard's emotional outbursts in *Liberty Valance* is consistent with Smith's way of acting in the Capra classic.

As part of his program for civilizing the West, Stewart also embodies controversial qualities of masculinity that relate to his earlier Capra roles. Stewart's idealism, emotionalism, vulnerability, reliance upon women, and self-exposure clash in almost every apparent way with the conventional view of masculine aggression and domination represented by Wayne. Obviously inclined personally toward Wayne's creed of the male hero, Ford still sees Wayne's character, Doniphon, as an anachronism in modern society. As a sign of Stoddard's greater value as a social type to the new times of law and civilization, he achieves great public success and even wins the girl, leaving Doniphon to suffer the fate of fading into irrelevance and anonymity in the town he once dominated.

However, Ford develops his connection to Capra according to his own aesthetic and ideology. Elements in the popular Stewart characterization of American innocence undergo serious alteration in the Ford film. One of the most ironic and profound changes that contrasts Stewart's roles in the two films involves Stoddard's evolution into the kind of pompous, hypocritical, and patronizing senator that Smith combats in the Capra film. With his return to Shinbone, it becomes immediately clear that after a successful career as a politician, Stoddard has grown into a less corrupt version of Senator Joseph Harrison Paine (Claude Rains) in *Mr. Smith*. Stewart's moral deterioration suggests Ford's uncertainty about the pragmatic and political durability of Stoddard's idealistic innocence in a corrupt world. For Ford, the individual must incorporate and assimilate some experience of evil to achieve inoculation against being consumed by evil. Ransom's self-righteousness, therefore, ultimately leaves him drastically vulnerable to the debilitation of serious corruption.

Ford also clearly anathematizes the loss of individual moral responsibility that the conformity of modern civilization often requires. He presents the collapse of Stoddard's moral character as truly regrettable. Stoddard's failure to live up to the promise of his own idealism and to match the heroism and strength of the man who made him a success, Doniphon, leaves the Stewart figure forever vulnerable to Hallie's contempt. As they leave on the train out of Shinbone at the very end of the film, Stoddard indicates how he noticed that the kind of cactus rose Doniphon once gave her as a token of his love had been left on Doniphon's coffin. We do not need to hear who put it there, although Hallie readily confirms our suspicion.

Ford's development of Stewart in *Liberty Valance* constitutes a metacommentary on Capra and *Mr. Smith* as indications of cultural changes occurring in America in the mid-1950s, including new attitudes toward gender and race. Capra unleashed Stewart in *Mr. Smith* as a different kind of masculine power in American culture. Capra's film also insists, if even in the most tentative way, upon insinuating African Americans into the frame of American culture, thereby anticipating Ford's treatment of race in *Liberty Valance* through the character of Pompey (Woody Strode). Wayne's most devoted and loyal man, Pompey finds himself the object of Stewart's pompous paternalism during a class that Stewart institutes to educate the illiterate people of Shinbone, including Hallie. Treating him almost like a slave, Wayne takes Strode out of the school to get him back to work but at least indicates a form of love and respect for him as a human being. Ford, therefore, again demonstrates deep ambivalence about race and gender in a major film in a way that replicates the uncertainties and fears of the culture at the time.

For Ford, Stoddard's reformism fails to recognize that the permanence of evil, even in the reformer, creates the social necessity for some form of Doniphon's power and authority. Stoddard's hypocrisy and pomposity dramatize the failure of his moral imagination. He was supposed to change the system while embodying a new sensitivity about gender and the American hero; instead, he lives a lie in his understanding that it was Doniphon who shot Liberty Valance. Stoddard's failure indicates Ford's skepticism about the quality of his masculinity and the authenticity of his morality.

Ford's discussion with Peter Bogdanovich about Wayne and Stewart in *Liberty Valance* suggests his felt need to articulate a balance of the moral and social meanings of their roles. However, he also typically deflated any intellectual abstractions involving the casting of Wayne and Stewart. He told Bogdanovich:

> Well, Wayne actually played the lead; Jimmy Stewart had most of the scenes, but Wayne was the central character, the motivation for the whole thing. I don't know – I liked them both – I think they were both good characters and I rather liked the story, that's all. I'm a hard-nosed director; I get a script – if I like it, I'll do it.[5]

Also, Ford in *Liberty Valance* characteristically minimizes the woman's role, whereas in retrospect, Jean Arthur in *Mr. Smith* grows steadily more important as a force for change. Ford, thereby, keeps his western form as opposed to Capra's "populist" romantic comedy. In addition, the emphasis at the end of *Liberty Valance* upon the difference between legend and fact demonstrates Ford's consideration of the importance of media in creating social and cultural roles and values as in *Mr. Smith*.

The complexity of Stewart's cinematic image under Capra's direction helps Ford continue the modernization process in *Liberty Valance* that he initiated in *The Searchers*. While Ford's use of Capra testifies to Capra's influence and the depth and complexity of his work, it also says much about Ford's commitment to excellence and art that he got so much from this intertextual exchange with Capra that involved considerable differences as well as similarities regarding key issues of their times.

Smith and Saunders

Mr. Smith Goes to Washington begins as a conventional journey of initiation from innocence to experience. The film dramatizes a rite of passage from the country to the city that relates directly to some of our culture's most important literature, such as *The Autobiography of Benjamin Franklin* and Hawthorne's "My Kinsman, Major Molineux." The film's apparent narrative simplicity structures a complex process of creating a new kind of hero in a new relationship with a modern woman of equal significance and stature. The film therefore anticipates contemporary cultural and critical movements in film studies as well as other areas. Partly because of the interest in recent years in gender studies and feminism, it has become fairly common to emphasize the importance of actors in proffering through their work new gender positions and relations in film and society. Most early studies of this form of influence upon gender by actors tended to emphasize such figures as Rudolph Valentino, Marlene Dietrich, Greta Garbo, and Cary Grant.[6] More recently, Marlon Brando, Montgomery Clift, and James Dean have been hailed as revolutionaries for presenting complex representations of multiple masculinities.[7]

As part of this trend in gender and film studies, Stewart finally has been given credit for his pioneering work in helping to construct new perceptions of masculinity in film and culture. Both Ray Carney, in his authoritative and comprehensive study of Capra and culture, and Dennis Bingham, in his work on actors and masculinity, demonstrate how Stewart anticipated so much of the innovative work of the Method actors.[8] It would be hard to exaggerate Stewart's importance in this transformation of images of American masculinity. Moreover, one measure of his excellent performance in this film comes from comparing his work to the amazing achievement of the brilliant cast. Claude Rains as Senator Paine provides a sterling performance and becomes, as Carney notes, Paine incarnate.[9] However, the rest of the cast also is stellar: Jean Arthur as Clarissa Saunders, Thomas Mitchell as Diz Moore, the reporter, Edward Arnold as Boss Taylor, Eugene Pallette as "Chick" McGann, the political operative, among so many others from the classic Capra supporting cast. Stewart maintains his position in each scene with all of these acclaimed actors.

At the same time, even after recognizing Stewart's radical innovations in his representations of masculinity in Capra's films, it still needs to be remembered how much Stewart owes to Capra. If Stewart operates as a gravitational center of complex elements and forces of change, there can be little doubt that Capra helped considerably to put him there, discerning, positioning, and developing Stewart's genius as the personification of vulnerability and sensitivity in ways that other directors, including Ford, would emulate for several decades. Robert Sklar's insight concerning the metaphor of God as the director in *It's a Wonderful Life* certainly should apply as well to Capra's influence upon Stewart in their classic films, making Stewart a kind of chief angel and light among the stars in Capra's large portion of heavenly Hollywood.[10]

The image of Capra the director as God also pertains to the narrative situation of Stewart and his character Jefferson Smith in *Mr. Smith Goes to Washington*. The film opens with Smith in a kind of prelapsarian intellectual and psychological condition. Based on a story by Lewis R. Foster called "The Gentleman from Montana," Smith in the film, we recall, receives an appointment to the Senate after the death of the incumbent. The enthusiasm and adoration of the governor's children for Smith, the leader of the "Boy Rangers," influence the governor to make the appointment and to convince the political bosses of the state that the totally inexperienced Smith would be a popular but harmless tool of their interests. Consistent with his character, Smith speaks with a childlike innocence and naïveté, as though unable to distinguish between himself and the external world and strangely unaware of the processes of symbolization and differentiation upon which language depends. He still needs to mature and learn to engage reality through the mediation of language. Carney brilliantly emphasizes Smith's lack of verbal language and his dependence upon a physical as opposed to a spoken means of communication.[11] Boyish and adolescent, Smith also is emotionally immature, often evidencing unstable and extreme mood swings. He ultimately requires the help of Clarissa Saunders (Jean Arthur) to acquire the knowledge and the speech he needs to survive and to maintain his struggle for his goals. Interestingly, Saunders as a worldly woman of experience plays a complicated Eve figure with both phallic and maternal qualities of language, love, and authority that she bestows upon Smith.

The reliance Smith's inadequate speech places upon gesture and action focuses attention upon Capra's special genius of visualization. Carney suggests that, although in his earlier films Capra plays with extraordinary "visual moments," not until *It's a Wonderful Life* does he achieve a kind of fulfillment of his "visionary stylistics."[12] It seems to me, however, that *Mr. Smith* thrives as a classic film precisely because of the genius of Capra's organization and development of visual and narrative space in combination with verbalization through dialogue and speech. Unfortunately, throughout his career, Capra apparently fought bitterly with some of his closest collaborators over the responsibility for the ideas and the screenwriting involved in many of his major films. According to Joseph McBride and many others, Capra was ungenerous in dealings with writers who clearly were essential to his success. Most notable among these were Robert Riskin, who helped establish the famous Capraesque and "Capracorn" formula in several key early successes, and Sidney Buchman, a self-professed communist who had major influence on *Mr. Smith* but later got entangled with Capra over the director's dealings with him during the dreadful days of loyalty oaths and blacklisting. In addition, the history of the authorship of *It's a Wonderful Life* also involved similar disagreements.[13] Several factors contributed to Capra's attitudes on such matters, the most important probably being, as Carney and McBride suggest, an instinctive insecurity that stemmed from his impoverished immigrant origins and required serious ego boosting.

To me, the irony of such concerns over the authorship of Capra's films suggests an argument that misperceives the true genius of his greatest work. Classic Capra films go well beyond the wonderful Capra formula. As in the case of Ford, the uniqueness of Capra's style and success concerns how he synthesizes all of the various elements of film, including the scripts, to visualize something new and original for the screen. Thus, in the early scenes and sequences of *Mr. Smith,* obvious narrative conventions and cultural clichés become compelling visual material. Capra turns well-worn subjects such as the security and friendliness of small-town America, the journey of the country youth to the city, and the universal wish for instant success and fame into new experiences. His brilliant timing and organization of shots as well as his extraordinary visual development and presentation of Stewart as Jefferson Smith render such old themes in a new and vivid way. When the Boy Rangers say good-bye to Smith and present him with a gift of a briefcase to take with him to Washington, long shots, medium shots, and close-ups dramatize Smith's relationship to the boys who adore and venerate him. These shots immediately reveal the innate charm of Smith's youthfulness but also suggest potentially disastrous vulnerability in the volatility and naïveté that are part of this same innocence. Bathed in a light that exaggerates his adolescent youthfulness and emphasizes his all-American good looks, Smith's excessive emotionalism and intensity in this scene portend danger for him.

Moreover, the emotionalism of the scene and the physical presentation of Stewart anticipate his representation of what Kaja Silverman writes so brilliantly about: male moral masochism. In her lengthy study of this subject, Silverman includes a discussion of Capra's and Stewart's *It's a Wonderful Life.*[14] However, in Smith's farewell to the Boy Rangers, male moral masochism immediately manifests itself in Smith's manner and appearance. The investment of so much inner feeling upon a situation of inevitable farce and failure forecasts his position as a martyr in whom pleasure and pain intermingle in his unwavering devotion to what he and Paine call "lost causes," a phrase both associate with Smith's father. In his climactic collapse and speech at the end of the film, Smith of course refers again to lost causes and uses the term as an instrument of conscience that compels corrupt Paine into his own fit of self-recrimination and public self-humiliation. Earlier on the train to Washington, Smith and Paine talk in idealized terms about Smith's father, whose example of ultimate sacrifice establishes a model with which to beat themselves. Smith's father serves as an Oedipal figure of failed idealism who causes both men to internalize the aggression they feel against those who would block their efforts toward their different versions of perfection. Fittingly, a simple wipe signals the change of scenes from the hometown pleasures and juvenile celebration of Smith's appointment to a shot of the same speeding train cutting diagonally across the screen and taking Smith and Paine to Washington. The shot of the train not only illustrates the radical transition in time and place for Smith but also the likelihood that he will be overwhelmed and knocked over by the experience. The sequence initiates a process of exposing Smith's weakness and dismemberment. The shots dramatize his mind and character as well as the development of the narrative.

Similarly, Capra's dynamic composition of the visual frame and the mise-en-scène at the Washington train station perfectly renders Smith's new situation of both opportunity and entrapment. In addition to the excitement of meeting Senator Paine's aggressive daughter, Susan (Astrid Allwyn), and her flirtatious friends, Capra manages to compress other chaotic and confusing occurrences at the station within this amazingly brief time and limited space. Also at the station are the political hacks who have been assigned to handle Smith. They must work with the station's black porters, who ultimately outmaneuver them in a comic way that seems to entail an early if tentative and incomplete effort to give people of color a measure of identity and presence.

The tightly structured meshing of these ordinary circumstances at the station again displays Capra's brilliant direction in even rather mundane moments. Dialogue, jokes, ironic comments are all timed perfectly to punctuate the organization of the dramatic space. In this brief, early scene, Capra creates an extraordinary dynamism and energy within the movie frame that articulate the tensions between Smith and these women, who teasingly engulf him, and then Smith and the political operatives. After the women depart, Smith suddenly becomes breathtakingly aware of the Capitol dome through the narrow frame of the station door. He gets the men to look for just a flash at this site that has been available to them everyday for years. The concentration of attention and energy within the frame on off-screen space expands the imaginative domain of the frame while also adding to the intensity of energy within it. Thrilled and exhilarated by what he sees and by what he has become, Smith remains thoroughly oblivious to the dangers of his new situation. He is like the homing pigeons in the crate he brought with him to Washington. The diagonal and horizontal vectors of moving people and objects in the scene, such as a taxicab, and the visual tensions of the composition of the frame all emphasize Smith's sudden entrapment in an unfamiliar and hostile environment. "Things sure happen fast around here," he says.

Language and dialogue in these opening scenes of *Mr. Smith* contribute depth and irony to the visual situations in the form of several jokes about Smith as a Boy Ranger and a Daniel Boone figure lost in Washington without a compass. One political hack at the station mockingly grins at Smith and observes about Susan Paine and the other women who have been crowding and smothering him: "The wild life around here is a little different than what you're used to. They wear high heels." Such statements not only demean the new senator but also comment ironically on the contrast between the mythic pastoral and rural origins of American culture and what American society has become, leaving Jefferson Smith, a man with an oxymoron of a name, at a complete loss in his unfamiliar surroundings.

On the margins of all the action at the railroad station, the black porters have their own problems with the political hacks, ultimately leaving the most intrusive and offensive of these operatives, Chick McGann (Eugene Pallette), holding the crate of Smith's pigeons in his pudgy hands. Meanwhile, the young senator has disappeared to visit the city in the film's most famous montage of historical sites – a sequence constructed for Capra by his montage director, Slavko Vorkapich. Smith's escape comprises a release from the hectic tension of the scene and demonstrates the impulsive enthusiasm and innocence that predictably soon will be getting him into trouble.

Throughout *Mr. Smith*, multiple layers of finely constructed dynamic and mobile visual detail define scenes in coordination with the other crucial cinematic elements of sound, speech, and music. Capra's special genius remains the multidimensional complexity of his articulation of narrative space, as opposed to simply illustrating a continuous narrative line just for popular-audience consumption. The early scenes in *Mr. Smith* establish the style and pattern for the rest of the film of Capra's depth and originality as a director.

Similarly, the classic narrative continuity of the film invariably introduces destabilizing ideological and psychological elements that complicate the developing Smith–Saunders relationship. Smith remains the narrative focus of the film, but Saunders occupies and retains its ideological heart and center. It ultimately becomes her story as well as his. She steals the film and takes possession of its basic idea: Gender equality and opportunity as well as institutional reform and democratization are necessary for American democracy to survive and grow. The renaissance of the American female becomes necessary to transform and save the humanity of the American male. Several brilliantly directed scenes form the nexus for joining Stewart and Arthur into a couple who individually and together redefine gender in America. Capra's style of dense and complex visualizations and volatile narrative development focuses on the transforming nature of the relationships between men and women as represented by his star performers. Stewart and Arthur take gender roles and positions in the film that anticipate the development within the culture of a multiplicity of models for masculinity and femininity. While Stewart demonstrates the challenges facing the American male in a changing economic, cultural, and technological world of growing cities and bureaucracies, Arthur anticipates the emergence of a newly independent, professional, and aggressive American woman who exercises authority in the workplace while also challenging, altering, and sometimes breaking from the restraints of traditional domestic roles and responsibilities.

At the core of the film stands Stewart as a new American man radically different from what has been repeatedly opined as the traditional American male and hero in our culture, especially as represented in cinematic culture by such a figure as John Wayne in the Ford classics. In the psychoanalytical terminology of Dennis Bingham, Stewart epitomizes "the fragility of patriarchal gender constructions" and "the 'gentling' of white masculinity." Stewart's performance and presentation on screen form part of the effort "to rupture the unitary heterosexuality of conventional gender identities" and to break from "the smooth surface of the coherent 'masculinity' or 'femininity' of which every star persona is an individual version."[15]

One brilliant example of Capra's complex cinematic construction dramatizes Smith's masculinity as a form of radical oscillation between external aggression and internalized guilt. Stewart moves from being an embarrassing fool to a figure of humiliation and an object of pity. In the scene, Smith realizes that he has been duped by reporters and photographers into making a fool of himself by demonstrating birdcalls. A classic accelerated Capra–Vorkapich montage sequence shows Smith attacking people all over the city until he spots the reporter who organized his humiliation, a man dubbed "Nosey" by the other reporters, an unfortunate concession by Capra to public disapproval of the press. Smith pursues Nosey (Charles Lane) into the bar of the National Press Club. The organization of the action is brilliant as all the reporters come together as a buffer to receive the full brunt of Stewart's fury. However, once cornered into a chair by the very press that he has pursued, Smith must face the brutal and punishing truth of his ridiculous situation. The accelerated action of his earlier pursuit emotionally crashes into a marvelous mise-en-scène as his facial expression of fury changes into self-recognition. The lighting, costume, composition, and especially in this case, the language are all perfect. With the reporters peering down on him accusingly in his corner, Stewart's gritted teeth and angry expression fade rather quickly into mortification, self-awareness, and self-pity. His tousled hair indicate his confusion, while his frantic look of a besieged animal turns into a visual appeal for relief, pity, and affection. He shouts at them to tell "the truth" and be "honest" as opposed to just being "smart." Diz Moore, played by the great Capra and Ford character actor Thomas Mitchell, proceeds to tell him the truth about what "the people" found when they read their morning paper. "This morning they read that an incompetent clown had arrived in Washington." A reporter quickly adds, "Parading like a member of the Senate." Another reporter wonders what he knows about making laws and providing his constituents with the help they "need." Suddenly, Smith must face and learn the truth from his own lips. "I don't pretend to know." When told that the country needs leaders "who know and have courage" as never before, Smith's emotional roller coaster ends in disgust and self-loathing. The reporters' brutality increases as they deliver more of their truth that Smith will be expected to vote and act as told by the bosses. Then Mitchell delivers the final verbal blow: "You're not a senator. You're an honorary stooge. You ought to be shown up." Of course, "showing up" precisely describes the functions both of the photographers' cameras that expose Smith and of Capra's own nondiegetic camera apparatus that makes the actual film itself. Showing up suggests a visual revelation and exposure of disguise, weakness, and dismemberment.

Although they brazenly mock Smith, finally offering him a drink that will "taste better than the truth," showing up works both ways. Smith's humiliation mirrors their own weakness; the guilt he arouses as the victim of their cruelty suggests that together they form a community of the weak and dismembered. Concentrating on Stewart's tortured face, the camera brilliantly cuts to his back as he rises to leave, then focuses on the face of Mitchell, as prime accuser Diz Moore. Mitchell's expression changes from pleasure over his own aggressive wit and poisonous tongue to a glimmer of pity, thereby adding a stunning exchange of emotion and feeling between the two men. In this moment, Capra constructs the scene and sequence through an organization of looks, what Silverman and others term visual statements of psychic desire and sexual and gender difference.[16] The look of Stewart and the look of Mitchell constitute an aggressive–passive exchange in which Smith and Stewart alternate masochistic positions and reveal their mutual weakness and internalized guilt. The film reveals Moore to be no less dismembered and crippled than Smith except that he disguises his vulnerability with language and wit. Diz, an interesting epithet in itself for a reputed voice of the people, reveals himself in subsequent scenes in the film to be useless and inadequate as a journalist and as a suitor and potential husband for Saunders. As a journalist, he essentially functions as an irrelevant figure when not actually perpetuating the corrupt forces he thoroughly detests. Like Smith, the members of the press actually expose their own weakness when they act aggressively. Thus, Diz and the other outraged reporters finally must share in Smith's bad feelings over his awful and sudden downfall. Moore's guilt compels him to follow Smith out of the bar. As the camera tracks the two men heading toward the door, Mitchell says, "Hey senator, don't let it get you down. A hundred years from now, no one will know the difference."

Exhibiting still untapped depths of naïveté by going for help to Senator Paine and Susan, the very people who abuse him, Smith has turned the American hero and male into a thoroughly artless figure who operates without any understanding or insight into his true situation. He lives primarily in his own world of emotions and confusions, largely out of touch with reality. His vulnerability and innocence aggravate his emotional excess and personal weakness. In spite of his noble intentions, he epitomizes failure. Intense and sensitive, his mood swings and confusions undermine his fortitude and reliability.

Enter Clarissa Saunders: She radically alters our understanding of Capra and the development of gender in this film. Molly Haskell calls Saunders "a woman of both sense and integrity, halfway between Jimmy Stewart's fantastic idealist and the corruption of Washington politics."[17] In fact, instead of meeting Stewart halfway on a spectrum of values, character, and experience, Arthur, when we first view her, assumes a position in real opposition to Stewart. Her Saunders is the complete professional of great experience and worldliness. In her first scene, she stands by her desk as administrator/secretary in the new senator's office thoroughly dominating her realm, which includes the figure reclining on the couch, the reporter Diz. She is rough, skeptical, almost jaded, and easily capable of engaging Diz mentally and verbally, in spite of his reputation as the "poet" of the Washington press corps. Whereas Smith appears weak and dependent, Saunders maintains an aggressive authority that clearly counters traditional forms of femininity and maternalism.

Arthur's character at this point represents phallic power, the triumph of language, rationality, and authority over the vulnerable human body. She categorically represses any maternal nurturing that might subvert her position in a political and business world dominated by men like Senator Paine and Boss Taylor. Some of Arthur's most provocative and pungent lines assert the antimaternal, antinurturing nature of her role in its initial stage in the film. When Senator Paine beseeches her to continue working with Smith, she complains: "Well, I'm not a registered nurse." Asking her how Smith got in so much trouble so quickly with the press, Paine's manner hints at his suspicion that Saunders allowed it to happen as an expression of her own feelings and resentments about both Smith and her situation in the office. (It is worth noting tangentially that even in this brief exchange, Capra again demonstrates a style of cinematic complexity by contrasting Saunders's assertiveness in the midst of the visual signs of Paine's power in his office, such as the imposing array of photos on the wall, with the overwhelmed Smith's apologetic diffidence in a similar situation later in the movie.)[18] Of course, Saunders, believing Smith to be a fake, had set indeed him up with "Nosey," and she rationalizes her betrayal with a comment to Diz about resisting playing mother: "When I think of myself sitting around playing it straight for that phony patriotic chatter, me, carrying bibs for an infant with little flags in his face." In yet another antimaternal comment, she answers Paine's query about Smith's problems: "Look, I merely took him home. I didn't tuck him in and give him his bottle. That's McGann's job." Interestingly, she puts herself above the feminine mothering role by suggestively belittling and feminizing the gruff and beefy masculinity of the political operative who first met Smith at the station. She implies that in spite of appearances, her intelligence and independence make her stronger than McGann, an exchange of gender roles reinforced by his nickname, Chick. When the senator urges her to continue working with Smith, she proclaims that her qualities of mind and character free her from so-called maternal and feminine duties. "Look, senator, I wasn't given a brain just to tell a Boy Ranger what time it is."

Haskell maintains that while moving "effectively and pragmatically" through the inner workings of corrupt Washington, Arthur/Saunders has remained "untainted."[19] Yet Saunders has shown herself to be potentially quite corrupt. Nosey's offer of a bribe of a World Series pass that will be worth $15 in a week spurs her on to set up Smith. Paine convinces her to continue watching over Smith with the promise of financial and professional awards to come as his presidential ambitions progress. She tells him that her eyes have gone from being "big blue question marks" of idealism and hope when she first arrived in Washington to "big green dollar marks." He promises her a major "bonus" and says, "You'll get one of the biggest jobs in Washington." In essence, therefore, throughout the beginning of the film, Saunders has marketed and promoted her connection to Smith for her own advancement. Cynicism over Washington corruption, skepticism concerning Smith, and frustration over her own life cause her to act deceitfully.

The film suggests that Saunders's situation typifies the perversion of the values of honesty and loyalty by impulses of unbridled power and corruption in Washington. When her betrayal of Smith turns back on herself as a self-inflicted wound, the film demonstrates the consequences of giving such precedence to power and success. Saunders agrees to a request from Susan Paine to help her take Smith, who remains infatuated with Susan, from the Senate on the day when Senator Paine plans to introduce a bill, inspired by Boss Taylor, that would undercut Smith's sole cause of building a Boy's Camp in his home state. Saunders's temporary alliance with Susan in betraying Smith dramatizes the conflicts developing within her as she experiences new and contradictory thoughts and feelings toward the new senator. Disdain and contempt have been changing to curiosity and a growing, grudging affection and respect. Her decision to help Susan undermines this change and continues her service to people she despises. Work and power have superseded inchoate attitudes and emotions.

Thus, Jean Arthur stands as a pioneer in film in articulating women's professional life and position in the workplace in America in the middle of the twentieth century. In *Mr. Smith*, the sacrifice of important values that this position requires of her constitutes a subdued but crucial comment on the film's view of the ethos and myth of success in America. At the same time, her position also demonstrates a recognition of the autonomy, independence, and authority of contemporary women to make their own moral and political choices. Her initial disparagement of conventions and clichés of customary domestic roles proclaims her alignment in the film with what usually has been the male lead's values and position of toughness and power.

Jean Arthur's own insight into Stewart in comparison to Gary Cooper as male figures and actors succinctly encapsulates much of the academic and critical commentary about the cultural and social significance of Stewart's persona and image:

> Jimmy Stewart is marvelous, but Cooper's better. You get to know Stewart too well, and with Gary there are always wonderful hidden depths that you haven't found yet. Stewart is almost too much when he acts; I get tired of his "uh, uh . . ." – his cute quality. With Cooper it just seems to *happen*. I can't remember Cooper saying much of anything. But it's very comfortable working with him. You feel like you're resting on the Rock of Gibaltrar.[20]

This comment about Stewart's disconcerting emotionalism versus Cooper's reassuring solidity speaks volumes about their different conceptions of masculinity and heroic action. Arthur's words indicate her personal expectations. Her code of toughness resists Stewart's melodrama. Her statement thereby reinforces the reversal of gender roles and positions concerning herself and Stewart as actors as well as characters in the film. This consistency between their "real" and "reel" roles perhaps helps account for the brilliance of their performances and their success as a couple on the screen in articulating the profound social and cultural implications involved in their alternations between traditional male and female gender roles. To a considerable extent, they apparently were playing themselves.

Working to create a cinema for democracy, Capra proffers an important argument about the construction of male and female gender positions that oppugns assumptions in cinema and culture about unitary masculinity and domestic femininity. The film proposes a process of democratization that begins with individual gender and sexual identities and relationships as opposed to working for change from the top, so to speak, through the leadership and structures of political institutions, as the most obvious meaning of the film suggests. Politics and reform begin, the film shows, with the individual and the personal as well as the collective character of the people.

The process of democratization and transformation in *Mr. Smith* enters a vital stage in a wonderful scene between Stewart and Arthur that should be read in the context of their mutual exposure up to that point as the complete country boob and the thoroughly desensitized political operative. Significantly, the scene, which occurs at night in his office, concerns Smith's attempt to write a speech about feelings he cannot put into words. Trying to frame his thoughts, he stumbles, "Now . . . the . . . a" and then asks Saunders in frustration like a cartoon Westerner: "Dawg gone it, you ever have so much to say about something, you just couldn't say it?" In a sense, he operates at this moment in a kind of prelinguistic, or what Leland Poague terms a "pre-

Oedipal," state of personal and sexual immaturity.[21] Initially Saunders just wishes to fulfill her obligations to her bosses to keep Smith out of trouble by pretending to help him organize his ideas about a Boys Camp, though secretly she still believes him to be a phony and a fool.

The turning point in the scene and film comes to Saunders as a vision. At first she continues in the power role, breaking through Smith's narcissistic verbal incoherence by articulating his visual images. She plays the phallic mother who imposes symbolization, language, and discipline. Then specularity – her vision of him at this particular moment – undergoes a kind of revolution that completely transforms her perception and understanding of Smith. Up to this point in the film, specularity had signified Smith's dismemberment and castration. All the Washington scenes have tended to display him in his weakness and immaturity as a crippled man who thinks, speaks, and acts like a boy, a charming goof thoroughly unnerved, for example, by Susan Paine. Scenes of Smith repeatedly show him to embody lack, to be missing the strengths to make him a full man.

In the office scene all of this changes for the viewer, especially including Saunders as an intradiegetic or internal spectator who looks upon Smith and participates in the construction of his character. The transformation occurs when Smith moves to his office window, which forms a beautiful frame for the Capitol dome that caught his attention at the bus station. Smith literally enters that frame and immerses himself in the exhibition it offers of the dome. He becomes at one with his cultural environment and history. Body ego and psychic ego merge with ideology to overwhelm Saunders. Suddenly the scene is dominated, and reality defined, not by her speech but by his vision – in the double sense of his intellectual idealism and his appearance to her. Specularity, gender construction, and ideology cohere. Smith, rather than seeming weak, gains the authority to rewrite the visual text.

Until now the film's visual construction of sexual, social, and ideological relationships and hiearchies has stressed Smith's lack of masculine authority. Stewart's look to the camera, to other characters, and the audience invariably confirms his weakness.[22] Now Smith, standing before the dome, gains phallic authority. His appearance in the frame visually fulfills expectations raised by the narrative thrust and ideological tensions of the film. In this sequence, his words do not in themselves make him powerful but operate as merely one of the film's major semiotic modes of expression and articulation. He says that he wants his bill to capture that "spirit" of the Capitol so the "idea" of America can "come to life" for the boys of America. In isolation, this could be heard or read as a mere continuation of the kind of patriotic cant that has upset Saunders; but as part of the visualization of his look of authority, his words move her. It now becomes clear: He really believes. The vision of Smith engulfs his speech and absorbs Saunders into his world. She experiences a transformation that merges ideology and personal psychology. Sexuality and gender, identity and belief all come together for her. Smith becomes the object of her desire.

Silverman describes the visual linkage of psyche and ideology in a way that can be applied to this scene:

> [W]e are all dependent for our identity upon the "clicking" of an imaginary camera. This metaphoric apparatus is what Lacan calls the "gaze." The gaze does not "photo-graph" the subject directly, but only through the mediation of the screen, i.e., through the repertoire of culturally intelligible images. Unfortunately, all such images are ideologically marked in some way; at the very least, they are carriers of sexual and racial differences, but they also project values of class, age, and nationality onto those who are seen through them. (353)

In Silverman's description of the process, Smith finally achieves the authority of the dominant gaze in this scene by finding a means of visual and intellectual mediation that directly addresses Saunders in terms of her own self-image and inner needs. Enhanced by his proximity in the frame to the Capitol dome, Smith's mediated image at last conveys a sign of sexual difference and substance to which Saunders obviously responds in terms of her own sexuality. Just as the image overcomes the juvenile presexuality of Smith's persona, it also brings out feminine aspects of Saunders's nature. Accordingly, she responds with new interest to his words.

Moving from the frame, Smith preaches about wanting to articulate the meaning of "liberty" in his speech so that boys will understand and protect it:

> Liberty's too precious a thing to be buried in books, Miss Saunders – men should hold it up in front of them every single day of their lives and say, "I'm free, to think and to speak. My ancestors couldn't; I can. And my children will."

The shocking visual and verbal exchanges of energy and power in this scene between Saunders and Smith seem genuine and credible because Saunders secretly has been so vulnerable herself. The vision of Smith by the dome expresses what Saunders latently feels and believes. Throughout the film, her strength and independence have dissembled this basic vulnerability that stems from the vacuum in her life created by the absence of real belief and direction. The phallic dome also rather blatantly insinuates her need for love and sexuality. Motivated, therefore, partly by her own desires, guilt, and needs, she eventually becomes a convert to Smith and gains a new sense of purpose in her life. The change in her expression from skepticism to a muted form of belief brilliantly documents this transformation. Her expression switches to fear and near bewilderment with the realization of what the future could hold for Smith and perhaps herself.

As a sign of both Saunders's growth and conflict, Arthur, in one of Buchman's brilliantly written scenes, later says to Mitchell in her apartment: "I wonder Diz, if this Don Quixote hasn't got the jump on all of us." She asks the reporter "if it isn't a curse to go through life wised up like you and me." As an indication of the depth of her character, although Saunders now sees what the quixotic Smith sees of the American Dream, her intelligence still retains its critical edge.

In acceding to Smith's vision, a new sense of unity temporarily enters into Saunders's life. In terms of her own psychology and desires, her values and beliefs, she tastes a new quality of wholeness. Her aggressive independence suddenly finds mitigation in his gentleness and devotion. Her strengths of leadership, organization, and analysis combine with his depths of emotion, sensitivity, and compassion. She finds balance as a phallic figure, and he gains strength through the structuring of inchoate and incoherent feelings. The crossing of gender boundaries and reversal of roles create a unified whole. When Smith insists upon discovering that her first name is Clarissa, the tables have been turned on her powers of language. The naming helps to give her an identity in their relationship but also undermines her verbal and phallic authority; it feminizes her, as does the name itself, Clarissa. By insisting upon hearing it, Smith becomes the naming authority and the momentary voice of order and structure. This simple process also constitutes, therefore, an important complication of gender roles and positions.

In the context of these developments, Smith's comment that Saunders has achieved so much "for a woman" becomes less offensive, primarily as a sign of his maturing recognition of sexual difference and his awareness of others outside of his narcissistic vision of the world. He seems to look at her and see her for the first time. The comment obviously opens the door to the development of their relationship. It marks an important step in the film's argument of their shared psychic and social abuse by a dehumanizing system, and suggests how much more he has to learn about their shared situation. At the same time, her interest in his description of the romantic West suggests a promising expansion of her own imagination.

The potential for love and growth in the relationship between Saunders and Smith informs and deepens the significance of the split that occurs between them. The forces of gender, sexuality, and belief that temporarily bring them together and redefine them as individuals and a couple explode into differences that articulate the challenges that face them and the culture. After demonstrating how much Saunders and Smith can offer each other, Capra brilliantly splits the narrative to dramatize the cost to each of them of their separation. This division focuses the film on the objective of bringing them together with the implication of proposing national and cultural unity as well through a redefinition and reorganization of gender, sexuality, and ideology.

Capra dramatizes the division between Saunders and Smith in several key scenes that are carefully structured individually and as a coherent narrative line. The break in the narrative structure that establishes the division between them occurs when Susan Paine invasively telephones Saunders to elicit her help in diverting Smith's attention from crooked business that would affect his proposed Boys Camp bill. Susan's phone call intrudes upon and disrupts the unity and bonding that had developed between Saunders and Smith as they work together. The several scenes that follow develop that disruption, leading ultimately to Saunders's flight from the havoc and misery of Smith's destruction. The dialogue and lines in these scenes are so sharp and clever that some possessiveness on a director's part over final authorship would be understandable. However, Buchman's great script still provides only one crucial element of the cinematic totality of the film's achievement in these scenes.

Surface banter between Arthur and Thomas Mitchell especially stand out in two scenes of vital importance for their development of personal relationships in the film. Both scenes dramatize subtextual meanings and conflicts: Subtle suggestions of the barren relationship between Saunders and Diz emphasize the depth of her developing affection for Smith and indicate a concomitant change in her own character from a tough-working woman to one with incipient strengths and longings that need to be addressed. Thus, in her apartment Saunders tells Diz that she can't stand the thought of the blows "below the belt" Smith will suffer in his political battle – an obvious recognition of the machine's intention to ensure Smith's continued impotence. She complains about that "dame" Paine's hold over Smith, and says about the prospect of seeing Susan in the White House with her father: "Imagine reading 'My Day' by Susan Paine in the neck." Arthur's wonderful acting and mimickry of Susan Paine's affected speech and contrived glamour, especially in contrast to Eleanor Roosevelt, convey the mixture of her feelings of jealousy and concern for Smith.

In a subsequent bar scene, Diz and Saunders ostensibly have gone for dinner, but their humorous inebriation becomes symptomatic of their alienation and her need for Smith. In a sharp reversal of character, Saunders confesses to new maternal feelings around Smith's initiation in the Senate. "I felt just like a mother sending her kid off to school for the first time . . . hoping he can stand up to the other kids." Just as the scene comes dangerously close to turning maudlin, Buchman's script and Capra's direction inject wonderful humor into it. Saunders becomes angry over her own train of thought. Her tone switches to the exact opposite, tough part of her character. "Say, who started this?" Drunkenly, Mitchell responds: "I'm just waiting for a streetcar." "Well, cut it out, see. Who cares, anyway?" Claiming that only her squeamishness rather than real affection prevents her from "being party" to Smith's impending "murder," she insists again on quitting her job. After hiccuping a couple of times, she proposes marriage to Diz, who drunkenly responds, ". . . 'is a good idea." Consisting basically of a prolonged take and two-shot, the scene ends with Saunders repeating Smith's earlier romantic lines about the prairie and the beauty of the West. Diz confesses that he has never seen the West that she describes; she admits that she hasn't either. He pleads, "Do we have to?" Saunders snaps out of her reverie and delivers her punch line like a shot: "No, I can't think of anything more sappy!"

Following these two scenes, Arthur and Mitchell return to her office to clear it out that night in anticipation of her imminent departure and their immediate marriage. There, they find an exuberant Smith delighted over his day with Susan Paine. Slowly coming to realize Saunder's condition and bitter mood, he is genuinely shocked by her tone and demeanor. She ridicules and mocks him and Susan. "Well, what are you looking at? You didn't think I was a lady, did you?" In blind anger and frustration, she produces papers that reveal how Smith has been duped by everyone: the senator, Susan on their day together, and even Saunders herself. Shouting that he doesn't have a chance "in nine million years" of beating the forces arrayed against him, she grabs onto his loosened tie and clutches him. "Go home! Don't stay around here, making people feel sorry for you." The visual and dramatic organization of this scene perfectly realizes the multiple tensions and conflicts of the moment. The two-shot of her grasp on Smith cuts to a deep-focus shot that captures all three of them together but apart, with Smith in the foreground and Diz barely holding himself up by the wall in the background, looking exactly like what he described in the bar, a man waiting for a streetcar – an amazing image that becomes dramatic and compelling in this setting of tension and pain and separation. The visual read of the film is powerful and clear. Distraught and in a rage between Smith and Diz, Saunders, in spite of her words, does not want to pursue her impulse to spend the rest of her life with the intoxicated reporter who personifies the modern urban man of alienation and displacement, whom Poe and Baudelaire saw as the "man of the crowd."

Saunders and Diz then leave the dazed Smith in his office, and Capra creates another brilliant shot and scene. We cut to a long shot of the office hallway covered by disturbing patterns of artificial lighting and darkness and rectangular shapes that evoke a feeling of lifelessness and loss. Saunders literally stumbles in physical pain and anguish, her steps echoing through the hall as she makes her way to the wall, where she stops with Diz in pursuit. The camera cuts closer, but we see only her bent back and lowered head against a wall. A two-shot shows their bent figures and shadows; their backs are black against the white wall and the dark shadows. Showing none of her face and only a portion of his profile, the scene becomes a portrait of her inner pain. The camera movement from a distance to a place right behind them accesses that pain for us. The setting tells all about her internal feelings, including the physical reaction to their drinking. Diz realizes with a glance back to Smith's office that there will be no marriage that night. "Okay, come on, I'll take you home," he says. She nods weakly and cries. They walk shakily with each other's help. The final long shot of the hallway shows the two figures leaning into each other as faceless condemned souls.

This sequence of scenes with Jean Arthur dramatizes her emotional and moral isolation as a result of her treatment of Smith and her separation from him. Similarly, Smith also proceeds on his own to suffer exactly the kind of awful defeat that Saunders predicts. Whereas her journey becomes an allegory of life without love or purpose, his path proceeds through the bowels of the corruption and misery of the political state. His journey covers a landscape of dangers to democratic thought and life that actually started obviously and ironically with his own ignorance, ineptitude, and weakness.

It would be difficult to exaggerate the prescience of *Mr. Smith Goes to Washington* in presenting this particular pilgrim's progress through American political institutions and life. Close to the beginning of a new century and about sixty years after its release, the film's picture and study of democracy and politics in America resonates today with even greater truth and accuracy and intensified emotional ambivalences and intellectual complexities than when it opened in 1939 for a special Washington audience of the political and cultural elite. The excesses of the film that clearly were designed to simplify and make a point for a mass audience have become today's reality. Capra's propensities to exaggerate have turned into prophecies of serious relevance to contemporary life and politics.

To be sure, the film adheres to an unreal Manichean conception of Smith's innate puritanical goodness versus the world's corruption. Nevertheless, this surface simplicity contains structures and patterns that pertain at least as much to today as it did to Capra's era. Boss Taylor's (Edward Arnold) control of the system translates into today's stranglehold over political institutions by special-interest and action groups that impede reform and change. (At the same time, of course, at least until the end of the film when he and his machine personify the horrific actions of totalitarianism, Taylor somewhat resembles a traditional power broker who represents the interests of various groups and people in his state that are beyond Smith's limited concerns or even understanding.) Also, the prolonged paralysis of political processes and agencies in the film compares to the frustration today of finding the means to create political solutions to serious problems. The film's suggestion of the historic use of scandal and deception to disguise real political issues becomes in our time almost the inevitable basic material of political discussion and action. Furthermore, the story in the film of Smith's meteoric rise to notorious attention seems exaggerated until we consider events and personalities of the past two decades involving such figures as Oliver North, Newt Gingrich, and even President Clinton. Similarly, the importance of trends and movements in the film accurately forecasts emphasis today on discerning and creating mass tastes and moods.

Most important, the pernicious abuses of media for propaganda and manipulation, which seem farfetched in this film even in the age of totalitarian state regimes, now prove to be even more powerful in both the discussion and determination of events. In *Mr. Smith Goes to Washington*, Capra's compression and prolongation of time to coordinate events with public reception and responses defy the credibility of the point he wishes to make about the importance of the media upon the political process. Thus, in crosscutting between events and their consequences involving Smith and his supporters as opposed to Taylor and his machine, the technique of rapid montage in this instance defies reality, although it works in Sergei Eisenstein's sense of intellectual constructions to dramatize the meaning of events.[23] Temporal and spatial restraints cast doubt on the realism of the montage of people organizing so quickly for and against Smith during his filibuster of nearly twenty-four hours. Of course, other cinematic techniques work perfectly to demonstrate the power of the media to shape events; for example, the technique of classic cinematic ellipsis neatly compresses into a few highlights and moments a long congressional process of investigation calculated to defame and destroy Smith.

Using these various techniques, Capra obviously wishes to emphasize the importance of media in a totalitarian age of mass culture and opinion. However, what looked like exaggeration during Capra's era seems understated in our age of instant, round-the-clock global news and media intervention into events. What Capra unrealistically tried to propose could occur within the period of a day now transpires within moments on television. The media create a culture that contains and organizes events and their consequences in a way that transforms the events themselves in terms of the media's ability to present them. Now media culture mediates events so quickly as to influence the perception and understanding of reality. In this respect, Capra's world has been realized in ways that he never could have completely imagined when making *Mr. Smith*.

Also, Capra's development of Boss Taylor and Senator Paine and their relationship involves important subtle touches. As Boss Taylor, Edward Arnold seems so powerful that his dominance initially invites skepticism, whereas Senator Paine's squeamish complicity in corruption belies his deeper complexity. However, as part of the film's mise-en-scène, acting and direction turn Rains and Arnold's scenes into tense encounters of psychological and political realism. In a crucial scene, the two men stand in a simple long take and talk. There seems to be almost no movement, but every gesture or even intimation of a facial movement or finger position resonates with meaning. Arnold uses a combination of sarcasm and contempt to manipulate and persuade the senator. His rhetorical strategy with Paine follows a logic that is based upon sound psychology. Paine cannot separate from Taylor without also being destroyed; he cannot dissociate himself from a political career of representing the interests that made him a success. The courage and power to make that kind of stand are foreign to this political man of the moment, who deserves Arnold's disdainful and mocking repetition of the public epithet for the senator, "The Silver Knight." Arnold's power and Rains's pusillanimity make this scene a crucial segue to an even more important confrontation between Stewart and Arnold. Senator Paine's capitulation to Taylor in this scene sets up Smith, who, in the adjoining hotel room, seems like a helpless sacrifice.

However, even this bit of melodrama between Stewart and Arnold has a moment of genuine cinematic brilliance. With Stewart seated and Taylor over him in a position of absolute dominance, Taylor sends forth a rhetorical assault to persuade Smith to join forces with him. He talks patronizingly, as though addressing a "drooling infant" – a term he once used to describe Smith. Taylor also uses promises about how much Smith could achieve and get "If you're smart," a refrain thumpingly repeated throughout his talk. Instead of being intimidated, Smith rises from his seat and stands in all of his youthful ignorance and innocence over Taylor. When Taylor affirms that he practically controls the votes and work of Senator Paine and many others, reverse shots first show the solid anger and determination on Stewart's face and then concentrate on Arnold's corpulent face as Smith says, "You're a liar." No excessive sign of agitation ripples across Taylor's round face and no overbearing reaction emanates from his stolid bulky frame, but just the slightest little downward movement of his eyes and lips casts a sense of shadow and darkness over the scene and indicates his total understanding of the situation. Arnold manages without any major dramatic action to convey that as Boss Taylor he could not care less about Smith or his insult; the new senator remains beneath Taylor's contempt or consideration. Only one thing matters: Smith's impulsive innocence and explosive volatility pose a genuine threat that must be eradicated.

At this point, of course, Taylor becomes a thoroughly barbaric and dictatorial figure, a ruthless totalitarian gangster eager to destroy anything in his path. He proceeds to execute a systematic program of destruction that ultimately includes not only lying and character assassination but bullying and beating children and suppressing freedom of speech and expression. He becomes evil incarnate, a comic-book figure representing the worst fascistic threat to democracy at home and abroad. Unfortunately, the heavy-handed montage technique and simplistic presentation of the conflict between obvious evil and good weaken Capra's case for democracy by falling into bad melodrama and overstatement; yet the tactics of totalitarianism and oppression that Capra dramatizes actually are mere child's play compared to events overseas in totalitarian regimes both then and today. True, left-wing screenwriter Sidney Buchman saw the end of the film as a typical Capra profanation that ruined his theme about the underdog individual versus the oppressive state. However, in spite of such criticism, the reaction of opponents of the film to its representation of the condition of American politics at the time suggests the amount of courage its production and release actually required of Capra. Much of the right-wing press as well as many established leaders publicly attacked the film for its portrait of the workings of the Senate and its analysis of the system and processes of American politics.[24] After all, Capra in 1939 depicted the emergence of a homegrown fascist dictatorship within America. He certainly cannot be accused of minimizing the danger or understating the case or in any way trying to apologize for such dangerous indigenous forces.

Capra responds to this perceived threat not with a political program or a strategy for revivifying the American idea. Instead, he chooses to save American democracy by regenerating American character through the transformation of our understanding of what it means to be an American man and woman. He redefines our ideas of heroism. Smith, as a masochistic, martyred Christ figure, in conjunction with a woman who sees herself as something of a soldier, becomes the living force for political and cultural renewal. A New Yorker and former photographer's model whose real name was Gladys Greene, Jean Arthur apparently chose her professional acting name from Jeanne d'Arc and King Arthur.[25] In the film, she plays a Joan of Arc role in her attempt to encourage Smith in his battle of reform. However, in spite of their best combined efforts to defeat Paine and Taylor by persuading the Senate and the people of the righteousness of their cause against the bosses, they obviously fail in terms of traditional politics. The ending, as already noted, depends upon a thoroughly melodramatic development in the form of Paine's breakdown, attempted suicide, and overwrought confession to the Senate to being corrupt and unfit to serve. At first glance, this rather unrealistic end appears to justify Buchman's argument that Capra's proclivity toward violence proves the deeper point of the absence in the film of a meaningful political alternative to counter Boss Taylor's fascism. However, the logic of the end of the film works in terms of the psychology of martyrdrom and redemption and the ideology of renewing American manhood through a reconstruction of gender relationships.

At the end of the film, when Paine proves that the political process fails because public opinion has turned on Smith, the final and winning appeal from Smith concerns not political principles but the matter of lost causes that goes back to the beginning of the film, when both men remember Smith's father's dying loyalty to these causes. Smith arouses Paine's guilt for again abandoning his ideals. Just as Paine apparently failed Smith's father years ago, he now fails the son. The impossible ideal of lost causes as the measure of moral political behavior satisfies Paine's masochistic need for pleasure from moral punishment. For Paine, loss of faith in such causes does not end the pain of his conscience over such causes. Suffering from a form of moral masochism similar to that infecting Smith, Paine is compelled by his guilty conscience to emulate Smith's martyrdom. Both yearn to be punished for failing to live up to a transcendent fallen martyr, Smith's dad. Paine, therefore, contributes in an important way to what Charles Wolfe terms the "spectacle of martyrdom" in the film.[26] As Bingham says:

> With Smith's instinctive identification with lost causes and signifiers of dead men – even down to the style of hat that his father wore during his crusades on the day he was killed – the narrative strains toward a giving over of self, martyrdom as the culmination of Stewart's surrendering gaze.[27]

The key difference between the two men concerns Paine's historic disavowal of his pain, guilt, and weakness. Throughout his life, the "Silver Knight" maintained his resemblance to a father figure to the nation and to his daughter. As a mature man in the film, he already has undergone his personal Oedipal journey and has emerged as a stalwart public advocate of classic American masculine solidity, detachment, and rigidity. As part of his Oedipal code and national presence, he must maintain masculine silence regarding potential inner weakness. However, Paine's hidden weaknesses manifest themselves in his relationship to his daughter. In a manner of speaking, he violates her. In spite of his pompous protestations about the effrontery of Chick's suggestion, he allows her, as discussed above, to be used to distract Smith from attending a Senate action concerning his Boy's Camp. Spoiled and self-indulgent, she becomes generally tarnished by his corrupt world and by his double failure to protect her from this world and to set an example for her. Such failure confirms the corruption of his moral manhood and his subservience to Boss Taylor. Rather than being mere expediency, his use of his daughter Susan indicates a profound weakness of Oedipal authority and integrity. Years of disavowal and denial of such corruption have inured him to the psychological and moral costs of such hypocrisy. Confronted with the moral example of Smith, the accumulated guilt and the weight of so much repression and disavowal come crashing around him at the end. A glimmer of potential defeat suggests itself as some of the senators during Smith's filibuster start to wonder about potential deeper meanings to the situation. In the game of classic Washington politics, Paine predominates; but in the game of martyrdom and moral masochism, Paine confronts the master in Smith.

In contrast to Paine, the pre-Oedipal Boy Ranger makes no pretense of traditional classic manhood. He thrives on exposing his weakness and vulnerability.[28] In his climactic moment in the Senate after filibustering for nearly twenty-four hours without any opportunity for rest or relief, Smith's eyes point upward to heaven. His weakened physical bearing, agonizing exhaustion, and look of desperate surrender make him the embodiment of symbolic crucifixion and martyrdom. His look to heaven of total loss and vulnerability translates into a gaze of recognition concerning the destiny of his life and the meaning of the film. He triumphs in the spectacle of his masochism. It may be Stewart's most famous and important moment in film, a capstone in his representation of the moral masochist that helped establish his continuing influence in changing perceptions and understandings of masculinity in America.

In this scene, Smith's look to heaven means the victory of moral masochism and weakness over the forces of monolithic masculine aggression and domination. This look dramatizes the redefinition by Lacan of castration as a visual phenomenon; as Silverman says, Lacan's theory "repeatedly locates lack at the level of the eye, defining castration as the alterity of the gaze" (155). The visual strategy in the film of castration as a visual phenomenon that acknowledges difference also involves a political and psychological strategy of rejecting Taylor's and Paine's values. Smith's ability to take punishment as a moral masochist exceeds Paine's capacity to dish it out; his martyrdom overcomes Paine's mastery of political manipulation. In the midst of the filibuster battle with Smith, Paine even confesses to Taylor that "I hit him from the floor with everything I knew." He adds, "Besides, I haven't got the stomach for it anymore." Paine's admission of his weak stomach for Taylor's tactics signals the collapse of his ability to function. He stands trapped in impotence as the failure of his own brutality transmogrifies into an intensified masochistic craving to take the place of his victim. Smith thereby fulfills the kind of program that Silverman advocates of saying "'no' to power" by acceding "to his castration, his specularity, and the profound 'otherness' of his 'self'" (389, 388).

In rejecting the classic Oedipal resolution of sexual and gender tensions, what Silverman terms "the murderous logic of traditional male subjectivity," Smith directly challenges the most basic and fundamental assumptions of power in the country and its institutions (389). Through his actions in the Senate, he battles and wins over the institutionalization of classic Oedipal authority and succession. He becomes the kind of "marginal male" that Silverman proffers who can "absent [himself] from the line of paternal succession" (389). In other words, Smith directly challenges not only the basic political and cultural structures of the country, he also undermines the sexual and gender foundations of those structures. After instinctively rejecting Taylor's bullying overtures for him to be smart by accepting the rewards of the corrupt system, Smith directly engages the entire national enterprise by challenging the conditions of manhood and the cultural definitions of heroic masculinity. He insists on retaining his idealism, naïveté, youthful innocence. In Taylor's terms, he refuses both to be smart and to grow up.

A powerful element of Capra's genius in this film concerns the consistency and coherence of his development of this revolutionary program of change through gender and sexuality. Capra dramatizes a radical plan of gender reconstruction by having Smith, in Silverman's term, "occupy the domain of femininity" (389). The governing gaze that encourages and empowers Smith to act emanates from Saunders in the gallery of the Senate. While Harry Carey in the role of vice-president (and hence Senate president) looks upon Stewart's character benevolently and paternally but without active commitment, the greater energy in the scene comes from Arthur. Smith's battle with Oedipal authority effectively counters the ambiguous approval of Carey's look and reinforces the importance of Saunders's support in the gallery. Smith's moral masochism inspires her with a mission worthy of her soldiering. His abject dejection compares to her marginalization in the gallery. Both of them are weakened by the isolation and separation imposed upon them. Capra turns their shared weakness into a strength by suggesting a potential wholeness through their relationship with each other. His passion, idealism, faith, and emotion require her intellect, analytical power, personal strength, organization, and focus. Together as a couple they can achieve the kind of relationship for life that Capra explores again in *It's a Wonderful Life*.

Nevertheless, to some in the audience, Saunders's secondary position in the gallery may suggest that her real function in the film is merely to serve as a vehicle for Smith's ultimate triumph.[29] She makes him into a man, while having to remain on the sidelines in a subservient position. In fact, however, she validates his redefinition of the masculine by aligning him with the feminine in reconsidering the structuring and outcome of the Oedipal narrative. Gender construction allows alternatives to Paine as the male and to Susan as the self-indulgent narcissistic daughter. Without denying Saunders's relegation to the gallery, it also needs to be emphasized that the film really proposes their mutual displacement and incompleteness when apart. The film's ideology declares their equality while also reflecting pervasive gender discrimination in society. For Capra, the continued vulnerability of Smith and Saunders demonstrates their common humanity and establishes a bond with the audience. They adhere to a common democratic humanity. In his articulation of a democratic aesthetic, it is important to Capra to maintain the humanity of his characters and to resist the temptation to turn such ordinary figures into the very thing that his films reject: supermen and -women who supersede pragmatic and democratic values.

Capra's commitment to a convincing democratic aesthetic for film became even more tenacious with the Second World War. The outbreak of the war soon fulfilled the fears of many concerning film's fascist proclivity for celebrating power and violence. Just five days after Pearl Harbor, Capra became a major in the Signal Corps to produce the documentaries about the war that eventually became the classic *Why We Fight* series. To prepare for his work of making documentaries to explain democracy's stake in the outcome of the war to ordinary soldiers and, at Roosevelt's suggestion, to the public as well, Capra viewed and studied Nazi propaganda – most important, Leni Riefenstahl's classic *Triumph of the Will*. Riefenstahl's documentary has become a seminal work of fascist aesthetics. Ostensibly a film documenting the Nazis' 1934 Nuremberg Party Congress, *Triumph of the Will* merges modernistic cinema and propaganda to propound fascistic ideologies of racial superiority, violence, technology, and death. Of course, Capra's own films contain many of the same techniques and elements that can be found in *Triumph of the Will*. Montage, the manipulation of space and time, the use of composition and the editing of shots to emphasize a particular point of view and ideology all were pioneered by Capra, among many others in Hollywood. However, the development and application of these techniques to serve a fascist ideology made them different in Riefenstahl's film. Seeing *Triumph of the Will* at the Museum of Modern Art, he remembered: "It scared the hell out of me. My first reaction was that we were dead, we couldn't win the war." Capra said he responded just like the defeated Austrians and Czechoslovakians. "That picture just won them over." He remembered thinking, "How can we possibly cope with this enormous machine and enormous will to fight?" As McBride says:

> As a filmmaker, Capra was impressed by Riefenstahl's orchestration of the spectacle, which had been staged specifically for the film itself – by her grandiose, mythic imagery, by the hypnotic rhythm of her editing and use of music to add a further dimension of barbarian emotional power to the endless marching, flag-waving, and speechmaking. He considered *Triumph of the Will* "the greatest propaganda film anyone has ever made."[30]

Capra told Bill Moyers that Riefenstahl "promised supermen stuff" to the German people and particularly to German youth.[31]

The ideological structure of *Mr. Smith Goes to Washington* anticipates Capra's reaction to viewing Riefenstahl. Capra's film constitutes an ideological and aesthetic antithesis of Riefenstahl, a modernistic cinema for democracy and the ordinary man and woman as opposed to a super race. Capra certainly proffered something quite different from a fascistic ideology of domination, death, and destruction; he hoped for a democratic cinema of openness and renewal. *Mr. Smith* relates that aesthetic project to the search for democracy in other structures and relationships, including, most especially, the basic relations between men and women – a view of democratic politics epitomized by Whitman's poetry and ideology of the mid-nineteenth century.

However, a gender gap between the reality and the promise of the film's democratic ideology has been apparent since the film first appeared: Saunders's greater strength, superior intellect, more powerful personality, and larger presence cannot overcome the gender bias that favors Smith's incompetence over her achievement. Nonetheless, Smith's idealism and Saunders's strength constitute a beginning for realizing a democratic ideology of increased equality and opportunity. Capra saw a democratic aesthetics of cinema as inevitably involved in such renewal.

One important scene in the film symbolizes the birth of a new force of democratic cinema and culture for national renewal through the combined efforts of Smith and Saunders. The scene occurs in the Lincoln Memorial, where Saunders finds the defeated Smith in tears. Having been betrayed by Paine and defeated by Taylor, Smith retreats to the monument before planning to flee Washington in disgrace. The script simply dismisses the near impossibility of finding him at that precise moment with Saunders's explanation that she had a "hunch" as to his whereabouts. In the film's famous earlier scene at the memorial, it is a national house of worship to democracy; in this later scene, it is darker and funereal. Before Saunders arrives, Smith weeps in total isolation and abandonment. One enormous pillar of the monument separates him from the off-screen public space. The darkness and shadow delineate the national and individual psyche. Signs of life and vitality are totally absent. When Saunders enters this space, however, her presence, speech, and influence turn the tomblike womblike. The Lincoln Memorial becomes a source for new life for the democracy.

In this scene, Saunders, although a mother figure, also remains a soldier with a strategy for Smith's return to the battle against Taylor and Paine. Once again, her words shatter his narcissistic universe of impotent inaction. She provides the phallic authority and energy to overcome his passivity and defeat, while also enacting her new role of nurturing and caring mother. Smith and Saunders together revivify democratic values and structures through their decision to take action.

At the same time, the use of shadow and light in this scene serves not only as a sign of the emergence of new life from darkness but also as a metaphor of cinema's visual power through a democratic aesthetic to instigate national, aesthetic, and individual regeneration. The dark and gray tones of the shot signify the form and elements of photography and film. The scene suggests the potential transformative power of modern media to renew cultural and aesthetic tradition, institutions, and life. Also, the association in this scene of

Saunders with mothering a wounded Smith contributes to the idea of the regenerative force of film for creating new life. Jean Arthur, therefore, transforms the setting of the Lincoln Memorial into a kind of national mise-en-scène and shrine devoted to what Lucy Fischer terms "cinematernity," meaning the fusion of cinema and motherhood.[32] Film as the modern medium of renewal and Lincoln as the symbol of the tradition of renewal merge in the promise of continued regeneration. Smith's bitter words concerning the hypocrisy of other words about democracy "carved in stone" around the capital add to the theme of envisioning the truth as opposed to only writing or speaking or hearing it. Saunders specifically notes how the Boy Rangers will "look" up to him for better answers than simply surrendering. Also, she relates such looking to "doing something," to turning abstract words and ideas into a real program for democratic renewal.

Capra's effort to conceptualize and put into practice this kind of democratic aesthetic would continue in his classic film of the post–World War II era, *It's a Wonderful Life*, with a new couple that film critics and students also have been talking about for half a century: George Bailey and Mary Hatch of Bedford Falls, New York.

George and Mary

Based on a seemingly unpublishable short story, "The Greatest Gift" by Philip Van Doren Stern, *It's a Wonderful Life* credits four people for the film's screenplay: Frances Goodrich, Albert Hackett, and Capra, with special help from Jo Swerling. Apparently many others – including celebrated writers such as Dalton Trumbo and Dorothy Parker, as well as relatively unknown ex-Marine Michael Wilson (who would later win an Academy Award for *A Place in the Sun*) – also were called upon for help without receiving much public or official recognition for their efforts. Acrimony and squabbling were so intense that, according to McBride, "The Hacketts never wanted to see *It's a Wonderful Life* because of their dislike of Capra, whom Goodrich called 'that horrid man.'"[33] Obviously, an influx of such major professional help on the script and the dissatisfaction of the participants with the experience and result indicate serious problems with the screenplay. Even thinking that more patchwork by more writers could repair and turn this script into a finished work of art suggests a basic failure to recognize inherent conceptual and structural weaknesses in the screenplay.

A concatenation of inconsistencies, inaccuracies, and incongruities leaves much of the screenplay incoherent. From the beginning, a simple mistake anticipates these structural difficulties. The film begins with a winter snow scene on Christmas Eve in Bedford Falls, a small, upstate New York town. The camera swings up to the heavens where flickering stars dramatize a discussion involving Chief Angel Joseph's concerns about the man who is the

Figure 5. Donna Reed and Jimmy Stewart playing at love and life in *It's a Wonderful Life* (RKO / Liberty: The Museum of Modern Art / Film Stills Archive).

object of all the prayers below, George Bailey. As Robert B. Ray points out, we are told in the opening that Chief Angel Joseph will give Angel Second Class Clarence Oddbody "one hour to learn about George before descending to earth to help him." Instead, there occurs "a long, *film noir*-like flashback, covering George's life" that exceeds the "promised time limit" by taking "nearly 100 minutes," an unfortunate oversight in a major film.[34] From this opening scene, the relationship of the film's heavenly figures to the people on Earth remains vague, owing not to the script's concern for profound questions of theology but because of a failure of art and imagination. Also, in spite of Silverman's best efforts to psychoanalyze the symbolic significance of the names and the relationships of the film's heavenly and earthly beings, the allegorical meanings of the names and characters in the screenplay remain murky.[35] Other basic incongruities continue to deflect the impact of the film: Although George and Mary grow up in this small town in upstate New York where privacy seems impossible, the film repeatedly finds them apparently losing all touch with each other – yet rediscovering each other when it suits the development of the plot. In one of the greatest scenes, not only in this film but in American film history, when George and Mary dance the Charleston at the high-school graduation party for his younger brother Harry (Todd Karns), they act as though they have not spoken to or seen each other for years; yet he admits to having passed her regularly on the street, and we know their relationship goes back to the time when they were children and she swore her eternal love for him.

In addition, George's brother goes to college and returns home after four years with a wife, not having told anyone about the marriage even though it will radically influence George's life. On the day George and Mary Hatch (Donna Reed) marry, we learn that Thomas Mitchell's character in the film, Uncle Billy, has apparently not been to the wedding (without anyone noticing his absence) until George and Mary head for the train station to go on their honeymoon and realize there has been a run on the bank, indicating the inevitability of a similar disaster on George's Building and Loan association. Instead of going on their honeymoon, they sacrifice their money to save the association. George totally forgets about his young wife until the end of the day, when after saving the Building and Loan with the couple's own money, we see that Mary has managed to take over the abandoned and devastated old Granville house, where they had cavorted on the night of Harry's graduation party, and turn what will be their future home into a honeymoon fantasy.

The concluding part of the film also hinges on what can be seen as an incongruity, as Leland Poague discusses it. The problem concerns the loss by erratic and eccentric Uncle Billy of several thousand dollars of Building and Loan funds. George immediately assumes that the loss necessarily will result in his own prosecution and imprisonment for theft or negligence. Poague writes, "A long-standing puzzle of the film, at least for me, is the logic behind George's decision to accept responsibility for Uncle Billy's lapse of memory in the matter of the $8,000. . . ."[36] As Poague suggests, this problem possibly could be explained by seeing it as part of George's psychological tendency to assume guilt and responsibility for the events and people surrounding him. However, it also could be argued that the film itself never really negotiates this particular matter credibly. Difficulties such as these make the script's coherence problematic and have raised questions among critics over the years.[37]

One persistent literary reference in the film also raises questions of intention and audience. In the beginning of the film, Clarence, George's guardian angel, has been reading Mark Twain's *The Adventures of Tom Sawyer* prior to being asked by his superior angel, Joseph, to study George's life in preparation for helping him on Earth. Since Clarence does not yet have his wings after two hundred years of trying, he does not have an angel's vision and has difficulty finding George Bailey and his brother Harry as well as their friends as young children sliding on shovels on the ice. He requires the help of an angel who has the power to look back to when George was just twelve right after the First World War. Joseph literally focuses the view for Clarence like a projectionist or camerman. The innocent joy of the children caught up in the visual and cultural cliché of rural winter sports during the early part of the century maintains the nostalgic mood established by the stylized Currier and Ives type of illustrations used in the film's opening credits. The script obviously evokes Twain and Tom Sawyer to maintain a sentimental feeling and attitude toward the past. This is a romanticized remembrance of small-town boyhood adventures and rites of initiation as Twain and his great literary friend, William Dean Howells, sometimes nostalgically recalled their youth. Their writings helped embed such ideas into the American imagination. This view of the past helps create a sense of comfort and complacency for readers and moviegoers.

However, such complacency is about as far from the real meanings of *Wonderful Life* as it is from the deeper significance of Twain's greatest works. In the film's ice-sliding scene, for example, George's brother slides through the ice and almost drowns. George jumps in and saves him but suffers an infection in his left ear that leaves him partially deaf for the rest of his life. In contrast to suggestions of security and pleasure, the scene really presents danger, death, and disability. Thus, the thrust of the film radically opposes the putative innocence and joy of the Mark Twain of *Tom Sawyer;* however, it has everything to do with the Twain of *The Adventures of Huckleberry Finn, The Mysterious Stranger, A Connecticut Yankee in King Arthur's Court,* and many lesser-known works about the nightmare and terror of human existence and the perpetual hell of what he called "The Damned Human Race." This nightmare vision in Twain comes much closer to the inner reality of *A Wonderful Life* than popularized and sanitized readings of Twain.

An element of Twain that relates most immediately to the movie concerns the author's fascination for what Henry Nash Smith, among others, calls "transcendent figures" who enter into Twain's work as superhuman beings with omnipotent powers, just as heavenly figures intercede in Capra's film.[38] Twain's transcendent figures often dramatize the weakness and vulnerability of the human race and portend death and destruction, as in the mass slaughter that concludes *Connecticut Yankee,* the killing of Boggs by Colonel Sherburn in *Huckleberry Finn,* the powers for evil by Satan in *The Mysterious Stranger.* The Twain of these works really helps bring out the deeper significance of *A Wonderful Life,* although the other-worldly figures in the film appear benign. As in much of Twain's work, the film attempts to contain and juxtapose the secure and sentimental with the dark and dangerous. As Charles J. Maland notes, the film structures different levels of meaning and intention.[39] Understanding the thematic connection to Twain helps establish the place of *It's a Wonderful Life* in American culture, even after recognizing the film's weaknesses.

Accordingly, *It's a Wonderful Life* stands as a flawed masterpiece of American cultural production, flawed as are almost all of Twain's great works, some of Whitman's poetry, and a great deal of Melville. Much of the literary achievement of these and many other figures suffers from deep structural and artistic difficulties. Undeniably, *It's a Wonderful Life* similarly has problems that cannot be overlooked; yet the aesthetic and cinematic complexities of the film's rendering of the tensions, ambiguities, and darkness at the core of modern American experience make it a major achievement.

Critics today tend to attack *It's a Wonderful Life* both on its own grounds as classic cinematic Americana and in terms of insights into the film via fashionable theories of ideology and psychoanalysis. The diversity of contemporary critical responses to the film suggests its depth and complexity. Some critics see it not only as vulnerable to the charge of failing to make its case for the average man but as managing to do the very opposite: The film, they argue, shows the average, ordinary citizen as a deluded victim of the phallic tyranny of patriarchal powers and an oppressive economic system and ideology. The dominant class maintains its hegemony through the false consciousness of myths that repress rather than liberate the people. As Ray says, "Its project was to summon support for the common life lived by the ordinary citizen, whose representative was George Bailey, 'a local boy,' in James Agee's words, 'who stays home, doesn't make good, and becomes at length so unhappy that he wishes he had never been born.'"[40]

For sure, the contradictions and conflicts in the film certainly reflect some of the difficulties Capra felt at the end of the war as he attempted to establish his economic independence and renew his aesthetic integrity through a new company named Liberty Films, which he formed with executive Sam Briskin and directors George Stevens and William Wyler.[41] Capra's state of mind during this period may help explain his inability to correct some of the film's flaws. Like Stewart and others, Capra was personally experiencing the very issues of the film in trying to put his life back together after the disruption of the unprecedented destruction of World War II. In Capra's particular case, however, the tensions of adjustment to peace and civilian life were aggravated by his sense of personal failure that compared to George Bailey's feelings in the film. As McBride writes, "The extent of Capra's identification with the character would have astonished those who knew him only through his successful public image and did not know that as he prepared his postwar comeback film he felt 'a loneliness that was laced by the fear of failure.'"[42] Evidently Capra had himself as much as George in mind when he emphasized failure in the film.

Capra, however, also clearly understood failure as a national theme. Some lines intended by Capra for Stewart, which would have been among the most powerful lines in the film, directly and immediately link the emotional theme of failure to issues of national identity, direction, and policy. Significantly, Capra eliminated these lines, as though afraid of offending his audience and cutting too close to the bone of hidden fears. George Bailey was to have spoken of failure in terms of one of Franklin Roosevelt's most powerful and idealistic rhetorical expressions of his whole national and international program: the Four Freedoms.

In a speech before Congress in early 1941, Roosevelt had articulated his vision of a nation and world at peace based "upon four essential human freedoms":

> The first is freedom of speech and expression – everywhere in the world. The second is freedom of every person to worship God in his own way – everywhere in the world. The third is freedom from want – which, translated into world terms, means economic understandings which will secure to every nation a healthy peacetime life for its inhabitants – everywhere in the world.
>
> The fourth is freedom from fear – which, translated into world terms, means a world-wide reduction of armaments to such a point and in such a thorough fashion that no nation will be in a position to commit an act of physical aggression against any neighbor – anywhere in the world.[43]

Roosevelt offered such an extraordinary program as a realizable possibility for current and future generations of Americans. "That is no vision of a distant millennium," he told his audience. "It is a definite basis for a kind of world attainable in our own time and generation."[44]

It would be hard to find a greater contrast with that idealistic vision than the words Capra gave to but took back from George Bailey. Capra had brilliantly dramatized the depths of George's pain and self-pity by reducing the powerfully moving and idealistic notions of Roosevelt to the pitiful level of George's physical and psychological condition. George's internalization of Roosevelt's vision emphasized his crippled psychological state more than the condition of his body. "I was a 4-F," he was to have said – his self-loathing accentuated by the implied comparison of his deafness, which kept him from the war, with the polio that crippled Roosevelt but didn't prevent him from leading the country and the world. So George would have delivered upon himself double blows of self-hatred as a failure to his country and a whining civilian in comparison to the president: "In my case it [4-F] didn't stand for Four Freedoms, it meant Four Failures. Failure as a husband, father, business[man] – failure as a human being."[45]

In contrast to Roosevelt's amazing idealism and goals, the horrors of the war and the difficulties of the peace to some degree explain Capra's disillusionment. Freud, in one of his most prescient and lasting essays, saw and explained the same phenomenon of disillusionment in Europe during World War I. In his "Thoughts for the Times on War and Death" (1915), Freud wrote: "In reality our fellow-citizens have not sunk so low as we feared, because they had never risen so high as we believed." Calling for greater reality in regard to expectations about human nature, Freud writes:

> In reality, there is no such thing as "eradicating" evil tendencies. Psychological – more strictly speaking, psychoanalytic – investigation shows instead that the inmost essence of human nature consists of elemental instincts, which are common to all men and aim at the satisfaction of certain primal needs.[46]

Freud theorized an extremely fragile foundation for civilization because of conflicts associated with its dependence upon eroticizing the "transformation of the egoistic impulses" into cultural altruism. So-called civilizing impulses inherently involve considerable hypocrisy because altruism in both the individual and the state never exists without unconscious contrary forces of destruction and death. For Freud, "cultural adaptability" equals "civilized hypocrisy" because of the perennial drive within the individual toward eroticizing external and internal aggression.[47] Disillusionment during the war originates in the inescapable linkage of idealistic altruism with the conflicting fear of death and the pleasure of aggression.

George Bailey's desire for his own destruction and disappearance from life – his wish that the angel Clarence grants him of never having been born, rather than simply dying – seems to dramatize the linkage Freud establishes involving death and disillusionment. Following Freud's line of thought, Bailey, disillusioned with his country and himself, redirects his natural aggression inward, away from his family and society, in a death wish of self-hatred and abandonment. Silverman essentially follows this argument with a feminist and Lacanian perspective, maintaining that at the end of the film Bailey – reminiscent of Smith, the moral masochist – learns to love the punishment doled out by phallic authority and to embrace the wounds of failure inflicted upon him. For Silverman, the dominant ideology and paternal authority have failed and only repress the individual. Paternal authority and the threat of castration equate to the death drive. In the current age of disbelief, succession through paternal authority fails to achieve loyalty; instead, it cultivates "dislocation from the paternal position and hence from the dominant fiction" of culture based upon "unimpaired masculinity" that disavows weakness and difference (106, 42).[48] Through the actions of Mary and their friends, George learns to love himself for his failures, and acknowledges the powerful paternal and ideological forces that put him in his position of weakness. He accepts and relishes his castration and reaffirms his allegiance to the system that has so repeatedly wounded him. According to Silverman,

He not only accepts these "wounds" as the necessary condition of cultural identity, but takes pleasure in the pain they induce in him. George thus steps over the narrow boundary separating exemplary male subjectivity from masochism, or to state the case slightly differently, the masculine norm from its perversion. (102)

For Silverman then, George's return to family and community constitutes an abnegation of his freedom and independence. Society's basic institutions are acceptable prisons for him because they provide more security than life on the outside, away from Mary and the children who mediate the oppressive power of the patriarchal state for the purpose of perpetuating the very institutions of pain and imprisonment.

Much of this interpretation hinges on the argument that George comes to love his failure and the punishment he receives for it. Another argument might accept Silverman's thesis that George and his generation "learn to live with lack" by accepting their vulnerability to the daily reality of the "abyss" of death (65). However, this alternative argument also would return to Capra's apparent original intent by emphasizing his recognition of the common democratic heroism of that ordinary generation's achievement. This achievement of common people involves facing and dealing with life's exigencies without denying one's humanity or the democratic institutions that empower people to engage existence to the fullest extent possible. Although superhuman "transcendent figures" are prominent in Capra's film, in contrast to a fascist cinema, such figures do not aver utopian social and political remedies based on illusions of personal and cultural grandeur.

Thus, at the end of *It's a Wonderful Life,* George really learns to love his life and the wonder of his existence after gaining an insight into what the alternative would be like of life without love, society, people, commitment, the values of democracy, and the willingness to sacrifice for causes and people greater than oneself. The movie actually insists upon his failures: It declines to trivialize them because doing so would entail dismissing the efforts and meaning of his life. Placing that personal story of failure within the broader national history of what Silverman terms the "ideological fatigue, induced by the historical trauma of World War II and the recovery period," *It's a Wonderful Life* anticipates the dominant intellectual trends of its time (106). These trends include a popularized Freudianism of accepting death, aggression, and unhappiness to appreciate life and peace; the existential movement that also was imported from Europe of confronting life in terms of freedom and being; and the national ideology of America's historic mission and responsibility to lead the free world. These intellectual movements help inform and articulate the issues of identity, manhood, moral authority, love, and sexuality at the heart of the film. Moreover, the film also frames these intellectual constructs of experience around the drama of the extraordinary social and cultural changes occurring in America after World War II. It especially anticipates and illustrates the revolution of gender positions in this period by continuing the transformations that Smith and Saunders initiated before the war. In *It's a Wonderful Life,* George Bailey and Mary Hatch advance the effort of the political pair in *Mr. Smith Goes to Washington.*

However, as individuals and as a couple, George and Mary also have changed considerably from their predecessors, Smith and Saunders. They no longer deal with the stuff of the Boy Rangers and a camp in the wilderness by Willet Creek. War and time have deepened and darkened the main characters and the issues. The film forecasts social and cultural contexts of considerable loss and dissolution. One of the film's most significant accomplishments involves its understanding of the crisis of the American family. *It's a Wonderful Life* indicates the growing failure of the family to cultivate security, freedom, and love resulting in an ensuing flight into social and cultural ennui and chaos. In the decades since George's nightmarish journey in which he loses his identity by abandoning his family and people, the flight from the family has become a national epidemic. By putting George in a situation thoroughly beyond his control and understanding, the same sequence of the film also dramatizes the emerging ideology of victimization and helplessness in American society. It leaves him absolutely dependent upon greater cultural and social forces, and estranged from those upon whom he most depends. This sense of victimization and helplessness therefore also vaticinates the elevation of social welfare as a new ethic for America to nurture individual and collective survival and security.[49] Despite the entrepreneurial and capitalistic proclivities that Capra evinced throughout his life, the ideology of social welfare and activism, as represented by George's leadership of his Building and Loan, accentuates the demonization of unregulated business and capitalism in *It's a Wonderful Life.* Potter (Lionel Barrymore), the owner of the bank and George's nemesis, exemplifies this repressive economic force, as does Boss Taylor in *Mr. Smith.* George's response to Potter's economic power to stifle the creativity and dreams of others compares to Capra's efforts, which we already have noted, to free himself at this time from the economic control of the major Hollywood studios.

Considering the cultural and historical differences between the world of Saunders and Smith and that of George and Mary, the continuity of Jimmy Stewart between both films is especially important. Stewart in *It's a Wonderful Life* continues the transformation of masculinity and gender that he initiated in *Mr. Smith,* and sustains his emotionalism and physical expression of inner feelings and fears.

An anecdote Stewart related not only confirms the importance of such emotionalism and expression to him as an actor and to his characters, but also validates some of Jean Arthur's insights into his personality. It involves shooting George Bailey's visit to Martini's bar after his emotional outburst at home regarding his fears about the missing Building and Loan money. Sitting at the bar, Bailey prays to God: "Dear Father in Heaven, I'm not a praying man, but if you're up there and you can hear me, show me the way." Stewart reports:

> In the middle of praying, I was overcome with emotion and started to cry. Frank [Capra] didn't know I was going to cry, you see. And neither did I. Afterward, Frank said, "I think I made a mistake, Jim. The camera was too far away when you cried. Do you think you could do it once more?" But because the emotion had been spontaneous, I didn't think I could do it over again.[50]

Capra had to work all night on an optical printer to enlarge the frames of the scene so that he could use them and capitalize on their affective power.

Stewart's brilliant emotionalism and sensitivity in developing the character of George Bailey has helped make this role something of a benchmark for some critics, not only in the Capra canon but also in the history of the transformation of gender in American film and culture. Such critics see Capra and Stewart in this role as going well beyond merely generating increased complexity in the representation of masculinity.[51] In making a case for the revolutionary way Stewart represents gender in this film, Poague uses Silverman's work to theorize on the predominantly feminine nature of Bailey's character.[52] Such an argument suggests something of the potential complexity of Stewart's portrayal of Bailey.

Stewart and Capra make George Bailey a figure of depth and intensity, a representative of a nation undergoing continuous revolution and change at midcentury. In combination with Donna Reed's wonderful portrayal of Mary Hatch, Capra and Stewart create a film that justifies Maland's statement that

> *It's a Wonderful Life* is clearly a culminating work. By that term I mean one of those rare works of narrative art in which an artist at last finds a form to express precisely the preoccupations he or she has been dealing with in a number of earlier works.[53]

Support for Maland's description of the film as "culminating" can be found in the way contemporary viewers of it continue to find *It's a Wonderful Life* so relevant to their own experiences.[54]

From the events of George's youth early in the film until the end, carefully constructed shots and frames structure intellectual, emotional, and psychological tensions that dramatize the complexity of George's masculine identity, the relationship between George and Mary, and the social and cultural contexts of their lives. The film turns these shots and scenes into a dynamic flow of changing relationships and meanings that are propelled toward one inexorable crisis: George Bailey's self-confrontation with all of his multiple failures and shortcomings, as well as with life's unfairness and injustice.

One crucial source of the film's compelling inevitability in the construction of character and theme can be found in its remarkable cohesion of the ideology of cinematic form and structure with its development of narrative and ideological context. As we recall, Sklar and others emphasize that an immediate central concern of *It's a Wonderful Life* involves the art of film. The opening metaphor of heavenly moviemaking introduces the subject of the cinematic and visual construction of reality. The film's pervasive self-reflection on the film process continues with the famous freeze-frame shot when George describes the suitcase he wants. By freezing the frame so that Clarence can study George's face and talk over the visual scene with Joseph, Capra brings attention directly to film as an art form and to the director's power to control and alter time and space.

Sandwiched between the heavenly dialogue of the angels and George's frozen frame, however, are still other scenes about moviemaking and the construction of vision. In the Gower pharmacy where young George works as a soda jerk and errand boy, he sees and reads a telegram informing the druggist that his son has died. This explains the druggist's drunkenness, which has caused him mistakenly to fill a poisonous prescription. Portions of these pharmacy scenes are shot through a series of framed shelves inside Gower's enclosed interior work area, which is hidden from the view of customers in the front.[55] The camera often observes Gower (H. B. Warner) through the shelves, but at various times, George needs to enter into the pharmacist's inner world or frame. In effect, these scenes proffer a discussion about vision and the framing and construction of reality. The framed shelves divide and arrange visual space and suggest how the perception of reality depends upon the organization of such space. They also serve as a visual metaphor for a particular way of organizing reality through film: Viewing reality through the shelves compares to cinematic framing. The scenes illustrate the psychology of viewing films.

The lesson of the scenes as self-conscious visualizations of the filmic process becomes most obvious in a painful episode when George returns to the pharmacy without having delivered the poisoned prescription to the waiting customer. Gower still does not realize his mistake and begins to beat George, who cries in self-defense and holds his hands up to protect his "sore ear." When George finally blurts out through the blows that Gower has made a terrible mistake, the pharmacist realizes that George has saved him from killing someone and is overcome with gratitude and grief.

However, just as important as this drama of the beating, Mary has been involved in the whole scene from her stool at the soda fountain, hearing George's cries and imagining the brutal blows delivered upon George inside

Gower's hidden work area. The way Mary repeatedly winces and recoils over the sounds vividly exhibits her own pain over hearing George's cries. Separated from the action but a part of the larger scene, Mary psychologically now becomes a voyeur. Capra's shooting and editing in effect put the viewer inside Mary's consciousness as she hears, imagines, and envisions George's beating. She seems to share the audience's perception of the action as a movie as witnessed through the frames of Gower's shelves. To represent how the beating scene feels and how it affects George and Mary, Capra organizes it as a film. The dramatic intensity of the beating as shown through segmented frames compares to the complexity of the filmic viewing process. The fragmentation of framing fractures vision and experience in a manner that reinforces the crippling punishment of George's pain within the frames. In sum, Capra renders the psychological meaning and impact of the beating scene in the form of a movie that the audience sees but Mary hears and imagines. He uses the compartmentalization and fragmentation of framing as a means for conveying how film operates to reenact both difference and loss through the appearance and disappearance of visual reality. Moreover, representing Mary's impeded vision through a series of such fragmented frames dramatizes the fragmentation of her developing psyche as well as George's. A world of infatuation and wholeness – what Lacanians would call the imaginary, or the narcissism of the mirror stage, in which all experience appears unified – has been shattered. She now appreciates the difference between the immaturity of believing oneself to be the world and being just a limited part of it. In contrast to George, who will go through life as a perennial moral masochist, Mary will become an active agent in her own development and her relationships with others, especially George. She will initiate actions and move aggressively to fulfill her ambitions, including marriage to George and keeping her family together.

Accordingly, in the pharmacy beating scene, Capra conceptualizes and envisions a theory of how film as an art form operates psychologically and structurally in its representation of characters and in its interaction with the audience. He delineates this theory as a relationship between the framing of fragmented cinematic vision and the psychology of the ephemerality of the viewing experience. He then illustrates the theory by showing how George and Mary literally are constructed psychologically by the moviemaking process. His film therefore anticipates the insights of such critics as Stephen Heath and Colin MacCabe into the relationship of film to psychoanalysis, semiotics, and ideology.[56] The drama of the changing frames in the pharmacy proposes a connection between the psychology of the viewing experience and sexual difference and organization. It suggests the basis in the psychology of vision of a tendency to internalize or externalize aggression and love. It also suggests the idea of gender as a construction, yet indicates extraordinary fluidity and variety in that construction between individual experience and the formation of character.

As part of the film's development of this theme of vision, Mary appears with glasses in the film's famous, nightmarish "Pottersville" sequence when George discovers how his nonexistence has changed people's lives. Although some consider her need for glasses ludicrous, the glasses simply suggest that never knowing George would affect her vision of the world. Also, Mary Ann Doane notes that glasses signify the cliché of unattractive women; women are supposed to be seen and not look or think.[57] However, Donna Reed both looks and thinks; moreover, so does George's mother (Beulah Bondi). When his mother sends George off to visit Mary, she insists that she knows how Mary feels about him because even though they have not discussed the matter, she has "eyes." Thus, Mary acquires a power and determination that also pertain to Jean Arthur's Saunders. Both women are the engines of difference and action, whereas the Stewart characters are visionaries and dreamers who remain isolated in their own worlds.

The emphasis in the pharmacy scene on Mary's look at George contrasts with the way Violet, the other girl in the film, looks only casually as an indication of her attitude in general toward life and men. Significantly, in a later scene when all the participants are grown, George decides to give Violet (Gloria Graham) a loan to help her get a new start in life. They make this transaction in his office where the camera, but not the other people in the Building and Loan, observes the action. As in the pharmacy scenes, the location of the camera inside a space hidden from others indicates the problematic nature of vision and the fragmentation of reality and experience. Inside Gower's office, Violet kisses him for his kindness. When they walk out of the office, all eyes turn to the two of them, including those of the bespectacled bank inspector who just happens to be visiting on the day before Christmas when Uncle Billy loses the money. The look of these spectators emphasizes the closeness of George and Violet, the lipstick stain on his cheek, and a recollection for some of a flirtatiousness since childhood between George and the somewhat notorious Violet. Simply as a statement about vision, the scene between George and Violet dramatizes the uncertainty associated with perception and reality and the connection of vision, sexual difference, and guilt.

Early into *It's a Wonderful Life*, when excitable George as a boy races to the Building and Loan to ask his father's advice about Gower and the poisoned medicine, he sees banker Potter's hearselike carriage outside the building, a sign of death and loss. George then intrudes in his father's office to see him literally begging Potter for more time to pay off a loan. Shot from an angle and position that emphasize the father's humiliation, the scene, some say, envisions castration. Similarly, the connection of specularity to sexuality and gender continues throughout the film in the stares Violet gets from the men, including George, as she walks down the street. George looks at Violet that way as he walks downtown in search of excitement on the night he eventually follows his mother's suggestion to go to Mary Hatch, the girl with answers to unspoken but important questions.

Perhaps the most visually memorable and provocative linkage of the look and gaze in the film concerns George and Mary and the eyeline match between Stewart and Reed at the high-school dance. The long shot and the close-up of her smile at George, who stands above the others, reaffirm the visual tone of their relationship, which goes back to the Gower pharmacy scene. She is radiant and beautiful. At the same time, she also continues to do her own looking and in her own way to act self-confidently without mimicking Violet's self-conscious flirtatiousness. Later, the shot of Mary addressing a restless and ambivalent Stewart from an upstairs window of her house as he paces nervously on the street below works like a visual emblem of her power and elevated position in their relationship. The following scene, with the two of them sharing a phone call from the potential suitor, Sam Wainwright (Frank Albertson), seems to be about hearing because they both try to listen to Sam on the telephone. However, the shot of them emphasizes not only her beautiful face but also the intensity of her restless eyes. Her facial movements and penetrating look construct their shared desire. The telephone, a sign of physical separation, compounds what their eyes and looks express about desire, the explosive frustration of their distance from each other even though they are close enough to kiss.

The cut to a rather crude single shot of a woman shouting congratulations on their wedding day anticipates the extreme change of mood of a marvelously framed shot of both of them and then Mary alone looking through a small rear window of the taxicab taking them to the train station for their honeymoon. The scene out that window is the run on the bank. The shot of Mary looking by herself as George races off to the Building and Loan is made more interesting by the heavy rain that washes on the window, turning the downpour into a trite metaphor for Mary's inner tears and the change in her life as George's wife.

In spite of the power of George's speech and the ensuing dialogue at the Building and Loan over the effort to save the association, the visual organization of Mary's role constitutes the scene's most powerful statements. After watching from her cab window George race away, she enters the chaos of the office. One shot finds her barely visible, circling around the crowd. Another locates her as having moved in line with her husband as he pleads with the people to keep their money in their Building and Loan. Another deep-focus shot aligns her directly with George as his backup. After George follows one person toward the door in an effort to persuade him and the others through his rapid speech to pause and think, we get the great shot of Mary across the office raising their honeymoon money in her hand. "How much do you need?" she asks, and the visual sign and her voice begin the change in the group's mood. Although George's speech dominates the scene, these shots of Mary document her greater power as a character and force: She becomes the foundation of their relationship. In the next scene at the old Granville house, which Mary unbelievably converts from a disastrous wreck to their romantic honeymoon place, Capra rather remarkably concentrates not on her physical beauty but on the house, exhibiting what she has imagined and done in each area. Her vision rather than her body becomes the object of the camera. Later in the film, her coy charm in helping George figure out that she is pregnant proclaims her continued mastery of their relationship.

The visual organization of the scene at the Building and Loan anticipates the great, climactic scene years later on Christmas Eve when George comes home thinking that he and his family have been ruined by Uncle Billy's loss of the company's money. This scene in its entirety is one of the most moving and powerful in American film history. It also may be one of the most important in its suggestiveness about the impending collapse of the American family in the face of accumulated pressures involving economics, security, and gender.

When George enters the house, the family busily works on preparing for Christmas and has no clue about the catastrophe of the lost funds. As the scene develops, George's increasingly violent and ill-tempered behavior indicates his growing hysteria about his situation. However, the scene also suggests that such submerged violence perhaps has erupted at other times, as when he earlier berated Uncle Billy for losing the money. It hints that George may have other secrets, such as drinking under duress, as he does later that night at Martini's, or even retaining an interest in Violet. He becomes increasingly agitated as the scene progresses. Seated in a living-room armchair with tears in his eyes and total devastation on his face, he holds and hugs the youngest boy, Tommy. Mary, looking down upon him from her position of authority by the Christmas tree, sees George with a tear-drenched, tortured face, desperately clutching Tommy to his chest. Nevertheless, her look remains absolutely calm and strong; her face registers concern without revealing extreme emotion but also without losing any of its sensitivity, beauty, and warmth. Although Mary says nothing, her look and presence put her in command, while George's visible anxiety compounds the chaos. She looks with stable authority, and he stays lost.

After learning that his youngest daughter, Zuzu, has been sick, he starts to bound upstairs to see her, but the knob on the bannister comes off in his

Figure 6. Donna Reed as Mary Hatch, a woman who sees and acts in *It's a Wonderful Life* (RKO / Liberty: The Museum of Modern Art / Film Stills Archive).

hand, adding to his frustration: This loose knob has been a sign for years of the poor condition of the house and of his finances. The scene upstairs between him and Zuzu works beautifully as a calming interlude to the crushing and encircling tensions of the family scene. His effort to show Zuzu that he can heal the fallen petals of a flower, which he actually hides in his trousers, movingly relates to his own twisted feelings of helplessness. Sitting on the bed with her, feeling her forehead for her fever, asking her in a whisper to try to sleep – all of these actions present an impressive maternal aspect to his nature, especially under the circumstances. His genuine concern and tenderness provide a powerful counterpoint to the violence of his hidden emotions. Zuzu's whisper that she is not sleepy, like little Tommy's pride earlier over his burp, seem so genuine as to add considerably to the effectiveness of the overall scene. Downstairs again, he insults a schoolteacher who calls on the telephone to inquire about Zuzu; his misdirected assault on her clearly signals to Mary that his rudeness involves something beside his obvious concern for Zuzu. Mary actually tries to wrestle the phone from him. Janie's continued pulsating practice on the piano and the general commotion drive him to distraction.

After verbally attacking the children and overturning a worktable holding models of his failed dreams of construction, George stops in horror over his behavior. Breathing heavily, he turns to face his family. Shadow and darkness cover him; alternating reverse shots, showing him isolated from his family, painfully dramatize the damage he has done. The children are frozen in fear and looking at him in dread; their terror is as genuine as his own fear and self-hatred. He tries to apologize, but his empty effort to undo the damage only heightens the tension, increases his isolation, and aggravates the children's fear. In choking anguish, he urges Pete to ask his question again and demands that Janie return to playing the piano. "Janie, go on. I told you to practice. Now, go on, play!" As Janie responds with a tortured, "Oh Daddy!" her mother huddles closer to the children and looks at George accusingly. "George, why must you torture the children?" she asks. Her words and attitude are absolutely authoritative and final, totally isolating him. "Mary!" he appeals helplessly. He has been unable to bring himself to articulate the circumstances causing his distress; now the silence rigidifies his isolation and abandonment. Disheveled and alienated in his own home, he moves in mobile shadow and darkness from right to left past the camera and toward the door. In the next shot – the room in strong light, the children standing by Mary – she moves to the right toward the telephone. Even before George actually leaves the house, Mary begins the process of finding out what has happened and of trying to correct it. A slow wipe to another scene keeps her on the phone at home but has her share the frame with her husband. George, in yet another example of terrible judgment in a crisis, has gone for help as a supplicant literally on his knees to Potter, who secretly has hidden the lost money. The striking reversal of gender roles in these Christmas Eve scenes continues the impulse toward powerful change set forth in the relationship between Smith and Saunders in *Mr. Smith*. Mary's presence and command could hardly contrast more with George's disastrous loss of control.

It has been widely suggested by many film scholars that the cinema as an aesthetic form redesigns and re-creates woman in order to suit its own demands and needs of specularity. Woman is shaped and formed according to how film wants literally to shoot and display her. Thus, Heath expounds upon cinema's "institution of the image of the woman": "Cinema has played to the maximum the masquerade, the signs of this exchange femininity, has ceaselessly reproduced its social currency."[58]

Figure 7. An ending built on belief and action in the widely discussed family Christmas scene in *It's a Wonderful Life* (RKO / Liberty: The Museum of Modern Art / Film Stills Archive).

However, it seems to me that Capra's classic films *Mr. Smith Goes to Washington* and *It's a Wonderful Life* dramatically contradict that notion of cinema as an art form that predetermines content and subject regarding women and gender. The intelligence, authority, and power of Saunders and Mary as played by Arthur and Reed challenge the assumption of the inherent bias of cinema toward the demeaning display of women. The women in these films insist upon revolutionizing and transforming gender. In doing so, they are at the forefront of Capra's strategy for creating a cinema for democracy.

The aesthetics of *It's a Wonderful Life* structures the debate for a democratic cinema and culture. The film relates the visual organization of reality to the construction of systems of belief. *It's a Wonderful Life* is about mind and reality as well as vision. Robert B. Ray's understanding of the relationship of vision and ideology to reality in *It's a Wonderful Life* may help explain his argument that the film really concerns the collapse of the American

Dream. He says, "More than any other character of the movie, George Bailey recognized that the American Dream was no longer a given, that it depended on the will of its adherents." Ray then proceeds to quote from a scene in the film that we have discussed. "'We can get through this thing all right,' he pleaded with the Building and Loan customers during a run on the bank. 'We've got to stick together, though; we've got to have faith in each other.'" Seeing George as the community's greatest doubter and skeptic and the one most vulnerable to adopting a kind of agnosticism about values and beliefs, Ray also writes: "The truly subversive point about *It's a Wonderful Life*, then, was its recognition that a man could have so many of the things promised by the American Dream (wife, children, job, friends, house, car) and still be unhappy." Ray further notes that for George "the American myth had suggested that he could have it all."[59]

A key element in Ray's argument concerns the dichotomy it establishes between a manifestly "given" external reality about America and an America constructed through belief and myth. He wavers between seeing myth as historically verifiable belief systems and viewing it as the creation and interpretation of experience. In contrast to Ray, it can be maintained that *It's a Wonderful Life* actually argues that the American Dream never has been a "given" but always has worked as a creation from the vision of people. Such people followed George's lead and supported him during the potential run on the Building and Loan. Under George's rhetorical influence and Mary's vivid example of visible dollars in her hand, the people really operated pragmatically, as William James defined that term, by treating ideas like "cash" for their value and what they can purchase in the way of truth and individual and social benefit.[60]

Furthermore, as a prime doubter of the myth, the one in the town who continually talks of escaping and making his own way, George also functions as the leading seeker of the truth, the pilgrim, who tests and then evidences the strongest commitment to his faith. Thus, his fall into the pool with Mary when the gymnasium floor cracks open during the graduation party, his slide into the ice to save his brother, and his jump into the river to save Clarence are all forms of baptism that ultimately represent his faith in the human race. As in Jonathan Edwards's "Sinners in the Hands of an Angry God," his feet slide as a test of his faith. George's ideology as his brother's keeper culminates in his joining Mary in a commitment for life.

The answer to his dilemma about the value of his life does not rely only upon the ending, when all of his friends, at Mary's instigation, surround him with love and prove their faith in him. The answer has resided all along in the film's opening frames and shots, only George didn't quite see it or hear it. In the opening frame when his family and community pray for him, we know they are creating the environment for his salvation and justification.

The heavens answer because the action and support of the people individually and as a society are part of the beginning of any answer. As Robert Sklar
says,

> Indeed, there are two miracles in *It's a Wonderful Life*, one divine and one hu-
> man, or social. The social act (collections of many individual acts) frames the su-
> pernatural, calls it forth, and then completes it; the two are so entwined in the
> film's structure that one could not occur without the other.[61]

To some, this exchange between a mythical heaven and a distressed people merely dramatizes the operations of the dominant ideology of acceptance
and conformity as opposed to the collective will and action of the people.
Thus, Silverman approvingly quotes Michael Renov's suggestion that the resolution to the film's crisis of belief can be associated with a form of "propaganda," an "interpellation" or calling by greater forces to accept one's fate
with pleasure (106). If the conclusion entails a form of propaganda as presumed, it should be emphasized that Capra's version of propaganda works
assiduously to humanize its main hero and to display him in all his weaknesses rather than to deify him in the manner of Riefenstahl's aesthetic.
George Bailey's accumulated weaknesses and failures manifest themselves
like plagues on himself and his family: business practices that enable an im-
balanced incompetent like Uncle Billy to endanger him and his family's future; hubris that allows him to take a largely uncompromising moral and
political attitude toward greater opposing forces; timidity and fear that keep
him from fulfilling his potential. No matter how hard he has tried, George
ends up looking vulnerable to others, especially Mary. The movie drowns
him in its exposure of his weakness and inevitable failure. Mary doesn't deny
or disavow it. She has seen and known it at least since the experience at
Gower's pharmacy.

Failure, however, has never been all that she has seen. Other qualities also
obtain between George and the children, George and the community, George
and herself. To Potter and others, including himself, George invariably will
look like a failure. In the context of the conventional cultural definition of
success and power, such a conclusion becomes inescapable. The film is all
about what success and triumph mean in America – success, of course, as
money and power. What Mary also sees in George is a man who will never
stop trying to be human in spite of the beating he will receive for it. What
audiences, therefore, have seen in George is the American – naïve, idealistic,
the battler for enduring causes, the believer in himself and the future. Even
the interference of the angels cannot guarantee results but only emphasizes
George's need to find himself. In presenting George in all of his frailty and
helplessness, the film really follows a classic paradigm of faith and conversion. With all of his weaknesses, George embodies the tenacity of the exis-

tential courage to be and therefore can be saved through his own actions and the community. He represents his culture as an ordinary man who ultimately accepts his failures, except for the one mistake he almost made of quitting. Of course, this is precisely Capra's point. Never quit!

In his unfailing weakness, George still draws strength from the cultural tradition of his pilgrimage as an individual and a member of the community. The pilgrimage, of course, relates directly to American culture. Taking a cue again from classic American figures such as Whitman, for Capra American democracy remains a system of faith; the religion of *It's a Wonderful Life* continues to be democracy as it was in *Mr. Smith,* where the Lincoln Memorial functions as the national house of prayer and regeneration. In following a path of earlier democratic figures from our literature and culture, George does not walk alone.

As an argument – what Silverman terms propaganda – for faith in the individual and the democratic community, the film explores and reveals the inherent weaknesses of its hero and program. In its antiutopian revelations of the challenges and obstacles to democratic fulfillment, it offers a pragmatic argument that only action fulfills faith. It never promises a return to Eden but only a rationale for the continuing search for it. Moreover, it specifically suggests that reconstructing gender relationships provides the strongest foundation for reform and renewal in the culture as a whole. In *It's a Wonderful Life,* Mary's strength and character provide the most important vehicle and force for that democratic journey. In Capra's idea of gender and American democratic culture, the weakness and vulnerability of the ordinary male hero elicits the assertive strength of women who fill the vacuum. The resulting relationship constitutes a radical challenge to putative patriarchal privilege. It undermines conventional conceptions of male representation and domination. George remains ordinary, the common man, the democratic hero. Stewart's great achievement and genius in *Mr. Smith* and *Wonderful Life* involve his ability to maintain this portrayal of democratic heroism and to endow his characters with such sustaining human qualities of everyday life.

The alignment of George's ordinary humanity with women's inferior status in the office, in the Senate, in the community, in business emphasizes the incompleteness of American democracy. The secondary status and unfair treatment of Saunders and Mary testify to the continued need for revolution and transformation in America – for greater democratization. Mary and Saunders are visual and emblematic Jeremiahs proclaiming and demanding equality, opportunity, liberty. Their brilliant achievements in the films radiate the inadequacy of the system. They embody injustice, especially considering their participation in creating a greater complexity and multiplicity of representations of masculinity through their support of Stewart. They advertise and promote the need for change.

Mr. Smith Goes to Washington and *It's a Wonderful Life* give Jean Arthur and Donna Reed, Clarissa Saunders and Mary Hatch, important platforms from which to set forth the beginings of such change. In these two films that deal directly with the importance of media and cinema, film as an art form serves the cause of women. In these Capra films, the ideology of the cinematic form works with the democratic impulse to dramatize the need for the kinds of changes that have occurred in the decades since their production. Film empowers. The cinema for democracy modernizes and transforms American culture partly through its revisioning of gender and the masculine and feminine in America.

Like America itself, *It's a Wonderful Life* and *Mr. Smith Goes to Washington* remain unfinished efforts, works in progress. *Wonderful Life* echoes *Mr. Smith* and then establishes its own voice in proclaiming that Mary and Saunders deserve the right to be on center stage giving the address in the Senate and running the Building and Loan.

That'll be the day.

CHAPTER 4

REVISIONING HEROIC MASCULINITY: FROM FORD TO HAWKS AND ZINNEMANN

War Wounds: Sexual Politics and American Heroics

The stage from Tonto to Lordsburg repeats a great deal of history, but it also makes history. The story of John Ford's classic *Stagecoach* (1939) continues the mythical American journey of individual and communal regeneration. It takes a composite of various basic American character types and turns them into a transitory community capable of working and fighting together to achieve a common goal. The film's treatment of the Apaches as the stereotypical Indian enemy, Mexicans as comical or exotic others, and African Americans as markedly absent from American consciousness also says much about the popular self-conception of America during this period and how much both Ford and the country would change by the time of his last films, such as *Cheyenne Autumn* (1964), which so sympathetically advocates the cause of the Indians. Besides starting a hopeful transition toward a new future for some of the white people aboard the coach, the journey in *Stagecoach* resonates with another idea of the American myth as a flight from past oppressions, including in this instance the repressive moral conformity and emotional constraints of civilization as embodied in the faces and attitudes of the women who drive away the prostitute Dallas (Claire Trevor) and the alcoholic "Doc" Boone (Thomas Mitchell). The women in this scene project a form of late-1930s political correctness of such venomous harshness as to suggest Ford's own latent hostility toward women as authority figures. In any case, almost all on the stage are in flight from some form of despair and loss.

However, the film also inaugurates a particular movement of reimaging heroic American masculinity. This movement occurs as part of the broader dialogue within American culture and film regarding the relationship of American gender and heroism to American character. It concerns the emergence of a particular pattern of intertextuality in the Hollywood Renaissance involving a continuity of directors, actors, images, and ideologies.[1] The shot that begins this particular history of masculinity and gender in American film occurs relatively early in *Stagecoach,* right after we see the stage rapidly make its way over a rise in the rough New Mexico road.[2] From a camera position on that rise, we see the stage suddenly pull up short, and a cut from the general point of view of the stage shows what obstacle in the dusty road caused Andy Devine, the stage driver, to stop so abruptly. There stands the Ringo Kid (John Wayne) shouting "Hold it!" He twirls his rifle in his right hand as though it were a pistol and holds the heavy saddle from his lame horse in his left. His body dominates the frame, showing him from above his waist. His broad chest occupies the center of the shot. This is our first impression of Ringo. As Gary Wills says, "The shot that introduces Wayne has become famous." Wills adds that Edward Buscombe "calls it 'one of the most stunning entrances in all of cinema.'"[3]

The historic subsequent shot, however, indicates what Ford wants his audience to feel and think about the Kid. With explosive intensity, the camera suddenly breaks from the hold of its medium distance to a smashingly rapid zooming close-up that goes right up to Wayne's chin and nose, as though embracing Ringo. Wayne's hat casts a shadow over the left side of his face so as to emphasize the lighting on his right side, which softens his features and adds to the impression of his youth. This shot of him not only signals the arrival of the main figure in the film but also a rebirth of Wayne's career that began a new movement of complexity regarding heroic masculinity in American film. At the age of thirty-two after nearly ten years of making around eighty low-budget westerns, the six-foot-four Wayne received new life when Ford cast him in this role as Ringo. In spite of his age, the subsequent close-up shots of Wayne, especially within the stage and during moments at important stops along the way, reaffirm his innocence and youth. Years later Wayne's image would mature into the greater, darker, more ominous hero of *The Searchers* and *The Man Who Shot Liberty Valance*.

Besides emphasizing a youthful softness to Wayne's face and features, Ford's direction and shooting in *Stagecoach* dramatize a new vulnerability in Wayne's role as the victim of violence and social prejudice. In beautifully timed and coordinated cutting and editing, Ford shows Wayne cramped on the floor of the stage, in between the seated travelers who face each other. He lowers his chin and hides his face beneath his hat to protect himself from the dust and wind. When he looks up, his face often serves as a visual mediator of the interlocking looks and glances of the other travelers. These shots again emphasize his youth and his social distance from most of these other people. In especially interesting shots, when he peeks up from under the brim of his hat as the stage surges and sways over the rolling and irregular high desert road, he looks almost feminine, seeming more like a coy Marlene Dietrich than the embodiment of rough-and-ready masculine self-confidence.

Already too old for this constructed image of youthfulness to last much longer, Wayne moved on to the more senior roles that steadily established his ultimate Hollyood image of aggressive strength, physical dominance, and personal charisma. The important drama of transition from the youthful persona of Ringo to the mythic western figure of dark granite in later movies occurs, as Wills and others state, not in a Ford film but in Howard Hawks's *Red River* (1948).[4] In *Red River* the Wayne character, Thomas Dunson, enters middle age after building an empire of hundreds of thousands of acres and several thousand head of cattle – which Hawks modeled on the dominating, real-life King Ranch in southern Texas – only to find all his work worthless unless he can move the cattle north over the Chisholm Trail to be sold in Missouri. In the beginning of the film, a younger Dunson leaves a wagon train in the midst of hostile Indian territory to set off on his own to start his cattle empire. He takes his sidekick, Nadine Groot (Walter Brennan), but leaves behind his girlfriend, Fen (Coleen Gray), because of the danger. Hours later he and Groot figure from the smoke miles behind them that the wagon train has been attacked; still later, after fighting off their own Indian attack, Dunson realizes that Fen must be dead because the Indian he has just killed wears the snake bracelet that he had given her before leaving the wagon train. At about this point, a young boy, crazed by the death and destruction of his family by the Indians, wanders across Dunson and Groot. Dunson adopts the young boy, Matthew Garth, but only after beginning his lessons in manhood by taking the orphan boy's gun, slapping him, and instructing him never to trust anyone. The three join together under Dunson and locate the area for Dunson's ranch and empire, land he takes from Mexicans who, as he insists, took it from the Indians.[5]

Red River then cuts to a period almost fifteen years later, after Dunson has built his empire but must sell his herd. Wayne now appears middle-aged, visibly indicating through his physical movements the cost to his body of years of tough ranching, range riding, struggling with the land and environment, and fighting and killing contenders for control of his empire. In contrast, Matthew is now played by Montgomery Clift as a young man in his prime. More important, he clearly exhibits the qualities and features of sensitivity, vulnerability, and innocence that characterized Wayne's portrayal years earlier of Ringo in *Stagecoach*. While *Red River* demonstrates the progression from young manhood to maturity of Wayne's character, Dunson, it also uses the physical bearing and appearance of Montgomery Clift to establish a line back to the youthful Wayne that Ford helped to create in *Stagecoach*.

On the face of it, Clift, who in *Red River* was appearing in a film for only the second time, would seem to be the exact opposite of the older Wayne – smaller, sensitive, boyish, and homosexual – a fact apparently unknown even to others in the film, according to a recent conversation I had with Harry Carey, Jr. However, Clift came prepared with an Academy Award nomination for his first film appearance, in Fred Zinnemann's *The Search* (1948). Nervous himself about portraying an older man, Wayne worried that Clift was not experienced or powerful enough to play against him. As reported by Hawks, Wayne complained to him: "That kid isn't going to stand up to me."[6] Clift not only stood up to Wayne, he created a presence and force so great as to bring out Wayne's role. Clift plays Matthew Garth with such depth and clarity in this performance as to indicate the roots of that role in Wayne's own image and character of Ringo in *Stagecoach*. Clift's performance, therefore, dramatizes the prominence of Wayne as one original source for the development of the growing complexity and multiplicity of representations of masculinity in film. Gerald Mast delineates this connection between the images of Clift and Wayne in the evolution of Wayne's persona. Discussing how "the inflexibile indomitability of John Wayne became one of the dominant traits of his screen being after Hawks developed it" in *Red River*, Mast writes:

> Wayne had never played quite this kind of role before *Red River;* he was far more often the romantic, beautiful young outlaw – for example, the Ringo Kid in John Ford's *Stagecoach,* made just seven years earlier – more like Clift himself. Once Wayne had played this unbendingly hard (yet vulnerably insecure) male for Hawks he would play variations on it forever (and would seem as if he had played it forever).[7]

Mast's reference to *Stagecoach* properly demonstrates the seminal influence of Ford on the Hollywood Renaissance. The intertextual connection between Capra and Ford, discussed in Chapter 3, now extends to Hawks. Ford's image of Wayne in *Stagecoach,* which reappears in *Red River* in the person of Montgomery Clift, goes on to become the giant characters in Ford's later classics: Ethan Edwards in *The Searchers* and Tom Doniphon in *The Man Who Shot Liberty Valance.* The professional and personal relationship between Hawks and Ford sustains this argument of intertextuality. Ford's tough-guy sarcasm and irony dissemble his considerable respect for Hawks and what he could learn from him and his work. As Ford reputedly told Hawks after seeing Wayne in *Red River:* "I never knew the big son of a bitch could act." That line was attributed to Ford by Hawks in a conversation with Joseph McBride about the progression from Ringo to Clift in their movies:

> Ford put Wayne in *Stagecoach.* I put him in *Red River.* Wayne did a hell of a job in *Red River,* and Jack Ford said, "I never knew the big son of a bitch could act." So every time I made a picture with Wayne, Ford would come around and watch.[8]

Hawks also has expressed unbounded admiration for Ford, proclaiming: "I learned right in the beginning from Jack Ford, and I learned what not to do by watching Cecil DeMille." Hawks says that together he and Ford learned to "cut down the dialogue on every scene" and to go with "the visual stuff."[9]

Besides duly appreciating the special bond with Ford, Hawks also fully recognized the unique nature of their relationship with Wayne: "John Wayne represents more force, more power, than anybody else on the screen. And I think both Ford and I succeeded in making pretty good scenes with him."[10] Wayne's on-screen force and power that Hawks so greatly admired achieved their greatest fulfillment in the later Ford films. However, as already noted, much of the unique authority in those roles in *The Searchers* and *The Man Who Shot Liberty Valance* came out of *Red River* and what those concerned – Wayne, Hawks, and Ford – learned from it. Wayne's image of superhuman masculinity in these later films incorporates at some level the complex ambivalences and ambiguities of character that Clift develops in *Red River* from Wayne's earlier classic Ringo. An unresolved tension and dialogue involving these different versions of masculinity lend credibility to Wayne's maturer roles. This history of conflict and difference in the construction of the Wayne image and character also suggests the developing complexity of an ideology of masculinity in America.

Hawks's *Red River* flows not only through a visual landscape of the West but also through a region of the American mind, an intellectual frontier of images and ideas of heroic masculinity and American culture. Over the long haul, most of the territory for these imaginative and psychological landscapes would go to Ford, leaving Hawks with an important realm of his own in the middle. The film *Red River* divides those landscapes so that, in terms of chronology, psychological development, and interpretive meanings, charming Ringo stands on one side and demonic Tom Doniphon on the other. Hawks's development of his own smaller empire on this cinematic landscape of multidimensional meanings articulates important issues concerning the construction of heroic masculinity in the context of American society during a period of great transition following the Second World War. His effort in *Red River* to establish a meaningful narrative and ideology of heroic masculinity on a middle ground between what would become Ford's dramatic extremes raises the question of manhood in a democracy that so concerned Capra. Hawks's idea of heroic masculinity in the Hollywood Renaissance continues Capra's interest in the relationship of manliness and the hero to democracy in America and to the cinema of democracy. In Capra, questions about heroic manliness and the ordinary hero lead to other questions about women, and the need for liberating and unleashing the American woman as part of the enterprise of democratizing and broadening the idea of America. This, however, is not Hawks's answer in *Red River,* although the issue of women becomes central in many other Hawks efforts. Instead, *Red River* really concerns the difficulty of becoming a man.

In *Red River,* Wayne and Hawks consider masculinity in terms of total authority and power. However, the values of democracy still impede and inhibit their freedom to pursue this idea, so they tentatively address Wayne's role of the tyrant and proceed cautiously in having him assume the mantle of the despot. The antagonistic and competitive nature of Dunson's relationships leads to such tyranny. Even the humorous banter between Dunson and Groot (Brennan) dissimulates basic affection and loyalty with aggressive competitiveness. In spite of his age and the danger, Brennan asserts that he will accompany Dunson on the thousand-mile Chisholm Trail. He then outthinks Dunson by being prepared to tell him that his services as a cook are necessary because the current cook cannot be relied upon for the trip. Interestingly, Groot's age puts him in a domestic and secondary position that feminizes him from both Wayne's and his own perspective. Ironically, his situation compares to that of Fen, who died when Wayne left her behind with the wagon train. In this psychological context, the joking about Groot's toothlessness has a sexual connotation, though Hawks and Wayne undoubtedly would scoff at such a connection. Wayne responds to Brennan's argument about going on the drive with a genuinely funny facial expression that concedes the older man's triumph. Wayne's face also registers a degree of self-irony that indicates a potential depth to his character and his acting.

Although Dunson reasonably expresses concern about the dangers and hardships of the cattle drive, the actual filming proved arduous. Shot outdoors on location, the challenge of driving the cattle was real for the people in the film, and this realism helps make it a classic of the genre. Hawks found this part of the filming challenging and exhilarating: "When you have to shift 3,000 head of cattle every time you shoot a new scene, that's hard work."[11] Hawks also recalls that in the interest of giving greater credibility to the historic accuracy of the cattle drive, rarer longhorn cattle were placed in front of the more readily available white-face cattle. Hawks said "we bought Mexican cattle, hand-fed them, and made a hell of a lot of money selling them after the picture was over."[12]

However, as the film develops, the greatest challenge to Dunson's completion of his task concerns neither the physical dangers of driving the cattle, the harsh and unpredictable extremes of the weather, nor the miserable conditions; the greatest challenge and obstacle is human. *Red River* turns out to be less about cattle, Indians, or weather than about men, politics, and Dunson himself. Even the event of greatest physical danger to the men and the herd on the drive, the stampede in the middle of the night, results from a weakness of human character. Bunk Kennelly (Ivan Parry), a cowboy with a compulsive sweet tooth, sets off the herd to stampeding because of the noise he causes by accidentally scattering all of the chuck wagon's pots and pans while trying to treat himself to an off-limits sugar fix. The stampede scene in the film is a Hawks triumph, a powerful and exciting presentation of action and chaos to compare with the best of similar action efforts of other directors. Hawks impressively builds the tension before the stampede with a coyote's incessant and pitiful howling that aggravates the herd's restlessness and stirs up the men's anxiety. He personalizes the scene by focusing before the stampede on the character of one particular cowboy, Dan Latimer (Harry Carey, Jr.). Dan will be horribly crushed and killed by the stampeding cattle when he falls from his horse. Hawks uses shadow and light in the cowboy camp to develop the suspense and tension of the impending disaster of Bunk's actions as the sweet-toothed cowboy approaches the wagon and reaches for the sugar. Hawks maximizes the drama when the clattering and crashing pots and pans keep the whole camp in agonizing suspension, waiting for the nervous cattle to explode. His dramatic cutting and editing in this sequence anticipate the extraordinary montage of the nightmare stampede.

Although the stampede dramatizes the most likely form of physical danger on a cattle drive, the wild scene also builds toward another kind of danger when Dunson insists on whipping Bunk for causing the stampede and Dan's death. By concentrating on Dunson's violence and extremism, Hawks keeps the viewer's sympathy for Bunk without dimininshing the importance of his mistake. Bunk stands in darkness and absolute isolation. Clearly, the depth of his self-condemnation and hatred exceeds the feelings of most of the men – except for Dunson. Bunk's genuine remorse and guilt make him quite human and sympathetic. His flaw is understandable even if the consequences of his actions make his behavior unpardonable. Through careful plot construction and beautifully timed editing and visual organization, Hawks manages to show the cowboy operating on several moral levels. He steals the sugar and causes the catastrophe, accepts his guilt but cannot accept a form of punishment that he and the others regard as grotesquely excessive. By so quickly and clearly insinuating such underlying complexity into this simple character and event, Hawks greatly increases the tension of Bunk's encounter with Dunson. Bunk's resistance to the whipping gains the support of the other cowboys; Dunson, insisting on executing this punishment, thus thoroughly alienates himself from his men. In the end, it is Dunson and his problems – not Bunk, Dan the dead cowboy, or the runaway cattle – that are the climactic focal point of the stampede and the extended scene. The external chaos and disaster of the stampede dramatize the internal chaos of Dunson's growing paranoia and his obsessive need to control his men and the drive.

A milestone for Wayne in his performance in this film concerns his demonstration of the perverse turnings of mind and character that alienate Dunson from his men. As already noted, his exhibition of dark and interior psychic forces comprises a dramatic move toward significant growth as an actor and figure that can be better appreciated when compared briefly with the innocence and simplicity of the Ringo Kid in *Stagecoach*. Throughout *Stagecoach*, Ringo registers no reaction to or even awareness of Dallas (Trevor) as a prostitute. In the controversial meal scene at the stagecoach's first way-station stop, the travelers cruelly remove themselves from Dallas. Ringo's friendliness toward her indicates no awareness of her real situation. Similarly, no sign of acknowledgment appears as he walks her home in the Lordsburg red-light district, making him either the greatest gentleman or silliest fool in the West. As Tag Gallagher says, "We are not sure whether Ringo is noble or stupid, whether or not he knows Dallas is a whore, but his unflinching simplicity as he walks with her perfectly offsets her confusion."[13] Ringo's supportive reaction at this time to Dallas's outburst indicates his genuine regard for her, a response that is consistent with the concern he showed for her throughout the journey. However, he still dramatizes very little of his inner feelings or character. When compared to the performance in *Stagecoach*, Wayne achieves much greater depth and intensity in *Red River*. The failure by both Hawks and Wayne to sustain and fulfill that level of intensity in the film involves other issues of the film's meaning and development.

Several scenes in *Red River* suggest Wayne's maturity and growing ability to present a deeper and darker side to his character. Most of these powerful scenes involve the men's mutiny toward the end of the film. After the stampede and whipping incident, the drive becomes increasingly difficult. Some of the men want to turn back; others argue for a different route, to Abilene, where they have heard about a new railroad line that Dunson cannot be sure exists. Dunson deems the men who want to abandon the drive potential deserters to be handled according to military justice. He won't sleep for fear that the men will endanger the venture by leaving with indispensable supplies. Even Groot worries about Dunson's state of mind as sleeplessness exacerbates his proclivity toward isolation and mistrust. When Cherry Valance (John Ireland) brings back some deserters, Dunson decides to hang them. Led by Matthew, the men defy Dunson, shooting and wounding him to prevent him from killing Matthew. Matthew then takes control of the herd, leaving Dunson behind.

For Wayne and Clift, the mutiny scenes mark important advances in their careers. While Clift gains in stature by rising to the challenge of dealing with Wayne, for Wayne the scenes represent a new dimension to his acting and his film persona. In them, Wayne fulfills Dunson's pathological radical individualism. He establishes a precedent for himself of embodying the world and the law in himself, of being a godlike hero. Playing off of Clift, Wayne's strength achieves fresh intensity in its intimation of an element of human vulnerability. The fusion of superior strength with suggestions of vulnerable sensitivity demonstrates a new potential in Wayne's power.

The mixture of absolute power and vulnerability achieves its greatest tension and most eloquent expression first when Matthew and the men actually mutiny and then when they go off with the herd. Relatively early in the complex narrative, the enlarged written text of "Early Tales of Texas" that appears on the screen for the audience refers to Dunson as a "tyrant." However, his effort toward the end of the film to enforce his own justice by hanging the deserters involves his most tyrannical act, exeeding all of his previous bullying and intimidation. The tightly controlled dialogue during this scene, when Matthew interferes, saving the condemned men and taking over the herd, contributes greatly to the drama. The pointed brevity of the exchange between Wayne and Clift exemplifies how Hawks's economical direction strengthens a scene. Dunson says, "I'm gonna hang 'em." With an extraordinary intensity that Clift projects through the discipline of his look and expression, Matthew responds: "No, you're not." Dunson asks, "Who'll stop me?" "I will," says Matthew.

Given the structure, movement, and power of the film to this point, the narrative turn in this sequence is brilliant. The man who has played God and has acted like a mythic superman faces an open rebellion of his power and authority. He will lose everything he has striven to achieve. The scene is astounding, however, for its controlled intensity and the absence of overacting. Confronting Clift, Wayne reveals multiple levels of emotion and belief. He stands totally alone yet remains the strongest of them all. He watches all he has built disappear but conveys greater inner resources of strength and capacity for pain. Preparing to take the cattle, Matthew tells Dunson that "I'll get your cattle to Abilene." The issue now has exceeded the material reality of the cattle and the years that went into building the empire. Dunson and Matthew might as well remain silent because their facial expressions, body language, and physical intensity express so much more than their words.

Wayne only glances at Clift, just barely recognizing his existence but suggesting a deeper, internal anticipation of future reprisal. Dunson says that preventing the cowboys from killing him proves Matthew's softness. He says, "I'm gonna kill you." Through much of the scene, we see only Wayne's back and Clift's profile, but we also get Clift and Wayne at angles to each other in tense opposition. The scene ends with a prophetic and powerful long shot of a pathetic Wayne with his back to the camera in the middle ground of the frame standing over his shadow, obviously hindered by his physical and psychological wounds, looking at the men leaving with his herd. Wayne evokes complex and contradictory emotions as Hawks creates in this scene a compressed, metaphoric history of the rise and fall of paternal authority.

Supposedly, Clift felt that he had lost this scene to Wayne and that Wayne had dominated it. Hawks reports that Clift

> thought he had a great scene, but Wayne never looked at him or anything – he just looked off and said, "I'm gonna kill you." Monty didn't know what to do. Finally, he came out of the scene and came around to me and said, "My good scene certainly went to the devil, didn't it?" I said, "Anytime you think you're gonna make Wayne look bad, you've got another think coming."[14]

Although Wills challenges this account and accuses Hawks of "fabulating," in retrospect Clift is much stronger in the scene than he apparently realized.[15] Clift bears the thrust of Wayne's attention, and both men are stronger for it. The moment truly elevates the visual complexity of Wayne as a hero.

A similar intensity repeats itself at the very end of the film when Wayne finally catches up with Matthew and the other cowboys. The man who buys the cattle from Clift at the end of the trail is appropriately called Melville, a name that recalls the tyrannical and insane individualism of Captain Ahab in *Moby-Dick*. The kindly presence and figure of the actor who plays Melville, Harry Carey – the smiling vice-president of *Mr. Smith Goes to Washington* (and real-life father to the man portraying Dan, crushed in the stampede) – softens the connotations of the author's most famous character. Nevertheless, the association of Melville with the madness, tyranny, and expansionism of Ahab still sets an intellectual and emotional stage for Dunson's vengeance and his expected killing of Matthew.

In the scene, Dunson approaches on horseback followed by the anonymous riders he has accumulated to help him settle the score. That he rides well in front of these men is an indication not only of his emotional intensity and personal stake in the events but also of his continued separation and isolation from the human community. Meandering throughout the town are the cattle that Matthew has delivered and sold. Dismounting, Dunson continues to approach Matthew, cutting through the cattle with that signature walk that no other actor has quite been able to duplicate. He does not even stop moving to shoot the one cowboy who tries to interfere, the gunman Valance (an ironic foreshadowing for Wayne of his later movie with Ford); he only alters his stride a bit, executing a kind of timed dance movement to shoot Valance, a motion that remains so unique and special to Wayne.[16] When Dunson finally encounters Matthew, he fires his gun in frustration in an attempt to get Matthew to shoot back: As Melville (Carey) earlier said, Matthew would never kill the man who adopted him and became his father.

However, in a discussion of this scene, Mast brilliantly analyzes its structure and Clift's place within it, bringing fresh insights to the film:

> Matthew emerges from the hotel into the sunlight – loose, casual, relaxed. This coolness and looseness will dominate Clift's playing throughout the final scene – implying Matthew's absolute confidence in what he alone knows about Dunson. He knows Dunson, and he knows he can trust him.[17]

Although Mast seemingly overlooks Matthew's and Groot's admitted and visible fear on the final phase of the cattle drive that Dunson would catch up to them and wreak his revenge, Mast's excellent description of Matthew's mood, dress, and demeanor makes the point that Matthew acts so confidently partly out of the expectation that Dunson will not shoot. The final scene certainly fulfills that expectation. After failing to get Matthew to shoot, Dunson finally succeeds in getting him to fight and even to knock Dunson down. At that point, the second woman in the film, Tess Millay (Joanne Dru), effectively stops the fighting by firing at the two of them to force them into a reconciliation to which Wayne suddenly greedily accedes. Hawks has famously explained this end by asserting that both characters were so strong and important, he just didn't want to kill either one of them: "I certainly would have hated to kill one of them. It frustrates me to start killing people off for no reason at all."[18] Concerning the ending, Hawks told McBride:

> I still don't believe in killing people and making a picture end with death. . . . People have talked about the ending of *Red River* – hell, with the characters that I had and their relationship, that was the only ending you could possibly use. Anybody who says it different isn't a student of characters. Because Wayne had a distinct character, and Monty Clift had a distinct character, and the only way they could end up was just the way they did. If they couldn't understand that relationship, why then, they. . . .[19]

From the way Mast describes Clift and the way Hawks discusses the film, it would seem the ending of the film was inevitable: Dunson would spend all those years building an empire, lose it to the orphan he found in the high desert, chase him down, and then let Tess use a gun to force them into making up.[20]

Clearly, Matthew, as played by Clift, understands Dunson's dilemma over the possibility of killing his adopted son. Conceivably, Matthew's sudden insouciance over Dunson's arrival after earlier indicating real fear involves his own acceptance of death and his fatalism. He now has the courage to die rather than kill his father. These diverse conflicts and complexities – resolution and courage in facing death, confidence in the outcome of the conflict, even fatalistic indifference – all play out in Clift's development of the role of Matthew.

In contrast to Clift, Wayne's murderous entry into this confrontation simply collapses. This time Wayne loses the scene. Moreover, the loss sustains a pattern of loss throughout the film in the development of Wayne's character. As a collaborative effort between Hawks and Wayne, Dunson presents but cannot sustain his interior complexities. The extraordinarily original inner energy of this new Wayne hero continually dissipates in chaotic compromise with the implications of his inner drives and conflicts with society. These tensions evaporate or scatter in confusion in order to satisfy conventional expectations of democratic manhood. Unsure as to how to be an Ahab embattled with God, Wayne unsuccessfully tries at the same time to be a democratic Ishmael with a grudging recognition but little genuine respect for the common man.

Confusion and uncertainty over the portrayal of Dunson manifest themselves throughout the film. In several scenes, Wayne simply falls short of fulfilling his insidious potential that would make him either Ethan Edwards or Tom Doniphon. Unable to take that additional step, he also finds himself incapable of falling back to Clift's position as the putative democratic hero. In the beginning of the film, when Dunson and Groot see the fires of the wagon train behind them, Wayne's unconvincing expression of grief, guilt, and loss invites a comparison with his handling of the similar scene in *The Searchers*. Ethan Edwards's sustained mixture of thoroughly conflicting and contradictory feelings and attitudes of hatred and love, grief and anger, guilt and desperate loyalty are largely absent in Dunson. Dunson almost shrugs off Fen's death although the expressed relationship with her calls for an extremely different emotional response. Wayne's depth and intensity of emotion also seem shallow after Dunson finds on the arm of an attacking Indian he kills the coiled-snake bracelet he had given to Fen. In both scenes, Wayne conveys confusion over what he should be feeling and revealing of himself. He remains unable to find an adequate position between the ruthless independence his character suggests and conflicting demands for a more conventional emotional response. Similarly, in another early scene with Matthew as a boy (Mickey Kuhn), Wayne communicates uncertainty as to how to treat and feel about this dazed and abandoned orphan who has just seen his family killed. The scene compresses the difficulty throughout the film of representing manhood with genuine emotion and compassion. The film resolves the confusion in this particular scene when Wayne gives the armed boy a sharp and ugly slap. Wayne here still has not found a tone, voice, or attitude for the development of the forces he and Hawks have set into motion in the character of Dunson.

Over the years, many critics have explained the narrative structure, relationships, and some of the difficulties involved in *Red River* in psychoanalytical terms of father and son conflicts and unresolved Oedipal tensions. A recent article in *Sight and Sound* on "Ten essential cowboy movies," which describes the film as "the greatest" of all "Westerns which actually centre on cowboying," also notes that "along the way" on the Chisholm Trail "is played out the Oedipal conflict between Wayne and Montgomery Clift."[21] Similarly, Leland Poague argues that "thematically, *Red River* can be seen as yet another variant of the Oedipal fable in Hawks."[22] As a story about growing up, striving for manhood, and dealing with the conflicts between father and son, the film undeniably invites analysis in such Freudian terms. Moreover, the confused but central role of the character of Tess Millay (Dru) also develops and sustains Oedipal tensions and difficulties. Tess not only intercedes between Dunson and Matthew in the last scene by firing a gun to stop their fight, she performs this function after she has served as a sexual intermediary between them. Wayne goes to Tess after Matthew and she already have established a relationship. Wayne makes the amazing proposition that she give him a son – institute, in other words, a trade-off of sons: Dunson will not kill – do in – his adopted son if Tess agrees to give him another. Tess thus plays both mother and wife, an unresolvable situation in this context, and one that has to end in chaos.[23]

However, Tess's role also emphasizes the confusion of sexual organization and roles between the men. Acting as both father and mother, Dunson found young Matthew wandering in the desert and adopted him. In a sense, he created him out of himself and his ego; only the feminized Groot observed the event. Moreover, we recall that when Matthew grew up and appeared on-screen in the person of Montgomery Clift, the film experienced a form of return to Wayne's own youth as a performer as well as a character. Psychologically, Wayne in his role as father to Clift plays father to himself. A heavy narcissistic circle surrounds and defines their claustrophobic relationship. The enclosed narcissistic bond of love between the two men suggests a form of affection that Hawks himself adamantly rejected when asked about the "homosexual subtext" in his work.[24] "I'd say it's a goddam silly statement to make," Hawks said. "It sounds like a homosexual speaking. People attribute all kinds of meanings and everything."[25] Nevertheless, as Mast notes, the "contrast between Dunson–Wayne's stereotypic 'maleness' and Matthew–Clift's soft and beautiful 'femaleness'" establishes "a metaphoric paradigm of the meaning of 'maleness.'"[26] Undeniably, in responding to and developing an affection for Matthew, Dunson acts on an impulse within his own nature. Clift helps Wayne as both actor and character develop that impulse in Dunson. In contrast to Wayne, Clift seems to work with the understanding that the most intense drama occurs within Wayne's psyche as a conflict of different aspects of his own personality and as a tension of sexual divisions within his own mind.

Thus, Clift helps Wayne redefine the nature of masculinity. They work together as mutually dependent opposite forces within the same mind and within the same culture. As Mast says,

> But the power of Clift's soft beauty could never have played this metaphoric role, giving a shape and a focus to this Hawks narrative, without a shift and a more precise definition of the established persona of John Wayne.[27]

Given Dunson's failures as a leader and father figure, the movie dramatizes a redefinition of manhood and reversal of roles. Matthew the son and softer figure gets the job done while the father suffers impotently in his own narcissism. This reversal of roles and questioning of masculinity constitute a major accomplishment for the film.

However, Wayne's repeated moments of serious uncertainty and the film's frequent lack of clarity and coherence suggest that the conflicts of sexuality and identity in *Red River* remain largely unconscious and unresolved. Often such unconscious tensions concern and expand upon the ambivalent role and situation of women in the film, especially in their relation to men. The coiled-snake bracelet, with its Edenic imagery, connects many of these sexual elements. The bracelet originally goes to Fen, the woman whose death evokes an ambivalent response in Dunson. After retrieving it from the Indian, Dunson gives it to Matthew, only later to find it on Tess. The snake bracelet symbolizes the sexually coiled relationships of the film, including the conflicted sexuality of Dunson himself. (Ironically, Clift faces a similar bracelet as a sign of conflicted sexuality, parental relationships, and the unconscious a few years later when he plays the founder of psychoanalysis in John Huston's film *Freud*.)

With Tess's involvement at the end of *Red River*, Dunson and Matthew never surpass their difficulties by completing their confrontation. The end of the film shatters any attempt at resolution and represses the tension. This failure of Oedipal resolution entails a broader political failure to propose a means in the film to mediate such tensions; they simply get dismissed. *Red River* tries to joke its way out of the difficulties with the suggestion that Matthew and Tess will marry, and Dunson finally will learn to stop telling people what to do. Just as Hawks felt compelled to keep both men alive at the end of the film, they also apparently simply avoid the question of determining authority and responsibility. The political and psychological logic of this conclusion would anticipate a return of the repressed in both men to fight another day.

The failure of individual leadership turns the center of energy to the group. With Dunson a toppled dictator and Matthew uncommitted to lasting leadership, the true hero of this film becomes the community of men on the drive. The democracy of the cowboys contrasts radically with Dunson's tyranny and with the silence of the nameless ruffians and shooters he recruits to reclaim his herd.

Two very different ways of shooting, editing, and constructing film articulate Hawks's view of two very different political and philosophical positions regarding the relation of the individual and the group. His contrasting techniques dramatize how film asethetics inherently relate to ideology. In one memorable scene, Hawks's camera captures Dunson's narcissistic way of seeing the world and his possessive relationship to all that is in it. With Dunson leading the cattle drive, a dazzling single shot involves a counterclockwise pan that begins with his point of view of the men and cattle and ends with Matthew looking at him. According to Mast,

What is striking about the maneuver, however, is not merely its visual idiosyncra-
cy but its complex manipulation of narrative point-of-view – no other Hawks shot
attempts in a single shot to show simultaneously that there are two physical points-
of-view which are really a single spiritual point-of-view.[28]

The shot, as Mast indicates, creates a double point of view that really exhibits and accentuates the narcissism of Dunson's individual view. Dunson certainly does not differentiate between himself and what he considers his personal human creation, Matthew, or between himself and the entire world as
encapsulated in his vision of the ranch. The shot therefore represents and typifies a fascistic, self-enclosed, totalistic worldview that incorporates everything into itself. The cattle as consumers (grazers) that are being moved to
be consumed also symbolically extend Dunson's way of thinking that insists
upon incorporating everything within itself. As Edward Buscombe's recent
Sight and Sound article suggests, psychology and politics merge as Dunson
exemplifies an extreme capitalistic hunger for growth and expansion, a point
also made years earlier by Robert Sklar.[29]

In contrast to this pan shot that dramatizes the workings of Dunson's
mind and ideology, the film also emphasizes montage sequences of the cowboys to articulate a democratic ideology of community and cooperation. The
most famous montage concerns the "yahoo" sequence as the men set off on
the cattle drive. Undoubtedly corny, the chorus of yahoos and cries and the
organization of close-ups and action shots magnificently convey the excitement of the group enterprise. Other editing sequences in *Red River* also create a sense of unified community effort, including the stampede montage.
The editing of the men's confrontation with Dunson when they mutiny provides a further example of art and ideology working together. Action rather
than extended speech makes the scene; as already noted, clipped and brief
dialogue here adds to its dynamism. One exception in this scene to such verbal control emphasizes Hawks's belief in style and discipline as signs of masculine strength and heroism. This occurs when one of the men to be hanged,
Teeler (Paul Fix), loses control of himself and wants to kill Dunson after
Wayne's character already has been overcome and rendered harmless. Teeler's emotionalism and uncontrolled speech and action suggest a core of weakness and cowardice. His language and behavior run counter to the style of
strength and economy that Hawks prefers for a democratic hero. Thus, the
director uses montage and editing throughout *Red River* as a means to develop an ideology of participation and involvement, and works to create a democratic aesthetic that makes his art consistent with that ideology.

One important example with interesting results of his effort to create a
democratic cinema occurs early in the film, when Dunson describes to Groot
and to young Matthew how his ranch, the Red River D, will look after they
work on it. The sequence wonderfully illustrates how internal vision can be

translated into external reality. Hawks not only externalizes Dunson's inner consciousness in this sequence, he also aestheticizes time and organizes space to present Dunson's ideological vision. So several lines of movement – internal into his consciousness, external over the landscape, horizontal through time, and vertical as ideological belief – work together in this scene. The sequence begins with Dunson speaking for himself, Groot, and Matthew as he looks off in the distance and explains how the visual geography and landscape will change with years of work. The overlapping shots visualize and document his words, turning his ideas and vision into reality and showing how ideas, energy, and human will can transform reality. Cinema aesthetics become a rhetorical strategy to create an ideological and cultural context for the scene.

However, the use of voice in this sequence problematizes this rhetorical strategy and dramatizes the potential complexity of the relationship between aesthetics and ideology. The scene begins with Wayne's voice attached to his person and his character. He speaks as someone with a presence and a particular vision of how he relates in specific ways to the world. We identify the voice with him personally and with his specific plans for the future. The images we see of the development of the ranch, such as the location of houses and barns and the growing numbers of cattle and horses, match this voice. As the sequence develops, however, and the shots continue to visualize and illustrate his words, the language takes a different tack toward abstraction. Concomitantly the voice turns into a kind of documentary or detached voice-over, gaining an identity that becomes distinct from his person and body, and achieving a transcendent authority. This transcendence parallels the growing abstraction and detachment of the actual language, whose verbose and self-important rhetoric dramatically exceed the dynamism and reality on-screen. Wayne's speech turns into political bombast and exaggeration as it emphasizes the importance of this ranch in feeding people, hungry Americans who, the speech suggests, are themselves advancing the nation and building the country for progress, prosperity, and the welfare of future generations. Now as the voice expresses such general sentiments, the screen shows the thousands of cattle that have been produced on the ranch to feed the population. Suddenly we see a herd of cattle destined for slaughter for a remote and abstract market of consumers.

The speech and voice-over in conjunction with the visual images are propaganda. The artificially altruistic language contradicts the blatantly aggressive greed and exploitive nature of the very man issuing the ideas, Dunson. The transcendent vision and voice in their detachment and abstraction are intrinsically antidemocratic; they function totalistically and unrealistically in the effort to manipulate and dominate mind and perception as opposed to the creativity of a democratic aesthetic.

This fissure in the ideological and aesthetic meanings of the scene continues the basic difficulty in *Red River* of sustaining the film's democratic aesthetic and impulses. The film cannot find solid ground upon which to construct and present its underlying ideological commitment to the ordinary
hero as represented by the cowboys who complete the drive. It has difficulty
dealing with the vulnerability and weakness of the democratic hero. Recognizing such vulnerability invites exposing deeper psychic wounds of masculine identity, which the film prefers to deny and disavow. The denial occurs,
of course, because in *Red River* softness and weakness relate to the feminine,
and succumbing to the feminine in oneself or in a relationship engenders
deeper weakness, vitiates resilience, and promotes complacency. This fear of
facing the feminine makes it impossible for the film to achieve one of its major goals: setting forth a hero who combines the sensitivity and softness of
Clift and the power of Wayne. At the same time, the film also persuasively
rejects the authoritarianism of the absolute leader such as Dunson. Thus, *Red
River* finds itself in a great dilemma of trying to define heroic masculinity in
a democratic culture while binding itself so completely in contradiction as
to make it impossible to do so. As Molly Haskell says, "Where the Hawks
ethos was vulnerable . . . was in the manhood theme that runs, like an adolescent anxiety dream, through most of his films."[30]

Psychoanalytically, the failure of *Red River* to deal with weakness or softness as a misleading and fallacious sign of the feminine also places the film
in deeper difficulties. As Haskell says of Hawks in general:

> You don't have to reach for Freud or Lacan to find such theoretical staples as fear
> of castration or the temptation to regress or the instability of the ego. Sex-role slip-
> page is everywhere: men cry over each other; women want to escape domesticity
> and act like men.[31]

Despite Haskell's caveat regarding Freud, the insights of psychoanalysis into
gender prove useful in trying to understand Hawks. Freud discusses the masculine fear of the feminine, which pervades Hawks's work, and argues "that
a passive attitude to men does not always signify castration and that it is indispensable in many relationships in life." Freud says that such fear of passivity and dismemberment creates a crippling resistance to the feminine in oneself, and that "The rebellious overcompensation of the male produces one of
the strongest transference resistances."[32] Unresolved Oedipal ambivalence
about sexual identification, gender, maleness, and the feminine interfere with
the wish in *Red River* to construct the kind of ordinary, vulnerable democratic hero that Capra creates with such credibility. Unlike Capra's heroes, Dunson in particular cannot turn to the main woman in this film, Tess, because
her position between him and Matthew has been so greatly compromised,
primarily by Dunson's own actions and attitudes. Dunson, of course, cannot

find completion or fulfillment with any woman in any potential relationship that might require compromise with his illusion of masculine invulnerability. *Red River,* therefore, often falls back on a kind of embarrassed laughter and humor to hide its insecurities. Such laughter and joking that occurs at the end of the film compares to the humor in Sam Peckinpah's *The Wild Bunch,* a film that Hawks intensely disliked.[33]

A recent biography of Hawks by Todd McCarthy strongly suggests a basis in Hawks's personality and behavior for the kind of resistances to the feminine and to emotional relationships that are displayed by Wayne's Dunson. As McCarthy describes them, Hawks's sexual, love, and family relationships indicate a deep-seated repulsion against maintaining strong, emotional bonds with the women in his life and even with his children, who often seem to have been neglected or forgotten by him. His womanizing apparently worked as a means for avoiding emotional depth and commitment as well as the responsibilities of mature relationships. McCarthy describes how this attitude manifests itself in Hawks's work:

> But Hawks was profoundly uninterested in what came after, in the realities of married life and the complexities of mature emotions, and he displayed this indifference in his work by avoiding the depiction of married or settled couples to an extent unmatched by any other major Hollywood director. Until the end of his career, Hawks was almost singularly obsessed with how a new couple sparked until they clicked; after that, he didn't care.[34]

All of these difficulties that suggest certain limitations in Hawks's work and life have not escaped the notice even of critics who consider him to be one of the great American directors. As McBride says,

> Hawks's work can be faulted for its narrowness of thematic range, in contrast to the breadth of vision one finds in the work of Renoir or Ford or Rossellini, and the lack of thematic development in his work over such a long career is evidence of a self-centered, relatively unquestioning personality.[35]

However, Hawks partly overcame these roadblocks to aesthetic completion and fulfillment through the invention of an ingenious and original comedy style that enabled him to circumvent what he preferred not to face in much of his art and life: the need to reaffirm the feminine in oneself and in life to achieve mature individuality and masculinity. Humor becomes a great strength for Hawks when it indicates more than an unconscious, nervous response to sexual difference or a failed disguise for the fear of weakness and the feminine. Humor works effectively for him in certain conscious forms and genres to structure and mediate the questions of absence and lack. Hawks's comedy plays with the conventions of gender that articulate concerns over complexity and difference. By reversing conventional gender roles and expectations, he exposes and enacts insecurities over the instability of gender. His comedy replicates the processes of psychic instability and insecurity: The women are strong and aggressive but the men debilitated. Hawks's comedy, thereby, illustrates Freud's important emphasis on the arbitrary nature of the gender definitions of masculine and feminine. In *Three Essays on the Theory of Sexuality,* Freud stresses that "observation shows that in human beings pure masculinity or femininity is not to be found either in a psychological or a biological sense." He maintains that associating gender purely with aggression for men and passivity for women confuses biology and sociology. "Every individual on the contrary displays a mixture of the character-traits belonging to his own and to the opposite sex; and he shows a combination of activity and passivity whether or not these last character-traits tally with his biological ones."[36] Whereas in *Red River* ambiguity and insecurity about gender lead to confusion and repression, Hawks in his screwball comedies channels his discomfort with male weakness and limitation to address the issue straightforwardly: He simply treats the weak male as a ridiculously comic vision of emasculation and turns the woman into the aggressive, powerful, and confident being he values. As Haskell says:

> Where most directors were keeping female characters virginal and pure in deference to the Production Code, Hawks's women were openly sensual and direct; they saw what they wanted and went after it. If the Hawksian male was involved in an existential drama of self-worth, in the ultimate battle of life the women were in the evolutionary driver's seat.[37]

Gender and sexual insecurity erupt from the hidden subtext of *Red River* to outrageous representation in both *Bringing Up Baby* (1938) and *I Was a Male War Bride* (1949). In many ways a model for the screwball comedy of zany action and incongruous and contradictory dialogue and behavior, *Bringing Up Baby* simply turns the professor, played by Cary Grant, into a totally foolish figure in his thoroughly passive relationship with Katharine Hepburn. Grant becomes impossibly malleable before her energy; yet, with his handsome charm, he brilliantly exploits and balances all of these tensions of gender and sexuality. Similarly, *I Was a Male War Bride,* which was made just a year after *Red River,* conducts a relentless attack on the male body; the story has Grant undergo continuous pain, difficulty, and embarrassment, all leading up to the final humiliation when Ann Sheridan puts him in a woman officer's uniform with a horse's tail for a wig. The film works beautifully by so directly demeaning and assaulting masculinity. Pushed into continually crippling situations, Grant, dressed as a woman, wonderfully exemplifies gender ambiguities as a cross-dresser who looks so much like a man but finds himself in the classic feminine position of needing help from the person he loves and has married, Sheridan.

Pauline Kael helped to make a name for herself by ridiculing this film and all those associated with or favorably inclined toward it, including Hawks and male critics like Andrew Sarris (Haskell's husband) and Peter Bogdanovich.[38] Her dismissive and derisive attitude toward the film misses all it says about the postwar psyche of American men. This criticism also fails to appreciate how accurately the film forecasts the impending sexual and feminist revolutions that have changed America so radically.

The story of the film grows out of a real event and situation at the end of the Second World War. Free-French Captain Henri Rochard (Grant) finds himself on a mission in Heidelberg, Germany, where he becomes reluctantly dependent upon the help of WAC Lieutenant Catherine Gates (Sheridan). Escapades and happenings that are typical of Hawks's comedies abound, beginning with the gender reversal of roles when she drives their motorcycle while he occupies the sidecar. They nearly drown in cascading river water. At a charming hotel, he endures an endless, nerve-wracking night trying to sleep in a chair but still gets unfairly blamed by her for sexual aggressiveness. Forced to hide outside her window on a canopy that promptly gets rolled in, he falls. Compelled to change into clothes much too small for him, he looks idiotic. Eventually, Catherine completes his military mission, adding to his humiliation. Nevertheless, they end up in a haystack, in love, and marry – only to find that the congressional Public Law 271 covers the non-American brides of male personnel yet makes absolutely no consideration for a reversed situation of a male from another country marrying a woman in the service. The movie, thereby, develops an important subtheme concerning the crippling influence of bureaucracy and regimentation upon love and freedom.

In spite of the humiliations he suffers and the failure of his initial efforts to resist or escape her, Grant never crosses a boundary that violates proper respect for her. Sheridan, in turn, acts with flawless grace, poise, and charm, presenting a character of considerable strength and self-confidence. Poague notes of them that like "most Hawks couples" their "courtship" combines the "intellectual" with the "erotic" and the "physical" to create "a relationship based on mutual attraction and respect."[39] Without needing to articulate a code of manly heroism, Hawks can engineer the fluid nature of gender boundaries, roles, and definitions to emphasize the importance to him of structure and the need to respect difference and limitation. Having been unable in *Red River* to delineate a middle-ground position for a democratic hero of ordinary human proportions, Hawks surrenders his hero in *Male War Bride* to a comedic and chaotic culture that turns him into a joke. His situation accentuates through the female lead the importance of the qualities of independence, strength, and self-reliance that she possesses. In the end, the incoherence and disorder of the comedy proves the necessity of discipline and organization, whether inspired by a man or a woman. As the title suggests, in this film the woman maintains the structure that ultimately overcomes chaos and allows for coherence and love.

Thus, a dismissive attitude toward *Male War Bride* also mistakenly minimizes the significance of the film's argument that beyond the fun of playful incoherence, only structure and direction can nurture and sustain love and freedom. The alternative of a world without structure or leadership, a kind of radical democracy or anarchy, seems impossible to Hawks for the completion of a cattle drive, the making of a worthwhile and successful film, or the survival of a culture. Following the horror and catastrophe of world war, Hawks's democratic aesthetic of cinema emphasizes the need for balance between individual freedom and order. Even though he often had difficulty framing a program for democratic culture, Hawks's most effective and appreciated films usually demonstrate such constructive creativity from the group, as in *Red River,* from its energetic female leads, or from its most solid heroes, such as Humphrey Bogart in *The Big Sleep* or *To Have and Have Not.*

Accordingly, in spite of Hawks's limitations that various critics have addressed over the years, he still participated with Ford and Capra in the creation of a cinema for democracy. For many film critics and historians, the nearly forty Hawks films that are still available include some of the absolute best films in each of the different genres in which he worked. Some of these films include *Tiger Shark* (1932), *Scarface* (1932), *Twentieth Century* (1934), *Only Angels Have Wings* (1939), *His Girl Friday* (1940), *To Have and Have Not* (1944), *The Big Sleep* (1946), *Red River* (1948), *Gentlemen Prefer Blondes* (1953), *Rio Bravo* (1959), and *El Dorado* (1967). As Haskell says of Hawks's greatness as a director and his special contribution to American film genres:

> Hawks's genius was to be able to merge plot and moral dynamic, gesture and character, across a broad field for a very long time. He did indeed hit a high-water mark in every genre. *The Big Sleep* (1946) is the film noir everyone remembers not for its indecipherable plot but for its unforgettable and crystal-clear double-entendres, particularly the racetrack dialogue between Bogart and Ms. Bacall; the 1938 film *Bringing Up Baby* is the most frenetically paced of all the screwball comedies; *Scarface* is the most violent (and most heavily imitated) gangster film of the '30s.[40]

The Puritan under Siege: Masochism, Masculinity, and Moral Leadership

For F. O. Matthiessen, the literary achievements of the American Renaissance were also great cultural achievements because they spearheaded a flowering of democracy. The originality and energy of the literary works of the renaissance generated new life in a democratic culture through their consciousness of the values of the common man, the ordinary individual within various social, cultural, and geographic contexts. At the same time, as Matthiessen understood the work and contribution of these authors, the imaginative and artistic complexity of their endeavors, energized by the structured tension of the democratic aesthetic, also made their writings a powerful source of cultural renewal in a democracy: Their commitment to artistic excellence and intellectual achievement, as much as to the values and bonds of ordinary humanity, distinguish their contributions from work done primarily to appeal to a mass audience. Such original works of imagination and complexity challenge and engage the culture rather than merely reflect or copy it.

Similarly, the great films by the directors in the Hollywood Renaissance play a role of renewal as complex works of cinematic art. As film, they operate as heterogeneous texts on several channels and levels of communication to a broad democratic audience. They represent a democratic aesthetic of artistic integrity that encourages a diversity of interpretations for cultural renewal, as opposed to the rigid indoctrination and manipulation of propaganda.

The importance and meaning of this democratic aesthetic sometimes become clearer in its absence or denial – as, for example, in the scene in *Red River*: already discussed in some detail, wherein Dunson speaks and imagines for Matthew and Groot how the Red River D will look after years of their work on it. The scene warrants revisiting, as it dramatizes the challenge of articulating a democratic ideology through film. It also expresses an ideology for the particular story of *Red River* that relates to the broader ideology of American history and American culture at the time of the film's production. As we recall, Hawks exhibits on the screen the changes and developments on the ranch as Wayne reports them. The separation of the voice from Wayne's body and the compression of years of change on the ranch into overlapping images on the screen give Wayne's off-screen narration a transcendent quality. The voice-over articulates and authorizes an omniscient power that controls time and the future; it also controls intepretation for the viewer. The transcendent form of the voice-over thus countermands the democratic altruism of Wayne's statement – the cattle feed a hungry America – by suggesting a contradictory ideology of power. The antidemocratic manipulation of the voice-over reveals the contradiction between Dunson's statement of national purpose and the film's artistic structure and aesthetic, which emphasize his aggressive and aggrandizing nature. The voice-over becomes, in Kaja Silverman's term, an "acoustic mirror" that melds the viewer and Dunson's words with the images on the screen.[41] It creates a kind of aural suture that incorporates the viewer in the film's hidden ideological and psychological text as represented by Dunson's aggression.

Accordingly, the voice-over associates and identifies Dunson/Wayne with the dominant ideology of America at the time of the film. In "calling" or "hailing" as in interpellating the interest of the viewer and listener, the voice-over fuses the film's expansive ideology of the West and cattle with the post–World War and Cold War ideology of growing American influence around the world. This places Dunson and the viewer within the broader, burgeoning dynamism of American national interests in this volatile era.

Red River also articulates a confused ideology of American manhood during the early days of the Cold War. It proposes a contradictory ideology of continuing aggressive heroic masculinity while acknowledging the importance to the culture of the democratic hero in the figure of Montgomery Clift. The Hawks and Wayne ideology of heroic masculinity leaves little room for mediation between the absolute masculinity of Dunson and the sensitivity of Clift. The failure to deal with the Oedipal tension between Dunson and Matthew creates, as we discussed earlier, an ideological vacuum in the film that ultimately allows for the perpetuation of Dunson's values. Disregarding the implications of this ideological and psychological tension, Hawks and Wayne avoid either of opposing paths that could help develop Wayne's character: One path leads to complicating and deepening the character of Dunson by developing the sensitive qualities in him of Matthew that Clift learned in part from Wayne's earlier portrayal of Ringo in *Stagecoach*. The other involves a deeper and fuller exploration of the interior darkness in Dunson that Wayne eventually achieved in his later films with Ford. The direction actually taken in *Red River* – toward shallow humor, confusion, and denial of conflict – performs a kind of psychoanalysis for Hawks and Wayne by presenting and dramatizing in disguised form profound fears of vulnerability, weakness, and the feminine that vitiate their commitment to a true democratic hero. Thus, the film's tortuous ending anticipates the reaction of both Hawks and Wayne to another film of the era.

A few years after *Red River* appeared, the reaction of Hawks and Wayne to Fred Zinnemann's *High Noon* (1952) brought to the surface some further indication of their values, attitudes, and ideology in *Red River*. Hawks hated the idea and theme behind *High Noon* so much that he made another film in response to it: *Rio Bravo* (1959), a western starring John Wayne as a hero with, as Gerald Mast says, a "commitment to a vocation" that merges with "a commitment to a personal definition of honor and integrity as well as an existential assertion of personal meaning and value."[42] According to Hawks:

> *Rio Bravo* was made because I didn't like a picture called *High Noon*. I saw *High Noon* at about the same time I saw another western picture, and we were talking about western pictures, and they asked me if I liked it, and I said, "Not particularly." I didn't think a good sheriff was going to go running around town like a chicken with his head off asking for help, and finally his Quaker wife had to

save him. That isn't my idea of a good sheriff. I said that a good sheriff would turn around and say, "How good are you? Are you good enough to take the best man they've got?" The fellow would probably say no, and he'd say, "Well, then I'd just have to take care of you." And that scene was in *Rio Bravo*.[43]

Hawks then added that "we made *Rio Bravo* the exact opposite from *High Noon*."

John Wayne's reaction to *High Noon* is even more significant in terms of surfacing his understanding of the relationship between values of heroic masculinity and American ideology. Wayne hated what he saw as the message of the film: A marshal finally rejects the law and his town after experiencing the cowardice and disloyalty of the entire community of people who previously seemed to be his friends and supporters. Wayne was especially upset that Gary Cooper played the lead role of Marshal Will Kane in the film. The marshal's final act in *High Noon* of throwing his badge in the dirt and leaving the town seemed to Wayne "like belittling a Medal of Honor." Wayne summarized the plot and significance of *High Noon* as follows:

> [F]our guys come in to gun down the sheriff. He goes to the church and asks for help and the guys go, 'Oh well, oh gee.' And the women stand up and say, "You're rats. . . ." So Cooper goes out alone. It's the most un-American thing I've ever seen in my whole life. The last thing in the picture is old Coop putting the United States marshal's badge under his foot and stepping on it.[44]

Wayne's narrow view of Cooper as a man and as a representative American in *High Noon* and Hawks's disdain for the film render some additional insight into the source of the confusion behind their development of Dunson in *Red River*. Wayne's anguish over Cooper's role establishes the connection in his mind between the sexual politics of heroic masculinity and the cultural politics of Americanism. For Wayne an ideology of American heroism involved playing a role with aggressive masculine values. Complexity, contradiction, ambiguity ran counter to his ideology of masculinity and Americanism, making it nearly impossible to deal with Clift without enacting an extreme violence that seemed inappropriate to Hawks. Fortunately, in other films, Wayne proved capable of violating his own taboos to develop complex elements within his personality and his screen persona.

In an important sense, of course, both Wayne and Hawks were absolutely correct in their interpretation of what they saw on the screen when viewing *High Noon* – a black-and-white western, like *Red River*, of a dismal town of cowards turning its collective back on an old marshal who was marrying a beautiful blonde who was much too young for him. The problem, however, for Wayne and Hawks was that they looked at the film rather than read it. As Wills notes, Wayne "misremembered" parts of *High Noon*.[45] Even the language Wayne and Hawks use to describe their reactions and interpretations reveals the superficiality of their consideration of the film. They were viewing it as a rather simple and obvious story of immediate and direct impressions of reality and experience, as opposed to seeing a complex artistic effort to reimagine and reconstruct reality. As Colin MacCabe says of art and film in general: "The central nature of the artistic activity becomes the presentation of a reality more real than that which could be achieved by a simple recording."[46] Thus, for other viewers of *High Noon*, Zinnemann created a major artistic work of great imagination and cultural significance. Even the history surrounding the film's production as well as the diverse reaction to it indicate a much greater complexity than either Wayne or Hawks would allow.

Ironies abound in Wayne's concern that Cooper could damage his career with his role in *High Noon*, for some parallelism exists between their careers. In the first place, Cooper, according to Todd McCarthy, earlier had turned down the Dunson role in *Red River* because "Dunson was too mean and unsympathetic for an audience to tolerate." In spite of this decision, Cooper went on to achieve the kind of stature in *High Noon* that Wayne failed to attain until *The Searchers*. It could be argued that *High Noon* dramatically advanced Cooper's reputation from being somewhat diminished through its association with the kind of puerile costume role and film he chose instead of *Red River*: Cecil B. DeMille's "pre-Revolutionary War 'Western' *Unconquered*" (1947).[47] The enormous gap between Cooper's achievement in *High Noon* toward the end of his career and his work in earlier westerns and adventure films that he did for DeMille, such as *The Plainsman* (1937) and *Unconquered*, compares to the distance between Wayne's early cowboys and his lasting work with Ford and Hawks. Perhaps Wayne's frustration over his own career, which may have fueled the bitterness of his reaction to Cooper in *High Noon*, gained intensity with his awareness at some level that *High Noon* signaled a need for him to reconceptualize heroic masculinity in America in order to remain relevant and real.

All that Hawks disdained in DeMille as a director occurs in those films starring Cooper.[48] The antithesis of a democratic aesthetic, DeMille's films present history as a mindless pageantry of ideological clichés, racial stereotypes, and narrative conventions that are contrived to inhibit thought and stifle the imagination. Even Cooper cannot escape the tasteless exhibitionism, mindless romanticism, and petty sensationalism that characterize DeMille's work. Like the characters in Woody Allen's *The Purple Rose of Cairo*, Cooper is trapped inside DeMille's frame, subject to the propagandistic view of history and experience that governs the director's aesthetic. With American history decoratively packaged around sexual fantasies and racial taboos, film and history become a lifeless sequence of staged events within an enclosed ideological system of self-serving values and beliefs. The contrast between Cooper's role and performance as Marshal "Wild Bill" Hickok in *The*

Figure 8. Walking alone: Gary Cooper, the embodiment of the American hero at war with his own society in *High Noon* (Stanley Kramer: The Museum of Modern Art / Film Stills Archive).

Plainsman and as Marshal Kane in *High Noon* involves a virtual rebirth: Cooper grows from a morally and emotionally dead physical object in a totally unreal dramatic and historic environment to a figure of international cultural and historic significance.

Cooper in *High Noon* brought more than his extraordinary presence and character to the role, a significant accomplishment in itself. He also brought his politics with him in a way that added to the film's credibility for conservatives among both the Hollywood establishment and the public. The association of Cooper's image on the screen with his political views becomes a factor in understanding the film, in which the politics of his screen image serves as an additional element of signification.

The matter of politics made Cooper's role in *High Noon* even more problematic for Wayne. The two occupied similar positions in the political history and ideology of Hollywood and America. As conservative voices, Wayne and Cooper, along with DeMille, Walt Disney, and Adolphe Menjou, were among the 1,500 people who in 1944 founded the Motion Picture Alliance for the Preservation of American Ideals (MPA). This group in 1947 inaugurated the right-wing response within the Hollywood community to the Cold War by inviting the House Un-American Activities Committee (HUAC) to investigate the influence of communists in the film industry. MPA came to support the ousting and blacklisting of reputed communists or sympathizers. Robert Sklar describes the alliance as "an organization of politically conservative movie workers who proposed to defend the industry against Communist infiltration." Sklar notes: "The MPA provided HUAC with something no outside critics ever had, a body of supporters within the industry willing to testify publicly against their colleagues."[49] Given his understanding of the meaning of *High Noon* and his knowledge of the people and events behind its production, Wayne certainly would see Cooper's role in *High Noon* as an extreme departure from their conservative political leanings and previous actions.

High Noon encapsulates the various contexts of American ideology and culture after the Second World War. The film structures a transition in the Hollywood Renaissance to the issues of the Cold War. It marks a confluence of many different forces and movements in film and in the wider culture. All of the historical, political, and cultural forces that converge in *High Noon* also manifest themselves in the various interpretations and multiplicity of meanings of the film.

In *High Noon, cinetext* – the multiple semiotic and expressive modes of a film – and context merge. *High Noon* as a visual and aural text proves inseparable from the social, cultural, and historic forces related to it. Historic and cultural background are interfused within the text itself and are intrinsic to its meaning. The Second World War, the Cold War, and the domestic crisis over loyalty and communism comprise the fabric of *High Noon,* partly because of the way the film operates metaphorically and symbolically for all these forces from beginning to end.

The movie's director, Fred Zinnemann, was born and raised in Vienna, where his father, a doctor, and his mother expected him to be either a great concert violinist, or failing that, a successful lawyer. However, while studying law in Vienna, he committed himself to film after seeing Erich von Stroheim's *Greed* (1924) and King Vidor's *The Big Parade* (1925).[50] Although successful in Hollywood throughout the late 1930s and 1940s, nothing he did before quite anticipated his success in *High Noon*. Zinnemann's direction of *High Noon* helped transform the simplicity of the classic western genre into a myth that structures and amplifies the ambiguities and complexities of life for the Cold War generation. Based on John W. Cunningham's story "The Tin Star," the screenplay for *High Noon* was written by Carl

Foreman, who had been a communist during the years of the Popular Front in America. Although Foreman left the party, he also felt compelled to leave the country for England, because of the blacklist that prevented him from working.

The events that give *High Noon* its special meaning often seem quite remote from our times and the western genre. The history of the several decades since the film's release also inevitably influences current critical perception. The United States has changed so dramatically since then: Decades of social and cultural transformation have altered ways of thinking, while various movements and countermovements over these years make the era of the Cold War seem distant. However, to movie audiences in the early 1950s, the events that frame and shape *High Noon* determined and defined the psychology of the times. A basic delineation of the major historic events of the period suggest why they proved so intimidating and compelling. Moreover, the events of the Cold War also need to be considered in the light of the universal exhaustion and disillusionment of the world war, as well as the general awareness that nuclear bombs had introduced a new form of terror into human history.

To some historians and philosophers, the Cold War was rooted in irreconcilable differences between the cultures of the East and West that made conflict and tension inevitable.[51] Nevertheless, the first signs of the transformation of the postwar peace into the conflict between the West and the East involved the installation of puppet regimes in Eastern Europe. President Truman in 1945 demanded of Soviet Foreign Minister Molotov, "Carry out your agreements."[52] Within two years, however, the Cold War already was firmly entrenched in response to what was seen as continued Soviet aggression and domination. The Truman Doctrine, the Marshall Plan, and the building of the North Atlantic Treaty Organization established a permanent response to the new conditions. Winston Churchill's famous address in Fulton, Missouri, summarized the new world situation, although many at the time were still shocked by his bluntness:

> From Stettin in the Baltic to Trieste in the Adriatic, an iron curtain had descended across the Continent. Behind that line lie all the capitals of the ancient states of Central and Eastern Europe. Warsaw, Berlin, Prague, Vienna, Budapest, Belgrade, Bucharest, and Sofia, all these famous cities and the populations around them lie in what I must call the Soviet sphere, and all are subject in one form or another, not only to Soviet influence but to a very high and, in many cases, increasing measure of control from Moscow.[53]

Casting an insidious and ominous shadow over the new realities and dangers of the Cold War was the mysterious and dark figure of Joseph Stalin, the dictator of the Soviet Union. As David McCullough writes:

That Stalin was also secretive to the point of imbalance, suspicious, deceitful, unspeakably cruel, that he ruled absolutely and by terror and secret police, that he was directly responsible for destroying millions of his own people and the enslavement of many millions more, was not so clearly understood by the outside world at this point as it would be later. Still, the evil of the man was no secret in 1945.[54]

Certainly, by the time of *High Noon,* the evils of Stalinism were widely known, although it would take the invasions of Czechoslavakia, Poland, and Hungary to convince some of the most stalwart and devoted of American and European leftists to abandon their faith in communism and the Soviet Union as an alternative to the West. Throughout the 1950s, the public became steadily more aware of the numbers of massacres and purges and the millions who had died under Stalin's rule. To most Americans, this knowledge of the history of terror under Stalin, along with the fall of China, the Korean War, and the acquisition of nuclear arsenals by the Soviet Union, contributed to the sense of terror and impending doom that defined the Cold War.[55]

These accumulating Cold War tensions, in combination with perceived dangers concerning internal espionage and subversion, resulted in a so-called Second Red Scare of investigation and action that was instituted at several levels of government and throughout American society. Among the most damaging domestic abuses of this era were what became known as "witchhunts" conducted under the auspices of Senator Joseph R. McCarthy of Wisconsin.[56]

Despite such legal abuses and violations of decency and fairness at home, the fear of the devastation to humanity and human rights by Soviet aggression and communism was justified. Stephen Whitfield succinctly summarizes volumes of work on the Cold War:

> The animus against Communism was not concocted of phantasms; it was rooted in reality. If judged in the light of liberal democratic ideals, of the promise inherent in personal autonomy and of the conventions of ordinary decency, Communism *was* evil. Indeed, the system that the Bolsheviks had created in the Soviet Union and had imposed beyond their borders was even more hideous in its devastation of humane values than many of its most vocal opponents in the 1950s realized.[57]

Similarly, Walter A. McDougall argues:

> There *were* Communists, Communist sympathizers, and ex-Communist sympathizers (those Truman called the "Reds, phonies, and 'parlour pinks'") in positions of influence, as proven by the Alger Hiss case and atomic spy rings. No one knew how many there were or how deeply they were entrenched, and what is more – one point McCarthy had right – the allegedly compromised government agencies seemed uninterested in running checks on their own people. Hence the

strange spectacle of a national panic over Communist infiltration of an administration that was rallying the world to a bold anti-Communist stand![58]

Obviously, the circumstances of the Cold War that affected America and
the world also had a great impact upon Hollywood. There, extreme right-
wingers were joined by genuine conservatives in feeling that the movie industry was vulnerable to the influence of the Left. During the Second World War,
Hollywood had made at least three strongly pro-Russian films that reflected our alliance against the Nazis: *Mission to Moscow* (1943), *The North Star*
(1943), and *Song of Russia* (1944). Moreover, there was general public
awareness of the sympathies of many politically active and reform-minded
people in Hollywood to the Left.[59] However, as McDougall says, "a flood
of articles, books, and films – starting just after the Nazi invasion of Russia
on June 22, 1941 – *instructed* Americans to smile on the Kremlin."[60] Thus,
while the devastation of the Second Red Scare upon so many institutions in
the country, such as universities and schools, also was enormous and dreadful, the public exposure of those in the film industry in Hollywood seemed
to make actors, screenwriters, directors, and producers especially vulnerable.

As the Cold War solidified, one American steadily emerged as a dominant
figure to provide leadership and to convey a sense of security and control:
Dwight D. Eisenhower, the Supreme Allied Commander during the Second
World War, who became the thirty-fourth President of the United States in
1952. Eisenhower had been chosen in 1950 to lead the major allied military
response to the Soviet threat in Europe, the newly formed alliance known
as the North Atlantic Treaty Organization (NATO). As Stephen E. Ambrose
writes, "Leaders on both sides of the Atlantic unanimously agreed that Eisenhower was the 'only man' who could take command of NATO forces." Eisenhower, considering "this to be the most important military job in the
world" because of "what I definitely believe to be a world crisis," naturally accepted President Truman's offer to lead NATO.[61] At the center of the
American and allied victory in the Second World War, Eisenhower now became the focus of the forces involved in the transition to the era of the Cold
War. Eisenhower saw his position as a continuation of the "crusade" he had
led in the war against fascism in Europe. His vision of his role in this process
and his understanding of the world situation at the time helped to shape public understanding of the meaning of the Cold War and its moral and political stakes. Eisenhower became a focal point for national and international
belief and action. He helped to create the public motivation for action in the
Cold War and to inspire a sense of belief and faith in the potential outcome
of that action. As Ambrose writes, "The specter of the Europe that he had
liberated being overrun and enslaved by the Red Army – a prospect that
in late 1950 seemed entirely possible – was too painful to contemplate." Ac-

cording to Ambrose, Eisenhower told a friend, "I rather look upon this effort as about the last remaining chance for the survival of Western civilization."[62]

As Whitfield emphasizes, a new "ideal of consensus" based on these postwar developments formed around the figure and leadership of Eisenhower. Eisenhower literally "seemed to embody" such consensus.[63] Given his biography as a military leader and his personal set of beliefs and values, the new national accord he helped to shape emerged directly out of the historic ideology of consensus of America based on traditional American values and ideals. This ideology also included fairness, decency, and human rights. Thus, within this system of belief Eisenhower could be seen as not only the leader of the free world against communist expansion abroad but also as a mitigating force at home against the excesses of the Red Scare. As Whitfield argues, hope for real substantive leadership from President Eisenhower concerning the danger from reactionaries such as Senator McCarthy to civil liberties and rights proved rather illusive. Nevertheless, to those looking for such leadership, Eisenhower seemed the one person who could make a difference. As Whitfield writes:

> Another sign of the fragility of civil liberties was that the Anti-Defamation League of B'nai B'rith chose to celebrate its fortieth anniversary in 1953 by giving a Democratic Legacy Award to President Eisenhower – not because he had done so much to enlarge the definition of an open society, but because he had done so little. Bestowing such an award, the donors hoped, might quicken the president's interest in civil rights and liberties.[64]

As Whitfield notes, Eisenhower accepted the award on national television and "was suddenly inspired" by the occasion to explain spontaneously his "objections to McCarthyism," the movement that was consuming not only so much national attention but so many innocent lives as well. As Whitfield details Eisenhower's ad lib, the president's organization of ideas centered on his feelings about the American West, especially the West of his hometown, Abilene, Kansas, where "Wild Bill" Hickok achieved fame as the marshal. In his remarks, Eisenhower clearly was thinking of the devastating results of McCarthy's tactics upon the nation and so many people:

> "Now that town had a code," Ike reminisced, "and I was raised as a boy to prize that code. It was – meet anyone face to face with whom you disagree. You could not sneak up on him from behind – do any damage to him – without suffering the penalty of an outraged citizenry. If you met him face to face and took the same risks he did, you could get away with almost anything, as long as the bullet was in the front."

To Whitfield, Eisenhower thought about this issue in terms of the "frontier moral," so that, according to Eisenhower, in this country, if someone dislikes you or accuses you, he must come up in front. He cannot hide behind the shadow. He cannot assassinate you or your character from behind, without suffering the penalties of an outraged citizenry.[65]

Regardless of how one judges Eisenhower in general or on the particular matter of civil rights – and Ambrose is devastatingly critical of him on civil rights and civil liberties[66] – the symbolism Eisenhower embodied and used remains important to understanding the nature of American character during the Cold War era.

In terms of visual symbolism and imagery, if one examines documentary footage of Eisenhower both in the Second World War and as the leader of NATO, comparisons with Gary Cooper in *High Noon* seem credible. Especially when pictured wearing his officer's cap, Eisenhower's profile and his solidly handsome and rectangular face, as well as his physical bearing and presence, all strike a powerful resemblance to Cooper. With Eisenhower's image on the screen, whether in intimate close-up or amid a group of admiring soldiers or citizens, World War II and the world of the Cold War become reduced ideologically and psychologically to High Noon in America. In the American public consciousness during the Cold War, the world stage turns into the Abilene of Eisenhower's youth or the Hadleyville of *High Noon*. Eisenhower and the marshal merge; the survival of America and Western civilization and the violent threat to a Western town meld into the same danger, fear, and effort; ultimate danger from opposing and contradictory forces both outside and within the community confront the single, supreme leader who stands above all. Psychologically and metaphorically, the world of *High Noon* becomes one with the felt experience of these years.

Carl Foreman, the blacklisted screenwriter of *High Noon*, emphasized that it was a western about Hollywood, meaning the period of the Red Scare and the blacklist: "I used a Western background to tell a story of a community corrupted by fear, with implications that I hoped would be obvious to everyone who saw the film, at least in America."[67] At the time of the film's release, and on many occasions since, critics have noted how the antipopulist position of the film puts it in opposition to a classic Marxist defense of the people. In *High Noon*, the burden of blame falls on the people who abandon the marshal. Robert Warshow dubbed this aspect of the film "a vulgar anti-populism."[68] Similarly, Whitfield comments that "no film could be more remote from the cultural sensibility of the Party than this Western, which repudiated the populism integral to the Communist faith in the 'masses.'"[69] Thus, different and opposing views of *High Noon* receive credibility: The screenwriter emphasizes the venality of those who instituted blacklists and witch-hunts; others reveal the contradiction between left-wing ideology of the masses and a narrative theme that attacks the weakness of the people.

In a view akin to the suggestion of the resemblance between Eisenhower and Cooper, Douglas J. McReynolds and Barbara J. Lips see Marshal Kane as a postwar figure with "a clear sense of duty complicated by weariness, self-doubt," the object of what "an American collective consciousness had seen projected onto its ideal soldier."[70] For McReynolds and Lips their perception of Kane as a veteran, an "ideal soldier" needed for another battle, also sustains their idea that one key to the film is concerned with "the transfer of patriarchal authority from one generation to the next and, second, with the perceived role of women in the exercise of that authority." They relate this transfer of authority to the "Cold War/McCarthy days" and the Eisenhower administration.[71] Their discussion of transitional patriarchal authority, the role of women, and Cold War politics suggests an ideological context for the Oedipal conflict at the heart of both *Red River* and *High Noon.* Indeed, throughout *High Noon,* Cooper finds himself engaged in a generational battle with Harvey Pell (Lloyd Bridges) over both authority and sexuality concerning Kane's former girlfriend, Helen Ramirez (Katy Jurado). At different points in the film, Pell expresses jealousy concerning Kane's past relationship with Helen and his superior paternal authority and respect in the town. Ramirez even tells Pell directly that he has "big, broad shoulders" but he will never be a man the equal of Will Kane. Rather than try to help Kane fight the gunmen who want to kill him, Pell petulantly abandons him and even fights him. He accuses Kane of being "sore about me and Helen Ramirez" when Kane obviously was totally unaware of their affair. In a sequence with Oedipal and Freudian connotations concerning maturity, one gunman tells another to "grow up," while Helen in a following cut says the same thing to Harvey, who responds with an emotional outburst that makes her point. Thus, Lee Clark Mitchell notes "how highly charged the conflicts are in *High Noon* between fathers and sons – sons who desperately want adult prerogatives yet disdain expectations for adult behavior."[72]

All of these different views of *High Noon* feed into what probably has become the strongest understanding of the film in the popular imagination in countries around the world: the image of the American hero drawing a line in the sand to oppose aggressive forces of evil and corruption. Two cartoons from different eras and very different parts of the world demonstrate this appreciation for *High Noon.* One cartoon from 1956 is labeled "High Noon" and shows a marshal walking down a Western street with the "Suez Saloon" written on the local bar on one side of the street and a sign for "Nasser & Co." hanging from a storefront on the other side. An even more graphic, dramatic, and memorable illustration of the lasting, overall impression of the film shows Cooper as Marshal Kane on a sign in 1989 for Solidarnosc or "Solidarity," the movement that sparked Poland's rebellion against communism.[73]

What Zinnemann calls the "visual style" of the film strongly supports this theme of the isolated loner in a struggle against evil forces. Filming in black and white establishes a graphic sense of stark contrast and difference that accentuates Kane's abandonment and radical separation from others. Also, shooting in black and white identifies such isolation with current events – McCarthyism, blacklisting, communism – giving the film a feel and look of newsreels and news photographs. As Zinnemann says, "When it came to choosing the visual style, Floyd Crosby – a great photographer – agreed with me that it should look like a newsreel of the period, if newsreels had existed around 1870. . . ."[74] While the technical achievement of the film inspires John Howard Reid to call *High Noon* Zinnemann's "masterpiece" and "the greatest western since *Stagecoach*," more writers focus on the way Zinnemann's close attention to detail and camera position fulfill the issue of isolation.[75] As Alan Stanbrook says, "At the heart of Zinnemann's films lies a preoccupation with identity and individuality. . . . The intense isolation of Zinnemann's characters was embodied in its most quintessential form in *High Noon*."[76] However, the significance of Cooper's character concerns not only his obvious isolation but also the nature and meaning of his isolation and identity.

Will Kane thrives so powerfully as a loner in our film and cultural history because of the clarity and depth of his representation of a particular kind of loner: the Puritan on a moral mission who never loses touch with his society even when alienated from it or embattled against it. He never transcends that society. The great paradox and dilemma of Kane's lonely isolation concerns how in that isolation he still embodies his culture. Kane not only never becomes a superman, he grows stronger as a human being and character the more we see of his vulnerability, common humanity, and his fear. The genius of the film involves the visual, narratological, and ideological construction of his dilemma of deadly isolation and constant engagement. He takes his place with other figures in our past as a living Jeremiah who typifies the culture through his estrangement from it.

Accordingly, Cooper's Kane becomes part of a tradition of the Puritan and moral saint and soldier that goes back to our historic and cultural roots, finds sustenance in our early years of nationhood, and flowers during the period of the American Renaissance. So, while antipopulism separates the film from the Marxist critical tradition, it typifies the tension between the individual and the community in the myth and ideology of America. Kane exemplifies the culture rather than follows the group; he serves as a model of moral independence to inspire group action and unity. As big as he is, Kane grows still bigger as the rebel Puritan saint. Though he remains visually at the center of the film's action, Kane is part of a historic tradition of individuals who culturally occupy the margin, like Thoreau on the Fourth of July or Whitman wherever he walked and thought. Another paradox in the film concerns how the dissipation of personal independence ironically corrupts and cripples the unity of the group to act. Zinnemann perceptively dramatizes the way the fear of independent moral action leads to a cracking and crumbling of communal cohesion and the collective psyche. Kane becomes a Jeremiah for our times over moral integrity and individuality, and Cooper's great genius as an actor and Zinnemann's as a director is in part how they manage to show the physical and emotional costs of such independence on Cooper's face and body.

By so emphasizing the Puritan sensibility of moral conscience as the crucial factor to individual character and the key to social redemption, *High Noon* moves in direct opposition to another ideology and aesthetic of the Cold War era that discusses ethical and ideological matters in terms of collective and group security. In contrast to Zinnemann's *High Noon*, Robert Rossen represents a thoroughly different tradition of relating film, aesthetics, and politics. Born, raised, and educated amid the violence and turmoil of New York City's Lower East Side, Rossen, a former boxer, directed such socially conscious films as *Body and Soul* (1947), *All the King's Men* (1949), *Island in the Sun* (1957), and *The Hustler* (1964). He articulated a social and artistic philosophy that probably comes much closer to reflecting emerging trends in the early 1950s. Rossen told HUAC: "I don't think that any one individual can indulge himself in the luxury of individual morality or pit it against what I feel today very strongly is the safety and security of this nation."[77] Commenting about this statement by Rossen, Whitfield notes that, of course, "'individual morality' is precisely what Kane" represents.[78] Differing strongly with Rossen's view, *High Noon* argues that greater danger stems from the absence of such individual conscience.

The centrality of *High Noon* to the intellectual, social, and ethical conflicts of the times can be further demonstrated by suggesting the film's relationship to the work of David Riesman. Riesman's method of studying and analyzing American social character, behavior, and values during the 1950s proposes the psychological and social importance of conscience in providing structure for stable individuals in a cohesive society. His language of the social sciences transforms traditional moral values and ideals into concepts and constructs for social analysis. Thus, Riesman's essays that appeared during the years immediately surrounding *High Noon* articulate a social philosophy as well as a method of analysis; they establish a bridge to the putative values and beliefs of America's historic past.

Moreover, Riesman's vocabulary of individual and social conscience suggests crucial insights into the meaning of *High Noon*. Indeed, the film seems to be almost a dramatization of what Riesman describes in several essays, as well as in *The Lonely Crowd*, as the "shift" in the "character structure of

Figure 9. Gary Cooper under siege as the surviving remnant of Puritan conscience and leadership in *High Noon* (Stanley Kramer: The Museum of Modern Art / Film Stills Archive).

modern man" from a "type" Riesman termed *inner-directed,* "whose source of guidance in life is an internalized authority," to one designated *other-directed,* who is "dependent on external authorities."[79] In the early 1950s, Riesman described the inner-directed individual as originating with the Renaissance man and the Puritan in the age of frontiers and exploration. In "The Saving Remnant," Riesman maintains that the inner-directed type was "self-piloting" with an "internal psychic 'gyroscope' which, installed in childhood, continues to pilot the person as he struggles to master the exigent demands of the frontier" (101). Self-disciplined, self-governed, self-reliant, and self-promoting, this individual contrasts with the corporate other-directed type who emerged in the early decades of the twentieth century. Dependent for approval from the group, obsessed with security and approval, and feeling overwhelmed by helplessness and vulnerability, this contemporary character constructs a self-image based upon consumerism. Riesman writes, "Today, the helplessness foreseen by a few thinkers, and sensed even in the earlier age of frontiers by many who failed, has become the common attribute of the mass of men" (103).

Riesman cites several factors to account for this profound shift in character – the end of frontiers and individual enterprise, the rise of leisure over work, the explosion of monstrous bureaucracies and institutions:

> These changes in the nature of work and leisure have made themselves felt most strongly among the middle classes of the American big cities in the last twenty-five years or so. It is here that the character that I call other-directed appears to be concentrated, a type whose source of direction is externalized. (104)

Riesman, of course, maintains that such psychological dependence and the internalization of corporate authority for the other-directed person not only condemns the person to a lifetime of insecurity but also dooms democracy:

> It is my tentative conclusion that the feeling of helplessness of modern man results from both the vastly enhanced power of the social group and the incorporation of its authority into his very character. And the point at issue is not that the other-directed character is more opportunistic than the inner-directed – if anything, the contrary is true. Rather, the point is that the individual is psychologically dependent on others for clues to the meaning of life. He thus fails to resist authority or fears to exercise freedom of choice even where he might safely do so. (106)

As noted earlier, recent versions of this social theory of conformity and helplessness have been articulated by such thinkers and critics as Christopher Lasch.

No matter how one feels about Riesman's thesis, in *High Noon* Zinnemann and Cooper dramatize a world in which one man of inner-direction, Marshal Kane, confronts a society of other-directed conformists who are morally crippled by fear and helplessness. Not unimportant for either Riesman's thesis or the contemporaneity of the film is the fact that in the end the only convert to Cooper's brand of individualism will be his wife, Amy Fowler (Grace Kelly). With this act of union and support, the great age difference between Kane and Amy gains special meaning. The Old Puritan, the saving remnant who embodies the traditions and values of the past, earns through his example the loyalty of this new representative of her rising generation of independent women. Ironically, by rejoining Kane, she triumphs over her past and asserts a new independence. As in Capra, two are stronger than one. Although Bruce Kawin questions the ideological meaning of Cooper's heroism and sees Amy as a vehicle for the postwar drive back to female domesticity, his view of the film echoes Riesman's perspicacious concern for women to propel their liberation by resisting pressures toward moral conformity.[80]

In another irony, early in the film Amy asserts her independence by deciding on her wedding day to leave Kane rather than violate her Quaker principles of nonviolence by staying while Kane fights the men who have come to town to kill him. She also acts out of fear and self-interest, believing flight to be a better alternative than a gunfight, especially since Kane technically has stepped down as marshal. She simply wants to take the advice of others to run before the train arrives with killer Frank Miller (Ian MacDonald). They can get away, she thinks, and begin their married life. Amy ultimately abrogates her initial act of independence from her husband when she returns to him. Her return can be interpreted as a positive act of strength that enables her to fight aggressively and even use a gun to save her husband's life and their future. As opposed to angrily and fearfully fleeing the town and abandoning her husband, she moves toward a truer form of independence that Riesman proposes as an alternative to the extremes of inner-direction or other-direction. In so doing, she also follows the example of Helen Ramirez, Kane's Mexican ex-mistress, who truly pioneers gender and ethnic autonomy as a sexually and economically independent woman. However, before Amy's act of reconciliation transpires, Kane must stand alone.

Time, of course, functions as a major dramatic element on Cooper's lonely search through the town. Time works as his inexorable boundary and enemy as he fights the deadline of the noon arrival of the train carrying Miller. The similarity in *High Noon* between the approximate screen time of one hour and twenty minutes and the actual time of the events in the story has generated considerable discussion. This parallel time structure adds considerably to the film's sense of realism; but the compressed time frame of *High Noon*'s story also invites a manipulation of the action and visual material of the narrative to develop the drama and tension Zinnemann seeks. Within the approximate eighty to eighty-five minutes of the story, Zinnemann repeats patterns of shots that involve incessant crosscutting throughout the town to develop conflict, character, narrative, and theme. Unfortunately, such manipulation often seems painfully self-conscious. Zinnemann's direction often becomes heavy-handed, with melodramatic shots of such things as the railroad tracks on which the killer's train will arrive, the innumerable clocks anticipating the noon arrival of the train, the empty chair from which the former prisoner promised five years earlier to kill Kane, and the man whose crass resemblance to Adolph Hitler seems an excessive penalty for being an enemy and critic of Will Kane. The Academy Award–winning score and song by Dmitri Tiomkin also become somewhat grating in their ceaseless throbbing and pulsating tempo. Such stylistic excesses at times recall the 1950s television parodies of Hollywood by Sid Caesar, Carl Reiner, Imogene Coca, and Howard Morris.

In the final analysis, however, the use of time institutes a powerful existential motif and theme in the film. Forcing his characters to deal with time and the inevitable reality of death, Zinnemann emphasizes the existential challenge to choose and to grapple with the meaning and relevance of one's own life. His aesthetic lapses and failures of style and execution ultimately diminish in the face of his and Cooper's successes in the film. The visualization of pain and abandonment becomes a major achievement. Despite Zinnemann's excesses, his style aspires to and maintains an impressive degree of visual subtlety, depth, and intensity. As noted above, amid ever-increasing isolation and vulnerability, Cooper's power as a character and figure grows steadily, almost with each shot and sequence. He also expresses a range of emotion and awareness that testifies to the director's genius for using close-ups to gain access to interior feelings and thought. Zinnemann brilliantly conveys psychological change through physical movement. Some of the most powerful sequences in *High Noon* involve tracking shots and close-ups of Cooper as he walks the streets of the town seeking help. The more Kane searches, the more intently and probingly does the camera examine the inner core and character of the hero. Zinnemann and Cooper collaborate to establish an aura of anguish and heroism.

French semiotician and writer Roland Barthes published a famous sketch in the 1950s on "The Face of Garbo";[81] in contrast, *High Noon* could be called "The Face of Cooper." The intensity and consistency of Zinnemann's focus on the face and figure of Cooper make *High Noon* into a kind of visual poem of the development and transformation of a man at middle age, when he would seem to be complete and total.

From the film's beginning, several scenes illustrate vital themes and motifs that develop steadily into a visual and aural climax of inner turmoil and ultimate victory. This sequence of scenes establishes the film's psychological and ideological pattern of shattering Cooper's assumptions about reality and challenging his strongly held beliefs. Proposing a new beginning for Kane, these major scenes also inaugurate a process concerning the reconstruction of an American hero; moreover, they introduce Kane to the reality of his own vulnerability and lack, meaning his psychic and social incompleteness. The scenes work like dramatic and psychological building blocks after the film's opening shots establish the basic thrust and conflicts of the narrative.

The film opens with parallel actions in powerful opposition on several important levels. Zinnemann positions the film's ideological and psychological parameters by opening with the meeting outside of town of the men who come to help Frank Miller kill Kane in town. He then crosscuts to the scene of Kane's wedding to Amy Fowler. Unknown danger from the opening scene encroaches upon the domestic peace and harmony of the wedding. Significantly, from Kane's perspective, he seems to have everything: a beautiful and young wife, the admiration of good friends and supporters, a promising new future. At this early point in the film, Kane personifies plentitude and fulfillment: He has it all – love, security, and bright prospects. This scene is disrupted by the news that Frank Miller unexpectedly has been pardoned and is due to arrive on the noon train in less than an hour and a half. Kane initially takes the advice of his friends, most notably the town's political leader, Jonas Henderson (Thomas Mitchell), to flee immediately. However, outside of town, he stops his speeding wagon and tells Amy they must go back in spite of their fear.

Thus *High Noon* begins by dividing the world into two spheres, with the external endangering the internal domestic realm of peace and love. The split enters their marriage when Kane returns to his office with Amy and tries to explain his actions to her. This is one of those scenes in the sequence mentioned above that constitutes the thematic, psychological, and aesthetic heart of the film. He draws his line in the sand here with her by insisting that he has to stay in town and fight. His first point, however, is not honor and some kind of masculine code: He tells her that he really has no choice but to fight because there is not enough time to get away from the Miller gang. The couple would be helpless in any other setting. In other words, he makes a completely rational and honest assessment of their situation and decides to act accordingly. Kane uses plain and direct language consistent with his role as the American pragmatist and man of action. (In contrast, Judge Percy Mettrick [Otto Kruger] uses complex logic and decorative rhetoric in a separate scene to rationalize his flight while at the same time taking down his American flag from the wall.) Thus, to Kelly's frightened insistence that they flee because fighting at this stage of their lives makes no sense, Kane succinctly explains his understanding of the situation, telling her how the gang plans to kill him. He presents the facts as he sees them: It would be stupid for him to leave himself and his wife at the mercy of the gang on the road or in another town. "They'll just come after us. Four of them. And we'll be all alone on the prairie." She pleads that they have an hour, and he asserts more forcefully: "What's an hour? What's a hundred miles?" Fleeing will keep them in fear and danger the rest of their lives. "We'd have to run again. As long as we live."

Close-ups and careful timing steadily develop the tension in this scene. The camera focuses primarily on Cooper since his argument with Amy involves a debate with himself as well. After rationally considering his situation, he convinces himself and makes his decision like a soldier and man of action. He moves to the left to pass her and go outside to begin the necessary action. Kelly intercedes, and the camera cuts to her in close-up. She makes her final plea in personal terms that change her line of argument from ideas to character and emotion. She accuses him of trying to be a hero. That just barely stops him. In his own mind at least, he knows that argument not to be true. "I'm not trying to be a hero. If you think I like this, you're crazy." That line evokes his strongest emotion and loudest voice. His face retains the soldierly strength of an Eisenhower but also suggests the beginnings of an inner tear of the psyche that will become a chasm by the film's end. When she intensifies her appeal by holding him and reminding him that they just have been married, he remains unmoved and determined. "You know, I've only got an hour and I have lots to do," he says, trying to dismiss her at last so that he can get to work. Her final action, however, is an ultimatum of her own, her own line in the sand. She will not wait an hour to see if she will be a widow or a wife. The scene concludes with their separation.

Propounding the film's major themes of moral conflict, choice, and commitment, the fight between Cooper and Kelly in his office marks a new beginning for them involving what Stephen Heath terms the violence of any narrative beginning.[82] Their conflict helps propel the narrative in a new direction that concomitantly initiates the transformation of their characters and relationship. Although their conflict domesticates and personalizes the moral debate in the form of a love relationship, the restraint and maturity of Cooper's controlled determination establish the pattern for his performance of a lifetime. Equally important, the authority of his presence ironically accentuates the impending tragedy of his losses and emphasizes his increasing awareness of his limitations and weaknesses. In addition, the scene establishes the quality and strength of Amy's moral character as well as her instinctive drive for independence.

The severity of the split between the new husband and young wife also foreshadows the harsh divisions still to come. In spite of his intelligence and his courage to act against the advice of his friends and the pleading of his bride, he really cannot appreciate how the crisis before him will turn into one not of mind, intelligence, and the will to act but of faith. He will be left entirely alone and be brought to the extremes of despair and anguish as he comes to realize that his effort does not seem to mean anything to anyone but himself. Believing that he acts for everyone, he finds himself alone. Looking for validation from the townspeople, he grows aware of his total disagreement with them. Expecting to gain legitimacy for his efforts through their approval, he becomes the object of their ridicule and the cause of their embarrassment. No longer certain as to how to measure or know the truth, he finally has to act totally upon faith in himself, a self that has been reduced to its minimum in minutes. Through Cooper's performance and Zinnemann's direction, a life of solidity and purpose gets completely reversed.

Also as a tribute to the performance and direction, the profound absence of excessive histrionics or emotionalism from Cooper intensifies the rendering of the steady deterioration of Kane's confidence and real power. His outer appearance of stability therefore compounds the great irony of his misplaced confidence in his ability to control life and to achieve the support of his friends. During his office confrontation with Amy, when he still believes rationality and intelligent decision making work, he says to her, "This is my town. I've got friends here." If there will be trouble, "Then, it's better to have it here." However, the nature of the situation turns the drama into a test and trial of individual action as opposed to a validation of rational collective behavior. The film dramatizes how the town's collective intelligence and rationality ultimately succumb to fear. The townspeople begin to analyze their situation and choices rationally, but they yield to inner, unconscious collective doubts. *High Noon* emphasizes the tendency of the unconscious to govern beneath a mask of rational behavior. The surrender to fear in the unconscious inspires the cultivation of debilitating illusions. The film therefore illustrates the community's collective death instinct. The citizens believe in a hope for salvation that displaces a real danger with an illusion of security. Such action signifies the town's inevitable destruction.

Cooper and Zinnemann convey such complexity partly through their exercise of what some current critics term "the look" or the organization of the visual space of the scene. Heath defines and explains the look as a relationship of spatial position and organization that maintains "a kind of perspective within the perspective system, regulating the world, orientating space, providing directions." He identifies three "factors" of the look: the camera's look at the profilmic totality to be filmed; the spectator's look at the film; and the "intradiegetic" looks of the characters within the film. "Classically, cinema turns on a series of 'looks' which join, cross through and relay one another."[83] For Heath and others, the look, in delineating difference, distance, and separation, invariably relates to the visualization of sexual difference and identity.

In *High Noon*, Cooper's look as constructed and directed by Zinnemann – his appearance to the camera, the spectator, and the film's other personae – structures the transformation of his character. It becomes a visual articulation of catastrophic change and isolation; it visually speaks for the situation Kane faces of increasing complexity that will challenge the strength of his ego and character to operate under conditions he never previously imagined. When Cooper speaks in the beginning of the film, he expresses a singular subjectivity. He articulates an "I" of confidence that suggests a secure identity and sense of self, presenting himself initially as a thoroughly coherent and consistent ego – the solid American. As the film progresses, however, his speech remains coherent, but his look articulates an ego under siege. As he addresses other characters, his "I" retains its independence and identity, but the "eye" reveals a body in pain and a psyche in a living hell. His look delineates growing fear and separation; it exposes dread. Thus, in the scene with Kelly early in the film, although Cooper speaks with the voice of paternalistic authority, his look dramatizes the beginnings of new psychic and social realities.

Similarly, in a subsequent scene with Harvey Pell (Bridges), the young deputy whose great animosity toward Kane stems from professional and sexual jealousy, Cooper's look again structures the scene's splintering paternal politics of Oedipal anxieties. In this second scene that helps establish the psychological pattern for the rest of the film, Cooper's look at once conveys fatherly humor, paternal exasperation, masculine fellowship and bantering all mixed with an inner apprehension that suggests deeper psychic division. The Oedipal tension that began with Kelly continues in this scene with Bridges. Cooper again works and talks with intelligence and rationality but also with considerably less patience, reflecting both the way he normally would work with a younger man and the ongoing passage of time. Soon they encounter the basic tensions at the heart of Pell's character: his insecurities about sexuality and his manhood. Both matters involve Kane because Pell follows him as Helen Ramirez's new lover. Pell also wishes to emulate Kane by becoming marshal. His inability to fulfill these roles only feeds his frustration. Moreover, Kane's discipline and reserve hide his inner meltdown but also exacerbate the tension of Pell's adolescent need for attention and an emotional response. Although more physical action occurs in this scene than in the earlier one with Kelly, the major burden for the action and meaning of the scene finds expression through Cooper's look.

Similarly, Cooper's look as articulated by his facial and physical expression dominates the church scene, when Kane confronts the townspeople only to find himself betrayed by his closest friend, Jonas Henderson (Mitchell), who tells him to leave town in order to save it from inevitable violence: Citizens should not endanger themselves because the killer hates the marshal for arresting him. Cooper's look in the face of surrounding moral devastation continues to function as the visual organizing principle for much of the rest of the film, including the shots of his face and body as he walks through town alone.

Throughout the film, Cooper's struggle for self-control gains poignancy and intensity as he deals with his growing fears and sense of defeat. A tug-of-war – like the children's game outside the church – between control and loss, strength and terror, plays out across the lines of his face and through his rigid body. Initially showing him in a confident and complacent mood, the film immediately explodes his false sense of security. Instead of enjoying the comforts and pleasures of a new life with his bride, he confronts a challenge that requires his reconsideration of his life and past. As the visible target for murder, he goes from respectable stability to perpetual movement. He experiences a violent new beginning that leads him to see himself in terms of his difference and separation from everyone he has trusted. Psychologically, this new beginning or rebirth involves a severing; he suffers a form of dismemberment. Suddenly, Kane's identity becomes a function of his difference from the community rather than his adherence to it. His movement alone through the town compels the formation of a new sense of self. This experience constitutes his real awakening to his own existence as an individual with a self-determined identity. He undergoes a midlife transformation and becomes his own man, a rebel-hero, as demonstrated by his final rejection of the town. Intuitively, Hawks and Wayne reacted to this implication behind "Coop's" rebellious act of discarding the badge into the street.

In contrast to Hawks and Wayne, Clint Eastwood's *High Plains Drifter* (1973) suggests a different view of the social and psychological meaning of *High Noon*. Eastwood says his movie imagines what would have happened had Cooper died: The town's fear of acting in the face of death and violence results in evil and chaos and the arrival in *High Plains Drifter* of a mythic, transcendent figure of monolithic terror, justice, and power.[84] Eastwood confirms the idea in *High Noon* of a sick town's demise through its sacrifice of a courageous moral leader.

Existentially, Kane's transformation into his own man also will require him to accept his individual existence by confronting the reality of his likely death. Cooper has been preparing for physical death through a series of smaller deaths, all of which were brilliantly enacted on his strong but anguished face: his humiliation in the town bar; hearing his coffin nailed together as he gets a shave; finding himself barred by his friend's wife from asking the friend for help; standing totally alone and growing pathetically smaller as Grace Kelly and Katy Jurado abandon him in the street. In his office, he writes his will, his face again dramatizing the opposite of power: death, failure, abandonment. Now concerned about how he looks only to himself, he projects a deep awareness of his end. In this moment of unspeakable loss, he gains himself by accepting his condition with the courage to act as he sees fit.

Kane has progressed from disavowing lack, denying weakness, and negating difference. He has gone beyond believing that masculine intelligence can supplant lack, that individual integrity can overcome all weakness and vulnerability, that paternalistic and well-intentioned authority can heal all wounds. In the end, however, he retains his faith in himself and in his courage to act. He remains the exemplary American Puritan in his moral leadership and intensity.

Kane's situation, therefore, stands in stark contrast to the fragmented figures of crippled masculinity in Zinnemann's other classic film of male identity, released the following year. *From Here to Eternity* (1953) projects the collapse of masculinity in the absence of Kane's system of belief and identity. For the three heroes of the film – played by Burt Lancaster, Montgomery Clift, and Frank Sinatra – male masochism as a structure for male bonding and affection substitutes for permanent heterosexual relationships of love and work. Sinatra and Clift play supreme male masochists who seem to thrive upon the punishment they can accept; Lancaster functions as an aggressive male force. For Robert E. Lee Prewitt (Clift) and Angelo Maggio (Sinatra), punishment from another man incorporates the paternalistic state into the individual psyche. They treat themselves as innately guilty and needing punishment from a father figure for self-fulfillment. Moral masochists in deriving pleasure from their punishment, they also gain a feeling of moral superiority from their pain, which helps give each of them a sense of unique individuality based on their own personal codes of behavior. Ultimately passive and receptive in their experiences of life and their relationships to others, they find it impossible to play an active role of responsibility with women. Thus, the film's frequent exchanges of genuine affection often transpire between men, as when Sergeant Milton Warden (Lancaster) fondles Prewitt's hair as they sit drunkenly in the middle of a road.

Similarly, the emotional climax of the film occurs in a spontaneous communal ritual of grief instigated by "Prew" (Clift) when he bugles taps to commemorate Maggio's death. This is a beautifully constructed sequence that becomes genuinely touching in its expression of the sincere emotion of the men. Again, Zinnemann's mastery of the look through brilliant filming and editing organizes the sequence. His intercutting between shots of individual soldiers and the men as a group dramatizes the military unit as the interweaving of so many separate entities, each of which comes alive when they unite as a caring force. Prewitt in tears plays taps so well that the men realize they are participating in a special moment that really amounts to a tribute to them all. Through his playing, they are all connected spiritually and emotionally as men and soldiers to the special friend who died so unnecessarily and so unfairly. Even Warden looks up and stops his work to pay attention to this ceremony; he too must show respect for the dead man and the bugler. Lancaster's look renders a kind of sanction and approval to the unique expression of emotion during this ceremony. He walks outside the barracks to listen to the end of taps. Although they never actually see each other until the end of the sequence, the organization of the look in the scene becomes so moving and powerful partly because of the way it connects Clift and Lancaster. Individually so charismatic, together they strengthen each other and the group. Their look unites them in a grief that engages death in an effort to fill in the gap left by the deceased friend with their new sense of common humanity. Zinnemann makes the look connecting Clift and Lancaster a concrete representation of the abstract unity of all the individuals in the group.

The intensified look of Lancaster and Clift and the montage of the men as individuals and as a group become a cinematic counterpart to Whitman's triumphant symbolism in his poetry of unity and continuity in the face of death and loss. The intercutting of cinema that breaks and fragments visual experience (as in Gower's beating of George in *It's a Wonderful Life;* see Chapter 3) enacts the sense of death, disappearance, and loss memorialized by Prewitt's playing. Moreover, Zinnemann's mastery of montage as a means

Figure 10. Montgomery Clift in *From Here to Eternity,* the emergence of a new American hero of sensitivity, depth, and lonely alienation (Columbia: The Museum of Modern Art / Film Stills Archive).

for organizing narrative space through the look here aesthetically sustains and develops the feeling of unity that love and grief can convey. The same rhythm and organization of the intercutting that evoke death also create a renewed sense of life and continuity in the faces and reactions of all the men, while Lancaster's look of authority and respect provides the whole sequence with an aura of credibility and coherence.

With tears running down his face, Prewitt concludes taps and salutes. In a brilliant touch, Zinnemann's long shot shows Clift walk past Lancaster as he returns to the barracks. The shot diminishes the size of the individual men as though to emphasize the significance of the group and event at this moment. The two do not mark each other or exchange greetings: Verbal expression might entail unmanly recognition and approval of weak emotionalism;

meanwhile, ordinary language should not contaminate this unique arousal of deep feelings. In a scene that so originally expresses so much genuine emotion, the return at its conclusion of emotional disavowal dramatizes with a touch of irony the dilemma of heroic masculinity in America.

The intensity of emotion between the men in *From Here to Eternity* manifests itself again in a painful scene at the end of the film when Warden cruelly and impulsively jumps from a difficult conversation with Karen Holmes (Deborah Kerr), his married lover, to see if a passing soldier happens to be "Prew," who has been violating Army rules with his unauthorized absence. Clearly, Warden wishes to be with Prewitt, who occupies his inner thoughts, leaving Karen to a dubious future: She will have to return to her ruined husband, Captain Dana Holmes (Philip Ober). Caught in comparable uncertainty is the prostitute who becomes Prewitt's girl, Alma "Lorene" – played by Donna Reed in stark contrast to her performance as Mary in *It's a Wonderful Life*. Interestingly, the look that connects Clift and Reed when they first see each other in a crowded house where soldiers and women meet works like a conscious replication of the visual exchange between Jimmy Stewart and Reed at the high-school party in the earlier film. The contexts of the meetings are radically different, however, as are the characters and their situations; the visual similarity and continuity of the two scenes serve to emphasize their profound differences of content and meaning. In *From Here to Eternity*, Alma achieves the working-girl independence that was denied Mary but in a form that leaves her in a much greater quandary of abandonment and loss, with only lies and fantasies about her relationship with Prewitt to substitute for real love and a life of real meaning to her.

For Zinnemann, moral masochism in men such as Prewitt and Maggio seems to equate with prostitution and self-destruction in the women. They are finally all powerless in their mutual masochism. They are martyrs without a cause greater than themselves except for their own weakness and victimization. For Warden, however, authority and power are self-justifying as the only means for survival in a culture and time of violence. Early in *From Here to Eternity*, Warden tells Prewitt that room no longer exists for the independent and self-reliant individual. The film's obvious choices – a meaningless martyrdom, the accommodation of oneself to lack and limitation by losing one's identity in the group, or a commitment to aggression and power for their own sake – all constitute forms of inner death.

Significantly, another film of this period with a more optimistic outcome and outlook than *From Here to Eternity* also examines heroic masculinity in the context of a reconsideration of the values of democracy in the climate of the Cold War. Like *High Noon*, Elia Kazan's *On the Waterfront* (1954) studies such heroic masculinity as part of a broader search for belief in the modern age.

CHAPTER 5

AN AMERICAN CONSCIENCE: ELIA KAZAN'S LONG JOURNEY HOME

Terry Malloy's sanctuary, his place of refuge, in *On the Waterfront* has been the tenement rooftop where he keeps his pigeon coop and cavorts with neighborhood youngsters who still revere him as a hero, boxer, and founder years before of their gang, the Golden Warriors. To anyone familiar with immigrant, urban, and proletarian literature and film, the symbolism of the rooftop suggests escape from the streets, the quest for freedom and transcendence, a search for solitude and privacy. With its inherent limitations of space, security, and comfort, the roof also often dramatizes confinement and failure in the search for freedom. In Henry Roth's classic immigrant novel *Call It Sleep*, for example, the rooftop entails all of these symbolic meanings as part of a metaphoric cosmology that incorporates the terror and evil of the basement with the hope for rebirth on the roof. So Terry (Marlon Brando) naturally will head for the roof to seek solace for himself in one of the final sequences of the film after he has testified before the State Waterfront Crime Commission against the corrupt bosses and racketeers of the longshoreman's union. By so testifying, of course, Terry has violated the great code of the mob and streets against ever informing, especially when it means turning against one's own. As a "stool pigeon," or what the corrupt union boss Johnny Friendly (Lee J. Cobb) calls a "cheese eater," Terry now feels totally dejected and alone, even though the murder by the mob of his brother, Charley "the Gent" (Rod Steiger) helped motivate him to testify. Even the police who escort Terry home after his testimony ridicule him as a "canary," and a friend won't acknowledge him on the stairs of their tenement. Bounding up the stairs from his police protection, Terry enters his apartment, a perfectly stark and miserable setting that epitomizes the realism and power of this film in depicting the depressing conditions of the people associated with the waterfront. Waiting for Terry in the apartment is Edie Doyle (Eva Marie Saint), who has become his girlfriend. The sister of a popular longshoreman who has been murdered by the mob, Edie has forgiven Terry for his unwitting complicity in that murder. Edie tries to comfort Terry, but he, in his depressed restlessness, needs to get away. He moves to the window, and Edie follows him, so that the camera pans to the left, emphasizing the drabness of the scene by revealing clothes hanging on the wall and some unevenly hung framed pictures. Among these is a photograph of a boxing match, probably one of Terry's more memorable fights during his career when he still hoped, as he said in his talk with his brother Charley in the back of a car, to be a champion "contender." Now Brando sits, with his back to the camera, on the inner base of the cramped and confining window. In a brilliant touch that maintains the authenticity of Kazan's intensely realistic representation of urban life, after Edie tries to soothe his feelings, Terry exits through the window to use the fire escape to get to the roof.

Coming toward the end of the film, the ensuing scene on the roof has a symphonic quality of inevitability. It brings together all the elements of the film to that point in a moral and ideological climax that anticipates the violence of the concluding confrontation between Terry and Johnny Friendly. The visual detail of this rooftop scene comprises the aesthetic fulfillment of the propelling force of the narrative and characters in the film. The concreteness of the scene synthesizes into a coherent whole the issues of conscience, character, love, and ideology that make *On the Waterfront* such an important film for this period of history.

When Terry reaches the roof, he encounters Tommy (Thomas Handley), one of the young boys who has idolized him. The crying, distraught boy heaves a dead pigeon at Terry. The camera focuses on the boy's small frame in a medium close-up single shot. He is a duplicate of Terry years before – a city street kid. Without education or serious guidance, he only knows what the streets and the life on the docks have taught him. Throughout the course of the film, he angrily has watched Terry steadily change and form new relationships and get new ideas. Tommy clearly suffers as much confusion and conflicted feelings as Terry. The boy cries, "A pigeon for a pigeon," and Terry dreads the anticipated discovery that his birds have been killed.

In this scene, Kazan turns the roof into an elevated cinematic stage with the city's skyline as an in-depth, multidimensional backdrop for a mise-en-scène of despair. Filmed on location on the Hoboken, New Jersey, waterfront in extremely cold and cloudy weather, *On the Waterfront* documents the depressed living and working conditions for the dockworkers. The film never loses its artistic integrity or its intense visual originality in presenting and representating their lives; shot starkly in black and white, the film unrelentingly emphasizes the bleak circumstances of these people. Based on widely publicized events of crime and labor corruption on the docks, *On the Waterfront*, like *High Noon*, uses black and white to impart a quality of newspaper documentation. Thus, even in its evocation of some freedom in the open air, the roof still wreaks of confinement. The tight and cramped spaces atop the tenement suggest danger for anyone who goes there. Everything is old and

Figure 11. Elia Kazan: American conscience and identity in turmoil (The Museum of Modern Art / Film Stills Archive).

marked by urban grime. The foggy and cloudy atmosphere and the poverty all add to the sadness. Sometimes a momentary escape, the roof also serves as an urban plateau of moribund expectations.

In a high-angle shot, Terry, holding the dead pigeon that the boy Tommy has thrown at him, cuts across the roof. Brando, wearing an unbuttoned rough shirt with a wide tie loosened at the collar, appears as strong in this scene as he has been throughout the film. The shot emphasizes the steadily developing stockiness of his body that somewhat softens him and gives him even more of a working-class quality than the pure animalism and vitality of his figure and performance in his first film with Kazan, as Stanley Kowalski in Tennessee Williams's *A Streetcar Named Desire* (1951). He holds the bird with a tender detachment, evincing by his facial expression and body language conflicting feelings of dread, grief, fear, and denial. Brando here demonstrates a quality of fragility and sensitivity without making the scene pathetic or gruesome. Brilliantly and beautifully, Kazan cuts to a shot from within the bird coop while Terry, body poised in anxious anticipation, looks through the wire and into the structure. While the coop's chicken wire obviously exaggerates the feeling of confinement that pervades the whole film, the shot in deep focus captures the congestion and confined spaces of the roof. Also, the inclusion in the shot of the crosses of television antennae and power lines perpetuates the theme of crucifixion that images of crosses and spikes have symbolized throughout the film.

In a graceful visual movement, Brando moves to the right to get into the coop and then goes to the left once inside; at the same time, the camera, which remains stable for this shot, continues to present the roof in deep focus. This deep-focus shot of Terry in the foreground and the roof extended beyond him marks the significance of Eva Marie Saint's appearance on the roof in the background, a vision of blond innocence and softness, almost saintliness, moving with some care and trepidation toward him. With shoulders bent and head bowed, Terry ever so carefully and sadly opens the door to the sheltered part of the coop to see the extent of the boy's actions and damage. Moving into the frame in full body in the distance but like a hovering angel in black and white, Edie comes ever closer to the grotesque carnage. The wonderful Leonard Bernstein film score plays its most sympathetic and appealing theme as we cut again to a shot from behind Edie as she strains to get a sense of what has happened inside the coop. In an intermediary position between the spectator and the action, Edie adds to the tension and uncertainty of the moment. A close-up from behind the chicken wire catches the beginning of her sense of shock as she gets closer and comes to realize that indeed something awful has happened. Then Kazan renders an original shot from the side of her lower legs that while seeming to be high angle, because it reveals Terry a bit below in sorrow on the floor, also captures the psychology of being so low by showing her legs on the dirty roof. Shot from this angle and position, the camera is with both Edie and Terry, as she looks upon Terry from the door. The camera declines to exhibit the dead birds fully but uses the reactions of both Terry and Edie to convey the horror.

Up to this point in this scene and sequence, the Academy Award–winning combination of Kazan's direction, Budd Schulberg's screenplay, Boris Kaufman's photography, Richard Day's art direction, and Leonard Bernstein's score develops the narrative and the film's excellent synthesis of internal feelings and external social conditions. Now, however, Kazan's direction takes the scene, it seems to me, to another level of intensity and meaning in just a few brief lines and shots. The development of Edie's character and her relationship to Terry from the beginning of the film focus and structure the crucial dramatic change that occurs between them at this point.

Much of the film's force and energy has been directed toward Terry's moral self-recognition in this scene on the roof. To a great extent, the energy and vehicle for this moment of truth has been Edie in her developing relationship with Terry. Throughout the film, Edie has been an extraordinary combination of conflicting roles and values, all of them beautifully fulfilled by Eva Marie Saint in what was her first major film performance and critical triumph. As an innocent and virginal convent girl whose longshoreman father has removed her from the filth and crime of the docks and streets, Edie has been an angel of conscience, strongly influencing Terry's character with the example of her purity, honesty, and idealism. She acts, thinks, and speaks with the kindness and authenticity of a sincere teacher or social worker. However, as the sister of Joey Doyle, who was killed by the mob because of his resistance to the bosses, Edie has been a holy terror throughout the film, working with unrelenting intensity to avenge her brother's death. She has been an engine of justice and retribution, demanding that Terry take responsibility for the implications of his involvement in that murder when he allowed himself to be used by the mob to call Joey to the roof to be killed, even though he was not actually privy to the killers' plans. At the same time, as an object of desire, a beautiful young woman who arouses and reciprocates Terry's feelings of love and compassion, she greatly complicates her relationship to him. In all of the scenes with Brando, Saint coherently develops these various elements of her character and role. It is the unity of her sexual, moral, and psychological entanglements with Brando that makes her performance so strong and convincing.

The scenes between Brando and Saint are still today unique combinations of charm, sensitivity, and sexuality. Even Kazan, a hard-nosed director not usually given to romance or sentimentality, says, "My favorite scenes in the film are the love scenes between Marlon and Eva Marie Saint."[1] The genuine potency of their relationship in conveying an explosive mixture of realism and passion, strength and tenderness, love and fear, despair and renewal would be hard to equal with other famous on-screen Hollywood couples. Brando and Saint are special together in this film, starting with their first encounter when Brando flirtatiously spars with her over giving up a brass check thrown by a dock boss that will enable her father to work in what is known as the "shape-up" system. When told that she is Joey's sister, the look on his face, his hesitation, the movement of his head, and the subtle mutual recognition that occurs between them anticipate their relationship for the rest of the film. In a following scene, their walk on a freezing day through a foggy park – a fog created in part by fires built by Kazan and Day for effect and warmth – inspires extraordinarily creative performances from Brando and Saint. Brando's improvisation in the scene, when he spontaneously puts on Saint's white glove, has aroused discussion ever since by leading critics such as James Naremore about his trying on a new character or gender with this female apparel, or even experimenting with a new morality with the fit of the glove.[2] Brando's rough charm in this scene boggles the mind. He must seem believable as a thoroughly contradictory character. He has to show himself to be truly rough but at the same time must possess the potential for self-examination, inner pain, and moral growth. To be credible, he must come across as uneducated but intelligent and capable of learning. As Naremore says:

> Brando's every look, movement, and gesture, is keyed to the essentially adolescent confusion of the character. Throughout, he oscillates between violence and child-like bewilderment, making visible Terry's conflict. . . . The film's strategy is to make Terry a synthesis of these two groups: a hero virile and independent enough to beat up the mobsters yet sensitive and caring enough to win the heart of Edie.[3]

Saint's performance, on the other hand, helps structure the conflict within Terry and helps shape Brando's overall performance. Edie is determined but utterly accessible, strong and compulsive in her quest for justice but also open and kind. Brando and Saint create an original and exciting combination.

Another scene between the two of them that helps build momentum to the climactic rooftop scene occurs after Edie has sought out Terry, again on the roof, to find out about her brother's death. They go to a neighborhood bar and have their first drink together, which seems to be her first taste of alcohol. Whereas in the earlier park scene Brando's brash, boyish, showing off only hints at deeper elements to his character, in the bar he emphasizes that side of Terry to Edie, revealing a vulnerability and sensitivity that she cannot resist. Brando's acting in this and related scenes has changed representations of masculinity in film ever since. Saint continues to draw out his intelligent sensitivity. After dramatic reverse shots of them at the table in the bar, Kazan sets up a wonderful two-shot, with Edie's lovely white profile above his anguished dark face as he tries to explain himself to her. She reaches down and caressingly touches his face, again revealing that sympathetic side of her nature that her father fears will cause her to act impulsively. While Schulberg's remarkable dialogue indicates the potential for love between Edie and Terry, the softer musical theme associated with Edie and love in Bernstein's powerful score adds to the great unity of mind and emotion in the scene.

At this point, of course, Edie remains unaware of the extent of Terry's complicity in the mob and the death of her brother, but Brando's face slowly and systematically indicates the depth of his inner conflict and anxiety over the issue as his feelings of care and responsibility for Edie steadily grow. Later, he feels compelled to confess to Father Barry (Karl Malden) that "I'm the one who set Joey Doyle up for the knock off." In the midst of such awful poverty, crime, and violence, Edie and Terry give their relationship a quality of innocence and fresh promise. In perfect psychological consistency with the development of their relationship, the bar scene ends when one of the mob finds Terry, gives him a message from the boss, and Edie suddenly doubts him. She then reacts angrily, like a disappointed mother, castigating him in a way perfectly designed to cultivate his sense of conscience, guilt, and need for her approval. The creative energy of their performances makes their relationship seem at once inevitable and impossible. The truth they project with and about each other also makes them receptive to what Kenneth R. Hey terms the mythic element in their relationship. In his brilliant article about *On the Waterfront,* Hey asserts this quality of myth between Terry and Edie, especially when she returns to the roof to give him Joey's jacket after "Kayo" Dugan (Pat Henning) also has been killed wearing it. Karl Malden's powerful jeremiad-sermon over Dugan's body, to the workers and mobsters assembled in the ship's hold where he was slain, invests the jacket with religious meaning. Malden's sermon – based on a real sermon by the man who was the model for the dockside priest – evokes the mystery of Jonah in the belly of the whale.[4]

Later, Terry breaks down the door to Edie's apartment, in frenzied inner conflict over his love for her, his confused loyalties to his brother and the mob, and his guilty conscience. The visual action of this scene has been repeated in other films, most successfully in the bathroom scene in Martin Scorsese's *Raging Bull.* The camera emphasizes the rectangular, boxlike confines of the apartment, as awful and miserable as Brando's room. The Bernstein score now reaffirms the tension and conflict between them through its harsh and pulsating quality. To the right of the screen, Brando batters the door off its frame and chain. To the left is Edie, all blond and white, looking like a kind of bird or creature in frightened retreat from the dark, intruding figure of Brando. His whole body dramatizes coiled inner tension, conflict, and turmoil. He is so violent and powerful and she so passive and vulnerable; yet there can be no doubt in this scene of her power to influence him through his developing conscience and love. Even in defensive retreat, Edie has the power to organize and direct Terry's emotions and actions. Wearing a white gown that matches the whiteness of her bed, she says without fear and with definite authority: "I want you to stay away from me." He gestures back with a wonderful rhetorical movement of his right arm as though addressing an enormous group and force: "I know what you want me to do, but I ain't gonna do it, so forget it." She moves from the bed: "You let your conscience tell you what to do." Looking like one besieged by a steady chaos of challenging doubts and fears, he yells back: "Will you shut up about that conscience. That's all I been hearing." The very explosiveness of his statement reveals his conflict and ambivalence, his inarticulate awareness of his dilemma. Interestingly, she responds that she has "never mentioned the word before," indicating how it now has become part of Terry's own inner thought processes and vocabulary. He screams at her, "Edie, you love me!" As she retreats into the interior rectangular space of the wretched flat, she articulates the complexity of the dilemma for Terry that love and emotion cannot always answer other issues of conscience and morality. "I didn't say I didn't love you. I said stay away from me," which of course proffers the very rejection that would now make Terry act as she would hope and expect, according to his conscience. Edie, who also is caught in her own conflicts involving her brother's death, genuinely desires such separation yet at the same time wants him for her own fulfillment. Terry responds in a way that dramatizes his dependence upon her: "I want you to say it to me." They kiss and collapse melodramatically into each other's arms behind a wall that holds a cross, the religious sign sealing the connection between their love and his mission of redemption. As they kiss, a mobster's voice calling Terry to find his dead brother's body echoes up through the alley and into the apartment, confirming the omniscience in this neighborhood of the mob as well as its shameless violence.

Moreover, this crucial scene in the apartment also signals the commingling of all the film's forces of love, sexuality, conscience, and social action. Terry's relationship to Edie complicates and intensifies his intention to act against the mob. Terry acts now out of his need for Edie's love and approval as well as his hatred of the mob that has killed their brothers. His decision indicates maturity and manhood – his break from the gang to act on his own inner values and beliefs.

Throughout the film, Edie has been both the motivating force and the vehicle in influencing and manipulating Terry's behavior. She has used love and desire to internalize a profound sense of guilt and conscience in Terry. Acting in concert with Father Barry, Edie has installed a conscience in Terry in a manner redolent of the influences of conscience upon Mark Twain's most important characters.

After this extraordinary development and buildup of moral character, Edie, in the final rooftop scene that opened this discussion, suddenly draws back. She tells Terry that he must consider his own safety and get away from all the unending dangers to him on the docks. Thinking of her possible future with him now that the men who killed her brother have been exposed, she says he might need to consider going inland to a farm. Brando merely repeats the one word "farm" with so much derision and disdain as to speak volumes. While her voice pleads off-screen, the camera focuses on Brando's lighted profile and shoulders as he sits crunched on the surface of the roof.

His body intimates the grief he feels over Tommy's slaughter of the birds and his own isolation as well as his growing resolution and determination. The mood of Bernstein's score also changes from the sadness that accompanies Terry's discovery of the dead birds to a more inspirational, martial sound of a trumpet evocative of a solitary power that slowly awakens and grows. Edie's desperate tones convey not just alarm and concern for his safety but also the added complexity of her own assertion of authority over him. As she talks and realizes that he is not really listening, her frustration suggests her emerging awareness that maybe she has succeeded too well in helping Terry to develop into his own man, beyond even her influence.

With the camera still in close-up on his face, the lighting, music, and dialogue articulate Terry's developing consciousness of his choice for action. He looks off, and the camera cuts to the harbor and a ship pulling out to sea. Whether coincidental or planned by Kazan, the vessel and its direction serve as a synoptic theme both for the film and for Kazan's life and career. In the scopic regime of Terry's gaze toward the harbor, the ship's movement out to sea and potentially away from America to Europe assumes special meaning. Terry's look indicates premeditated action, and the ship helps contextualize this impending action. In combination with Terry's decision to act and assert himself, the ship's pulling out constitutes a comment about American history. It opens a discussion about the exchange of culture and values between America and Europe and invites a reconsideration of the meaning of the entire journey to and settlement of America. The vision of the ship points to a need to revision America from the perspective of Europe and human history in general as a way to start rethinking the meaning of the American experience. In heading away from America and quite probably back to Europe, the action at this point in the film suggests a reconstruction in a grander way of Terry's journey, one that approximates Kazan's own experience. Terry will not retreat inland to a life on a farm; for him, it is ludicrous, inconsistent with all of his previous experience. In the light of his actions and development, the film can thus be seen as indicating not a retreat from America but a reaffirmation of the whole experience of making and discovering America.

With the music growing ever stronger, Terry rises to take up the longshoreman's hook that he has implanted like a weapon on the wooden door of the coop. The hook signifies Terry's work, his manhood, his wounds, and his impending martyrdom in the form of the beating he will receive from Johnny Friendly (Cobb) and his men. Anticipating and dreading such violence, Edie in the climactic roof scene exclaims, "What are you trying to prove?" He answers, "They always said I was a bum. Well, I ain't a bum, Edie. Don't worry, I'm not going to hurt nobody. I'm just going to go down there . . . and get my rights."

Throughout the film, Brando has played Terry as a kind of dull thinker, an introvert who mulls things over but never has had the opportunity until meeting Edie to express his inner thoughts and feelings. Accustomed to taking second place to his older brother, who also has been mocked by Friendly as a "deep thinker," Terry now can assume his place as a man and speak his own mind. Pondering his decision to challenge Friendly, Terry pauses and faces Edie, no longer afraid to confront either her or himself. He nods "Okay" and scratches at the jacket of martyrdom that, as noted above, has been passed from Joey Doyle to "Kayo" Dugan and now to Terry, who will wear it in the fight on the dock with the mob in the concluding scene. As Hey writes:

> In the final scene, these visual and verbal references come into play. As Terry staggers to the warehouse door to meet the awaiting gray-haired man, he carries the longshoreman's hook, a suggestion of the cross Christ carried as well as the burden placed on the shoulders of longshoremen. Terry wears a sacred cloth, the coat worn by previous martyrs. He is bleeding about the head, a visual allusion to the crown of thorns, and is enervated from the beating (flagellation) he has just received. Edie, who has by now fused the contradictory roles of lover and saint, tries to help Terry, but is restrained by Father Barry, who urges Malloy forward to his duty. He leads the longshoremen – the rejuvenated flock – to work while the scarred and evil Johnny Friendly remains outside the closing doors.[5]

Of course, Terry Malloy's story of achieving his individuality and independence as a man and citizen by informing against the mob has been widely interpreted as a surrogate narrative for Kazan's own experience in 1952 before the House Un-American Activities Committee (HUAC) of "naming names" and informing on former friends and colleagues who were either in the Communist Party or sympathetic to the communists. The events involving Kazan's relationship to the left and to HUAC have been documented, discussed, and debated by many, including Victor Navasky in considerable detail in *Naming Names;* moreover, Hey has done especially well in relating those historic events to the film itself.[6] However, the connection between *On the Waterfront* and Kazan's role as an informer before HUAC needs to be placed in the context of Kazan's life and work as well as the historic context of the times.

An Anatolian Greek born in 1909 in Istanbul, Turkey, Kazan came to America when he was four years old. After working his way through Williams College and Yale Drama School, he became part of the Group Theatre in New York City during the 1930s. Certainly one of the most innovative radical theater movements in American history, the Group Theatre was a source of creative dramatic energy that influenced the American stage for decades. Some of the most important talent in American theater, such as left-wing playwright Clifford Odets, emerged from this group. During this peri-

Figure 12. On his way to becoming a man and getting his rights, Terry Malloy (Marlon Brando) looks for his own truth and purpose with Edie Doyle (Eva Marie Saint), the force of conscience in *On the Waterfront* (Columbia/Sam Spiegel: The Museum of Modern Art Film Stills Archive).

od, Kazan joined the Communist Party. A member for less than two years, from 1934 to 1936, he left largely out of political and artistic frustration, especially bristling under the group's collective sense of intellectual and artistic regimentation. Although not a communist, he kept his left-wing sympathies and his aesthetic of social and political realism throughout the 1940s. In 1947 he helped found, with Robert Lewis and Cheryl Crawford, the extraordinarily important Actors' Studio that would, under the later directorship of Lee Strasberg, make the Stanislavski-based "Method" of acting so vital in America. It achieved unprecedented prominence largely through the work of such actors as Brando, Paul Newman, Montgomery Clift, Joanne Woodward, Lee Grant, Lee J. Cobb, James Dean, Shelley Winters, and Julie Harris.[7] During this period of the late 1940s, Kazan directed America's most important and successful plays on Broadway, such as *Death of a Salesman* (1949) and *A Streetcar Named Desire* (1947), and then directed films of comparable impact and significance. At the time, he could easily have been considered the country's most successful and important director.

Soon, however, the deepening hostilities between the East and West in the emerging Cold War and the resulting Red Scare of investigation at home changed or influenced the lives of most people connected with politics and the dramatic or cinematic arts in New York and Hollywood. Kazan developed a genuine distrust of the Soviet Union because of its aggressive Cold War activities, and an equally authentic dislike for communists at home for what he saw as their regimented and conformist loyalty to the party in Moscow; however, not until the Red Scare hearings and the HUAC investigations brought the situation to a domestic crisis did he have to deal with the matter. He hated the repressive threats of blacklisting and witch-hunting but also felt uncomfortable with what he sensed was either the arrogant elitism of some left-wingers, like Lillian Hellman, or the naïveté of some who had been his closest friends and associates, such as playwright Arthur Miller. Refusing to testify could mean sacrificing his future for people and a cause he detested; testifying would change his relationship to the creative community for the rest of his life and potentially leave him uncertain as to his own integrity, courage, authenticity. In a famous quote, he later said: "I went through that thing and it was painful and difficult and not the thing I'm proudest of in my life, but it's also not something I'm ashamed of."[8] As Hey says, "No doubt, Kazan confronted his unfortunate role as friendly witness with the perspective that he was trapped between two opposing and irreconcilable forces of evil, neither of which deserved his allegiance."[9] He testified twice in 1952, on 14 January and 9 April.

Although neither his appearance nor his friendly testimony was unusual at this time, Kazan did in fact take the unique step after his second testimony of publishing an advertisement-statement in the *New York Times* on 12 April 1952 as a way of responding to the "intolerable rumors about my political position [that] have been circulating in New York and Hollywood." The ad was both defensive and aggressive in justifying his action. Maintaining that "secrecy serves the Communists" and that supporting "the Communist Party is to have a taste of the police state," Kazan wrote:

> I believe that Communist activities confront the people of this country with an unprecedented and exceptionally tough problem. That is, how to protect ourselves from a dangerous and alien conspiracy and still keep the free, open, healthy way of life that gives us self-respect.[10]

Though Navasky claims that over the years the director became diffident about his testimony and hence tended to decline "to discuss his twenty-odd-year-old decision to name names," Kazan in fact expounds upon it in his autobiography with some of the vigor and self-confidence he demonstrated decades earlier in the *New York Times*. He emphasizes that "I had no regrets about my own actions" and "The truth is that within a year I stopped feeling guilty or even embarrassed about what I'd done . . ." (*Life* 463, 465).

At the same time, this assertion of a relaxed state of mind about testifying seems somewhat disingenuous in its contradiction of his comments about the experience in his extended interview in 1971 with one of his strongest critical advocates, Michel Ciment of France. He told Ciment: "I don't think there's anything in my life toward which I have more ambivalence, because, obviously, there's something disgusting about giving other people's names." On the other hand, he also emphasized in the interview, "I was convinced that the Soviet empire was monolithic":

> Since then, I've had two feelings. One feeling is that what I did was repulsive, and the opposite feeling, when I see what the Soviet Union has done to its writers, and their death camps, the Nazi pact and the Polish and Czech repression.

He also admitted how much of the "personal element" of his feelings of rejection by the party years earlier had played into his decision. He felt the party required conformity, obedience, and subservience from its members and adherents. Morever, "[t]here was no doubt that there was a vast organization which was making fools of the liberals in Hollywood." Kazan therefore had felt compelled, as he told Ciment, to refuse to act and perform as the party required: "But I would rather do what I did than crawl in front of a ritualistic Left and lie the way those other comrades did, and betray my own soul. I didn't betray it."[11]

Kazan's situation in this great crisis of belief, action, and conscience left him with an abiding sense of bitterness that he manifests in his insistence in his autobiography that the artistic and commercial success of *On the Waterfront* constituted a personal triumph and vindication for him: "So when critics say that I put my story and my feelings on the screen, to justify my informing, they are right. That transference of emotion from my own experience to the screen is the merit of those scenes" (*Life* 500). *On the Waterfront* received Academy Awards for best picture, screenplay, direction, photography, art direction, and leading actor and actress, as well as nominations for Bernstein, Cobb, Steiger, and Malden. For Kazan, these awards became badges of pride for his own troubled sense of honor. He took them as signs of moral and personal achievement as well as artistic triumph.

Kazan's feelings of vindication that grew out of this extraordinary success seem understandable and psychologically necessary considering the intensity of the anger, disappointment, and contempt so many felt and expressed toward him, first because of the way he informed and then because of his "chutzpah" over the way he publically defended his action. It also should be noted that Kazan's exceptional power and influence at that time as a direc-

tor marked his actions for special attention and comment. The intensity of
the bitter hatred directed toward him at the time can be sensed even today:
Nearly fifty years later, many in the Hollywood establishment not only could
not find it in themselves to overlook Kazan's past by awarding him the American Film Institute's Lifetime Achievement Award, but also used the repeated rejection of him for the award to reopen old wounds and reignite lingering moral outrage against him.[12] In confirming at various times that *On the
Waterfront* served as his vehicle for justifying himself during the early 1950s,
Kazan validated, as he notes, what had been a fairly obvious theory about
the film really since its release. As Navasky wrote years before the publication of Kazan's autobiography,

> Indeed, it can be argued that his film *On the Waterfront,* with its screenplay by
> Budd Schulberg (who also named names), makes the definitive case for the HUAC
> informer or at least is – among its considerable other achievements – a valiant
> attempt to complicate the public perception of the issue. The image of the inform-
> er is transformed from thirties-[Victor] McLaglen to fifties-Brando.[13]

Navasky's patronizing tone in this statement, made nearly thirty years after
the film's appearance, portends the recent actions by the American Film Institute and helps explain the depth of Kazan's ties to *On the Waterfront* as
a personal statement of moral and aesthetic vindication. Navasky also seems
to relish delineating the derision over the years that has been heaped upon
Kazan by those who felt betrayed by him and considered themselves morally superior to him as victims or as sympathizers of victims.[14]

The significance of *On the Waterfront* in Kazan's life and career is particularly well suggested by his use of the words "ritualistic" and "soul" in his
interview with Ciment. It can be argued that in the context of Kazan's agony
and anguish involved in his testifying experience, the film became not only
a justification and explanation for his action but also a ritual as part of a
broader and ambitious new search for identity and purpose. He was abandoning one system of belief and body of ritual for another, trading in lingering nostalgia toward the proletarian passion of the Left for a new idealism
about another political religion: America. In this light, *On the Waterfront*
becomes a transitional film that functions for Kazan as an important bridge
to personal fulfillment and identity within a refurbished American ideology.

In contrast to communism, the American ideology emphasizes values of individualism and self-reliance that more accurately reflected Kazan's beliefs and felt experience as he matured and succeeded: "I am an American, with a shameless drive for achievement and an aggressive stance in the world" (*Life* 218).

Accordingly, when Terry in the final rooftop scene looks off, sees a ship leaving the harbor, and thoughtfully informs Edie that he is going to get his rights regardless of the cost, it seems justified to argue that what appears to mark a culmination and climax in Terry's life also promises a transition and a new beginning for Kazan. Terry, who has boxed for others and made a spectacle and object of himself as a fighter, must now fight for himself. A neighborhood tough, he must undergo an initiaton into manhood in the sense of gaining identity, independence, and moral authority, all of the things the mob has tried to squeeze out of him. As Hey suggests, the "ritualized scene" in this final segment primarily concerns Terry's quest for his "rights"; but the search for rights in this film also involves achieving a new identity and value system.[15] In the parlance of the film, for Schulberg and Kazan, gaining manhood for Terry means acting on his obsession with overcoming the stigma of being a "bum."

For Kazan, Terry's declaration to Johnny Friendly, when they fight at the end of the movie, that "I'm glad what I done" constitutes a breaking of the bonds of the past, a snapping of the chains of a perverted and conformist conscience imposed on the individual by any group to secure unthinking loyalty. Through Terry, Kazan clearly hoped to exorcise the remaining shadow of the Left from his own psyche. The strength of the continued hold on him by old allies in the Left manifested itself in the energy behind his wish to get back at them through his triumph – suggesting that at some level he still valued their approval but also wanted to see them suffer for their attitude and actions toward him. Kazan writes:

> When Brando, at the end, yells at Lee J. Cobb, the mob boss, "I'm glad what I done – you hear me? – glad what I done!" that was me saying, with identical heat, that I was glad I'd testified as I had. I'd been snubbed by friends each and every day for many months in my old show business haunts, and I'd not forgotten nor would I forgive the men, old friends some of them, who'd snubbed me, so the scene in the film where Brando goes back to the waterfront to "shape up" again for employment and is rejected by men with whom he'd worked day after day – that, too, was my story, now told to all the world. (*Life* 500)

In breaking free and beginning a new phase of freedom, Kazan also initiated a journey and process of dual discovery and reinvention of both himself and America. In his mind, the two become interlocked and inseparable: Kazan and America. The meaning of his journey that begins with his work on *On the Waterfront* becomes clear in his attitude and feeling toward a film he made nine years later, *America, America* (1963). In his autobiography he asserts, *"America, America* is my favorite film," and *"America, America* is now my favorite of the films I've made" (*Life* 629, 658). The personal, aesthetic, and ideological significance of the film indicates that Kazan's journey involved moving into the future by revisiting the past. For Kazan, the physical counterpart of the spiritual, intellectual, and ideological journey of *America, America* began in 1955 the year after the release of *On the Waterfront.* It involved a return to Turkey and his roots; Kazan himself describes the venture in terms of a metaphorical "search for a new path" (*Life* 546). It was "about my uncle's journey from Kayseri to America; it would be the basis for the film *America, America"* (*Life* 615). The path and journey of the personal search also marked the beginning of preproduction for that film, which Kazan wrote and directed. He notes,

> For years I'd been thinking there might be a fine film, and one I had to make, in the story of my uncle Avraam Kazanjioglou, known in the rug trade as A. E. ("Joe") Kazan, who managed to come to this country at the age of twenty, put together some dollars, and in time brought his brother, my father, across the water, then, one after the other, the rest of the family – his sister, his half-brothers, and his stepmother, Evanthia, my favorite of them all. (*Life* 546)

An amalgamation of fact, history, autobiography, fiction, and immigration saga, *America, America* turns the individual's journey into the universal myth of coming to America. Shot in black and white with classic documentary footage of the immigrant passage, the film's narrative structure is framed by Kazan's authoritative voice-over and strong presence in the beginning and end. We get Kazan's story but also the story of America intermixed as one and the same.

At the core of the film rests Kazan's realization of the personal meaning to him, and the universal meaning to the world, of the myth and ideology of regeneration in the New World. To make this film of immigration, he returns to his roots in Turkey and discovers repeatedly what he could have been if not for America.

> I have many memories of that trip, but the most important one was my encounter with my cousin Stellio Yeremia, and the recognition I had that this man, almost precisely my age, was the self I would have been if I'd not been brought to America by my father. I found my discarded self. (*Life* 547)

Kazan later repeats the same thought with a bit more detail:

> If George Kazan had not brought his wife and two sons to America in 1913, I could have been there now, dressed as my cousin was dressed, hustling everywhere as he hustled everywhere, "invisible." If it hadn't been for my father's courage – a quality I had not until that day associated with him – I'd now be what my cousin was. (*Life* 643)

For Kazan, the cousin who stayed behind in Europe becomes a kind of alter ego, the "discarded self" who represents some lasting sense of his own identity. This discarded self in Europe becomes a new focal point in Kazan's world, concentrating his vision and imagination. He needs to go back to see what was lost and discarded to appreciate not only what he has but also what was personally lost and gained in America, including for him and the country during the Red Scare. Considering Kazan's confrontation with his lost self in Europe, we can gain further insight into the meaning of Terry's look from the roof to the harbor in *On the Waterfront*. In going to get his rights, he walks, as Father Barry urges, on his own two feet like his own man; but he also begins a process of revisioning America for himself and others as well. *On the Waterfront* and *America, America* become stories of individual renewal in American culture.

So to find America – to understand better the dream of self-creation in America – Kazan reverses the classic immigrant's journey to rediscover what was left behind in the Old World. Interestingly, his discarded self also entails a return of the Freudian "uncanny"; it is a hidden, unconscious self that never leaves but marks a permanent vacancy and negativity for Kazan, the hungry self of every outsider and immigrant to America.

However, before making the film of the return to Europe that would signal his second coming to America, Kazan undertook a thorough examination of conditions in America, as though to exhaust the sources at home for renewal. His explorations at home before *America, America* suggest patterns in social and cultural life of rigidity and stultification that were recalcitrant to reform and renewal. In his first great commercial and critical triumph as a film director, *Gentleman's Agreement* (1947), Kazan presented an aspect of New York life residing at the top of liberal and professional urban America. Based on the best-selling novel by Laura Z. Hobson, the film anticipates beautifully the marriage in contemporary culture of art and politics through the stylish and fashionable packaging of popular culture, liberalism, education, and reform. Gregory Peck's character represents the intellectual and cultural elite: A Gentile reformer and journalist working on a magazine series on anti-Semitism, he typifies a classic urban/suburban aristocracy. Besides so effectively representing a certain segment of the New York elite, the film also documents the emergence of Jews as a liberal force for democratization and change throughout society by its development of John Garfield's role as Peck's friend, a Jewish veteran who cannot find housing for his family because of anti-Semitism. With *Gentleman's Agreement* Kazan received his first Academy Award for direction; the picture also earned an Oscar for best film and received nominations for many of its performers. Interestingly, *Gentleman's Agreement* contains what must be one of the first proclamations in a public medium of self-initiated affirmative action: After becoming aware of the institutional anti-Semitism in the hiring practices of his own organization, the well-intentioned publisher of Peck's magazine decides to hire Jews aggressively to create better ethnic representation among his employees.

Kazan dramatized this New York intellectual, cultural, and social elite in *Gentleman's Agreement* after making *The People of the Cumberlands* (1937) and *A Tree Grows in Brooklyn* (1945) about people who are much closer to ordinary folk. From the world of fashionable liberalism in *Gentleman's Agreement,* Kazan's films from the late 1940s through *America, America* in the mid-1960s comprise a domestic survey of America that reflects his original proclivities toward social realism. A continuum of films covering a broad range of important American social and cultural themes can be discerned from *A Tree Grows in Brooklyn* and *Gentleman's Agreement* to an aesthetic highpoint and climax in *On the Waterfront* and on to his final films. These themes include race in *Pinky* (1949), underground urban life in *Panic in the Streets* (1950), sexuality and repression in *A Streetcar Named Desire* (1952) and *Baby Doll* (1956), the family and the West in *East of Eden* (1955), the corruption of politics and media in *A Face in the Crowd* (1957), loss of place and identity in *Wild River* (1960), and love and adolescence in *Splendor in the Grass* (1961). There also are important diversions to Mexico in *Viva Zapata!* (1952), concerning peasant revolutions, and to Eastern Europe in *Man on a Tightrope* (1952), about communist repression.

After this extensive tour of America as a social condition and cultural phenomenon, Kazan still felt compelled in *America, America* to seek out his so-called discarded self in Europe as a means to understand his own identity and relationship to America. The discarded self Kazan finds in Europe becomes a kind of a primal psychic force for an education in the myth and ideology of America. Considering the film's title, it is ironic that all of *America, America* takes place in Europe or at sea, except for the final sequences of the journey and deliverance to America and New York. The absence of America as a physical presence through almost all of the film emphasizes and dramatizes America as an idea and a vision of the European mind and imagination.

In contrast to the vision and dream of America, *America, America* documents Europe as a series of endless prisons of ethnicity and gender. Conceived and developed by Kazan, *America, America* presents individual and group ethnic origins in Europe as an inescapable destiny and catastrophe for freedom. The Greek minority remains Greek forever without any real equality or opportunity to achieve true security and advancement; Turks are Turks – always dominant and in charge as the majority and the power in their own country; and Armenians, tragically, are condemned to powerlessness and perennial victimization. A suffocating atmosphere of oppression, denial, poverty, and hopelessness, therefore, consumes the film. Even an unattractive character like the young hero's father, among so many other unhappy figures in the film, becomes sympathetic in his failed efforts to overcome his ignorance and limitations in order to make the best decisions for his family. Obsessed with his paternal responsibilities, he operates in real darkness. The very boundaries and enclosures of culture, economics, thought, and life make it impossible to acquire the knowledge to crumble those confining walls. In *America, America,* however, the greatest constriction of life and possibility falls upon the women, who exist in near servitude. This depiction of women in the film contrasts with what seems to be Kazan's predominantly sexist attitude toward women as detailed in his autobiography.

The cinematography and editing of *America, America* dramatize the rigid ethnic and gender boundaries that help make change and growth impossible. Kazan's signature style exploits the potential of light and shadows in black-and-white filming and editing to emphasize the sense of entrapment and enclosure in Europe. The aesthetics of the film perfectly cohere with this contrast of ideologies between oppressive Europe and America as the land of rebirth. Years of filming in black and white to achieve a sense of social realism culminate in *America, America.*

As a result of the palpable oppression of Europe, *America, America* becomes a visual celebration of an ideology of consensus and renewal in America. It dramatizes what Werner Sollors sees as the dangers of institutionalizing myths of special ethnic origins based on ideologies of biological and ethnic determinism.[16] The film articulates a visual argument for dissent over descent, to use Sollors's terms; that is, the importance to freedom of individual rights to dissent, as opposed to rigid traditions of origins and descent that define life for everyone forever. *America, America* advertises the importance, to paraphrase Ben Wattenberg, of universalism.[17]

America, America proffers a response to Terry Malloy and others like him in suggesting where they can go for their rights – to help create a culture that venerates the individual, a society of the marginalized that retains its open frontiers of opportunity of various kinds for all. Thus, Terry Malloy's desire to escape the shabbiness of his existence and achieve a form of rebirth into manhood involves a search for a cultural ideology to cultivate and engender such transformation. In *A Life,* Kazan discusses the theme of regeneration in *On the Waterfront* in terms of religious redemption, an idea that suggests the existence of a broader system of belief beyond just the individual. Redemption, he says, strikes home to the hopes of people in general and helps to explain the success of *On the Waterfront.* "My guess is that it's the theme, that of a man who has sinned and is redeemed" (*Life* 528). He adds, "Redemption, isn't that the promise of the Catholic Church? That a man can turn his fate around and by an act of good heart be saved at last? . . . Yes, that a man can, no matter what he's done be redeemed – particularly if he has a sympathetic young woman as his confessor" (*Life* 528). Certainly part of the originality of *On the Waterfront* derives from its dramatization of that yearning for redemption, including the linkage of redemption to love and sexuality, as Kazan suggests, in the Terry and Edie relationship. However, the genius of *America, America* puts that yearning within a historic and cultural context. Similarly, it also needs to be noted that another element of the special success of *On the Waterfront* involves the way it embodies the yearning for redemption and its fulfillment in Brando. Through his own body, figure, manner, and action, Brando institutes a theme of regeneration. Partly because of the triumph of the interaction between him and Eva Marie Saint, Brando achieves a transforming performance as an actor that sustains and reinforces the change that Terry undergoes.

Brando not only portrays Terry so well, he also helps to alter, through his acting, the ideology of heroic masculinity in America. Although his was but one of many acting triumphs in *On the Waterfront*, Brando gave the only performance, it can be argued, that helped install in the culture a new articulation of masculinity – one that has changed acting in America and also remained a major influence upon gender. His unique sensitivity in *On the Waterfront* certainly undermines any unitary and monolithic masculinism that, it has been said, pervaded Hollywood's representations of masculinity – with several notable exceptions, such as many of Jimmy Stewart's performances. Brando in this film especially becomes an oppositional character who challenges stereotypes and conventions about sexuality and gender. To Graham McCann much of Brando's strength in his performance comes from the introduction of bisexuality into his character.[18] Certainly, for Brando and all of those he has influenced, from James Dean to Al Pacino and Robert De-Niro, a new attitude of openness and experimentation toward gender and sexuality contributes to the power of their rebelliousness and nonconformity as actors and stars. In ways that certainly seem unthinkable for classic Hollywood representations of masculinity by such figures as John Wayne, Clark Gable, or Spencer Tracy, Brando's efforts to signify his inner feelings through speech, facial expression, and his body indicate a new direction in expressing masculinity in film and the culture. Along with Montgomery Clift during this era, Brando helps articulate a new kind of American hero, with a depth of sensitivity and vulnerability that has established a new standard for characterization and performance. As McCann states, "*On the Waterfront* witnessed the affirmation of Brando's unique gift as an actor and, in the character of Terry Malloy, introduced one of Hollywood's definitive rebel males."[19]

Perhaps with a somewhat uncharacteristic generosity, Kazan credits Brando with such great genius and innovation in his portrayal of Terry Malloy that one almost could forget how instrumental Kazan was in helping to conceive and then construct this new model for heroic masculinity in America. Speaking particularly about the famous scene between Brando and Steiger in the back of a car, when Brando gives his memorable speech about being a "contenda," Kazan says:

> But of course the extaordinary element in that scene and in the whole picture was Brando, and what was extraordinary about his performance, I feel, is the contrast of the tough-guy front and the extreme delicacy and gentle cast of his behavior. What other actor, when his brother draws a pistol to force him to do something shameful, would put his hand on the gun and push it away with the gentleness of a caress? Who else could read "Oh, Charlie!" in a tone of reproach that is so loving and so melancholy and suggests that terrific depth of pain? I didn't direct that; Marlon showed me, as he often did, how the scene should be performed. I could never have told him how to do that scene as well as he did it. The same kind of surprising delicacy appears in his performance at the other most unlikely moment, when he finds his dead brother hanging from a meat hook in the alley. The first thing Brando does when he sees the body is not touch it. The body is hanging there and Marlon simply comes up alongside, putting his hand on the wall and leaning against it. He doesn't look at the body, but you know very well what he's feeling. (*Life* 525)

Leaving aside Kazan's self-deprecation, modesty, and generosity, it should be recalled that Brando has never matched his performance in *On the Waterfront,* his last effort under Kazan's direction. Instead, in the years since that film, the sensitivity and inner feeling that characterized his originality as an actor often have recoiled into a kind of chaos and loss – a form of rebellion without coherence, meaning, or direction. This inconsistency and diminution of his powers of performance in films with directors other than Kazan suggest his own reliance upon the director who worked with him in *A Streetcar Named Desire* and *On the Waterfront.*

Thus, it seems to me that the fluidity, elasticity, and experimentation of Brando's acting style achieved coherence and substance partly because of Kazan. Their relationship clearly involved mutual discovery and support. Together they reconsidered and reorganized the ideology of heroic masculinity in America as part of a reconstruction of the ideology and myth of America. For Brando and Kazan, heroic masculinity involves the exhibitionism of revealing the depths of one's pain rather than dissimulating that pain as classic hard-boiled masculinity. For Kazan and Brando, structuring and presenting the emotional and psychic costs of attaining masculinity qualify as success in acting and performance. Moreover, Kazan's direction helps to make Brando's isolation and loneliness more than a merely personal statement of despair. In *On the Waterfront,* Terry's relationship with Edie and the rhetorical strategy of Father Barry's jeremiad of redemption through reform and conscience place Terry's quest for individual identity and manhood within a greater American ideology of regeneration and consensus.

Terry's isolation recalls the crisis of Marshal Kane in *High Noon*. Although so much separates them, similarities remain. So different from the emotional solidity, paternal security, and moral independence of Gary Cooper in *High Noon*, Brando in *On the Waterfront* shares Marshal Kane's isolation over conscience. They both ultimately act on individual conscience against overwhelming odds of hostility and indifference.

Moreover, both Cooper and Brando are in the ironic positions of embodying their communities through their separation from them. They both find their internal struggles over conscience and action manifested and externalized in solitary walks on the periphery of the communities and people they represent. Their walks enact rituals of individual initiation that merge with rituals of cultural regeneration. They each signify the American as the loner, the liminal figure who brings powers of regeneration to his culture. Once again, the embodiment of the radical individual symbolizes cultural definition and meaning. By registering independence, self-reliance, and individual conscience, the hero achieves a form of rebirth and inspires regeneration in the national community. In the differences between them, Brando and Cooper promulgate a multiplicity of masculinities in American culture. They represent a broadening of heroic masculinity within a changing cultural context that includes sexual and gender diversity. As Pauline Kael says, "Brando represented a contemporary version of the free American."[20] Thus, the radical differences between Cooper and Brando in age, style, and cultural position suggest the range of the American cultural consensus. The representation by both Cooper and Brando of heroic masculinity in America makes one of the strongest arguments for the potential diversity of the American idea.

Among the directors in our study of the Hollywood Renaissance, Elia Kazan most immediately and personally advocated the idea of America in his films. Probably more than any of these other directors, he needed to find and create in the democratic cinema of his own invention a new self to regain the identity that he had lost through more than one discarded and abandoned self in his life. His construction of a unique democratic aesthetic of the common man paralleled his rediscovery of America for himself and for much of his generation. One of his greatest achievements in this simultaneous reconstruction of himself and his culture concerns his dramatization of the costs as well as the rewards to others, himself, and the country of that aesthetic and cultural construction.

CHAPTER 6

LOSING TOMORROW: GEORGE STEVENS AND THE AMERICAN IDEA

Women and Men of the Year

The five directors discussed in this study so far were all instrumental in creating a special period of artistic innovation in American cultural and film history. Beginning in the mid-1930s, John Ford, Frank Capra, Howard Hawks, Fred Zinnemann, and Elia Kazan achieved the kind of cultural renewal through film that earlier generations of Americans accomplished in literature, art, and thought. They created a democratic cinema of aesthetic complexity and depth during a time of extended and deadly challenge to democracy by totalitarianism abroad and antidemocratic movements at home. In contrast to the propagandistic cinema of totalitarian regimes, ideology and art cohere in their films to appeal to and challenge the general public as well as sophisticated *cinéphiles* of film and modernism. Advancing cinema as a heterogeneous art form of multiple channels of expression, these directors in the renaissance made films that are intertwined with American life, sometimes repeating and dramatizing some of the worst elements of the culture, such as the perpetuation of racist ways of thinking and acting. Thus, the artistic genius of these filmmakers and their focus on America make them the core of the Hollywood Renaissance.

George Stevens completes this group of directors. American culture, character, and history form the heart of Stevens's cinematic consciousness. His career extends from the era of classic Hollywood cinema to his less significant work during the last days of the Hollywood Renaissance in the mid-1960s. His artistic achievement, the range and depth of his works on America, and his influence upon Hollywood cinema and the film industry render him an important member of the renaissance.

Along with Stevens and the other directors in this study, many more directors also contributed to the cultural, aesthetic, and intellectual environment that made the Hollywood Renaissance. Such ethnics and roughnecks as John Huston, William Wyler, Billy Wilder, William Wellman, Preston Sturges (born Edmond P. Biden), and John Sturges, among many others, helped shape the renaissance. They all were brilliantly creative innovators and artistic leaders. Such works as Wyler's *The Best Years of Our Lives* (1946), Huston's *The Treasure of the Sierra Madre* (1948), Wellman's *The Ox-Bow Incident* (1943), and innumerable other films by these and other directors are indispensable works in this movement.

However, what distinguishes Stevens and the other major renaissance directors as a movement concerns their creation of an extended body of work that strives to engage all of the American experience. Artistic and cultural consciousness commingle. Their democratic aesthetic relates artistic originality to cultural renewal. Like the other renaissance directors, Stevens merges his sustained aesthetic achievement over so many years with exploring the uniqueness of American culture and character.

At the same time, Stevens ultimately occupies a special place in the Hollywood Renaissance by anticipating in his work the severity of the pending break between culture and consensus. His films often evidence the slippage concerning the capacity of the ideology of consensus to contain a changing American culture. Stevens's efforts over nearly three decades to articulate and visualize an ideology of consensus – which culminate in his classic epic of 1956, *Giant* – ultimately expose the incipient fractures and fissures in this order of values and belief, especially in regard to race but also concerning women, ethnicity, and class. Stevens's dominant aesthetic parallels his search for ideological cohesion. His style tends to emphasize in-depth, carefully structured compositions and an assiduously constructed visual order within a frame that encloses tension and controls change. The style becomes a counterpart to the ideology of consensus.

As noted at the beginning of this study, the most obvious weakness of the Hollywood Renaissance concerns the inadequate way it often tends to deal with race as well as gender. As was the case in the American Renaissance in literature and art a century earlier, the filmmakers of the later renaissance often tend to elide race in America from adequate consideration, thereby subverting and contradicting the idealism of the American idea. The insult of omission compounds the insults of denigration and subjugation. At times, films throughout this movement, by directors even of the stature of John Ford and Frank Capra, marginalize and promulgate stereotypes about African Americans, other minorities, or women. Such treatment of women and minorities also occurs in some of Stevens's films: His camera at times includes gender and race by dehumanizing and objectifying women and blacks. Some of his films dissemble their own prejudices as humor and trivialize the problems facing these groups. These kinds of representation highlight the intrinsic liberal dilemma of the conflict between belief and practice, exposing the crisis at the heart of the quest for consensus concerning the need for change and reform to include women and people of color. In much of his work, Stevens's conscious construction of consensus often exposes the failure of the liberal imagination to invent new structures and to consider new concepts for dealing with gender and race. The multiple visual and verbal texts of these films indicate the difficulty of revisioning and reconstructing a liberal ideology that incorporates people of color and independent women.

In spite of difficulties with assimilating difference into his frame of consensus, Stevens's artistic diversity in Hollywood challenges easy categorization of his work. Totally committed to film as an art form and to American film as an expression of a unique culture, he also directed many of Hollywood's most successful films. Working brilliantly in many different genres, his acclaimed films, ranging from the great musical *Swing Time* (1936) to the celebrated western *Shane* (1953), seriously engage critical and cultural consciousness. Thus, both his work and Stevens as an individual need further study and consideration.

Stevens himself stood out significantly as a unique individual in Hollywood. His special qualities of character made him a major force and leader in the film industry. The nature of Stevens's involvement in World War II and in the situation in Hollywood during the Cold War are of special importance in explaining his reputation and place in film and cultural history. His heroism and dedication to his mission and craft as a filmmaker in the Second World War and his role in Hollywood during the tumultuous days of blacklists, McCarthyism, and loyalty oaths suggest a great deal about him as a man and a director in the Hollywood Renaissance.

During the Red Scare in 1950, the conservative director Cecil B. DeMille, as discussed in Chapter 4, led an attempt to purge the Screen Directors Guild of America of people with either current or past sympathies for the Left. DeMille hoped to institute such political cleansing by listing all guild members who refused to sign a loyalty oath, intending to forward these names to the heads of all the Hollywood studios. Acting in concert with the House Un-American Activities Committee, DeMille also planned to include on that list the names of those people who were called to testify before that committee. The controversy over DeMille and the loyalty oath reached a climax at a historic and contentious guild meeting on 22 October 1950, when such figures as John Ford and Joseph L. Mankiewicz, the president of the guild and winner of several Academy Awards, all opposed DeMille's efforts. At the meeting, Stevens addressed DeMille, who had offended many with his insinuations of disloyalty concerning people with foreign-sounding names or liberal leanings: "By the way, C.B., when I was up to my ass in mud at Bastogne, how were the capital gains doing back home?"[1]

Stevens's pointed and powerful statement refers to the fact that whereas a superpatriot like DeMille had stayed home and prospered during World War II, Stevens from almost the very beginning of America's entry into the war had led in filming and documenting it, often under seriously dangerous combat conditions. From D-Day to the liberation of Paris and the fighting in between, to the gruesome and momentous combat at the Battle of the Bulge, to the liberation of Dachau concentration camp just a week before the German surrender, Stevens and his crew were there. As his son, George Stevens, Jr., reports, "In 1942 he joined the Army and was assigned by General Eisenhower to organize the motion picture coverage of the war in Europe. He assembled a team that shot much of the 35mm black-and-white film that we saw in the newsreels."[2]

George Stevens, Jr., joins others in arguing that the war made an important division in his father's work. He says about George Stevens's wartime experience, "Like others who served overseas he had changed. His changes were in his mind and in his heart and would show in his work."[3] Donald Richie, in his monograph on Stevens, also asserts a "postwar change" in the filmmaker.[4] Stevens's most memorable work before the war includes *Alice Adams* (1936), a story about growing up poor in a small town and a major vehicle for continuing Katharine Hepburn's rise to stardom; *Swing Time* (1936), a classic musical with Fred Astaire and Ginger Rogers that remains one of their greatest triumphs; *Gunga Din* (1939), a romance of India with Cary Grant, Victor McLaglen, Joan Fontaine; *Penny Serenade* (1941), about the difficulties of a young married couple, played by Cary Grant and Irene Dunne; and most important, *Woman of the Year* (1942), a very successful romantic comedy with Katharine Hepburn and Spencer Tracy, during the shooting of which they began their off-screen affair.

Stevens's major works after the war were, as his son says, "films that drew on his time at war and they were deeper than his prewar work."[5] These classic films now include what has come to be known as his American Trilogy, which surveys in depth the meaning of the American experience: *A Place in the Sun* (1951), an extraordinary film, very loosely based on Theodore Dreiser's *An American Tragedy*, that earned Stevens his first Academy Award for direction and includes a truly significant performance by Montgomery Clift as a sensitive loner as well as an impressive effort by Elizabeth Taylor; *Shane* (1953), an archetypal western, based on Jack Shaefer's novel, that starred Alan Ladd in probably his greatest role and received Academy Award nominations for Stevens and two of the cast, Jack Palance and Brandon de Wilde, as well as another for screenwriter A. B. Guthrie, Jr.; and *Giant* (1956), an acclaimed epic film, inspired by Edna Ferber's novel, for which Stevens garnered his second Academy Award for direction. The cast of *Giant* included Rock Hudson and James Dean, both of whom were nominated for awards, in addition to Elizabeth Taylor and Dennis Hopper. The film marked Dean's last performance before dying in an automobile crash. Other major postwar

Stevens films were *I Remember Mama* (1948), *The Diary of Anne Frank* (1959), and *The Greatest Story Ever Told* (1965). Many scholars and critics of American cinema believe Stevens achieved and maintained both artistic excellence and aesthetic integrity in the periods before and after the war. He always worked with extraordinary intensity. For example, a standard film encyclopedia notes of Stevens:

> Stevens was one of Hollywood's least productive directors in the quantitative sense. Intent on perfection and visual authenticity, he would spend many months, sometimes years, on pre-and post-production. He reportedly covered every scene from any possible angle, shooting at a ratio much greater than deemed necessary by most Hollywood directors. But the results, more often than not, justified the extra investment in time and money and Stevens scored a remarkably high average both with critics and with ticket buyers. For most of his career his work was held in continuous high esteem by the American critical establishment, although his reputation suffered a decline in the 60s. . . .[6]

Of course, the films of both periods reflect Stevens's special background and character, including what *Time* in its review of *Woman of the Year* dubbed his powerful "rugged roughneck" quality as a man and director. In what became *Time's* standard summary of his biography and work in its reviews of his films, the magazine said:

> George Cooper Stevens is an unassuming, long-jawed, rugged roughneck with an innate intelligence (uninfluenced by formal education), an extreme sensitivity and a fine flow of good humor. He was raised in show business. His father, Landers Stevens, oldtime Shakespearean actor, was proprietor of a popular Pacific Coast stock company.
>
> When Stevens went to Hollywood at 17 (1921), he had carried many a spear in his father's dramas, had stopped school after a year in high school, failed to make the grade at shortstop with the Oakland Acorns baseball team. Over his father's bitter remonstrances ("A cameraman's no better than a lousy stagehand"), he became the youngest and one of the best cameramen in motion pictures.[7]

The piece goes on to report that "Stevens learned his cinema technique on the roughhouse, two-reel comedy lots, where everyone from prop boy to producer had a hand in the story and no one knew how it was going to end." The review says that such work "is known as 'shooting off the cuff,' and Stevens does just that today with most of his pictures." *Time* also provides the additional background information that Stevens worked with Laurel and Hardy and Harry Langdon, the great film comics, on more than sixty shorts. According to the article, "One of them had an unforgettable sequence: Laurel & Hardy delivering a piano up an impossibly long, steep set of narrow outdoor steps." The article quotes Stevens on this sequence: "The first theater audience that saw it cheered so hard at the finish that the house had to run the two-reeler over again before the customers would look at the feature."[8] By 1930, Hal Roach felt Stevens could be moved from being a cameraman in Roach's studios to directing shorts. Within three years, Stevens was ready to direct his first feature, a sixty-eight-minute film called *The Cohens and the Kellys in Trouble,* the last of a series of comedy features about the rivalry between two families.

In the decade that followed Stevens's first feature, he directed a series of successful and popular films. Three of the most important – *Alice Adams, Swing Time,* and *Woman of the Year* – center in different ways on the changing situation of women in America. In each Stevens stars a powerful and gifted actress – Katharine Hepburn twice, Ginger Rogers once – to play women of great intelligence, charm, independence, and spirit. Rogers achieved a new level of excellence as a dancer opposite Fred Astaire in *Swing Time.* Nevertheless, in each of these movies, Stevens ultimately compromises the independence of his female characters and stars to conform to narrative conventions and social expectations, proffering an aesthetic that contains and controls change within the constructed vision of his cinematic frame.

Accordingly, by the beginning of World War II a pattern had been established in Stevens's work of a complicity between the ideology of his aesthetic practice and his cultural and political ideology that imposes a conservative compromise upon his basically reformist propensities. He creates an intensely original and complex world in his frame; but the borders of the frame also become the perimeter of his political and cultural imagination, thereby limiting and controlling change. In this collaboration between form and content, Stevens's camera tends to mitigate the thrust of his own narrative and ideology toward pluralism and diversity. As Molly Haskell says, "George Stevens had a way of taking projects or scenarios that in themselves were savage commentaries on the American Dream and directing them as if they were the dream fulfilled."[9]

Both *Swing Time* and *Woman of the Year* dramatically illustrate this pattern of visualizing the containment of change and difference. In *Swing Time,* we first meet Penny (Ginger Rogers) on a city street when she thinks Lucky (Fred Astaire) rudely wants to pick her up. He seems to be a rather foolish wolf. In a lively tracking shot, the camera is drawn to Rogers in her exchange of barbs with Astaire. In this encounter and in these shots, Rogers is in control and poised, generously exhibiting extraordinary beauty, grace, and self-possession. As Elizabeth Kendall writes:

> This is a portrait of a woman who has worked out a code of courtesy for city life, which she practices toward others and expects others to practice toward her. When they fail to do this, she doesn't hesitate to defend herself in any way she can think of.[10]

In terms of character, Rogers here anticipates the wonderful presence and independence of Ann Sheridan in Howard Hawks's *I Was a Male War Bride*. However, within moments a marvelous dance number with Lucky in the dance studio where she teaches exhilarates Penny but also begins a relationship with him that weakens her sense of autonomy. In the sequence of scenes, Lucky has followed her from the street to the studio. After initially causing her to lose her job because of his pretense of ineptness over learning how to dance, he saves her by the brilliance of his performance. Most of the dance occurs within the confines of a symbolically suggestive circle on the dance floor. When they dance over the elevated border of the circle, she obviously follows his lead. Stevens, therefore, has concocted a mise-en-scène of controlled desire and sexuality that eradicates the independence she has exhibited on the street. Her previously vibrant sense of self and autonomy now cannot be separated from her new identification with Astaire. Also, the narrative, which follows the basic formula of Astaire–Rogers musicals, focuses on her hopes to get Astaire to marry her. Although *Swing Time* after more than sixty years remains a charming and marvelous classic of the Astaire–Rogers musical form, the transition from the extraordinary woman on the street to the woman needing a husband for security and identity also says a great deal about the film's representation of gender and sexuality.

As testimony to her power as a woman and actress, Rogers throughout the film retains and expands upon her ability to convey emotion and sensuality. At the same time, the film also stifles that emotional power through the effort to control it. It does so partially by establishing a classic hierarchy involving the dominance of Astaire's masculine reticence over Rogers's strong emotionalism. He remains forever cool. Her blatant and expressive accessibility makes her vulnerable in a way that diminishes her attractiveness to him. With all of its playfulness, the movie adds an element of dramatic tension to the Rogers–Astaire relationship by manipulating her into a near disastrous marriage to the wrong man so that she can spite Astaire. Although the humorous impulse of the film suggests that the whole story should be taken lightly, it nevertheless dramatizes a situation of a woman's emotional and personal dependence that also should not be overlooked. As Kendall writes:

> As a contrast to Astaire's Lucky, Rogers's Penny completely inhabits her feelings, and feels free, at almost any time, to express them in ordinary words and actions. All through this second part of the movie she keeps signaling to Lucky that she's in love with him; she keeps offering him the gift of herself. She does this even when it's a risk to her pride.[11]

Swing Time really normalizes this remarkable situation involving Penny's wonderful "gift of herself" and Lucky's predicament of not being able to respond honestly to the genuineness of her offer. The film's narrative simply absorbs the contradiction over how she deserves to be treated and the reality of her subservient position in their relationship. The explosive energy, charm, grace, and utter originality of her character are all channeled into a narrative structure that controls Rogers's independence and self-expression. Kendall maintains that "In the course of the movie Rogers comes to stand for something more than the self-respecting working woman; she becomes the person who isn't afraid of the power of love."12 However, the movie demonstrates how that power of love turns on Rogers to weaken and even humiliate her into dependence. The fact that in the midst of filming *Swing Time*, Rogers and Stevens, according to Kendall, apparently "began an affair that would continue on and off for at least three years" adds still another dimension to the meaning of the role of women in the film and in society at the time. Kendall suggests this relationship may have influenced the tone and feeling of some of the numbers in the film. "Perhaps it was this personal involvement, doomed to marginality by Stevens's marriage, that lent such a melancholic tone to this 'Never Gonna Dance' number."13

In *Swing Time*, Rogers enters into a significant partnership with not only Astaire as her leading man and dancing partner but also with Stevens as her director. The partnerships form a kind of consensus but one that clearly limits and controls her. Stevens's frame articulates and defines those limitations for both Rogers the actress and her character, Penny. Ironically, Stevens takes Penny from a situation of independence and propels her into a courtship and marriage that was not available to the real, living actress.

In the same film, Astaire's most prominent dance number without Rogers personifies a cultural schizophrenia involving blacks. On its surface, the elaborate number indicates an attempt to pay homage to and celebrate the great African-American tap dancer Bojangles Robinson. In fact, the dancing constitutes a form of racial mimickry and stereotyping that speaks its own language of ridiculing and trivializing the humanity of the very individual and people it pretends to honor. Just as the film positions Astaire over Rogers, the dance number suggests the white dancer really possesses the greater talent. Once again, the frame and mise-en-scène intimate a subtext in contradiction with the surface meaning of the scene, a subtext that indicates the complex layers of belief and contradiction within the cultural consensus concerning race as well as gender. In a rather tendentious study of the roots of racism in American film in early Jewish blackface, Michael Rogin describes this scene in *Swing Time* as "phallic":

> A blackface Fred Astaire appears at the crotch of the giant black legs formed when chorus girls pry apart the shoes. Separated from Astaire and taken off by the chorus girls, the legs dance behind him as if they were his shadows. Blackface dresses up the trickster Astaire, whom we have seen black up and who remains

under burnt cork in the cardsharp scene that follows the dance. An homage to the African American tape dancer Bojangles Robinson, the number also quotes *The Jazz Singer*, for Astaire's blacking up seduces both women . . . between whom he is torn.[14]

Any doubts about the racism of the scene would have to be eliminated by a subsequent scene in *Swing Time* depicting an African-American male servant who is forced in the film to surrender his trousers to the ridiculous band leader Ricardo Romero (George Metaxa) who competes for Rogers's affection. The treatment of this black man follows a Hollywood pattern of presenting blacks as looking and speaking strangely. Ricardo's nameless servant, with his wide eyes, pronounced white teeth, slow movements, and mumbling speech, embodies Hollywood's hateful way of presenting African Americans during this era. *Swing Time*'s exploitation of this stereotype provides further demonstration of how Stevens's camera and ideology sometimes create their own obstacles to establishing an ideology of consensus in American culture. By juxtaposing the image of Astaire with Bojangles and the servant, the film renders a racial contrast. Astaire coolly and authoritatively controls his ebullience, joy, and spontaneity; he can enjoy and demonstrate the pleasure of jazz and of dance but keep his dignity and authority in tact. Astaire maintains his difference from and superiority over both women and black people who also dance. With all of his dancing and playing, he remains a white man.

A comparable exercise of control and authority also occurs in *Woman of the Year*. The movie begins with what appears to be a great propulsion toward change and accommodation to women's independence on the part of Sam Craig (Spencer Tracy), a top New York sportswriter who falls in love with Tess Harding (Katharine Hepburn), an international columnist of foreign affairs on the same newspaper with the kind of credentials and experience that would make her the envy of both Eleanor Roosevelt and Hilary Clinton. Obviously impressed with her as an independent and strong woman, Tracy finds her power attractive. It says much for his own sense of confidence and manliness that he enjoys his competition with her and at first feels challenged by her. Apparently, what Christopher Andersen calls the overt "real-life parallels" between the developing off-screen Tracy–Hepburn relationship dramatically reinforced the dynamic on-screen performances:

> Yet no one could ignore the simple fact that these two extreme opposites were falling in love. As with the characters they were portraying, the real-life scenario being played out was between a stubborn man of the people with his own unbreakable code of morality and an equally strong, financially independent woman who had, by her own account, behaved like a man in a world dominated by men.[15]

One scene in Sam's favorite bar brilliantly demonstrates Stevens's visual style of controlling change and containing conflicting and contradictory layers of reality within the visual frame. A mirror covers the wall of a bar owned by an ex-boxer, "Pinkie" Peters (William Bendix). In the scene, Pinkie in the middle of the frame tends the bar with his back to the mirror, in which we see his reflection. As he speaks, he looks to his right to Sam, whose reflection also appears in the mirror. Bendix seems more befuddled than usual as Tracy asks for the back booth; he then moves to the right of the screen, revealing Hepburn's image in the mirror – she too has been standing at the bar. With this simple movement and contrivance, the scene says a great deal about the way Stevens likes to suggest the depths of his frame. Layers of reality exist in the world he frames. The camera becomes a kind of social microscope penetrating multiple levels of interior meaning and hidden reality. Moreover, within that frame the world often changes, sometimes in extremely dramatic and radical ways. In this scene at the bar, for example, Tess's mere reflection in the mirror indicates the disruption of the established male order. Her insertion changes the social situation and order of the bar and radically alters the relationships within it.

In addition, the mirror not only gives visual and social depth to the scene but also suggests internal change in Sam's character and consciousness. With the reflection in the mirror of Sam's perspective from the bar and his happy expression concerning Tess, the frame indicates self-conscious changes in the psychology of this attractive bachelor. Sam literally sees himself undergoing a major transformation and apparently likes what he sees. The mirror reflects the change in his divided consciousness inspired by the woman who has helped re-create his mirror image; it also conveys the construction of individual and collective mental images of reality. The mirror, like the camera, dramatizes the power of consciousness to reinvent reality. Pinkie's mirror in the bar thereby reveals a process of constructing and reconstructing images of reality.

The dynamic and evolving reality of the mirror in the bar forecasts the explosive potential of Tess's presence. Indeed, she will foment a small revolution of values and attitudes concerning gender. While her presence requires that the men take special account of her as a woman, she enacts an additional radical turn by insisting on equality with them. Pinkie, feeling compelled to treat her with special courtesy as a woman, also cannot help but notice that she tries and almost succeeds in matching drinks with Sam until she ends up collapsed under the table, with the sportswriter still seated but not faring much better than she. As in their off-screen affair, in which Tracy needed, as the film's producer Joseph L. Mankiewicz said, a woman who "could match him point for point," Tess matches Sam, as well as his friends.[16] In so doing Tess surmounts a twice-closed circle of male narcissism: She both alters Sam's boyish adolescence and shatters the complacency and self-indulgence of the locker-room atmosphere of Pinkie's place that typifies male exclusiveness and resistance to gender equality. Thus, her presence initiates potentially long-term change on several psychological and social fronts. She acts as the transforming force in his masculine world, while he embodies open-mindedness and flexibility; together they seem to proffer great promise for future consideration of fresh alternatives to the way men and women can work and live together. Stevens's frame, therefore, works brilliantly as a classic window onto a reality of great depth and meaning, just as the later writings of film theorist Siegfried Kracauer suggests film should function.[17]

For Stevens, however, the frame also functions as a boundary for change, just like the dance-floor circle that encloses Rogers and Astaire in their first *Swing Time* number. The promise of a different kind of relationship between Sam and Tess does not really go anywhere: It remains in the bar mirror, merging into another image of yet another more deeply constructed reality of continuity and containment. At first promising great social change, the case for progress in the bar scene remains self-contained. The energy within the frame expends itself as the film emphasizes the dissolution of Sam and Tess's relationship and her ultimate defeat and destruction, rather than the creation of an atmosphere for personal and cultural growth.

Besides his tightly constructed mise-en-scène, Stevens uses classic narrative continuity and closure as a structured form to direct the film's incipient ideology of change. Instead of engaging and developing the explosive potential in the Tess–Sam relationship for reconsiderations of basic gender and sexual relations, Stevens's narrative undertakes a process of steadily demonizing Tess as selfish and self-centered – not a woman at all, as Sam eventually says when he feels compelled to assume the responsibility for caring for a poor Greek orphan that Tess adopts and neglects. Stevens steadily diminishes Tess's moral authority and stature as a person until the film becomes almost a parody of masculine bitterness and fear of female competition and abandonment. Rather than imagine a real new kind of "Woman of the Year," the movie commits itself to a strategy of destroying her while elevating Sam as the epitome of tolerance and maturity.

The film imposes multiple assaults and insults upon Tess. During the wedding ceremony of her aunt and widowed father, it seems as though God is castigating her for failing in her own marriage. She is then humiliated in the kitchen with a revised ending designed to win over women homemakers in the audience. As Andersen says, "Kate hated the new, blatantly sexist ending in which the strong woman finally 'gets hers.' Audiences, however, went wild for it."[18] Perhaps worst of all, the film ends with Sam speaking for her, acting as her voice of moderate liberation. When she begs to be allowed to be Mrs. Sam Craig and to return to him like a dutiful wife, he reminds her of the importance of her own independence. Like a good parent, he tells her to be herself but to do so in a balanced way. He patronizingly asks, "Why can't you be Tess Harding Craig?" With a new sense of maturity, she gratefully recognizes and appreciates his greater wisdom and generosity. The emphasis on his last name institutes a final linguistic frame for the film. She can be free but within his visual, verbal, and institutional strictures and expectations. The film thus compromises with most of the challenges it initially proposes to conventional sexual and gender relationships. A film with radical potential ends up anticipating *I Love Lucy*.

Stevens's efforts for visual and cinematic consensus culminate in *Giant*. The opening long take of the Texas landscape promises an endless horizon of expanding opportunities and promises; it dramatizes America as an idea for all. The film ends with an image of two boys in a playpen, the grandchildren of rancher Bick Benedict (Rock Hudson) and Leslie Lynnton Benedict (Elizabeth Taylor). One boy is as Anglo-American as Taylor and Hudson; the other is clearly part Hispanic, the child of Jordan Benedict III (Dennis Hopper) and his wife Juana (Elsa Cardenas). To the liberal-minded spectator, this vision of both children constitutes a breathtaking promise of the resolution of ethnic and racial conflict. Coming after a climactic and thunderous fistfight in an earlier scene between Bick and a prejudiced luncheonette owner who refuses service to a poor, brown-skinned Hispanic family, the final shot becomes genuinely moving. In the luncheonette scene, Bick intercedes on the family's behalf and takes on the owner; his own wife and family then watch him get the beating of his life, to the exuberant music of "The Yellow Rose of Texas" emanating from the jukebox. In both the concluding scene and the one at the restaurant, Hudson and Taylor, who have convincingly been steadily aged throughout the 197-minute film, are appropriately gray haired and look very much the distinguished grandparents their roles demand.

The fight scene turns Hudson's character into a crusader for equality. Filmed in the mid-1950s during the Eisenhower era, when the crusade a few years later for civil rights in the South seemed unimaginable, the scene and film make a truly powerful statement. Although the family in the restaurant scene is Hispanic, its role as the displaced embodiment and representative of all minority groups – including one of the most notoriously mistreated, African Americans – is quite obvious. Thus, *Giant* indicates a radical change in Stevens's sensitivity to race since *Swing Time,* a result perhaps of his experience with fascism and the Holocaust in the war. In any case, *Time* saw the film and these final scenes as a courageous statement for change and reform. It reviewed the film as a kind of jeremiad against racism and a call for liberal redemption:

> The director's passionate disgust – not for Texas, but for all that Texas signifies in this picture – comes to a burning point in the film's final frames; they constitute what is probably the most effective declaration against racial intolerance ever shown on the screen.[19]

Even more important than *Time*'s estimation of *Giant*'s value as a lesson in civil rights, the scene and the film attain no less than Elizabeth Taylor's own apparent endorsement when her character, Leslie, informs Hudson at the end of the film that he never looked more heroic or manly to her than when he fought and lost for a helpless Hispanic family.

Giant's visual ideology of consensus and its proposition for a continuing transformation of American culture and character to embody all peoples of the world still seem challenging, relevant, and radical near the end of the twentieth century; at midcentury, leaders like President Eisenhower and the two Texans who respectively dominated the U.S. Senate and House of Representatives, Lyndon B. Johnson and Sam Rayburn, probably found them unsettling. Released in 1956, the same year as John Ford's *The Searchers*, *Giant* also deals with racism and prejudice but in a very different way than the Ford classic: Stevens's film provocatively emphasizes the importance of continuing the centuries-old ideology of America as a haven for the world and the myth of its peoples as a unified amalgam of different races and ethnic groups. It proudly proclaims the ideology and creed of America's universalism.

It therefore seems both aesthetically and ideologically fitting that *Giant* was restored and released during the autumn of 1996, a year of vituperative struggle in the United States over affirmative action and immigration, especially immigration by the same dark-skinned peoples from the same areas below the Texas border for whom Hudson fights in the film. In contrast to *The Searchers*, the film envisions unity and discussion as opposed to division and continued violence for the nation's future. It's final image of both children united in Hudson's loving and affectionate look remains a national and cultural ideal and hope.

Moreover, the film's realism about the depth of Bick's initial ethnic and racial prejudices contributes to the credibility of the process of his growth. True to his character and his region, Bick's language and tone in his references to his Hispanic grandchild – calling him his "half-breed" and "muchacho" – retain an offensive edge that makes his gradual political conversion to a more liberal position believable. The language functions as a key to his changing mind and thought. By recognizing and articulating residual remnants of Bick's original values and attitudes toward ethnic difference, his words distinguish the film from propaganda and strengthen its plausibility and aesthetic effect.

In the final scene, at home on the ranch known as Reata, Bick sits next to Leslie on the sofa beneath an enormous painting of Texas ranch life that dominates the room, while Uncle Bawley (Chill Wills) opens the bar and indulges in the manly ritual of his eagerly anticipated first bourbon of the day. Bick growls to his gray-haired wife: "You really want to know what's got my goat?" As he speaks, Stevens cuts to a close-up of the little Mexican American's unabashadly adorable face – America's promise and hope for the future. "My own grandson don't even look like one of us, honey. So help me, he looks like a little wetback!" Leslie's appropriate but half-hearted admonition of her husband for his crude language punctuates his speech, but the tone of her "Jordan!" registers her understanding and appreciation of the true acceptance and love in Bick's words and voice. With Uncle Bawley happily holding his bourbon and the painting hanging on the wall over the couple, the sound-track music resonates with its own approval of Bick's newly acquired tolerance. The camera then cuts again to the children: The darker-skinned boy, standing next to his blondish cousin, rattles the playpen rail and gurgles exuberantly, signaling his intentions to break free in the near future. Bick hunches forward and approvingly says, "Little muchacho fires up, don't he." He then adds, "Well, I'm sorry, Jordan Benedict the Fourth, but there's times when a man just has to be honest." As in *Woman of the Year,* repetition of the male surname at the end of the film signifies incorporation and inclusion; but this time, as spoken by Hudson, Stevens's theme rings brilliantly true. As Larry McMurtry writes in the Sunday *New York Times* article about the rerelease of *Giant:*

> Leslie Benedict's 25 years of dogged liberal argument don't really convert Bick; it is his grandson, the little brown one with the wonderful eyes, who converts him. Rock Hudson deservedly received an Oscar nomination for keeping all these tensions alive across the course of a long film. Bick Benedict is a man who was bred to control everything; in the end, morally better educated, he is forced to admit that he controls almost nothing.[20]

Contrary to *Time*'s claim of the film's disdain for the things Texas signifies, the scene – music, dialogue, painting, children, family, and friend – resonates effusively with warmth and love for this promise of a mythic Texas of racial harmony and love. It idealizes this Texas of the liberal imagination. Thus, as Uncle Bawley properly exits so that he won't violate a presumed Texan code of manliness by listening to Bick express his inner feelings, Bick confesses to Leslie that he considers himself a failure. She answers, "I think you're great." She happily admits, as previously noted, that all his riding and roping did not make him as big a man to her as he seemed on the luncheonette floor after fighting for the rights of a Hispanic family.

In *Giant,* Stevens's aesthetics tends to substitute for a coherent and systematic articulation and organization of political conflicts, differences, and possibilities for change. His aesthetic ideology at the end of the film concerning how *Giant* looks and feels supersedes how it thinks, meaning how the film propounds ideas and structures and develops themes. It transforms the ideology of consensus into an aesthetic vision that includes women, people of color, and immigrants; it mythologizes the symbols for change. It therefore returns to the mythological and symbolic mindset of *Shane,* advancing an aesthetic ideology and program as a strategy for cultural transformation and individual renewal. As Robert Warshow writes:

> The highest expression of this aestheticizing tendency is in George Stevens' *Shane,* where the legend of the West is virtually reduced to its essentials and then fixed in the dreamy clarity of a fairy tale.[21]

Similarly, in *Giant* both the Texas landscape and, in the end, the domestic scene at Reata are aestheticized as the symbols of consensus and renewal, substituting for the articulation of an ideology and program for action.

The climactic aestheticization of an ideology of consensus at the end of *Giant* follows and counters the thrust of the negative energy generated by an earlier scene, one that dramatizes the excruciating tensions of race and class that once divided the Benedict family and, by implication, still divides the country. This particular scene of internal family dissension and hostility anticipates the resolution of the later domestic scene. Its aestheticization of profound ideological differences and cultural divisions within the family and the country balances the final scene of harmony and unity with the Benedict grandchildren happily residing at the family home at Reata.

In the scene, the family assembles in a hotel room while all of Texas seems to be present in a nearby ballroom to celebrate and honor a drunken Jett Rink (James Dean), a cowhand who has become so powerful and important since the discovery of oil on what had been the little bit of land he had inherited on the Benedict ranch from Bick's volatile and jealous sister Luz (Mercedes McCambridge). Bick has alienated himself from the rest of the Texans by fighting Rink, in front of all of the guests at the celebration, following the oilman's racist treatment of Jordan's Hispanic wife, Juana, as well as his unfair bullying and beating of Bick's son, Jordan (Hopper), over the incident. Thus, the family has been compelled to leave the party and must deal with its own internal tensions in the isolation of the hotel room.

In spite of his defense of Juana, the prejudice and racism that Bick ultimately overcome in the film's concluding scenes manifest themselves acrimoniously in this scene. The conversation begins with Bick introducing discord by reminding Jordan that the latter always had a mind of his own. Bick then deepens the tension by stating the obvious fact that Jordan married a Hispanic woman – a comment that barely disguises his prejudice and bitterness, and intensifies the differences between them. Hudson speaks in a restrained and measured way that emphasizes the gap between Bick and Jordan over the issue of family and race at this moment in their relationship. His controlled speech suggests a stark contrast with both his son's demonstrably erratic nature and the implied emotional behavior of people of color. "You knew what you was doin' when you married in that direction," Bick says. "There's a lot of folks in this part of the country that's pretty jumpy about that sort of thing." Meanwhile, Bick clearly implies his own embarrassment and discomfort about the relationship. Jordan responds angrily that he only cares about his family's attitudes and beliefs: As far as he is concerned, it "all has to do with the people who ought to know better . . . like my own father"; it is "just simple truth . . . that's the way you think." Bick explodes in self-righteous indignation over this charge of narrow-mindedness, insisting that he has been fair toward all people and that no one has the right to address him with such disrespect: "You my own son can't sit there and tell me I'm not a fair man." Nevertheless, Jordan ultimately forces Bick to face the fact of his own prejudice and arrogance: Bick defended his daughter-in-law, Juana, only out of pride after Rink already had punched and beaten Jordan, whose hands were held behind his back by Rink's goons.

Visually, the scene is brilliantly constructed and filmed, almost as though it were a modernistic painting or even a still life of people made numb by events and spent emotion. This portrait of family tension epitomizes Stevens's visual style of framing and containing turmoil and change. The mise-en-scène positions the various family members in deep focus, at sharp angles from each other, with Bick in the foreground at the bottom of the frame. All of the figures seem to hang in the frame like a frozen mobile, a rigid balance of strains and anxieties that threatens to collapse at any moment. The dialogue, as already noted, ranges over questions of parental authority and respect, racism, marriage, personal responsibility, loyalty, and money. Furthermore, Stevens beautifully uses colors and graphic spaces in the mise-en-scène to accentuate stresses, differences, and emotional distances. The spectator can feel the strains of the dynamic tensions of forces, feelings, and ideas within the scene. Stevens times and organizes the minimal movement, physical action, and editing in the scene perfectly so as to exacerbate these anxieties and difficulties. He breaks this frigid vision of stabilized disunity and tension with cuts between the father and the rest of the family to highlight the conflict. The visual discord of this scene creates the impetus and energy for its ultimate resolution in the subsequent scenes of unity. The hotel scene provides additional evidence of Stevens's extraordinary gift for aestheticizing ideas and psychological differences in interior spaces as well as in exterior landscapes, as in the famous outdoor scenes of *Shane* and *Giant*.

However, the Stevens film in which aesthetics and ideology cohere most consistently and powerfully to make a work of true greatness is the one that helps to explain most completely the director's special place in the Hollywood Renaissance. In *A Place in the Sun,* mind and aesthetics meld into a powerful cinematic flow of extraordinary sensitivity and imagination; but this synthesis of art and ideas evokes an aura of pessimism, failure, and fear that marks a radical counterpoint to the drive toward cultural renewal and individual regeneration that characterizes much of the purpose and meaning of that renaissance.

In the Heart of Desire: A Nation of Loners

The values of democracy, the promise of rebirth, and the ideology of consensus at the core of the Hollywood Renaissance all seem at odds with the pessimism and darkness of *A Place in the Sun* (1951). Like its hero, George Eastman (Montgomery Clift), the film even seems out of place in the generally optimistic works of the Stevens canon. In *Swing Time,* Ginger Rogers giggles her way out of an impossible dilemma, refusing to let false pride ruin her life by making her treat a planned wedding to a ridiculous man seriously. In *Woman of the Year,* a classic happy ending overcomes unresolvable problems regarding sex, gender, and marriage. In *Shane* (1953), the myth of the West advances the promise of regeneration, and *Giant* optimistically asserts the univeralism of the American idea for all peoples.

In contrast, the title of *A Place in the Sun* must be taken ironically. Written by Michael Wilson and Harry Brown after the Patrick Kearney play based on Theodore Dreiser's *An American Tragedy,* the film never grants its hero George any place of sunlight without the intervention of shadow. The film really concerns George's free-fall into a bottomless pit of desire, an endless yearning for love, security, and completion. Whereas Dreiser's works delineate so intently and naturalistically the minutiae of social and economic life and corruption, *A Place in the Sun* never leaves George's consciousness and sensibility. From its beginning, the film reveals the world through the mirror of George's inner feelings and fears. He personifies desire, which manifests itself through the organization of cinematic space and time to dramatize psychic division and separation. In this role, Clift comes to embody a new kind of American hero for a different age and culture. Understanding Clift in this role helps to explain the erosion of the mindset that shaped the Hollywood Renaissance and the emergence of a new period and culture of fragmentation and separation.

As opposed to the strong subjectivity of Marlon Brando's assertion in *On the Waterfront* that "I'm just going to get my rights," or Gary Cooper's refusal to retreat before near-certain death, Clift lacks any solidity at all. He anticipates the fascination of the postwar era with desire and identity. The film begins with Clift hitchhiking on the road. In transition and thumbing a ride to a new place, his identity immediately seems a problem. In fact, in the opening shot, the young man's ambiguous identity is emphasized by having his back to the camera as he tries to get a ride. In theory, his orientation in the frame also means the viewer would have to guess or assume the actor's identity as Clift even as the film's credits appear at the same time. As the unknown figure stands on the side of the road, he epitomizes the displaced person of mysterious origins with an uncertain and precarious future. A speeding bus, a truck, and several cars urge him backward along the road, rendering the stranger especially vulnerable and abandoned at this time.

When Clift turns around to the camera, his face actually deepens the mystery of his identity that his situation on the road arouses. Clift's face conveys remarkably intense and vulnerable sensitivity. The thin face and piercing eyes instantly suggest emotional need and hunger. His expression evokes a quality of passivity and lostness as opposed to confidence, determination, and certainty. He is the stranger.

However, in this opening cut, Stevens also immediately establishes important visual and musical motifs that will come to resonate with significance throughout the rest of the film. The determination of the stranger's identity and place cannot be separated from related questions of gender and sexuality. Throughout the film, George will be surrounded by and consumed by women, and he will think and see himself through his body and the relationship of his body to women. Thus, as he faces toward the camera, his look concentrates on an object beyond the camera. As Clift's expression steadily reveals touches of wonder and awe, the camera physically and emotionally moves into a powerfully and provocatively intimate close-up that both sexualizes and feminizes his face and features, emphasizing a flagrantly feminine softness to his lips and a sensitive yearning in his eyes. The contending lines of visual action – his intradiegetic look up and off-screen and the camera's look and movement toward his face – create a visual motion and countermotion, an intimate collaboration of camera, field, and actor, until the rhythm and tension break with a cut from behind Clift. The shot from behind Clift reveals what so strongly fixes and sustains the young man's gaze and provokes such concentrated attention and wonder from him.

An enormous roadside billboard sign advertises a line of bathing suits with a full-bodied figure modeling a suit. The sign and figure take up nearly the whole width of the frame. The figure of the model and the sign hover over Clift, dwarfing and overwhelming him. The camera's look slightly to the left of Clift's back emphasizes the propulsion of the visual line of Clift's look up to the billboard. The progression from the camera's position and look to Clift's look beautifully organizes the spatial relationships of the frame and establishes a psychological continuity from the spectator in the audience, to the camera, to George and the advertising billboard. The organization of looks creates a coherent visual and physical space under the powerful figure on the billboard – a space of desire. The visual thrust of these looks toward the woman in the advertisement encounters her return look to Clift and the spectator, creating another visual countermovement in the scene.

The look and body on the sign clearly overpower Clift, the compactly built actor, and his character, George Eastman. The female figure dominates the sexual and visual space of the scene. Her extended body seems to thrust her feet into Clift's face, while her smile appeals beguilingly and warmly to him and the spectator. The scene here anticipates and typifies Mary Ann Doane's description of the "transformation from spectacle to spectator" in another film of the female who takes possession of the dominant gaze – *Humoresque* (1947) – thereby causing with her power "the male's impotence" through "this excess, the threat posed by her sexuality."[22] With Clift's back again to the camera, the look on the billboard encompasses and contains his look. The feminine image controls the meaning of the scene, thereby participating in the feminization of Clift's character and figure. Significantly, his look and reaction to this image do not suggest a sexual drive or sexual attraction but another kind of attitude of awe, admiration, and identification. He observes and witnesses the beauty of something for its own sake and for the empathy involved in his relationship to it.

As Clift continues to gaze up to the sign, his right hand and thumb held up toward his shoulder to signal for hitchhiking, the off-screen sound of a car horn echoes through the scene. He turns to the right, revealing his profile and face again. The camera cuts to the road. A speeding, open-topped Cadillac convertible races across the frame and leaves him behind despite the friendly honk. We realize later that the beautiful young driver was Angela Vickers (Elizabeth Taylor), the young woman who soon will return George's love and adoration in an orgy of mutual infatuation that ultimately will lead to his need to escape from and eliminate another woman, Alice Tripp (Shelley Winters), whose pregnancy makes any future happiness with Angela, as well as all of his ambitious dreams of success and prosperity, impossible. Well before those melodramatic events unravel in Alice's death and George's imprisonment and execution, the power and sweep of Angela's car in the opening scene by the billboard completes the visual and psychological organization of feminine space that encompasses George. With the billboard to the left occupying much of the space of the frame, the model's look dominating the visual field, and Angela's car rudely and loudly driving by him on the right, George finds himself surrounded by images of women. Looking off toward the car and its driver as they disappear in the distance on the road, George without realizing it sees his destiny.

In this opening scene, George has been silent, simply looking and responding. Amazingly, the billboard that has held such sway over him also speaks for him in a way, articulating his identity and prospects: "It's an Eastman," the sign reads – that being the name of the bathing suit company owned by the uncle who has invited George to leave his job as a bellhop in the distant city of Chicago to find employment in the firm. The billboard's writing continues the project, therefore, of reversing male and female positions and dominance by both speaking for George and naming him, declaring his presence and his prospects for the future as an Eastman. In marked contrast to the usual masculine and patriarchal responsibility of the father to impose the authority of his name, it is this sign of a woman that names George. A feminine force and voice here exercise the Oedipal "law of the father" that shatters maternal control and bonding through language and the imposition of the name. The sign's declaration, "It's an Eastman," reads like a birth announcement; its further linkage of the stranger to the billboard's image signifies the melding of desire, commodification, commercialization, and media in the film.

Of all the semiotic elements and actions of the camera apparatus that conspire to feminize George's identity – the camera's organization and construction of visual space, the physical and facial suggestions of his softness and passivity, his situational relationship to the billboard and its various signs and signifiers – the music erupts as one of the most important. As George looks to the billboard and then observes Angela's car pass, the musical theme and refrain from the Franz Waxman score resonate with the tone, mood, and feeling of the music for the so-called weepies or woman's films that were contrived for female audiences in the 1940s. By the time of the release of *A Place in the Sun*, weepies like *Humoresque*, for example, had become a readily identifiable subgenre and convention. According to Doane, the music in such films functions as an important form of communication in their complex signifying system: "[T]he register of the sign which bears the greatest burden in this yearning for a full language is that which authorizes the label 'melodrama' – music." Music, Doane maintains, comes closest to articulating an alternative kind of maternal language that stems from the connection between mother and child; moreover, the music in melodramatic weepies disrupts the objectification of the male gaze, the dehumanization of the female spectacle, and the institutionalization of sexual difference and distance. Thus it establishes an additional means of engagement for the woman in the film and the women in the audience that escapes appropriation and domination by the male gaze:

> Music marks a deficiency in the axis of vision. Because emotion is the realm in which the visible is insufficient as a guarantee, the supplementary meaning proffered by music is absolutely necessary.[23]

The musical theme announced in the opening scene of *A Place in the Sun* performs precisely this function, and throughout the film the music supplements the limits of vision by evoking and representing George's yearning for emotional sustenance and psychological completion through identification with the feminine. As Doane writes about such situations in the woman's film, "Gesture, music, and mise-en-scène are deployed to represent that which is unrepresentable – the 'ineffable.'"[24] The ineffable for George Eastman concerns the force of desire in his character and the film that yearns for unity, wholeness, and completion in the form of a woman. In addition, the film will introduce another musical theme for Alice Tripp that associates pain and lethargy and unhappiness with her body. This musical countertheme pursues and develops the issue of desire by connoting George's inevitable failure before the physical, psychological, and social obstacles to the transformation he wants; it becomes a musical sign of the body's inexorable failure to achieve wholeness.

Stevens thus constructs and organizes a system of looks and music in the opening of *A Place in the Sun* that visually and psychologically encircles the stranger, and turns this constricted space and time on the screen into a mise-en-scène of desire. Moreover, Stevens's delineation of desire in this scene establishes the nature of George's character and relationships, and structures the film's insight into the centrality of desire for the culture. Colin MacCabe's discussion of desire in film applies to explaining the importance of desire in *A Place in the Sun:* "Desire is only set up by absence, by the possibility of return to a former state – the field of vision only becomes invested libidinally after it has been robbed of its unity by the gaze of the other."[25] Psychologically in a kind of pre-Oedipal or prelinguistic stage and socially in a situation of displacement and transition, George personifies desire as lack of solid identity and emotional stability. The sign of the woman's body in the opening scene evokes desire in George by affirming his difference and separation from woman; at the same time, it holds out the potential for fullness and completeness by urging him both to identify with and want the female figure that overpowers him visually, physically, and emotionally.

For George, desire includes seeing himself as passive and feminine, to be adopted and cared for as a permanent dependent and love object. Standing before the bathing suit billboard, George enters, as MacCabe says about Lacanian theory, "into a signifying system which was always unstable, never finished." Interesting for film theory, the opening scene of *A Place in the Sun* emplaces George in a visually constructed environment of signs that institutes the fluidity of his identity as a man in terms of his attraction to the feminine. MacCabe notes that "the specificity of film was to be located in the field of vision" and that the field of vision helps forge the relationship of ego identity and subjectivity: "The ego was an imaginary production forged and reforged by the attempt to stabilise both subject and meaning, while the unconscious was the product of the fact that meaning could not be so stabilised." Thus, as the film initiates George's search for identity on the road, it begins with, in MacCabe's phrase, "an account of the processes of identification and disidentification, the methods by which fictions bind us into representations of both world and self."²⁶ Situated amid this mise-en-scène of desire, George embodies ambivalence in terms of sexual and gender organization and identification as well as the reconstructive interaction that MacCabe describes involving subjectivity and ego construction.

Equally important, in terms of George's association and identification with the woman and feminine in this scene, is that Clift and Stevens anticipate an important contemporary argument concerning the understanding of gender and sexual identification as "difference" rather than essential, innate, and intractable hierarchies of sexual nature or cultural structures. According to Bill Nichols:

> We must remember, though, that this notorious "lack" borne by women is an imaginary one (it only exists in the imaginary) and can only be a threat in any case to those who fear they have something to lose – namely, men. Women have nothing to lose because they "have" no thing but instead represent difference. There is nothing lacking in the real, there are no oppositions and identities that oscillate around "having" or "possessing." There are only differences. There are no lacks other than those instituted by desire; they can only be naturalized as "real" from within the arena of a phallocentric or sexist ideology, an arena large enough to enclose a great many psychoanalytic readings. . . .²⁷

Wishing to associate with women in terms of difference, identity, and society, George, as portrayed by Clift and Stevens, primarily yearns for female identification, support, and security, rather than retaining and rehabilitating his marginalized masculinity as a stranger on the road heading into an indefinite future of uncertain possibilities.

This interpretation of a few moments and shots of the opening scene of *A Place in the Sun* gains persuasiveness as the film steadily develops George's complex situation of desire. The remainder of the film confirms the notion of the fluidity and ambivalence of George's ego, subjectivity, and identification as a man who continues to see himself and think of himself through women and their bodies. George's sense of self and identity, his power to speak and act for himself and articulate his desires, and the determination of his sexual organization and gender are all fluid constructions of unconscious ambivalence about his place in the world.

The narrative thrust of *A Place in the Sun* dramatically and directly confirms George's assumption of a feminine position in the film. Most obviously, when George gets a position in his uncle's factory, he finds himself placed within a nearly all-female working force. When he enters the workplace to begin his new job as the only male on an assembly line that makes and packages bathing suits, the women look up and stare at him, totally reversing the usual priorities and power of the male situation and gaze. Even more blatant as gender and sexual reversal is a wolfish whistle directed toward him by one of the women, aggressively advancing the feminization of his role and position. The women he meets in the factory, including his supervisor, have strong ethnic identities and a suggestion of physical bulk and solidity. Portrayed as masculinized and working class, they contrast with Clift's physical proportions and sensitivity. Also, after he enters into the workplace, Alice (Winters) immediately notices him and casts the first glance his way. As his work progresses on the job, flirtatious eyeline matches between him and Alice equalize their situation. When George and Alice meet accidentally and then start to date in spite of the company rule against fraternization between employees of the opposite sex, their initial dialogue continues to feminize him and his situation. Alice notes that, being an Eastman, George seems different from all the women on the assembly line. "I'm in the same boat as the rest of yuh," he answers – a statement that casts him socially and psychologically with the girls (while heavy-handedly foreshadowing Alice's death on the lake). George clearly relates as one of the girls.

Insight into George's feminine situation in the Eastman factory can be gained by a comparison to the social and psychological state of women in Herman Melville's short story "Paradise of Bachelors and The Tartarus of Maids." In this story, Melville casts the economic and social subjugation of women as an extended metaphor for the biological determinism of reproduction. In the "Tartarus" portion, a young man who also happens to be a "seedsman" enters into a sexually suggestive valley; there he finds a paper mill manned by virginal maidens who operate the paper production in a way that clearly associates their work and the mill with sexuality and procreation. The whole process symbolizes not only birth and reproduction but also the dread of castration: Each of the maidens uses an "erected sword" for cutting the rags that make the paper.[28]

In A Place in the Sun, the Eastman assembly line compares psychologically to the industrial system in the Melville story. George, however, seeks this place and relishes his feminization; psychically, he already has been altered. Thus, a montage of overlapping images of the work environment and the production process beautifully interconnects George, his coworkers, and the assembly-line belt, all humming together as days and even months pass. A shot of a dark hole that spews forth packaged suits onto George's assembly line visually melds images of birth, biology, and industrial production into a climactic symbolism that links sexuality, reproduction, and the way the industrial process incorporates and transforms libido and sexual identity. Visually indicating George's feminization, the montage enmeshes him within a female system of production, where he loses one identity and gains another in the industrial/sexual machine.

George soon works in a white short-sleeve T-shirt that reveals his upper body and again exhibits his compactness. The shot of him in his T-shirt emphasizes his body, while the whiteness suggests his relative blankness or incompleteness – a tabula rasa. Like a gender chameleon, George belongs and fits in with his female coworkers, just as women will fit into the gender-defining bathing suits that he packages on the assembly line. Thus gender as semiotic inscription can be rewritten and revisioned on the white text of George's body by the combination of psychology and environment.

In another suggestive juxtaposition, Stevens in the factory montage shoots Clift positioned beneath a workplace sign of the same advertisement of the bathing-suit model that first attracted his attention on the road. This low-angle shot establishes a continuity that also develops the meaning of the girl in the bathing suit as a kind of emblem of sexual chaos for George. Her presence advances all of the associations of sexuality and gender that were suggested in the opening scene. Now with George literally occupying a place within a woman's world, the girl in the advertisement once again represents the power of woman in determining his way of being and seeing himself.

George's feminine identification finds reinforcement through his connection to the production process of women's bathing suits. The bathing suit defines and shapes the body by influencing, through the balance of nudity and masquerade, how the body should look. Women remake themselves according to images of fashion and desire, as George's uncle suggests at one point in a comment about the tastes of American women. As part of the fashion industry, the production and marketing of bathing suits institutionalize the organization of gender and identity, especially for George in the film. This process reassures George in his association and identification with the feminine. His place in this industrial and social system enacts and externalizes his internal desire to see himself in terms of the feminine.

However, the medium that best merges George's psyche with the social and industrial complex involves the system that mass produces images of women. Desire for George relates to the signifying chain of desire perpetuated by the assembly line of female models and poses that appear in the advertisement over his head, changing with the calendar as the days and months pass. Part of the production process, the models as signifiers of desire are interchangeable just as the assembly-line workers are dispensable productive parts. The models and workers, including George, are fetishized beings without totality or individuality. The models embody the psychological and industrial process of manufactured tastes. They promote internalized desires and needs for consumption to match the demands of the system. George works beneath the iconic Eastman bathing-suit girls and aligns his identity and being with the advertisements. In his T-shirt, his body extends to the seminudity of the bodies in the sign. He stands at the altar of their carefully contrived beauty, reinforcing their sexual and cultural significance. George enacts a semiotics of desire with his body as a text of sexual and gender signs that are constructed through the interaction of internal forces of desire in the psyche and the external forces of culture.

As George operates in this system, a confirming voice and image appear by him in the figure of his female supervisor, Mrs. Kovacs, who informs him: "Now you're in business." George now finds himself immersed in the business of manufacturing and redesigning women, but also in business for himself in the process of self-reconstruction according to his feminine impulse. Also, George works within Alice's lost and lonely eyes and expression. Her sad-dog stare places him within her look and solidifies his containment within the female gaze that emanates from her and others, including the supervisor, Mrs. Kovacs, other workers, and the ubiquitous "Eastman girls" in their ever-changing bathing-suit advertisements. Meanwhile, Waxman's music retains its importance in the factory scene for developing the film's significance: As Alice looks at George, the strains of her musical theme become ever more ominous.

Another crucial as well as classic visual sign of the irresolvable forces contending for control of George's mind and character occurs in the middle of the film. As he sits alone in his room, outside a huge neon sign atop a high building garishly flashes the name Vickers – as though the viewer really needs to be reminded at this stage of George's inner thoughts toward the beautiful young woman from this wealthy family, as opposed to his wrenching anxiety over the pregnant Alice. More important, on the wall is yet another picture of a woman, only this time it is not an Eastman model but *Ophelia* – a copy of the popular pre-Raphaelite painting by Sir John Everett Millais of the young Shakespearean heroine who drowned without any stylish bathing suit. Another of literature's great sacrifices to a failed and complicated love, a dead Ophelia stares heavenward from her pool in the frame on George's wall.[29] Besides the obvious foreshadowing of Alice's death by drowning, the painting has some other important connotations for the meaning of the film. It accentuates the dilemma of George Eastman as a kind of Hamlet caught in a nightmare of his own sexual and gender ambivalence. *A Place in the Sun* was released only a few years after Laurence Olivier's heavily Freudian interpretation of *Hamlet* (1948) had received adulatory critical and popular attention. Also, the genre and style of the painting itself has come to be considered significant in feminist theory as the embodiment of Victorian-era demonization and destruction of women within a neurotic male syndrome of defining women as either whores or goddesses.[30] Finally, the presence of a copy of such a painting in George's room inevitably invites discussion of the theme of the cultural and aesthetic meaning of duplicating images of art in the modern age. The reproduction of such images of high art in a film that highlights the industrial and commercial reproduction of images of women in contemporary media and advertising accentuates the co-optation and absorption of all forms of art and expression within the modern industry of desire.[31] The image of the lost Ophelia achieves its place in the sun as yet another commodified and fetishized object of desire.

With all of the psychic pain enacted in the film's scenes of desire, probably the most moving and touching moments in *A Place in the Sun* come from the social scenes of George's alienation and the related love scenes with Angela (Taylor). In these, Stevens's visual style and aesthetic vary somewhat from his usual emphasis on depth and long takes; instead, there is an interactive involvement in George's situation and his relationship to Angela. A detailed choreography between the camera and cinematic space articulates both George's lonely isolation and the developing merger of his personality with Angela's through their mutual infatuation. Exemplifying Stephen Heath's theory of "narrative space," Stevens reconstructs and reorganizes the visual regime to relate George and Angela's story.[32] Departing from his usual stress on structured vision in the frame, Stevens edits and cuts more than usual in these scenes to effect what D. N. Rodowick calls in his theoretical and critical terminology "the coding of relations of spatial mobility and continuity which guarantee the clarity of vision offered by classical narrative."[33]

Thus, in the scene when George visits the home where he first meets Angela and encounters society, the camera perfectly marginalizes and alienates him in the midst of family and company. The camera presents him in deep focus in what seems to be a foyer of exaggerated length, so as to distance him from the family and minimalize his size and presence. The ensuing shots quickly situate him in isolation and separation – over sofas, in strained discomfort in an armchair, in awkward conversation – until Angela's entrance from the same foyer through which he appeared. The wonderful close-up of his look at her repeats his awe in the opening scene. With his unfashionable sport jacket scrunched up at its collar, he cranes his neck to glance over the back of the chair to observe her. As he rises totally unnoticed and useless, another shot positions him in deep focus and alone between his uncle Earl Eastman (Keefe Brasselle) and Angela. The scene ends with him almost left behind, like the furniture, as all the others depart for their evening activities.

George returns to the Eastman house in a later scene under somewhat similar conditions after being forgotten by the family while he has worked with Alice in the factory. The invitation to the Eastman party comes after Earl, passing through the workplace, spots George and reassures him that he has had "his eye" on him all along – a repetition of the film's theme of visual possession and control. George escapes Alice's possessiveness in the factory and their off-work relationship to go to the party. Again, Stevens creatively constructs narrative space to emphasize George's situation of isolation and abandonment. The camera takes him around the room in a kind of slow dance of life as a misfit and loner. Each space he takes, he occupies alone, completing a circle of loneliness with a sheepish smile of despair. Long shots, medium shots, close-ups, moving-camera shots, and long takes all structure his separation from society.

Then, in a classic Stevens frame and composition, George retreats to the billiard room and plays alone, with the door slightly ajar. A quickly passing Angela catches the sight and sound of a great shot he makes with the cue stick behind his back. She enters, says "Wow!" and her flirtatiousness with the mysterious and beautiful loner begins. Throughout their relationship, his passivity arouses her passion and sensuality; from the beginning, she plays the aggressive role. Artfully displaying herself in her attractive evening dress, she circles the table and asks him, "Why all alone? Being exclusive . . . being dramatic . . . being blue?" Spoken with soft sensuousness, her words project onto him her melodramatic and adolescent qualities of narcissism that will characterize their relationship. With a hint of an onanistic connotation to his self-absorption with a cue and balls, he answers that he is "just fooling around" – although, ironically, fooling around is clearly what *she* does. She says that she will just watch as he plays, and once again George finds himself under the gaze of a beautiful woman; but this time, of course, Angela controls the spectacle. She not only assumes the dominant role in their relationship now, she also intercedes between him and his mother, Hannah (Anne Revere), whom he telephones at his uncle's urging. The transfer of affection from his mother to Angela now begins in a way that ensures even deeper and more profound dependence upon the younger woman. Meanwhile, of course, the Angela theme of the Waxman musical score provides the emotional glue to thicken their instinctive feelings for each other.

In probably the film's most provocative and sensual scene, George and Angela attend another party later in the film. George now wears evening clothes and has become her obvious escort and companion. As they dance check to cheek to the soft strains of the Angela theme, Stevens visually articulates their emotional and psychological intimacy through a series of overlapping intercuts that fuse their bodies and identities. A mark on Taylor's right cheek highlights her dark beauty. In an extraordinary two shot, they seem to become one person as the curve of his nose matches her bridge. A rather funny shot of two young people joined at the nose, it still captures a quality of adolescent intimacy and desire – one that she confirms with her sudden eruption of immature self-consciousness that others are watching them as he expresses his love.

They go off to be alone. Angela says how much their love scares her; then George, realizing that they cannot remain together because she leaves for vacation, asks, "But what's it going to be like next week?" – words that again

Figure 13. The sensitive stranger, George Eastman (Montgomery Clift), calls his "momma" and arouses the interest of Angela Vickers (Elizabeth Taylor) in *A Place in the Sun* (Paramount: The Museum of Modern Art Film Stills Archive).

emphasize his secondary and dependent position in their relationship. In reverse shots and intense close-ups that Stevens uses to magnify the couple's infatuation, the director brilliantly captures the youthful feeling of a world of their own separated from reality. Taylor's next lines remind us that Angela really is a schoolgirl, a debutante thinking about her summer. She tells him the family will be up at their beautiful house at the lake for the summer, and George can visit on the weekends "when the kids from school are up there." Taylor then breathlessly speaks lines that reemphasize her character's active and provocative role in this relationship: "If you don't come, I'll drive down here to see you. I'll pick you up outside the factory." She then pauses and looks at him with a marvelous touch of sexual suggestiveness and transgression in her voice and eyes. "You'll be my pickup. Oh, we'll arrange it somehow." Hearing these words, George, in a virtual fit of happy hysteria and joy, buries his face in her bosom and hands. His emotionalism and need render him thoroughly passive and dependent upon her love. "I'm the happiest person in the world," he says, playing the secondary and responsive part. "If I can only tell you how much I love you. If I can only tell you all." During the entire scene, he sounds dependent and feminized. Her re-

Figure 14. A modern American tragedy of desire: Montgomery Clift and Elizabeth Taylor look to an impossible future and dream in *A Place in the Sun* (Paramount: The Museum of Modern Art Film Stills Archive).

sponse marks the climax of his dependence upon her love and body: "Tell momma, tell momma all."

Of course, throughout the development of this teenage affair of the heart and of class, the reality principle, in the body and figure of Alice Tripp (Winters), functions with its promise of inevitable doom and death. Alice's failed attempts to have an abortion dramatize the despair and death at the core of her relationship with George. The blatant presentation of abortion as a possible result of sexuality represents an exercise in realism controversial for its time. Stevens shoots this part of the film in dark and ominous film-noir tones that advance the symbolic fatalism of George and Alice's affair. He also ingeniously films and directs Winters to embody a nagging and painful physical reality that articulates the film's countertheme of the body as a vehicle of death and loss as well as of life and love. Stevens portrays Alice's body as thoroughly recalcitrant to pleasure and fulfillment. Winters's performance, invariably reinforced with the deadeningly lethargic strains of her music, is designed to arouse the audience's ire against her: She epitomizes the victim to the point of turning even the spectator against her for interfering with the potential happiness of George and Angela. However, her role remains indispensable as the agent of the body's death and as the embodiment of the frustrated love, joy, and fulfillment that help define desire. Quite beautiful herself, Shelley Winters triumphs as Alice by allowing herself to be physically and psychologically contrasted with the glamour and vitality of Taylor.

The visual, physical, and symbolic tensions and oppositions between Taylor and Winters are so extreme, profound, and intense that Alice's ultimate death and George's conviction and execution finally seem anticlimactic. Similarly, Frank Marlowe (Raymond Burr), the vengeful, crippled prosecutor, proves irrelevant as a gruesome castrating force hoping to impose a form of superego or conscience upon George. Using a boat as a courtroom prop from which to accuse George of drowning and murdering Alice, Marlowe seems a weak imitation of Melville's Ahab. Marlowe can never achieve real stature because George already has condemned himself, even though Alice's fall from the boat and drowning finally were accidental.

All along, the real judge and executioner in the film have been George's vision of himself. From the beginning, George has been different, guilty, and emasculated, wishing only to be beautiful, loved, and protected. As Stevens apparently realizes, George's desire can be described in Freudian terms of unresolved Oedipal tensions of divided subjectivity, an unstable ego, and ambivalent gender identification. George's desire insists on identification with the imaginary closeness and security of the feminine as opposed to classic Oedipal distancing and displacement that establishes rigid male demarcations between the ego and reality. The priority the film places upon a Freudian interpretation of George's guilt in terms of youthful sexuality and regressed development gains offical expression in a late scene at Angela's school. Wearing her school uniform, Angela listens with other female students to a lecture about growing up. The lecture, whose language echoes the popularized Freudianism of the day, seems directed especially toward her to explain and simplify the film's meaning. While hearing that the "imagined problems" and "sheltered immaturity" of youth impede the young from mature analysis, Angela peeks at a newspaper story about the pending verdict in George's trial for the murder of Alice Tripp.

George's failure to outgrow youthful narcissism propelled him into an unreal situation, and he will die for it. The film, however, exonerates Angela as a rich, young woman. She also gains exculpation in George's eyes. He continues to love her for what she is and what he wants to be – loved, protected, secure, happy. She remains the object and recipient of emotional, psychological, and cultural rewards that make her the center of a system of privilege that countless women in the rising feminist movement came to see as a form of insidious confinement and denial. George, however, can not bring himself to condemn her for keeping the place and position he wishes to occupy.

Figure 15. Losing himself: Montgomery Clift and Elizabeth Taylor kiss in *A Place in the Sun* (Paramount: The Museum of Modern Art Film Stills Archive).

In the end, Stevens once again seems characteristically ambivalent. The aesthetics of the beautiful impossiblity of George's dream as embodied in his brilliantly idealized relationship with Taylor constitute a statement of hope and love. From the beginning moments of the film, Stevens's camera brazenly loves Clift and Taylor both individually and as a couple. The camera even admires the challenge Clift issues to conventional structures of love and sexual organization as much as it relishes Taylor's pleasure in her own beauty, charm, and glamour. However, the same Stevens camera also must impose order on the potential chaos of their emotion and the uncontrolled democracy of their love: The unreality and narcissism of their desire endanger progress and society. Thus, even in the aestheticization of their ideology of love, the film ultimately seeks containment of their dangerous passion through their separation and George's self-guilt and execution. Stevens thus continues the pattern of his career of controlling the forces and impulses for change and difference that make his films and the crises confronting his characters so compelling.

With brilliant prescience, Stevens's special ideological achievement in this film concerns his anticipation of the obsession of postwar generations with desire as lack, absence, difference. This focus on desire differs from the issues of conscience, moral leadership, and authority that concern other Hollywood Renaissance directors such as Zinnemann and Kazan. Stevens in *A Place in the Sun* suggests instead the growing psychological and cultural importance of insecurity and fractured identity. As Graham McCann says, "The movie is centred upon the leading man's anxious search for himself." Affirming the prophetic importance of this role for several decades of American cultural history, McCann calls Clift "the first full-blown appearance of the definitive 1950s hero." According to McCann, Charlie Chaplin apparently also perceived the significance of Clift's role when he called *A Place in the Sun* "the greatest movie ever made about America."[34]

In so praising Stevens and Clift, Chaplin also could have been considering how much his classic *Modern Times* (1936) helped to establish a precedent in modern film for understanding man's dilemma of endless destruction in terms of desire. *Modern Times* ends where *A Place in the Sun* begins – with a loner and outsider on the road as the avatar of desire. In *Modern Times,* desire as opposed to class and economics also serves as the nexus for social problems. The Tramp's involvement with Paulette Goddard, the epitome of the commodification of desire during their romp in a modern department store, and the social organization and control of the body throughout the film entail Chaplin's brilliant insight into the inescapable and dangerous relationship of eros, death and culture.[35] Like the assembly-line system at the Eastman factory that commercializes desire and redesigns the body, industrial society in both films manipulates unconscious wishes and channels eros, recasting the life force into the service of useful, controllable, and enervated social functions. Whereas Chaplin's Tramp survives and moves on with Goddard, Stevens's young hero dies alone as a martyr to desire. Instead of cultivating his sense of self in a quest for maturity and renewal, the Stevens hero lives and dies as an example of what Christopher Lasch has dubbed the modern "minimal self."[36]

For Stevens, the end that George Eastman faces constitutes a failure of postwar democracy to create institutions for individual fulfillment and cultural renewal. A sign of personal and cultural displacement and isolation, George Eastman, like Chaplin's Tramp, portends a precarious future for democracy and the potential end to the promise of regeneration in America. The ultimate consequences for such failure could be imagined in one of Stevens's last films, *The Diary of Anne Frank* (1959). The history entailed in the final days of Anne Frank's life and family fulfilled the worst nightmares of those who, like Stevens, feared the triumph of a fascist aesthetic over the sources for renewal in democratic art and culture. To the mid-twentieth-century American imagination, the American Renaissance and the Hollywood Renaissance endeavored to meet the challenge of that fascist aesthetic with a democractic one that bridged art and experience and related aesthetic expression to democratic life and culture. Now, near the end of the century, it seems hard to tell if the fragmentation and displacement of the past several decades, including the movements for change during the Vietnam era, contain similar resources for renewal. It remains uncertain whether there will emerge meaningful and potent alternatives to the symbolism of George Eastman's lonely martyrdom to desire. Certainly the search continues for new forms of democratic expression and for a relevant language of moral renewal to counter the deadening discourse of a culture dominated by public relations and nihilistic fragmentation and "dissensus." At the same time, as in years past, the sources of renewal may be working in places where many of us would never think to look.

More than a half century ago, during the last days of the Great Depression and the beginnings of World War II, the environment of the Hollywood Renaissance seemed more like a cultural graveyard than a garden in which a democratic aesthetic could foster an efflorescence of cultural renewal. At that time, a generation of ethnics and roughnecks, as Peter Bogdanovich indicates, was too busy directing to be hindered by self-conscious doubts about their art and purpose.[37] They had to focus on their work. Through their artistic and technical creativity, these ethnics and roughnecks revivified the culture and democracy that made and nurtured them. Whereas today so much of popular culture dies at birth, the success and triumph of the endeavors of the Hollywood Renaissance remain visible on screens throughout the world every moment of the day. Although much of America looks elsewhere, much of the world continues to look to those screens for a promise of a future of opportunity and hope and a vision of how to get there.

CHAPTER 7

CONCLUSION:
FILM AND AMERICA AFTER THE
HOLLYWOOD RENAISSANCE

When F. O. Matthiessen's *American Renaissance* appeared in 1941, Americans still were suffering from the worst economic depression in modern times and were on the brink of fighting the most extensive and deadliest war in all of human history. President Franklin D. Roosevelt described the ultimate danger from overseas in his "Arsenal of Democracy" fireside chat of 29 December 1940. A year before the attack on Pearl Harbor, Roosevelt told his radio listeners:

> Never before since Jamestown and Plymouth Rock has our American civilization been in such danger as now. . . . If Great Britain goes down, the Axis powers will control the continents of Europe, Asia, Africa, Australia, and the high seas – and they will be in a position to bring enormous military and naval resources against this hemisphere. It is no exaggeration to say that all of us, in all the Americas, would be living at the point of a gun.[1]

Summarizing conditions at home, Walter A. McDougall writes:

> The 1930s were the first protracted period of economic contraction in U.S. history, and the first time that neither an open frontier nor an open world provided a safety valve. The West Coast was already settled, and the Great Plains a Dust Bowl. The collapse of credit and the rush to protectionism choked world trade. Savings disappeared, and not just traditional hard cases – Negroes and new immigrants – but even white farmers, factory workers, tradesmen, and shopkeepers despaired of opportunity. One result was a reflexive longing for old virtues, a return to an older small-town America quarantined from a world of economic distress and political extremism. But that old civic religion of democracy and enterprise now seemed impotent, tempting intellectuals to flirt with Communism or Mussolini-style fascism, and common folk to tune in to demagogues.[2]

As noted in Chapter 1, in this time of unprecedented danger and distress, Matthiessen looked to American literature of the period 1850–5 to find the core of the American experience. He went to this age of what he considered to be our greatest writers to explore and explain the sources for the sustenance and renewal of our democracy. He called this period a renaissance, which to Matthiessen meant a flowering of America's greatest literary expression and also its regeneration as a democracy.

Matthiessen saw no inconsistency in going to what he deemed the "best" literature to find the energy and the foundation for renewing the culture for all the people. The spirit and potential for such renewal, he felt, resided in the writers with the most imaginative, original, profound, and illuminating language of their times. To Matthiessen, of course, these were Emerson, Thoreau, Melville, Hawthorne, and Whitman. He stressed that these writers should be read and studied in the terms in which they saw themselves, as democrats creating a literature for democracy. They were avatars of democratic culture who incorporated in their works, and even in their very being, the American democratic experience.

In a recent study of this period, David S. Reynolds develops Matthiessen's case for the renaissance writers as a literature for democracy. However, he emphasizes the relation of these writers to the wider, general culture as opposed to their aesthetic complexity and genius. He notes that "the relationship Emerson perceived between popular and elite culture was hardly one of hostility or antithesis: rather, it was one of reciprocity and cross-fertilization – almost of symbiosis." He adds:

> It should be recognized that the major writers saw themselves as distinctly democratic artists committed, in Melville's words, "to carry republican progressiveness into Literature" and to immerse themselves so deeply in their time and culture that their works actually became, in Whitman's phrase, "the age transfigured."[3]

For Reynolds, the "literariness" of the American Renaissance "resulted not from a *rejection* of socioliterary context but rather from a full *assimilation* and *transformation* of key images and devices from this context."[4]

Through the artistic form of film, the Hollywood Renaissance also sought to engage the culture in all its dimensions and to provide a source for cultural and social renewal. Led by several great directors such as John Ford, Frank Capra, Howard Hawks, Fred Zinnemann, Elia Kazan, and George Stevens, this Hollywood Renaissance originated in the same era of national crisis and uncertainty that inspired Matthiessen's thesis concerning the renaissance of pre–Civil War writers. In this study, I have tried to show that the same kind of relationship between aesthetics and culture that helped to define certain writings of the 1850s as a literature for democracy also functioned a century later in Hollywood to create a cinema for democracy. The directors of the Hollywood Renaissance – along with a vast array of other directors, actors, production leaders, and industrial workers – created and sustained a system to perpetuate a democratic aesthetic of artistic complexity and originality as well as cultural depth and engagement. Working with film as a modernistic, heterogeneous art form of multiple channels of communication, these filmmakers justifiably earned the epithet of *auteurs*. They were artistic innovators, leaders with unique styles and visions. Their work synthesized popular-culture forms and elite sensibilities.

Thus, the great films made by these directors were as ineluctably intertwined with American culture as were the literary works of the earlier American Renaissance. Their films achieved a heightening of the strengths, weaknesses, ambiguities, tensions, and dangers of American culture as a whole. Like their predecessors in the American literary renaissance, the directors of the Hollywood Renaissance did not propose to transcend American culture through their own elitism or moral superiority; nor did they become so immured in the culture as to lose their identities within its various aesthetic, cultural, or political ideologies. Instead, the Hollywood filmmakers, like their literary progenitors, were fully engaged with the culture: They defined themselves and their differences with society in terms of America. American discourse dominated their thinking.

Although the films of the Hollywood Renaissance are distinct, individual aesthetic works, what Matthiessen terms "recurrent themes" and "interrelations" connect the films and directors to each other and to the culture. Significant works of aesthetic coherence and excellence, the films structure themes and issues, symbols and images, tensions and ambiguities that concern different levels, spheres, and arenas of cultural experience. The articulation and development of these themes and relationships help define the films and their directors as part of a cultural and aesthetic movement of great importance to American art and national identity in midcentury.

The nature and multiplicities of heroic masculinity in America operate as a major thread in the renaissance. The American hero as represented in the Hollywood Renaissance stands as an emblem of American character, but he also embodies the complexities of the modern revolution of gender and sexual relations. A quality of the Puritan loner continues to apply to many of these heroes. During the Hollywood Renaissance, the American hero tended to be a Puritan rebel, a moral consciousness at odds with the dominant culture for its failure to maintain and advance the American Way – like Thoreau, the rebel whose very rebellion epitomized the individualism and moral strength of the American Way and idea. The heroic figures in these films often tend to embody the intrinsic tension in heroic American masculinity concerning the conflict between speaking for and representing the culture by standing in opposition to it. Gary Cooper's Marshal Kane, acting on his own conscience regardless of the cost to himself and his community, and Marlon Brando's Terry Malloy, dismissing Edie's request to stop fighting so that he can go and get his rights, both personify in their different ways this paradoxical aspect of American heroic masculinity and individuality.

Through these films and characters, the directors of the Hollywood Renaissance often act as modern Jeremiahs in their insistence that individual moral conscience contains the potential to redeem the entire community. In performing the rites of conscience as one person, the individual saves himself and enables the regeneration of the community as well. By exercising radical individualism, the characters played by these actors help revivify the very culture that often misuses and estranges them. Thus, the priority the films place upon individual conscience dramatizes the historic clash in American history and culture between the individual and society. In the role of the Puritan rebel who embodies the values and ideals but also the conflicts and paradoxes of modern American consciousness and consensus, this heroic figure in these films operates vigorously and dynamically between the cultural center and its frontiers. The rebel-hero remains both key and marginal; like Wayne's Ethan Edwards, he occupies the heart of the culture but stands in a liminal position just outside the door. As represented by such heroic figures as Wayne's major characters, Cooper's Will Kane, and Brando's Terry Malloy, the same argument could be made regarding the Hollywood Renaissance directors that applies, according to Reynolds, to the American Renaissance writers: They were not "alienated rebels" but represented in their rebellion the very values and beliefs of the society.[5]

In the Hollywood Renaissance, the dynamic relationship between sexuality and gender revisions heroic masculinity. The spectacle of the male face and body continually subverts and complicates stereotypical notions of one-dimensional masculinity in American film. Jimmy Stewart pioneers in problematizing gender through his explosive emotionalism and anxiety in his major roles, but so also does Wayne in *Stagecoach*. The camera's embrace of Wayne when first we meet Ringo; the softness of Alan Ladd's face in *Shane*, perhaps more feminine than that of his costar, Jean Arthur; the spectacle of Burt Lancaster's torso in *From Here to Eternity* – all these signify the truth of Montgomery Clift's claim as Prewitt in the latter film that all men are different. "Prew" asks Alma "Lorene" (Donna Reed) if girls only want to tease a man to death without regard for the sensitivities of men's innermost feelings. His plea for liberation for men from crudely stereotypical images of masculinity demonstrates the intensity of the endeavor in the Hollywood Renaissance to complicate and diversify the whole notion of masculinity and heroism. The critical question for each heroic figure becomes, in Lee Clark Mitchell's phrase, "What does it mean to be a man?"[6] The range of responses to the question testifies to the multiplicity of masculinities in America as rendered through these figures in their films. Such diversity further suggests a somewhat underappreciated complexity to the whole issue of heroic masculinity in America. The determination and organization of this variety of masculinities concern, as Mitchell suggests, an interaction and negotiation "between sex and gender."[7]

The examples of Stewart, Wayne, Clift, Lancaster, Brando, and Cooper also suggest the complex uses of the spectacle and the gaze as articulations of gender in the Hollywood Renaissance. A fluidity obtains in many of these films over who controls the look or gaze as opposed to who functions as the object of such visual objectification.[8] Continuing alternations between subjectivity and objectivity compound the complexity of the controlling vision and complicate gender construction. This dynamic visual fluidity and flexibility over the domination of the look and the gaze add considerably to the potential complexity of narrative structure and ideology in many major films.

At the same time, the films of the Hollywood Renaissance emphasize what Leonard Kriegel calls an earned sense of selfhood. The sensitivity, emotionalism, and introspection of a Stewart, Brando, or Clift do not preclude the responsibility for the individual to achieve a constructed sense of identity and a meaningful place in the world. Achieved selfhood in such films frequently extends to the empowerment of women, often as a way of advocating true equality, as in several Frank Capra classics. In many of the Hollywood Renaissance films, women not only see and have vision, they also think and embody the film's moral, emotional, and intellectual consciousness. The moral independence of Grace Kelly's Amy as well as the ethnic and sexual assertiveness of Katy Jurado's Helen Ramirez in *High Noon;* the creative intelligence of Jean Arthur's Saunders in *Mr. Smith;* the emotional stability and moral vision of Donna Reed as Mary Hatch in *Wonderful Life;* the power of conscience of Edie as played by Eva Marie Saint in *On the Waterfront;* the rising feminist consciousness and liberalism of Elizabeth Taylor's Leslie Lynnton in *Giant* – all indicate a theme of powerful female consciousness, independence, and identity in the films of this movement. Moreover, the heroic actions, characterizations, and functions of these women in these films parallel the roles of the men as rebel-heroes and saints. Like the men, the women can be seen as figures of rebellion and redemption: By following their individual consciences, they help create the potential for collective redemption. This role of embodying heroic representation while also resisting moral conformity obtains for Amy, Saunders, Edie, and Leslie, among others. Like their male counterparts, these women best represent their culture and history when they have the strength to stand alone on the foundation of their own consciences.

Throughout this study, the dual concerns as to the revisioning of heroic masculinity and the changing situation and authority of women have entailed considerable use of Freudian and Lacanian interpretations of sexuality and gender. The concentration of post-Freudian theory upon the ego as a construction in language and culture, and the notion of the permanent destabilization of meaning and identity, help support and explain the argument for the mutability of gender and personality organization. This theory also has proven compatible with the dynamic and heterogeneous nature of film as a unique, multidimensional art form of changing visual images and forms and a diversity of sound. Indeed, the instability of identity and the ephemeral nature of reality infuse the films of the Hollywood Renaissance from the nightmarish sequence of *Wonderful Life* to the martyrdom of George Eastman in *A Place in the Sun.* The methodology and ideology of Freudian and post-Freudian psychoanalysis, therefore, help provide insight and structure to film's articulation of a cultural field as well as its aesthetic form of perennial change and transformation.

At the core of these explosive impulses toward change in the Hollywood Renaissance rests what Sacvan Bercovitch terms an ideology of American consensus and mission that proffers coherence and form. The films of the renaissance movement tend to structure this consensus around a system of beliefs that goes back to our initial discussion of the "American Creed" as delineated by Gunnar Myrdal and developed by a series of thinkers ranging from Daniel Boorstin and Max Lerner to Bercovitch. In this study's interpretation of that creed in the Hollywood Renaissance, the basic values and beliefs of the American idea include the following: the individual and collective mission to seek and achieve redemption and regeneration in America; individual and civil rights; equality of opportunity; and the universalism of America as a sanctuary and asylum, where all peoples of the world can belong together as one new people in the New World. Different variations of these themes resonate in the films of the Hollywood Renaissance from *Mr. Smith* to *High Noon, Shane,* and *Giant.*

However, though this ideology and creed provide the foundational stability for change by emplacing a coherent system of beliefs and values, a special genius of the ideology concerns how it organizes and directs change. Consistent with the Puritan tradition of the jeremiad, the rhetorical tension between ideals and reality constitutes a structure and mechanism for inspiring and managing change. The ideals of Myrdal's American Creed and Bercovitch's ideology of consensus provide the parameters and format for debate. The expression of the ideal and the consensus ideology, of course, help to articulate the meaning of failing and digressing from the creed; thus, the effort to maintain the American Creed and ideology of consensus explains failure in the very terms of the creed and consensus. Equally important, the rhetorical gap between the ideal and real organizes the perception of and discourse about social reality. The rhetoric, therefore, helps to control social change by expressing the need for change in terms of America's hegemonic ideology.

Similarly, the most important films of the Hollywood Renaissance often structure both narrative and ideology upon the tensions between American ideals and realities. These films articulate an extended pilgrim's journey that emphasizes the significance of ultimately achieving redemption and salvation in terms of the American idea. Such journeys through American consciousness often engage sinister and insidious dimensions of the American experience and psyche. During these encounters with the evils of the self and society, inner fear and anxiety sometimes become objectified in the form of women and minorities, a psychological and cultural phenomenon occasionally dramatized and even condoned in some of the most important films of the Hollywood Renaissance. At the same time, the journey in other films primarily involves either confronting failure and rejection (Jefferson Smith and George Bailey) or dealing mostly with fear and conformity (Will Kane and Terry Malloy).

Moreover, violence often becomes an expression of these tensions between moral idealism and the corruptions, demands, and realities of ordinary experience. Many of the heroes in these films envision a reality that justifies violent action in the name of a higher purpose for the individual and the society. These rebel-heroes in the movies of these directors begin, as D. H. Lawrence says of the classic American hero, with a kind of violent innocence. The volatility and exuberance of Jimmy Stewart's Mr. Smith and George Bailey, the moral wrath and fury of Wayne's Ethan Edwards and Dunson, the isolation and strength of Marshal Kane, and the explosiveness of Terry Malloy all evoke elements of violent engagement and encounter concerning moral consciousness.

Whereas ideology sometimes structures and sanctions violence in the Hollywood Renaissance, the ideology of consensus and the American Creed in the best films of the period also achieve lasting expression through debate and change. For the directors in the renaissance, ideology provides the medium for struggle and engagement between American ideals and realities. Such dialogue and dissension distinguishes the democratic aesthetic of the Hollywood Renaissance from the fascist aesthetic of totalitarian societies. The emphasis upon the common man, the ordinary life, and the bonds that bring people together in shared human experience also characterizes the democratic aesthetic of this renaissance.

Throughout the 1950s and early 1960s, the heroic masculinity and conscience of the Hollywood Renaissance characters played by Cooper, Wayne, Gregory Peck, or Spencer Tracy (among others) still resonated throughout the culture. For many, such figures continued to demonstrate the validity of the myth and ideology of America. Cooper's classic American independence and integrity, Wayne's evolution from boyish charm to its opposite as angry and anguished moral authoritarianism, and Brando's evocation of sensitivity and ethnic identity were all recognizable representations of American character.

These actors helped to ensure the stability and continuity of American patterns of belief and hegemony. In their roles and, for many, in their public lives, they provided some of the ideological and emotional cohesion that held the center together. They were an important element within the larger national consensus at the time that saw the world and judged experience in American terms of moral mission, leadership, and consciousness. Also, in many of their films as discussed in this study, they often speak for and exemplify an idealized consensus of universalism and renewal. The accessibility and pervasiveness of this consensus legitimize and give authority to their characters' independence and autonomy. In the logical circularity of all ideologies, these same actors also bestow credibility and authority upon the consensus as representatives of it.

Thus, in 1956 Ford and John Wayne and Stevens and Rock Hudson articulate in their different ways an ideology of America as a sanctuary and asylum for all peoples. In *The Searchers,* Ethan's "Let's go home, Debbie," and in *Giant,* Bick's acceptance of his "little muchacho" as a welcome and beloved grandson personify the effort to turn the family into a metaphor for American consensus. In these films, Ford and Stevens concretize in the imagery and symbolism of the American family and home, the abstract notions of Myrdal's American Creed of equality, democracy, rights, and universalism. The statements and actions in these films of Ethan and Bick gain considerable meaning and impact through the psychological, ideological, and dramatic processes of delay and conflict that mark their development as characters. In each case, the film's narrative fulfills itself through the transformation of the hero in a manner that also signifies ideological change for the culture. Demonstrating the prescience and hopes of both directors, these films appeared before the emergence of the civil-rights crusade of the 1960s that ultimately generated so much historic change for African American and other minorities.

Accordingly, such figures and themes in American film and culture help account for the belief that in 1960, as James T. Patterson asserts in his history of postwar America, the political center "seemed to hold."[9] A sense of confidence and promise imbued the thinking and feelings of many throughout the entire society who were involved in or believed in holding that center together. Patterson notes, "There seemed little reason to anticipate that the political center would shift very much in the days to come."[10] More than merely holding onto and maintaining the political center, the rhetorical strategies and programs of the early 1960s actually articulated the strongest and most expansive expression of the zeal of the liberal consensus.[11] As symbolic expressions of broad public policies with deep historic and cultural roots, John F. Kennedy's New Frontier and Lyndon B. Johnson's Great Society characterized the hegemony of the liberal consensus at its apex. The social idealism and economic optimism of both these programs seemed to promise, almost guarantee, a degree of economic, social, and political success and opportunity never previously believed possible even through the most sophisticated social engineering and management. Such programs and policies, therefore, stimulated great hopes and heady feelings of anticipation. For many, the age of entitlements of all kinds had arrived.[12]

However, as Patterson notes, within just a few years of the promise and optimism that initially greeted the ascendancy of President Kennedy, "the center seemed in some disarray, especially after mid-decade." According to Patterson, "The center that had more or less held in the late 1950s, cracked in the 1960s, exposing a glaring, often unapologetic polarization that seemed astonishing to contemporaries."[13] In the mid-1960s, the disastrous results of the New Frontier mentality in Vietnam and the flaming demise of the Great Society in the riots and burnings in the inner city signaled cultural collapse and turmoil. A sense of failure and confusion now suddenly permeated the whole society.

Thus, by the mid-1960s, visualizations of American ideology and culture, as seen previously in the consensus symbolism of *The Searchers* and *Giant*, showed fissures, then wider cracks, and finally shattering breaks and divisions. Unceasing and strident demands from a vast array of groups for deeper and faster social, cultural, political, and economic reform suggested the emergence of a time of profound transitions of all sorts throughout all levels and areas of American society and culture. From the perspectives of the marginalized, unseen, silent, and alienated in America, the relationship of the imagery and symbolism of home to the ideology of consensus and the American Creed seemed to dim steadily in its relevance to felt experience and daily needs. The everyday lives and concerns of the dispossessed and alienated, and often of much of the working and middle class, appeared remote from such idealistic expressions as Myrdal's American Creed.

The films of the Hollywood Renaissance also could seem remote, unrealistic, and patronizing to such people, especially women and people of color. Even within some of their most important films that develop a democratic aesthetic for cinema, the renaissance directors, as noted in Chapter 1, sometimes could not escape exhibiting and representing some of the worst aspects of American culture. Native Americans and African Americans sometimes were denigrated and demonized as embodying otherness, difference, and disunity, whereas women often were only vehicles for the salvation and regeneration of morally privileged and powerful men. Examples of such dehumanization abound in many Hollywood Renaissance films: Ford's humiliation of the Indian woman Look in *The Searchers* and his depreciation of the potential of the Woody Strode character in *The Man Who Shot Liberty Valance* reveal – in the very films that attempt to expose injustice and surmount discrimination – deep ambiguities and conflicts over race and gender that Ford shares with the culture. Likewise, Capra's dismissive attitude toward the maid, Annie (Lillian Randolph), in *It's a Wonderful Life* and Stevens's treatment of women and blacks in *Swing Time* and *Woman of the Year* represent unfortunate insensitivity toward minorities and women. Even as the male in the films of the Hollywood Renaissance underwent meaningful complication that revisioned heroic masculinity into new modes of sensitivity and emotional depth, the question of the place, situation, and condition of minorities and women remained and pressed for clearer expression and stronger conscious articulation. Ironically, both the presence and absence of this issue of the place of minorities and women in film and society vaticinated changes that soon occurred throughout the culture.

At the same time, mainstream values, beliefs, and patterns of life also seemed in transition for what had been considered the American cultural center. It is difficult to be as precise about the exact date of this collapse of this American center as Virginia Woolf felt about the emergence of modernism: "On or about December 1910 human nature changed," she said, proclaiming a revolutionary transformation in the break between historical tradition and the rise of a modernist culture of discontinuity, fragmentation, and the new.[14] However, at some point in the mid-to-late 1960s, the nation that had invented and reinvented itself since its founding and held together for more than two centuries seemed to be in a process of implosion. To some, it has been in chaos ever since – a kind of deep, black hole of negativity and destruction that subverts and impugns not only recent history but the past and our national identity. The collapse of the American center yet may prove as significant as the break between cultural tradition and modernism.

Interestingly, the rediscovery of modernism by intellectuals and academics coincided in the 1960s with the turmoil over foreign and domestic events, as though a modernist and soon a postmodernist ideology of the new and the absent could fill the vacuum left by the breakdown and sudden disrepute for some of the American idea. As innovators in the new art form of film, many directors in the Hollywood Renaissance anticipated this move to a modernist mode, including Ford in his melding of a modernist consciousness and the mythic West in *The Searchers*. Similarly, in his new biography of Howard Hawks, Todd McCarthy repeatedly describes Hawks as "a modern artist" and a figure of "modernity" and of "unceasing modernity."[15] In the 1960s, many also considered that modernism could energize creative forces for cultural renewal through new ways of thinking about all aspects of life, from sexuality and the family, to revolutionary technologies of thought and behavior, to reconceptualizing and rearranging relationships involving generations, gender, and groups in the new era. Also, the excitement generated by thinkers attracted to intellectual and artistic modes and innovations related to modernism – Marshall McLuhan, Herbert Marcuse, Norman O. Brown, Norman Mailer, and R. D. Laing, among so many others[16] – probably helped accelerate the collapse of the center not only through their aesthetic and cultural radicalism but also through their contribution to what Patterson terms "grand expectations." The radical vision of new social structures and behaviors and the zealous belief in new forms of consciousness all encouraged the growth of the optimism of the early 1960s that ultimately faded so dramatically and so precipitously.

The several months from the summer of 1967 to the winter of 1968 is as close as most students of the 1960s get to perceiving and identifying the exact time of the collapse of the American center. As Richard Slotkin writes,

> The seven-month period that began with the Newark and Detroit riots in the summer of 1967 and ended with the Tet Offensive signaled the eruption of a major crisis of politics and ideology which ultimately fragmented the conceptual and political consensus that had shaped our history since 1945. A political and ideological crisis of this magnitude naturally affected nearly every aspect of our cultural life and expression by calling into question some of the most basic elements of our belief structures, most particularly the belief that our political leadership and institutions of government are generally reliable, rational, and trustworthy, and that our political discourse provides both a reasonably truthful accounting of events and useful mechanisms for articulating and giving effect to the wisdom and will of the public.[17]

Slotkin here makes the political and economic institutions behind the war culpable for the collapse of the center.[18]

Slotkin's rhetoric contrasts somewhat with the emphasis different social thinkers and historians place upon other underlying technological, industrial, economic, and social forces for explaining the transformation of the culture at this time.[19] The values and beliefs of the myth of the frontier and ideology of consensus – mission, purpose, conscience, character, incorporation, expansion, domination – conflicted in the Vietnam era with the values nurtured and cultivated by the emerging technological society of consumerism and security. As early as 1951, Stevens's *A Place in the Sun* indicated a mood of incipient change in American character from placing priorities upon the search for consensus, the idealism of the American Creed, and the myth of renewal to a quest for security and anonymity within the "massification" of all aspects of American life. This turn in the development of American heroism and character proved symptomatic of other contexts and forces for change of all sorts.

During these Vietnam-era years of collapse, the culture and films of the Hollywood Renaissance also faded from view and evolved into a different kind of cinema of "dissensus" and fragmentation. Originating in the middle to late 1960s, postrenaissance films and culture interacted and produced each other, a process of aesthetic and cultural reconstruction aptly described by the title of a book by Robert Sklar, *Movie-Made America* – a phrase that inherently suggests the production and reproduction of many movie-made Americas over time.[20] While Mike Nichols's *The Graduate* (1967) proposed a transformation of middle-class values and life-styles, Arthur Penn's *Bonnie and Clyde* (1967) suggested a quality of moral equivalence to the violence and lawlessness of his characters that portended a pervasive skepticism concerning all social and cultural authority. Similarly, Sam Peckinpah's effort in *The Wild Bunch* (1969) to institute what Lee Clark Mitchell terms "a resurrection of the myth of a heroic West" ends in disaster and total destruction without resolving the issues of loyalty, commitment, discipline, love, and belief that concern it. The film also leaves unresolved the paradox, as Mitchell notes, that "restraint," which helps characterize and define masculine discipline and identity in the western, "can only be demonstrated through narratives of excess."[21] In societies that normalize excess, the restraint and discipline for mature manhood become anachronistic and irrelevant. Absent such restraint, popularized theories of the imploding cultural and political center in films of the 1960s made ideas of collapse part of the era's common knowledge and conventional wisdom, thereby helping to normalize, anticipate, and perhaps even encourage such chaos and cynicism.

Ironically, the very notion of a collapsed center for mainstream America seems self-centered. The crisis of the collapse of the liberal center of consensus suggests a kind of class and ideological conceit that elides embedded crises and miseries for marginalized peoples throughout our history. For Native Americans, the center collapsed several hundred years ago with the sight of the first white invaders's sails. For centuries of obliteration and oppression, nothing they tried or imagined could sustain their ways of life, cultures, and domains. Their center never was restored. Similarly, for Mexicans the center also dissipated with the intrusion of Anglo-American culture throughout the Southwest and West in the nineteenth century. Meanwhile, for African Americans, it could be argued, the concept of a center never even obtained: Originally brought to the country as slaves after already suffering captivity and enslavement in Africa, for many blacks a center of American origins as a source of pride and strength for character and independence never actually manifested itself.

The marginalization and alienation of minorities and women have caused many to reconsider or abandon the notion of a center in favor of a concept of a culture and society of greater diversity and equality. To some extent, the most vocal and articulate abandonment has come from academic fields and intellectual circles that previously helped to define and construct the center as a usable concept. To quote Sacvan Bercovitch, "the paradigm has become inoperative."[22] Bercovitch, of course, means a paradigm that structures a continuity through history and throughout culture and society, a model of coherent belief that inspires and holds the allegiance of people from all parts of society. An inoperative paradigm in this case means not only the rejection of a literary canon and tradition that articulate and substantiate national and cultural values and beliefs; this ineffective literary and historical paradigm reflects a redefinition of the liberal center as a restricted sphere for the privileged. The deprecation of the old paradigm also reconsiders the idealism of the American Creed as an ideological mechanism for the dissimulation of domination and co-optation as empowerment and participation. The values, ideology, life-styles, and realities of the post-Vietnam era involving civil and minority rights, gender, consumerism, and technology help explain the tendency of some who once occupied the center to disavow it.

Thus, for many the moral and intellectual consequences of this situation of a collapsed center have been dire. At least since the late 1960s, the alleged lack of any apparent or immediate resolution to this crisis of belief and action in modern culture consumes the consciousness of some with a pervasive dread. Such anguish derives from the conviction that the apocalytic prophecy of William Butler Yeats finally has been fulfilled in this land of pilgrims, a nation founded on the prediction of impending doom as a judgment for the failure to maintain a moral mission of leadership and inspiration to the world:

> Things fall apart; the centre cannot hold;
> Mere anarchy is loosed upon the world,
> The blood-dimmed tide is loosed, and everywhere
> The ceremony of innocence is drowned;
> The best lack all conviction, while the worst
> Are full of passionate intensity.

This vision of chaos and catastrophe inspires the feeling, in Yeats's words, that indeed "some revelation is at hand; / Surely the Second Coming is at hand." For some, the end in the form of Yeats's "rough beast" stalking the moral wilderness of contemporary life seems upon us.[23]

Also, the collapsed center displaces the moral consciousness of leadership and responsibility that the films of the Hollywood Renaissance so admired. As formulated and dramatized in these films, the Puritan rebel-hero gains psychic nourishment and moral strength in his conflict with the society that fails its own ideals and moral expectations. He grows stronger, not weaker, in his isolation through his embodiment of the very values and beliefs the society will not uphold. The absence of such individual strength through independence suggests what we earlier discussed as David Riesman's model of a new national character type of the other-directed person who becomes dependent upon others for moral approval. Riesman and many other social critics and thinkers, such as Christopher Lasch, worry that democratic culture cannot survive the absence of individual character to sustain it. George Bailey's nightmarish vision of his community as a carnal hell and Marshal Kane's isolation as a pariah are realized in a culture that nurtures insecurity and weakness. Psychologically impoverished and fearful individuals and fractured identities cannot maintain the kind of leadership that the renaissance era promoted. According to these social thinkers, moral conformity as opposed to individual conscience propels an endless search for acceptance and approval without adequate regard for moral consequences. The reconstruction of a workable center becomes hard to imagine without a democratic consensus based on individual conscience and renewal.

At the same time, it needs to be remembered that, almost by definition, America has existed with a destabilized center, a core that not only accepts but promises and thrives on challenge and change. Whether in the form of Thomas Jefferson's "tree of liberty" that feeds on the blood of revolution or in the processes of continuous immigration and assimilation, America always has been in the making.[24] Attempts to reconstitute a center should therefore include a commitment to seeing our history of continuity also as a history of deconstruction based upon perpetual change and transition. Understanding American history as an experience of difference, change, pluralism, and accommodation should facilitate efforts to reimagine and restructure a center that incorporates all peoples as Americans.

The attempt to reconceptualize precisely such a center based on the relationship of contemporary minorities, especially African Americans, to the dominant ideology of consensus and the American Creed can be seen as an overriding concern of Nathan Glazer, among many others. Glazer was part of a group of leading social thinkers who helped to initiate the basic discourse and define the terms of the relationship of ethnicity to the American center during the dominance of the liberal consensus. His most recent work on multiculturalism, *We Are All Multiculturalists Now*, can add considerably to the attempt in this study of American film and culture to relate the meaning of the cinema of democracy during the Hollywood Renaissance to the need today to reconstruct the American ideological and cultural consensus to incorporate minorities into a refurbished center.

Significantly, in his current reconsideration of the nature of American identity, Glazer begins by acknowledging his departure from his own orthodox model of classic assimilation and pluralism in America. He now accepts the argument that realities for African Americans differ markedly from the conditions for assimilation of earlier generations: "Black separatism is largely a reaction to what is seen as white rejection, of the failure of the larger society to integrate blacks."[25] Accepting that racism, history, and culture require a different model of assimilation for blacks, Glazer now rethinks his rejection years ago of multiculturalism, a term that to him means a recognition for some period of time of racial and ethnic differences as an institutionalized aspect of much of American life: "Multiculturalism is the price America is paying for its inability or unwillingness to incorporate into its society African Americans, in the same way and to the same degree it has incorporated so many groups" (147). He adds:

> It seems we must pass through a period in which we recognize difference, we celebrate difference, we turn the spotlight on the inadequacies in the integration of our minorities in our past and present, and we raise up for special consideration the achievements of our minorities and their putative ancestors. (159)

It should be reemphasized that for Glazer the current need to focus on difference derives directly from the failure of the dominant culture to meet the moral demands of its own values and creed in its treatment of African Americans and other minorities: "All this is premised on our failure to integrate blacks. Others are included in this process; but it is the response to blacks, their different conditions, their different perspective, that sets the model" (159). In making his argument this way, Glazer not only repeats the process of using the moral and intellectual power of the American Creed to promote change; he also structures and articulates his argument throughout his book in the moralistic and idealistic terms of the jeremiad, which infuse the forces for change with moral and psychological power. For Glazer, therefore, the moral tension between the ideals and realities of the American Creed still can articulate, motivate, and energize the forces for change.

In rethinking and altering his view of multiculturalism, Glazer once again repeats the vital conservative process of reforming the system in order to save it. His argument that now multiculturalism defines us all reaffirms Myrdal's notion of the conservative instinct of the American Creed to survive by recognizing, accommodating, and ultimately incorporating difference. Glazer's objective, therefore, remains the renewal of the American idea through a new means called multiculturalism with roots in a historic process of cultural change.

Thus, in making what to him is such a drastic break from his earlier position about pluralism and American identity, Glazer actually may be moving closer to a position identified with such thinkers as Bercovitch and Henry Louis Gates, Jr., who tend to view multiculturalism benignly as a modernized form of democratic pluralism and Americanism cast in language and rhetoric for today. At various times, they have suggested that today's multiculturalism looks as old and tested as the words and practice of Tom Paine, Crèvecoeur, and Herman Melville.[26] Similarly, a new collection of pieces on multiculturalism by leading thinkers on the subject uses a recent quote by cultural historian Lawrence W. Levine – widely known as partial toward the causes of minorities in both the study of history and in contemporary events – as an epigraph on its opening pages: "Multiculturalism means that in order to understand the nature and complexities of American culture, it is crucial to study and comprehend the widest possible array of the contributing cultures and their interraction with one another."[27] Levine's definition of multiculturalism seems to replicate efforts to place the movement within the broad tradition of achieving consensus and unity out of pluralistic diversity in America.

By acceding to the growing respectability of this form of multiculturalism, Glazer deemphasizes some other widely accepted definitions of the term that present multiculturalism as meaning an absolute equivalence between cultures. As one cultural journalist, Edward Rothstein, asserts, "Multiculturalism posits that there is no objective standard by which one culture can be judged superior to another, thus enshrining the principle of equality."[28] Rather than agreeing to such equivalence or even the permanent institutionalization of rigid demarcations among ethnic groups in America, Glazer essentially reaffirms the ideal of univeralism in the hope of ultimately achieving classic cultural amalgamation:

> Let us understand that more and more Americans want to be Americans simply, and nothing more, and let us celebrate that choice, and agree it would be better for Americans if more of us accepted that identity as our central one, as against ethnic and racial identities. (159)

Glazer's sermonic tone and style in this passsage warrants attention and discussion. After previously acknowledging with profound seriousness the great historic and cultural disparities between the opportunities for assimilation for earlier generations and the realities of difference and discrimination for African Americans today, Glazer's declaration of ideological and cultural continuity between ages and peoples contains elements of faith and prayer. The supplicating tone of his phrases "let us understand" and "let us celebrate" extols the continuation of a universal American identity as opposed to "ethnic and racial identities." He maintains the tradition of evoking an aura of religious prophecy when discussing the meaning of America. Indeed, the use of religious forms and ideas to articulate and structure conceptions of America go back to our very origins. In the context of Glazer's issue and argument, such language and thinking perhaps reflect his sense of a need to create a new reality through conscious and committed individual and group action. Thus, in Glazer's new model, multiculturalism continues the history of a rhetorical strategy of envisioning and presenting the American ideal as a form of moral consciousness. As now perceived and understood by Glazer, multiculturalism articulates and structures new ways to create access to the American Creed and to expand the ideology of consensus – a creed and ideology that remain the world's most prominent and promising continuing cultural and political ideology for individual regeneration in human history.

Glazer's accommodation to reality in reconsidering the value and importance of multiculturalism to American politics today helps toward reestablishing a meaningful and relevant center and returns the cultural debate to a historic strategy for renewal. Emphasizing the assimilation of African Americans recognizes that historically the American Way has advanced through the incorporation rather than the exclusion of diverse peoples.

With this vision of continued renewal in mind, it seems worthwhile to recall the journey Elia Kazan dramatizes in his film *America, America* (1963). Kazan discovers the meaning of America by returning to Turkey to find the "discarded self" of what could have been his identity and destiny without the opportunity for rebirth in America. His finding this discarded self in the face of a Turkish relative renders new significance to his American existence; it puts his personal history, his successes and failures, his gains and losses in a fresh perspective. In contrast to his opportunity for rebirth as an individual and a man in America, he envisions another life as a minority member in Turkey: It is a dark prison of ethnic determinism and confinement, a world of rigid boundaries in which blood origins and ethnic inheritances predominate; tradition and history rather than creativity, choice, individual genius, personal ambition, and renewal define character and life. Of course, Kazan's affirmation of the myth and ideology of America in his own story of discovery, creation, and reinvention particularizes what has become the metastory of becoming American.[29] In his own way, Kazan also replicates the earlier narratives of Puritan redemption that provided the first accounts of Americanization as a process of the acquisition of a new state of mind as well as new cultural and geographical environments.

Revisioning the classic immigrant journey to America to include multiculturalism opens America more to African Americans and other peoples. In making this argument, Gates, Bercovitch, Glazer, and others affirm a process that in fact refigures and reconstructs America at this moment. The process of greater incorporation and transformation already has engaged significant numbers of people who assert their commitment to broadening the American consensus and revivifying the American Creed, but not only through continuing immigration and assimilation.

Thus, in passages of great courage, honesty, and emotion, Keith B. Richburg, an African-American reporter for the *Washington Post,* describes the discovery of his America through a vision of his lost identity in Africa. As a correspondent covering Africa for the *Post,* Richburg describes being on the Rusumo Falls Bridge and watching countless dead float down the Kagera River in Tanzania, headed for Lake Victoria and oblivion. Numbers of dead float by every minute: "These were the victims of the ethnic genocide going on across the border in Rwanda. The killers were working too fast to allow for proper burials."[30]

Watching these dead in Africa, Richburg undergoes an emotional, psychological, and ideological transformation akin to what Kazan depicts of his time in Turkey. He reports that "I was seeing all of this horror a bit differently because of the color of my skin." Realizing that seeing "these nameless, faceless, anonymous bodies washing over a waterfall or piled up on the back of trucks, what I see most is that they look like me," Richburg has a near-mystical experience, a kind of epiphany concerning his own identity:

> Sometime, maybe four hundred or so years ago, one of my ancestors was taken from his village, probably by a local chieftain. He was shackled in leg irons, kept in a holding pen or a dark pit, possibly at Goree Island off the coast of Senegal. And then he was put in the crowded, filthy cargo hold of a ship for the long and treacherous voyage across the Atlantic to the New World.
>
> Many of the slaves died on that voyage. But not my ancestor. Maybe it was because he was strong, maybe just stubborn, or maybe he had an irrepressible will to live. But he survived, and ended up in forced slavery on plantations in the Caribbean. Generations on down the line, one of his descendants was taken to South Carolina. Finally, a more recent descendant, my father, moved to Detroit to find a job in an auto plant during the Second World War.
>
> And so it was that I came to be born in Detroit and that thirty-five years later, a black man born in white America, birthplace of my ancestors, standing at the edge of a river not as an African but as an American journalist – a mere spectator – watching the bloated bodies of black Africans cascading over a waterfall.[31]

He concludes this passage: "And so I thank God my ancestor survived that voyage." He then proceeds to summarize his reaction to the entire experience: "But most of all I think: Thank God my ancestor got out, because, now, I am not one of them. In short, thank God that I am an American."[32]

Of course, in giving voice to these emotions and in reporting this vision of finding his identity by discarding an imagined one, Richburg does not speak for or represent all African Americans. In fact, his rendition of this experience provokes and enrages many regardless of race. His efforts to put the events in his book in a meaningful historical and cultural context do not mollify his outraged critics, who see him as betraying his African past, severing his bonds with other African Americans, and perhaps subverting arguments for programs for significant change in matters concerning race.[33] In the face of such deep and acrimonious opposition to Richburg's comparison of the history and conditions for blacks in Africa and America, it should be reiterated that some recent studies of race by both white and black scholars emphasize change and progress at home in America amid persisting problems and crises. As previously noted, although Stephan and Abigail Thernstrom disagree with Orlando Patterson over tactics for instituting and realizing change by such means as affirmative action, they share a sense of amazement over what they consider to be dramatic advances in the United States since the Second World War in the improved economic, social, and political situation for African Americans and in relations between the races. They also decline to trivialize or minimize the challenges that remain for further progress regarding jobs, housing, status, education, health, and power. While reporting the continuing "bad news" for American blacks of poverty, crime, out-of-wedlock births, and the racial gap in educational performance, the Thernstroms still optimistically compare the present with the past and note that, once, "African Americans were a stigmatized group, assumed to be a permanent caste that would forever remain beyond the melting pot." Today, they add, because of changes in values, attitudes, and public policies over the past four decades, "That world has now vanished."[34]

Similarly, Orlando Patterson argues that "the main achievement of the civil rights movement was forcing the nation to apply the Founding Fathers'" values and methods to African Americans by fighting "centuries of racist discrimination" and then working "to improve the socioeconomic condition of all Afro-Americans." As part of this process of improvement, Patterson urges a realization for African Americans of a common American identity. Challenging the continued validity and relevance of "the terms *black* and *white* in reference to Americans," Patterson argues, "Afro-Americans are not Africans; they are among the most American of Americans, and the emphasis on their Africanness is both physically inappropriate and culturally misleading." He adds: "Afro-Americans, from a status of semiliterate social outcasts as late as the early fifties, have now become an integral part of American civilization and are so recognized both within the nation and outside it."[35]

The intensity and pervasiveness of such debate over race in America inevitably compel Richburg in his comparison of America and Africa repeatedly to ask himself: As an African American, for whom does he speak? Whom does he represent? The clarity of this reporter's vision and the strength of his own voice and identity suggest an answer that may resonate with many, especially those of whatever color and background who can identify with the myth of re-creating one's identity and one's past in the New World: For America.

NOTES

1. Ethnics and Roughnecks: The Making of the Hollywood Renaissance

1 F. O. Matthiessen, *American Renaissance: Art and Expression in the Age of Emerson and Whitman* (1941; rpt. New York: Oxford University Press, 1968), p. vii. Subsequent citations of this book will be to this edition and will be included parenthetically in the text.

2 The critical and scholarly landscape has been thoroughly transformed since Matthiessen's time insofar as scholars and critics have moved toward seeing America in terms of the "dissensus" and disunity of multiculturalism and the culture wars. Similarly, the diversity and complexity of critical theory as used by scholars and critics also reflect this transformation. See Sacvan Bercovitch, *The Rites of Assent: Transformations in the Symbolic Construction of America* (New York: Routledge, 1993).

3 John Dewey, *Freedom and Culture* (1939; rpt. New York: Capricorn, 1963), p. 124.

4 Stephen Heath, *Questions of Cinema* (Bloomington: Indiana University Press, 1981), p. 51. Similarly, Mas'ud Zavarzadeh, *Seeing Films Politically* (Albany: State University of New York Press, 1991), p. 70, says, "the continuity editing that marks the classic Hollywood film is subverted so that the material discontinuity of the film is displayed as a means for showing the arbitrary connection of the signifier with the signified, thus deconstructing the logic of representation: the ideology of the visible."

5 Jim Hillier, "Introduction: *Cahiers du cinéma* in the 1960s," in Hillier, ed., *Cahiers du cinéma: 1960–1968: New Wave, New Cinema, Reevaluating Hollywood* (Cambridge, Mass.: Harvard University Press, 1992), pp. 7–8.

6 Interestingly, two studies that similarly suggest an important historic break between old and new forms, styles, and ideologies in American films also appeared in 1967. See Gregory Battock, ed., *The New American Cinema: A Critical Anthology* (New York: E. P. Dutton, 1967); and Sheldon Renan, *An Introduction to the American Underground Film* (New York: E. P. Dutton, 1967).

7 Gary Wills, *John Wayne's America: The Politics of Celebrity* (New York: Simon & Schuster, 1997), p. 237. After making this largely unsubstantiated claim about Ford, Wills begins his next paragraph with the line: "Ford had a genuine interest in Irish literature, art, and acting. . . ."

8 For an important study of the ethnic basis of the Hollywood film industry see, for example, Robert Sklar, *Movie-Made America: A Social History of Amer-*

ican Movies, rev. ed. (1975; rpt. New York: Vintage, 1994); Neil Gabler, *An Empire of Their Own: How the Jews Invented Hollywood* (New York: Crown, 1988).

9   Michiko Kakutani in "Culture Zone: Ready for His Close-Up," *New York Times Magazine*, 28 July 1996, p. 14, concentrates on Wilder but also discusses other directors in a manner related to the Hollywood Renaissance: "It is Wilder's love of America and the American idiom, combined with an outsider's gift of observation, that animates so many of his movies – in every genre, from farce to suspense to satire – while defining the country as authoritatively as Capra's comedies or Ford's westerns. It is a vision of America as a promised land, where people can reinvent themselves, but also where they can 'become immunized, mechanized, air-conditioned.'"

10   Two crucial collections that concentrate on such reconsiderations of Matthiessen are Sacvan Bercovitch and Myra Jehlen, eds., *Ideology and Classic American Literature* (Cambridge: Cambridge University Press, 1986); and Walter Benn Michaels and Donald E. Pease, eds., *The American Renaissance Reconsidered* (Baltimore: Johns Hopkins University Press, 1989).

11   Sacvan Bercovitch, "The Problem of Ideology in a Time of Dissensus," in his *Rites of Assent*, pp. 354–5. All subsequent references to Bercovitch's essays in this collection will be to the edition cited in n. 2 and will be noted parenthetically in the text.

12   Gunnar Myrdal, *An American Dilemma: The Negro Problem and American Democracy* (1942; rpt. New York: Harper Colophon, 1962), 2 vols., I:3–4. All subsequent references to this work will be to this edition and will be included parenthetically in the text.

13   James T. Patterson, *Grand Expectations: The United States, 1945–1974* (New York: Oxford University Press, 1996), p. 21.

14   Stephan Thernstrom and Abigail Thernstrom, *America in Black and White: One Nation, Indivisible* (New York: Simon & Schuster, 1997), p. 51.

15   Patterson, *Grand Expectations*, p. 655. The Clark quote comes from Talcott Parsons and Kenneth Clark, eds., *The Negro American* (Boston: Beacon Press, 1965), p. xviii. See also Walter Jackson, *Gunnar Myrdal and America's Conscience: Social Engineering and Racial Liberalism, 1938–1987* (Chapel Hill: University of North Carolina Press, 1987), pp. 305–7.

16   See Thernstrom and Thernstrom, *America in Black and White*, pp. 18–19; Orlando Patterson, *The Ordeal of Integration: Progress and Resentment in America's "Racial" Crisis* (Washington, D.C.: Civitas/Counterpoint, 1997), p. 48.

17   Daniel Boorstin, *The Americans: The Colonial Experience* (New York: Vintage, 1958), p. 16.

18   Ibid., pp. 10, 13, 15, 3.

19   See the conclusion of Donald E. Pease, "*Moby Dick* and the Cold War," in Michaels and Pease, eds., *American Renaissance Reconsidered*, p. 153.

20   Ibid., pp. 120–6.

21   Roland Barthes, "Myth Today," in *Mythologies*, trans. Annette Lavers (1957; rpt. New York: Hill & Wang, 1972), p. 116.

22   Abraham Lincoln, Second Message to Congress, as quoted in Mark E. Neely, Jr., *The Last Best Hope of Earth: Abraham Lincoln and the Promise of America* (Cambridge, Mass.: Harvard University Press, 1993), p. 156.

23   For an excellent history of this concept of the relationship of American ethnicity and American culture, see Lawrence H. Fuchs, *The American Kaleidescope:*

Race, Ethnicity, and the Civic Culture (Hanover: Wesleyan University Press, 1990). See also Yehoshua Arieli, *Individualism and Nationalism in American Ideology* (Baltimore: Penguin, 1966); and Ronald Takaki, *A Different Mirror: A History of Multicultural America* (Boston: Little Brown, 1993).

24 Ben J. Wattenberg, *The First Universal Nation: Leading Indicators and Ideas about the Surge of America in the 1990s* (New York: Free Press, 1991), p. 9.

25 See K. Anthony Appiah, "The Multiculturalist Misunderstanding," essay-review of Michael Walzer, *On Toleration* (New Haven: Yale University Press, 1997), and of Nathan Glazer, *We Are All Multiculturalists Now* (Cambridge, Mass.: Harvard University Press, 1997), in *New York Review of Books,* 9 October 1997, p. 34. See also Henry Louis Gates, Jr., "Whose Culture Is It, Anyway?" *New York Times,* 4 May 1991, p. 15; and Sam B. Girgus, "The New Ethnic Novel and the American Idea," *College Literature* 20 (October 1993): 57–72.

26 See Diane Jacobs, *Hollywood Renaissance* (South Brunswick and New York: A. S. Barnes & Co., 1977), p. 11.

2. A Cinema for Democracy: John Ford and the Crisis of Modernity, Myth, and Meaning

1 Quoted in Ronald L. Davis, *John Ford: Hollywood's Old Master* (Norman: University of Oklahoma Press, 1995), p. 342.

2 Gary Wills, *John Wayne's America: The Politics of Celebrity* (New York: Simon & Schuster, 1997), pp. 67–76. In this chapter, subsequent references to this book will be to this edition and will be included parenthetically in the text.

3 Peter Bogdanovich, *John Ford* (1967; rpt. Berkeley: University of California Press, 1978), p. 34.

4 Tag Gallagher, *John Ford: The Man and His Films* (Berkeley: University of California Press, 1986), p. 340. Gallagher also is excellent for background and biography of Ford. Future references to this book will be to this edition and will be included parenthetically in the text. Also see Davis, *John Ford: Hollywood's Old Master* for the detailed bibliographical essay at the conclusion of the study.

5 Davis, *John Ford: Hollywood's Old Master,* p. 3.

6 Leo Braudy, *The World in a Frame: What We See in Films* (1976; rpt. Chicago: University of Chicago Press, 1984), p. 201, maintains, "In every film there are at least four films: the one written, the one cast, the one shot, and the one cut."

7 Herman Melville to Nathaniel Hawthorne, 16 April 1851, in *Moby-Dick* by Herman Melville, ed. Harrison Hayford and Hershel Parker (New York: Norton, 1967), p. 555.

8 See Braudy, *World in a Frame,* pp. 1–24.

9 Joseph McBride and Michael Wilmington, *John Ford* (New York: Da Capo Press, 1975), p. 148.

10 Many film theorists tend to divide into two schools of thought concerning the viewing of film. One school emphasizes the photographic and documentary idea of film as a window on reality, as seen in the early film work of Louis Lumière and the theories of film and objective reality of André Bazin. A second school sees film as a reconstructing and refracting of reality, as in the early work of Georges Méliès and the films and theories of montage and editing

of Sergei Eisenstein. For a discussion of this sort of contrasting view of film, see Siegfried Kracauer, *Theory of Film: The Redemption of Physical Reality* (London: Oxford University Press, 1960); and George Bluestone, *Novels into Film* (Berkeley: University of California Press, 1957).

11 Stuart Byron, "*The Searchers:* Cult Movie of the New Hollywood," *New York* 12 (5 March 1979): 45–6. The Hemingway quotation is from chapter 1 of *The Green Hills of Africa* (1935).

12 Peter Travers, "New Jack Cowboys," in *Rolling Stone* (10 June 1993): 73–4.

13 See Davis, *John Ford: Hollywood's Old Master*, p. 278.

14 Richard Slotkin, *Gunfighter Nation: The Myth of the Frontier in Twentieth-Century America* (New York: Harper Perennial, 1993), p. 467.

15 Richard Slotkin, *Regeneration through Violence: The Mythology of the American Frontier, 1600–1860* (Middletown: Wesleyan University Press, 1973), p. 95; and Lee Clark Mitchell, *Westerns: Making the Man in Fiction and Film* (Chicago: University of Chicago Press, 1996), p. 135.

16 Slotkin, *Regeneration through Violence*, pp. 96–7.

17 See Sacvan Bercovitch, *The American Jeremiad* (Madison: University of Wisconsin Press, 1978). See also his "The Rites of Assent: Rhetoric, Ritual, and the Ideology of American Consensus," in Sam B. Girgus, ed., *The American Self: Myth, Ideology, and Popular Culture* (Albuquerque: University of New Mexico Press, 1981), pp. 5–42.

18 Stout is quoted in John Demos, *The Unredeemed Captive: A Family Story from Early America* (New York: Vintage, 1995), p. 74. See Harry S. Stout, *The New England Soul: Preaching and Religious Culture in Colonial New England* (New York: Oxford University Press, 1986), pp. 77, 85. All subsequent references to *The Unredeemed Captive* will be to this edition and will be quoted parenthetically in the text as (Demos).

19 For a seminal analysis of this sermon and its significance that has influenced succeeding generations of Puritan scholars, see Perry Miller, "Errand into the Wilderness" in *Errand into the Wilderness* (New York: Harper Torchbook, 1964), pp. 1–15.

20 Wills, *John Wayne's America*, p. 271, quotes Marcus: "But the real Ahab of our films is not the pallid Gregory Peck of John Huston's *Moby Dick*. It is, as rock critic Greil Marcus noted, Wayne's Ethan Edwards. In *The Searchers*, says Marcus, 'Wayne changes from a man with whom we are comfortable into a walking Judgment Day ready to destroy the world to save it from itself.'" See Greil Marcus, *The Dustbin of History* (Cambridge, Mass.: Harvard University Press, 1995), p. 212.

21 See Bogdanovich, *John Ford*, pp. 92–3.

22 Mitchell, *Westerns*, p. 175.

23 McBride and Wilmington, *John Ford*, p. 159.

24 It should be noted that many might disagree with this assessment of Ford's influence upon Wayne's image and growth. For example, throughout *John Wayne's America*, Wills emphasizes Wayne's major responsibility in the self-creation of his public image and meaning to America.

25 I wish to thank Richard J. Perry, Professor of Anthropology, St. Lawrence University, for his help through personal correspondence in explaining the validity of Comanche terms and names such as "Noyeke" that are used in *The Searchers*. For further information, Professor Perry recommends, E. Adamson

Hoebel and E. Wallace, *The Comanches: Lords of the Southern Plains* (Norman: University of Oklahoma Press, 1952), as well as *The Political Organization and Law-Ways of the Comanche Indians* (American Anthropological Association Memoir 54, 1940).

26 Tony Tanner, "Henry Adams and Mark Twain," in *Scenes of Nature, Signs of Men* (Cambridge: Cambridge University Press, 1987), p. 89.

27 Leo Charney, "In a Moment: Film and the Philosophy of Modernity," in Leo Charney and Vanessa R. Schwartz, eds., *Cinema and the Invention of Modern Life* (Berkeley: University of California Press, 1995), p. 281.

28 Hayden White, "The Modernist Event," in Vivan Sobchack, ed., *The Persistence of History: Cinema, Television, and the Modern Event* (New York: Routledge, 1996), pp. 24, 31.

29 See McBride and Wilmington, *John Ford*, p. 150, on this point of Ethan's connection to Leatherstocking, especially as that tradition has been interpreted and developed by Henry Nash Smith in *Virgin Land: The American West as Symbol and Myth* (Cambridge, Mass.: Harvard University Press, 1950).

30 D. H. Lawrence, *Studies in Classic American Literature* (1923; rpt. New York: Doubleday Anchor, 1951), pp. 59, 73.

31 F. O. Matthiessen, *American Renaissance: Art and Expression in the Age of Emerson and Whitman* (1941; rpt. New York: Oxford University Press, 1968), p. 546.

32 Ibid.

33 Thomas Elsaesser, "subject Positions, speaking Positions: from holocaust, *our hitler,* and *heimat* to *shoah* and *schindler's list*" [*sic*] in Sobchack, ed., *Persistence of History*, pp. 153, 151.

34 Miriam Bratu Hansen, "America, Paris, the Alps: Kracauer (and Benjamin) on Cinema and Modernity," in Charney and Schwartz, eds., *Cinema and the Invention of Modern Life*, p. 387.

35 Matthiessen, *American Renaissance*, p. 625.

36 Charney, "In a Moment," in Charney and Schwartz, eds., *Cinema and the Invention of Modern Life*, p. 287.

37 See Richard A. Blake, S.J., "Going Home: The Films of John Ford," *Thought* 66 (June 1991): 179–95.

38 Sigmund Freud, "Mourning and Melancholia," trans. Joan Riviere, in Freud, *The Complete Psychological Works: Standard Edition*, ed. James Strachey (London: Hogarth Press, 1957), 24 vols., 14:246. All subsequent references to this piece will be to this edition and will be included in the text as *M&M*.

39 Peter Lehman, "Texas 1868/America 1956: *The Searchers,*" in Lehman, ed., *Close Viewings: An Anthology of New Film Criticism* (Tallahassee: Florida State University Press, 1990), p. 403.

40 Ibid., p. 404.

3. Gender and American Character: Frank Capra

1 Joseph McBride, *Frank Capra: The Catastrophe of Success* (New York: Touchstone, 1992), p. 29. See also Capra's autobiography, *The Name above the Title* (New York: Macmillan, 1971).

2 Richard T. Jameson, "The Lighthouse," *Film Comment* 28 (1) (January 1992): 24–7, at p. 24.

3 Wes D. Gehring, "Pushing the Capra Envelope: *Hero*," *Journal of Popular Film and Television* 23 (Spring 1995): 37. Other recent critics of Capra are often less kind to him in their assessment of the political significance of his films. See Frank Stricker, "Repressing the Working Class: Individualism and the Masses in Frank Capra's Films," *Labor History* 31 (Fall 1990): 454–67; Patrick Mc-Cormick, "Without Economic Justice, There's No Wonderful Life," *U.S. Catholic* 12 (December 1993):18–19.

4 Quoted in McBride, *Frank Capra*, p. 650.

5 Peter Bogdanovich, *John Ford* (1967; rpt. Berkeley: University of California Press, 1978), p. 99.

6 See for example, Christine Gledhill, ed., *Stardom: Industry of Desire* (New York: Routledge, 1991); Richard Dyer, *Heavenly Bodies: Film Stars and Society* (New York: St. Martin's Press, 1986); Andrew Britton, *Cary Grant: Comedy and Male Desire* (Newcastle upon Tyne: Tyneside Cinema, 1993); Steven Cohan and Ina Rae Hark, ed., *Screening the Male: Exploring Masculinities in Hollywood Cinema* (London and New York: Routledge, 1993).

7 See Graham McCann, *Rebel Males: Clift, Brando, and Dean* (New Brunswick, N.J.: Rutgers University Press, 1993); James Naremore contextualizes such actors within the broader history of acting in his brilliant study *Acting in the Cinema* (Berkeley: University of California Press, 1988).

8 Raymond Carney, *American Vision: The Films of Frank Capra* (Cambridge: Cambridge University Press, 1986), pp. 326–7; and Dennis Bingham, *Acting Male: Masculinities in the Films of James Stewart, Jack Nicholson, and Clint Eastwood* (New Brunswick, N.J.: Rutgers University Press, 1994), pp. 1–96.

9 Carney, *American Vision*, p. 324.

10 Robert Sklar, "God and Man in Bedford Falls: Frank Capra's *It's a Wonderful Life*," in Sam B. Girgus, ed., *The American Self: Myth, Ideology, and Popular Culture* (Albuquerque: University of New Mexico Press, 1981), pp. 212–13.

11 Carney, *American Vision*, pp. 337–41.

12 Ibid., p. 417.

13 See McBride, *Frank Capra*, pp. 234–5, 292, 410, 512–13.

14 See Kaja Silverman, *Male Subjectivity at the Margins* (New York & London: Routledge, 1992), pp. 93–106. Subsequent references to this book will be to this edition and will be included parenthetically in the text.

15 Bingham, *Acting Male*, pp. 4, 8.

16 For a discussion how such Lacanian terms as the look and the gaze tend to be used in film theory and criticism, see Silverman, *Male Subjectivity at the Margins*, pp. 1–12.

17 Molly Haskell, *From Reverence to Rape: The Treatment of Women in the Movies*, 2d ed. (1973; rpt. Chicago: University of Chicago Press, 1987), p. 122.

18 Carney, *American Vision*, p. 311, correctly analyzes the signs and signifiers in the office scene between Rains and Stewart as a way of establishing "the semiotic difference between the two figures," although he often tends to disparage such critical terminology. The earlier scene under discussion with Jean Arthur and Rains contributes to the complexity of this "semiotic difference."

19 Haskell, *From Reverence to Rape*, p. 122.

20 McBride, *Frank Capra*, p. 345. Bingham, *Acting Male*, p. 39, makes good critical use of this important comment by Arthur.

21 Leland Poague, *Another Frank Capra* (Cambridge: Cambridge University Press, 1994), p. 174.

22 See Silverman, *Male Subjectivity at the Margins*, pp. 127–9, 150–2, on the look and gaze.

23 See Carney, *American Vision*, pp. 341–2, on "Vorkapich's montage" as visual text; and see Sergei M. Eisenstein, *Film Form: Essays in Film Theory* (New York: Harcourt Brace Jovanovich, 1969).

24 See McBride, *Frank Capra*, pp. 410–24, for a discussion of the background and reactions to this political aspect to *Mr. Smith*.

25 Ibid., p. 342.

26 Charles Wolfe, "*Mr. Smith Goes to Washington:* Democratic Forums and Representational Forms" in Peter Lehman, ed., *Close Viewings: An Anthology of New Film Criticism* (Tallahassee: Florida State University Press, 1990), p. 318.

27 Bingham, *Acting Male*, p. 34.

28 Poague, *Another Frank Capra*, p. 183, notes that "Jeff could not work through the Oedipal crisis."

29 In contrast to critics who emphasize Capra's focus on masculinity, Poague, *Another Frank Capra*, p. 188, believes that in Capra's films, including *Mr. Smith Goes to Washington,* "Capra's deepest affinities are with the female characters."

30 As quoted in McBride, *Frank Capra*, p. 466.

31 Ibid.

32 See Lucy Fischer, *Cinematernity: Film, Motherhood, Genre* (Princeton: Princeton University Press, 1996), p. 4.

33 McBride, *Frank Capra*, p. 513. McBride (pp. 510–13), adds considerably more detail about the history of the story and the writing of the script.

34 Robert B. Ray, *A Certain Tendency of the Hollywood Cinema, 1930–1980* (Princeton: Princeton University Press, 1985), p. 183.

35 See Silverman, *Male Subjectivity at the Margins*, p. 103.

36 Poague, *Another Frank Capra*, p. 218.

37 See Jeanine Basinger, *The "It's a Wonderful Life" Book* (New York: Knopf, 1986); Richard Glatzer and John Raeburn, eds., *Frank Capra: The Man and His Films* (Ann Arbor: University of Michigan Press, 1975), and in particular James Agee, "*It's a Wonderful Life*" therein (pp. 157–9); Charles J. Maland, *Frank Capra* (Boston: Twayne, 1980); Leland A. Poague, *The Cinema of Frank Capra: An Approach to Film Comedy* (New York: Barnes, 1975).

38 Henry Nash Smith, *Mark Twain: The Development of a Writer* (1962; rpt. (New York: Atheneum, 1967), p. 136.

39 Maland, *Frank Capra*, p. 131; there, Maland maintains that *It's a Wonderful Life* "resembles *The Adventures of Huckleberry Finn,* the work in which Mark Twain finally managed to reconcile his personal ambivalence about the genteel and vernacular traditions by speaking through a young vernacular narrator."

40 Ray, *Certain Tendency*, p. 186; for Agee quote see his "*It's a Wonderful Life,*" in Glatzer and Raeburn, eds., *Frank Capra: The Man and His Films*, p. 157.

41 See Sklar, "God and Man in Bedford Falls," in Girgus, ed., *American Self*, p. 211, and McBride, *Frank Capra*, p. 503.

42 McBride, *Frank Capra*, p. 519.

43 James MacGregor Burns, *Roosevelt: The Soldier of Freedom* (New York: Harcourt Brace Jovanovich, 1970), pp. 34–5.

44 Ibid., p. 35.

45 McBride, *Frank Capra*, p. 519.

46 Freud, "Thoughts for the Times on War and Death," in Benjamin Nelson, ed., *On Creativity and the Unconscious* (New York: Harper Torchbook, 1958), pp. 218, 213.

47 Ibid., pp. 215, 218.

48 Silverman, *Male Subjectivity at the Margins,* p. 42, writes: "Our dominant fiction calls upon the male subject to see himself, and the female subject to recognize and desire him, only through the mediation of images of an unimpaired masculinity. It urges both the male and the female subject, that is, to deny all knowledge of male castration by believing in the commensurability of penis and phallus, actual and symbolic father."

49 On the crisis of the family and concomitant trends toward psychological fear and insecurity, see Christopher Lasch, *Haven in a Heartless World: The Family Besieged* (New York: Basic Books, 1977); and idem, *The Minimal Self: Psychic Survival in Troubled Times* (New York: Norton, 1984).

50 Jimmy Stewart, "Frank Capra's Merry Christmas to All," *Reader's Digest* 139 (December 1991): 81–5, at p. 84.

51 To Leland Poague (*Another Frank Capra,* p. 194), Bailey culminates a process that Elizabeth Kendall has identified as the centralization of women and the feminine in the work of Hollywood's major directors of the 1930s. See Elizabeth Kendall, *The Runaway Bride: Hollywood Romantic Comedy of the 1930s* (New York: Knopf, 1990).

52 See Poague, *Another Frank Capra,* pp. 194, 233.

53 Maland, *Frank Capra,* p. 131.

54 According to Jenny Diski, "Curious Tears," *Sight and Sound* 2 (August 1992): 39, "Capra's America is not that geographical landmass just above Mexico, but a mythological place in the geography of the mind. . . ." She maintains that Capra's genius encapsulates the multiple meanings of that myth: "Capra's *America* (the diametrical opposite of Kafka's *America*) is the place where tough-as-old-boots realists like myself can howl. It's a small compartment of the mind that retains unassailable notions of honesty, decency, goodness, fairness, and *how things ought to be.*" At the same time, she insists that "Capra is *not* an escapist." She maintains the primacy of *It's a Wonderful Life* as a work of art that melds imagination and social reality together. "I've never understood how *It's a Wonderful Life* is seen as a beacon of Christmas hope. It's one of the darkest films I know."

55 I wish to thank my students in "America on Film" at Vanderbilt University during spring 1997 (especially Will Geist) for their help in instructing me on the physical organization of this scene.

56 See Colin MacCabe, *Tracking the Signifier: Theoretical Essays: Film, Linguistics, Literature* (Minneapolis: University of Minnesota Press, 1985), pp. 65–8; Stephen Heath, *Questions of Cinema* (Bloomington: Indiana University Press, 1981), pp. 19–112.

57 Mary Ann Doane, "Film and the Masquerade," in *Femmes Fatales: Feminism, Film Theory, Psychoanalysis* (New York: Routledge, 1991), p. 27.

58 Heath, *Questions of Cinema,* p. 187.

59 Ray, *Certain Tendency,* pp. 212, 192, 193.

60 William James, "What Pragmatism Means," in Joseph L. Blau, ed., *Pragmatism and Other Essays* (New York: Washington Square Press, 1963), p. 26, says, "You must bring out of each word its practical cash-value, set it at work

within the stream of your experience. It appears less as a solution, then, than as a program for more work, and more particularly as an indication of the ways in which existing realities may be *changed.*"

61   Sklar, "God and Man in Bedford Falls," in Girgus, ed., *American Self,* p. 213.

4. Revisioning Heroic Masculinity: From Ford to Hawks and Zinnemann

1   I use *intertextuality* not simply as a term that suggests the "anxiety of influence" but also as a reflection of recent semiotic and psychoanalytic theories of film and literature. It emphasizes visual and literary relations between different texts; it concerns the perception and conception of the relationship between different systems of meanings in different aesthetic and cultural works. James Naremore, *Acting in the Cinema* (Berkeley: University of California Press, 1988), p. 263, discusses intertextuality as a system of "cues" that help create the viewers' response to a film based on such matters as genres, plot, and stars. See also Colin MacCabe, *Tracking the Signifier: Theoretical Essays: Film, Linguistics, Literature* (Minneapolis: University of Minnesota Press, 1985), pp. 113–50.

2   Written by Dudley Nichols from the Ernest Haycox story "Stage to Lordsburg," *Stagecoach* takes place in New Mexico in 1884, although it actually was shot primarily in Ford's favorite location, Monument Valley, as well as other locations in Arizona, Utah, and California. The indoor settings that feature adobe-style houses with vegas or wooden beams, low ceilings, and framed doorways reflect the Hispanic influence on New Mexico.

3   Gary Wills, *John Wayne's America: The Politics of Celebrity* (New York: Simon & Schuster, 1997), p. 90. See also Edward Buscombe, *Stagecoach* (London: British Film Institute, 1992), p. 9.

4   Wills, *John Wayne's America,* pp. 16, 129.

5   For a recent story about the history and legacy of the King and other cattle empires, especially in relation to Hispanics in Texas, see Sam Howe Verhovek, "Cattle Barons of Texas Yore Accused of Epic Land Grab," *New York Times,* 14 July 1997, pp. A1, A10.

6   Joseph McBride, *Hawks on Hawks* (Berkeley: University of California Press, 1982), p. 123. For background on Montgomery Clift, see Graham McCann, *Rebel Males: Clift, Brando, and Dean* (New Brunswick, N.J.: Rutgers University Press, 1993), pp. 31–78. The remark by Carey about Clift was made during discussions with him, 9–11 November 1997, in Durango, Colorado. See also, Harry Carey, Jr., *Company of Heroes: My Life As an Actor in the John Ford Stock Company* (Lanham, Md.: Madison Books, 1994).

7   Gerald Mast, *Howard Hawks, Storyteller* (New York: Oxford University Press, 1982), pp. 302–3.

8   McBride, *Hawks on Hawks,* p. 116.

9   Ibid., pp. 15–16, 25–6. Hawks also says he learned how to use the long shot from Ford (p. 84).

10   Ibid., p. 114.

11   Quoted in Mast, *Howard Hawks, Storyteller,* p. 298, from Hawks interview with David Austen, "Gunplay and Horses," *Films and Filming* 15 (October 1968): 25–7, at p. 25.

12   McBride, *Hawks on Hawks,* p. 121.

13 Tag Gallagher, *John Ford: The Man and His Films* (Berkeley: University of California Press, 1986), p. 151.
14 Quoted in Mast, *Howard Hawks, Storyteller*, p. 321, from Michael Goodwin and Naomi Wise, "An Interview with Howard Hawks," *Take One* 8 (July–August 1971): 19–25, at p. 21.
15 Wills, *John Wayne's America*, p. 146. According to Wills, "Anyone who has ever seen the movie should know that Hawks is fabulating. The scene where Wayne looks off into the distance was never a big one for Clift. Hawks set it up so Wayne could dominate."
16 Wills (ibid., p. 17) asserts that "Wayne, in one fluid motion, pivots while drawing his gun, downs the challenger, and completes the circle of his turn, his regained stride undeterrable as fate. Here was Manifest Destiny on the hoof."
17 Mast, *Howard Hawks, Storyteller*, pp. 326–7.
18 Quoted in Mast, *Howard Hawks, Storyteller*, p. 328, from Peter Bogdanovich, "Interview," *Movie* 5 (December 1962): 8–18, at p. 15.
19 McBride, *Hawks on Hawks*, p. 123.
20 John Belton strongly advocates the end of the film as not only successful but arguably one of the best in film history. Belton, *The Hollywood Professionals*, vol. 3 (London: Tantivy, 1974), p. 36, argues: "Yet the ending is one of the most perfect in all cinema; it has a beauty, logic, and integrity that is consistent both with what has gone before and with the positive qualities of Hawks's comic perception of man's relationship to other men and his environment."
21 Edward Buscombe, "C for Cowboys," *Sight and Sound* 6 (August 1996): 33.
22 Leland A. Poague, *Howard Hawks* (Boston: Twayne, 1982), p. 112. See also Clark Branson, *Howard Hawks: A Jungian Study* (Santa Barbara: Capra Press, 1987); and Robin Wood, *Howard Hawks* (London: BFI, 1981).
23 Wills, *John Wayne's America*, pp. 135–6, discusses the changes in Tess's role in the context of the development of Borden Chase's story and script.
24 Mast, *Howard Hawks, Storyteller*, p. 380, n. 17.
25 McBride, *Hawks on Hawks*, p. 147. Similarly, Wills, *John Wayne's America*, p. 145, insists that the love in the film is "not homosexual but familial."
26 Mast, *Howard Hawks, Storyteller*, p. 302. Mast, it should be noted, also says that the male–female contrast between Wayne and Clift "is not meant to imply any kind of overt or covert homosexual longings between them," although he also says that "Clift has never been more clearly and healthily beautiful in any other film."
27 Ibid., p. 302.
28 Ibid., p. 313.
29 See Buscombe, "C for Cowboys," p. 33; and Robert Sklar, "Empire to the West: *Red River*," in John E. O'Connor and Martin A. Jackson, eds., *American History/American Film* (New York: Ungar, 1979), p. 169.
30 Molly Haskell, "Film View: Screwball Existentialist, Male Bonder," *New York Times*, Arts and Leisure, 10 July 1994, p. 9.
31 Ibid.
32 Freud, "Analysis Terminable and Interminable," in Freud, *The Complete Psychological Works: Standard Edition*, ed. James Strachey (London: Hogarth Press, 1964), 24 vols., 23:252.
33 McBride, *Hawks on Hawks*, pp. 66–7. Hawks says, "I've seen so many people laugh at violence when it happens. Kind of hysterical laughter. It's the eas-

iest time for you to get a laugh. I'm getting goddam sick of these pictures, you know, nothing but violence. Peckinpah and I believe in exactly the opposite thing."

34 Todd McCarthy, *Howard Hawks: The Grey Fox of Hollywood* (New York: Grove Press, 1997), p. 392. For an insightful review of McCarthy's book that especially adds to our understanding of Hawks's relationship to women as part of his overall personality and character within the Hollywood system, see Gary Wills, "The Poses of Howard Hawks," *Atlantic Monthly* (November 1997): 141–3. For another excellent review of McCarthy and other books on film (Peter Bogdanovich, *Who the Devil Made It*; David Thomson, *The Big Sleep*; Jim Hillier and Peter Wollen, eds., *Howard Hawks American Artist*), as well as valuable insights into Hawks, see Michael Wood, "Looking Good," *New York Review of Books*, 20 November 1997, pp. 27–31.

35 McBride, *Hawks on Hawks*, p. 3. Probably the most famous attack on Hawks's overall work and significance can be found in Pauline Kael, "Circles and Squares," in Gerald Mast and Marshall Cohen, eds., *Film Theory and Criticism: Introductory Readings* (New York: Oxford University Press, 1974), pp. 516–29.

36 Freud, *Three Essays on the Theory of Sexuality*, trans. James Strachey, intro. Steven Marcus (1905; rpt. New York: Harper Colophon, 1975), pp. 85–6, n. 1.

37 Haskell, "Film View: Screwball Existentialist, Male Bonder," p. 15.

38 Kael, "Circles and Squares," in Mast and Cohen, eds., *Film Theory and Criticism*, pp. 516–29.

39 See Poague, *Howard Hawks*, pp. 49, 50. For another discussion of the positive aspects of the Grant–Sheridan relationship in the film, see Wood, *Howard Hawks*, pp. 85–8.

40 Haskell, "Film View: Screwball Existentialist, Male Bonder," p. 15.

41 See Kaja Silverman, *The Acoustic Mirror: The Female Voice in Psychoanalysis and Cinema* (Bloomington: Indiana University Press, 1988); and Sam B. Girgus, "Representative Men: Unfreezing the Male Gaze," *College Literature* 21 (October 1994): 214–22.

42 Mast, *Howard Hawks, Storyteller*, p. 358.

43 McBride, *Hawks on Hawks*, p. 130.

44 Quoted in Stephen J. Whitfield, *The Culture of the Cold War* (Baltimore: John Hopkins University Press, 1991), pp. 148–1. For a valuable interview with Zinnemann just several months before his death in which he discusses his view of the political atmosphere at the time of *High Noon* as well as other matters, see Brian Neve, "A Master of His Craft: An Interview with Fred Zinnemann, *Cinéaste* 23(1) (1997): 15–19.

45 Wills, *John Wayne's America*, p. 273.

46 MacCabe, *Tracking the Signifier*, p. 61.

47 McCarthy, *Howard Hawks*, p. 412.

48 For an important discussion of the cultural and aesthetic significance of Cecil B. DeMille, see Sumiko Higashi, *Cecil B. DeMille and American Culture: The Silent Era* (Berkeley: University of California Press, 1994). For Hawks on De-Mille, see McBride, *Hawks on Hawks*, pp. 15–16.

49 Robert Sklar, *Movie-Made America: A Social History of American Movies*, rev. ed. (1975; rpt. New York: Vintage, 1994), p. 257. Concerning the MPA see also Whitfield, *Culture of the Cold War*, p. 127.

50   John Howard Reid, "A Man for All Movies: The Films of Fred Zinnemann," *Films and Filming* 13 (May 1967): 4–11, at p. 5.

51   See John Gaddis, *We Now Know: Rethinking Cold War History* (Oxford: Clarendon Press/Oxford, 1997).

52   George Brown Tindall, *America: A Narrative History,* 2 vols. (New York: Norton, 1984) II:1213, 1189.

53   Quoted in David McCullough, *Truman* (New York: Touchstone, 1992), p. 489.

54   Ibid., p. 419.

55   See Tindall, *America,* II:1203–9.

56   On the "Second Red Scare" and the power of Senator McCarthy see Tindall, *America,* II:1209–13. Tindall's term, "Second Red Scare," puts the Cold War–era conflicts in the context of an earlier Red Scare that had followed the First World War.

57   Whitfield, *Culture of the Cold War,* p. 2.

58   Walter A. McDougall, *Promised Land, Crusader State: The American Encounter with the World since 1776* (Boston: Houghton Mifflin, 1997), p. 167. To be fair, McDougall goes on to provide a counterargument to this sense of the domestic threat of communism.

59   For a valuable bibliography on the impact of the Cold War upon Hollywood see Whitfield, *Culture of the Cold War,* pp. 101–51.

60   McDougall, *Promised Land, Crusader State,* p. 154.

61   Stephen E. Ambrose, *Eisenhower: Soldier and President* (New York: Touchstone, 1991), pp. 249, 250.

62   Ibid., p. 250.

63   Whitfield, *Culture of the Cold War,* p. 17.

64   Ibid., p. 146.

65   Ibid.

66   Ambrose, *Eisenhower,* p. 542, writes: "In civil rights, as in civil liberties, Eisenhower was not a reluctant leader – he was no leader at all. He just wished the problems would go away. With regard to civil liberties, the excesses of McCarthy and his supporters were so gross that the problem did tend to solve itself. With regard to civil rights, an area in which the depth of commitment by the American people was considerably less than the commitment to civil liberties, Eisenhower's refusal to lead was almost criminal."

67   Quoted in Gene D. Phillips, "Darkness at Noon," in *Major Film Directors of the American and British Cinema* (Bethlehem: Lehigh University Press, 1990), p. 117.

68   Robert Warshow, *The Immediate Experience: Movies, Comics, Theatre and Other Aspects of Popular Culture,* intro. Lionel Trilling (New York: Atheneum, 1975), p. 149.

69   Whitfield, *Culture of the Cold War,* p. 147.

70   Douglas J. McReynolds and Barbara J. Lips, "Taking Care of Things: Evolution in the Treatment of a Western Theme, 1947–1957," *Literature/Film Quarterly* 18 (July 1990): 203.

71   Ibid., pp. 202–3.

72   Lee Clark Mitchell, *Westerns: Making the Man in Fiction and Film* (Chicago: University of Chicago Press, 1996), p. 212.

73   From *Fred Zinnemann: An Autobiography: A Life in the Movies* (New York: Scribner's, 1992), p. 110.

74   Ibid., p. 101.

75 Reid, "A Man for All Movies," p. 8.
76 Alan Stanbrook, "A Man for All Movies: The Films of Fred Zinnemann," *Films and Filming* 13 (June 1967): 11–15, at pp. 11, 12.
77 Quoted in Whitfield, *Culture of the Cold War,* p. 148.
78 Ibid.
79 See David Riesman, "The Saving Remnant: An Examination of Character Structure," in *Individualism Reconsidered and Other Essays* (New York: Free Press, 1954), 99–120, at p. 99; all subsequent references to this work will be to this edition and will be included parenthetically in the text. See also Riesman (with Nathan Glazer and Reuel Denney), *The Lonely Crowd: A Study of the Changing American Character,* abridged ed. (1950; rpt. New Haven: Yale University Press, 1961).
80 See Bruce F. Kawin, *How Movies Work* (Berkeley: University of California Press, 1992), pp. 505–10. Also, see Riesman, "The Saving Remnant," in *Individualism Reconsidered,* pp. 115–18.
81 See Roland Barthes, "The Face of Garbo," in *Mythologies,* trans. Annette Lavers (1957; rpt. New York: Hill & Wang, 1972), pp. 56–7.
82 Stephen Heath, *Questions of Cinema* (Bloomington: Indiana University Press, 1981), p. 136.
83 Ibid., pp. 44, 119.
84 See Caryn James, "Critic's Notebook: Old West and Reality: A Showdown," *New York Times,* 23 July 1997, p. B3.

5. An American Conscience: Elia Kazan's Long Journey Home

1 Elia Kazan, *A Life* (New York: Anchor Doubleday, 1988), p. 525. All subsequent references to this book will be to this edition and and will be included parenthetically in the text as *Life.*
2 James Naremore, *Acting in the Cinema* (Berkeley: University of California Press, 1988), pp. 193–4.
3 Ibid., p. 205.
4 Kenneth R. Hey, "Ambivalence as a Theme in *On the Waterfront* (1954): An Interdisciplinary Approach to Film Study," in Peter C. Rollins, ed., *Hollywood as Historian: American Film in a Cultural Context* (Lexington: University Press of Kentucky, 1983), pp. 159–210, brilliantly documents the details of the origins of the film and the sources for it in journalistic investigations regarding crime and corruption on the waterfront. He maintains that Malcolm Johnson's original *New York Sun* articles on the waterfront included a portrait of Rev. John M. Corridan, the associate director of the St. Xavier School in Manhattan, who was known as the "waterfront priest." Among many of Corridan's attacks on the corrupt unions was a sermon, "A Catholic Looks at the Waterfront," that Johnson included in his book about the waterfront, *Crime on the Labor Front* (New York: McGraw–Hill, 1950). Hey also delineates the interest in crime on the docks expressed by playwright Arthur Miller and Budd Schulberg, especially as reflected in the efforts of such waterfront figures of reform as Peter Panto and William F. Warren.
5 Hey, "Ambivalence," in Rollins, ed., *Hollywood as Historian,* pp. 182–3.
6 See Victor S. Navasky, *Naming Names* (rpt. 1980; New York: Penguin, 1991). See also Hey, "Ambivalence," in Rollins, ed., *Hollywood as Historian,* pp. 159–89; and Whitfield, *Culture of the Cold War,* pp. 101–26.

7 For a comprehensive discussion of the Actors Studio, especially as it relates to *On the Waterfront*, see Naremore, *Acting in the Cinema*, pp. 197–212.

8 Quoted in Hey, "Ambivalence," in Rollins, ed., *Hollywood as Historian*, p. 164.

9 Ibid.

10 Navasky, *Naming Names*, pp. 205, 204.

11 Michel Ciment, *Kazan on Kazan* (New York: Viking, 1974), pp. 83–4.

12 See Bernard Weinraub, "From the Days of McCarthy, A Lingering Chill," *New York Times*, 16 January 1997, pp. B1, B6. The recent appearance of a new film version of Arthur Miller's 1953 play *The Crucible*, which was a metaphor for the witch-hunts during the Red Scare, also provoked renewed discussion of the Kazan controversy. See Edward Rothstein, "On Naming Names, In Life and in Art," *New York Times*, 27 January 1997, pp. B1, B7.

13 Navasky, *Naming Names*, p. 209. Victor McLaglen won an Academy Award for his starring role in John Ford's 1935 *The Informer*, set among the Irish Republican Army.

14 Ibid., pp. 206–7. See also the same author more recently on this subject in Victor S. Navasky, "The Demons of Salem, with Us Still," *New York Times*, Arts and Leisure, 8 September 1996, pp. 37, 58.

15 Hey, "Ambivalence," in Rollins, ed., *Hollywood as Historian*, pp. 169–70.

16 See Werner Sollors, "A Critique of Pure Pluralism," in Sacvan Bercovitch, ed., *Reconstructing American Literary History* (Cambridge, Mass.: Harvard University Press, 1986); and Sollors, *Beyond Ethnicity: Consent and Descent in American Culture* (New York: Oxford University Press, 1986).

17 See Ben J. Wattenberg, *The First Universal Nation: Leading Indicators and Ideas about the Surge of America in the 1990s* (New York: Free Press, 1991).

18 Graham McCann, *Rebel Males: Clift, Brando, and Dean* (New Brunswick, N.J.: Rutgers University Press, 1993), p. 3.

19 Ibid., p. 108.

20 Pauline Kael, "Marlon Brando: An American Hero," *Atlantic Monthly* 217 (March 1966): 72–5, at p. 73.

6. Losing Tomorrow: George Stevens and the American Idea

1 Quoted in Elia Kazan, *A Life* (New York: Anchor Doubleday, 1988), p. 389.

2 George Stevens, Jr., "Shooting D-Day," *New York Times Magazine*, 5 June 1994, p. 30.

3 Ibid., p. 32.

4 Donald Richie, *George Stevens: An American Romantic* (New York: Museum of Modern Art, 1970), p. 54.

5 Stevens, Jr., "Shooting D-Day," p. 32.

6 Ephraim Katz, *The Film Encyclopedia* (New York: Harper & Row, 1990), pp. 1091–2.

7 "Cinema: The New Pictures," review of *Woman of the Year*, *Time* 39 (16 February 1942): 84.

8 Ibid.

9 Molly Haskell, *From Reverence to Rape: The Treatment of Women in the Movies*, 2d ed. (1973; rpt. Chicago: University of Chicago Press, 1987), p. 127.

10 Elizabeth Kendall, *The Runaway Bride: Hollywood Romantic Comedy of the 1930s* (New York: Knopf, 1990), p. 104.

11 Ibid., p. 109.
12 Ibid.
13 Ibid., p. 111.
14 Michael Rogin, *Blackface, White Noise: Jewish Immigrants in the Hollywood Melting Pot* (Berkeley: University of California Press, 1996), p. 184. For further discussion of *Swing Time* in the context of movement between racial identities and disguises, see Susan Gubar, *Racechanges: White Skin, Black Face in American Culture* (New York: Oxford University Press, 1997), pp. 88–91.
15 Christopher Andersen, *An Affair to Remember: The Remarkable Love Story of Katharine Hepburn and Spencer Tracy* (New York: William Morrow, 1997), pp. 152, 147. The apparent fact that Stevens and Hepburn had had an intimate relationship years earlier and remained close does not seem to have hindered the development of what would become one of Hollywood's most famous loves between Hepburn and Tracy.
16 Ibid., p. 147. Ironically, Hepburn herself at first had difficulty dealing with Tracy's own heavy drinking.
17 See Siegfried Kracauer, *Theory of Film: The Redemption of Physical Reality* (London: Oxford University Press, 1960), pp. 27–40.
18 Andersen, *Affair to Remember*, pp. 153–4.
19 "Cinema: The New Pictures," review of *Giant, Time* 68 (22 October 1956): 110.
20 Larry McMurtry, "Men Swaggered, Women Warred, Oil Flowed," *New York Times*, Arts and Leisure, 29 September 1996, p. 27.
21 Robert Warshow, *The Immediate Experience: Movies, Comics, Theatre and Other Aspects of Popular* Culture, intro. Lionel Trilling (New York: Atheneum, 1975), p. 150.
22 Mary Ann Doane, *The Desire to Desire: The Woman's Film of the 1940s* (Bloomington: Indiana University Press, 1987), p. 99.
23 Ibid., p. 85.
24 Ibid.
25 Colin MacCabe, *Tracking the Signifier: Theoretical Essays: Film, Linguistics, Literature* (Minneapolis: University of Minnesota Press, 1985), p. 68.
26 Ibid., pp. 8–10.
27 Bill Nichols, *Ideology and the Image: Social Representation in the Cinema and Other Media* (Bloomington: Indiana University Press, 1981), p. 168.
28 See Richard Chase, ed., *Herman Melville: Selected Tales and Poems* (San Francisco: Rinehart, 1950), p. 224. See also Girgus, *Desire and the Political Unconscious in American Literature: Eros and Ideology* (New York: St. Martin's Press, 1990), pp. 93–5.
29 I wish to thank various students at Vanderbilt University who first pointed out the presence of this painting to me in the film, especially Paige Sudderth Polishook.
30 See Nina Auerbach, *Woman and the Demon: The Life of a Victorian Myth* (Cambridge, Mass.: Harvard University Press, 1982). Michael Parker of the Liverpool Institute of Higher Education, author of *Seamus Heaney: The Making of the Poet* (Dublin: Gill & Macmillan, 1993), first introduced me to the importance of Millais's painting and the pre-Raphaelite movement to psychoanalytical theory and cultural history.
31 Of course, Walter Benjamin, "The Work of Art in the Age of Mechanical Reproduction," in *Illuminations*, intro. Hannah Arendt, trans. Harry Zohn

(1955; rpt. New York: Schocken, 1969), pp. 217–51, and the ongoing body of work that has engaged this essay since its first appearance remain the indispensable discussion and development of the topic of the aesthetic and cultural significance of the "mechanical reproduction" of art.

32 See Stephen Heath, *Questions of Cinema* (Bloomington: Indiana University Press, 1981), pp. 1–75.

33 D. N. Rodowick, *The Crisis of Political Modernism: Criticism and Ideology in Contemporary Film Theory* (Berkeley: University of California Press, 1994), p. 184.

34 Graham McCann, *Rebel Males: Clift, Brando, and Dean* (New Brunswick, N.J.: Rutgers University Press, 1993), pp. 51, 49.

35 For an elaboration of this interpretation of Chaplin and *Modern Times*, see Sam B. Girgus, "The Moral and Psychological Dilemma of *Modern Times*: Love, Play, and Civilization in Chaplin's Last Silent Classic," *Thalia: Studies in Literary Humor* 16 (1996): 3–15. See also Kenneth Lynn, *Charlie Chaplin and His Times* (New York: Simon & Schuster, 1997), pp. 368–85.

36 See Christopher Lasch, *The Minimal Self: Psychic Survival in Troubled Times* (New York: Norton, 1984).

37 Peter Bogdanovich's recent book of interviews and analysis, which includes Hollywood Renaissance directors, tends to confirm the notion of their commitment to their work and craft. See Peter Bogdanovich, *Who the Devil Made It: Conversations with Robert Aldrich, George Cukor, Allan Dwan, Howard Hawks, Alfred Hitchcock, Chuck Jones, Fritz Lang, Joseph H. Lewis, Sidney Lumet, Leo McCarey, Otto Preminger, Don Siegel, Josef von Sternberg, Frank Tashlin, Edgar G. Ulmer, Raoul Walsh* (New York: Alfred A. Knopf, 1997).

7. Conclusion: Film and America after the Hollywood Renaissance

1 Quoted in Walter A. McDougall, *Promised Land, Crusader State: The American Encounter with the World since 1776* (Boston: Houghton Mifflin, 1997), p. 150.

2 Ibid., p. 148.

3 David S. Reynolds, *Beneath the American Renaissance: The Subversive Imagination in the Age of Emerson and Melville* (New York: Alfred A. Knopf, 1988), pp. 4, 6–7. See Joel Porte, ed., *Emerson in His Journals* (Cambridge, Mass.: Harvard University Press, 1982), p. 344; Herman Melville, "Hawthorne and His Mosses," rpt. in "Reviews and Letters by Melville," afterword to Melville, *Moby-Dick*, ed. Harrison Hayford and Hershel Parker (New York: Norton, 1967), p. 543; Walt Whitman, *Prose Works, 1892*, in Whitman, *Collect and Other Prose*, ed. Floyd Stovall (New York: New York University Press, 1964), 2 vols., II:454.

4 Reynolds, *Beneath the American Renaissance*, p. 7. Reynolds also sees the great variety and diversity of popular and literary renaissance works as enacting unresolved tensions between "liberating" forces of great imaginative potential and "disturbing" elements that threaten accepted "values." The classic writers also maintain this balance between imaginative liberation and social and intellectual disturbance. Reynolds states (p. 10): "The major writers sought in their central texts to incorporate as many different popular images as possible and to reconstruct these images by imbuing them with a depth and control they lacked

in their crude native state. Uniquely attentive to conflicting voices within their contemporary culture, they transformed a wide array of popular modes and idioms into literary art by fusing them with each other and with archetypes derived from classic literature and philosophy."

5 Ibid., p. 6.

6 Lee Clark Mitchell, *Westerns: Making the Man in Fiction and Film* (Chicago: University of Chicago Press, 1996), p. 152.

7 Ibid., p. 155.

8 For a discussion of this subject of the fluidity of the look and the gaze as it relates to the reorganization of gender, see Sam B. Girgus, "Representative Men: Unfreezing the Male Gaze," *College Literature* 21 (October 1994): 214–22, an essay-review of the following important works on the subject: Pam Cook and Philip Dodd, eds., *Women and Film: A Sight and Sound Reader* (Philadelphia: Temple University Press, 1993); Steven Cohan and Ina Rae Hard, ed., *Screening the Male: Exploring Masculinities in Hollywood Cinema* (New York: Routledge, 1993); Paul Smith, *Clint Eastwood: A Cultural Production* (Minneapolis: University of Minnesota Press, 1993); and Kaja Silverman, *Male Subjectivity at the Margins* (New York & London: Routledge, 1992).

9 See James T. Patterson, *Grand Expectations: The United States, 1945–1974* (New York: Oxford University Press, 1996), p. 440.

10 Ibid., p. 441.

11 See Godfrey Hodgson, *America in Our Time* (New York: Vintage, 1978), especially his chapter on "The Ideology of the Liberal Consensus," pp. 67–98.

12 For example, see Patterson, *Grand Expectations* (p. 452): "As these expectations expanded, millions of Americans began not only to anticipate ever-greater social and technological progress but also to believe that they had 'rights' to all sorts of blessings, including profound psychological satisfaction. They imagined, often narcissistically, that they could achieve great personal 'growth' and 'self-actualization.' What earlier generations had considered as privileges, many in this one came to perceive as entitlements. In personal life this meant rapid gratification; in policy matters it meant deliverance from evil. Anything, it seemed, was possible in this protean time in history."

13 Ibid., pp. 447, 457.

14 See Irving Howe, "The Idea of the Modern," in Howe, ed., *Literary Modernism* (Greenwich, Conn.: Fawcett, 1967), p. 15.

15 Todd McCarthy, *Howard Hawks: The Grey Fox of Hollywood* (New York: Grove Press, 1997), pp. 11, 13, 451.

16 See Gerald Howard, ed., *The Sixties: Art, Politics and Media of Our Most Explosive Decade* (New York: Marlowe & Co., 1995). See also Patterson, *Grand Expectations,* pp. 452, 479–85, 531, 537–8, 769, and 782.

17 Richard Slotkin, *Gunfighter Nation: The Myth of the Frontier in Twentieth-Century America* (New York: Harper Perennial, 1993), pp. 535–6.

18 Although also concerned about the social and cultural forces behind the transformations that helped cause the collapse of the center, Patterson also supports Slotkin's emphasis on the war in *Grand Expectations* (p. 769): "Nothing did more than Vietnam to subvert the grand expectations that many Americans had developed by 1965 about the capacity of government to deal with public problems."

19 For example, see Daniel Bell, *The Cultural Contradictions of Capitalism* (New York: Basic Books, 1976); and John Kenneth Galbraith, *The New Industrial State* (Boston: Houghton Mifflin, 1967). For a discussion of the psychological implications for the culture concerning the failure of great expectations, see Christopher Lasch, *The Culture of Narcissism: American Life in an Age of Diminishing Expectations* (New York: Norton, 1978).

20 See Robert Sklar, *Movie-Made America: A Cultural History of American Movies*, rev. ed. (1975; rpt. New York: Vintage, 1994).

21 Mitchell, *Westerns*, pp. 242, 167.

22 See Sacvan Bercovitch, "The Problem of Ideology in a Time of Dissensus," in *The Rites of Assent: Transformations in the Symbolic Construction of America* (New York: Routledge, 1993), pp. 354–5.

23 William Butler Yeats, "The Second Coming," from Richard Ellmann, *Yeats: The Man and the Masks* (New York: Macmillan/Dutton, 1948), p. 233.

24 See Jefferson to William S. Smith, Paris, 13 November 1787, in *The Political Writings of Thomas Jefferson: Representative Selections*, ed. Edward Dumbauld (Indianapolis: Bobbs-Merrill, 1955), pp. 68–9.

25 Nathan Glazer, *We Are All Multiculturalists Now* (Cambridge, Mass.: Harvard University Press, 1997), pp. 137; subsequent citations of this book will be to this edition and will be included parenthetically in the text. Glazer further states (pp. 136–7): "If under a regime of freedom in which racial discrimination is banned and often punished, blacks remain separate from whites, might that not be an indication of the fact that over these twenty years the desire to retain something distinctive that characterizes blacks – differences that have been created by a tragic history but which despite that have become valued signs of identity – has grown? The black of today is not the immigrant of yesterday (or of today, who assimilates probably at the same rate as the immigrants of yesterday). To many blacks, a high degree of separation in intermarriage, residence, and language may describe a faultline in American society that is a social reality rather than a problem."

26 See Henry Louis Gates, Jr., "Whose Culture Is It, Anyway?" *New York Times*, 4 May 1991, p. 15; see also Sam B. Girgus, "The New Ethnic Novel and the American Idea," *College Literature* 20 (October 1993): 57–72. Glazer also, of course, recognizes such historical continuity in the meaning of multiculturalism. See Glazer, *We Are All Multiculturalists Now*, pp. 97–9.

27 Quoted in Ishmael Reed, ed., *MultiAmerica: Essays on Cultural Wars and Cultural Peace* (New York: Viking, 1997), p. vii, from the *New York Times*, 21 August 1996.

28 Edward Rothstein, "Critic's Notebook: Culture Wars Go On, but the Battle Lines Blur," *New York Times*, 27 May 1997, p. B4.

29 For a discussion of this experience from the perspective of Jewish immigrants, writers, and thinkers, see Sam B. Girgus, *The New Covenant: Jewish Writers and the American Idea* (Chapel Hill: University of North Carolina Press, 1984).

30 Keith B. Richburg, *Out of America: A Black Man Confronts Africa* (New York: Basic Books/Harper/New Republic, 1997), p. x.

31 Ibid., pp. xi-xii.

32 Ibid., p. xiv.

33 For a sharply critical review, see William Finnegan, "Black Like Me?" *New York Times Book Review*, 30 March 1997, p. 9. See also Richard Bernstein,

Books of the Times, "Confronting Hard Truths about Ancestral Lands," *New York Times,* 17 February 1997, p. 20.

34 Stephan Thernstrom and Abigail Thernstrom, *America in Black and White: One Nation, Indivisible* (New York: Simon & Schuster, 1997), pp. 533, 532.

35 Orlando Patterson, *The Ordeal of Integration: Progress and Resentment in America's "Racial" Crisis* (Washington: D.C.: Civitas/Counterpoint, 1997), pp. 142, 81, xi, 81. See also Richard Bernstein, "Racism Is (a) Entrenched? Or (b) Fading?" *New York Times,* Arts & Ideas, 8 November 1997, pp. A11, A15.

FILMOGRAPHY

Alice Adams, dir. George Stevens (RKO, 1936)
All the King's Men, dir. Robert Rossen (Columbia, 1949)
America, America, dir. Elia Kazan (Warner Bros., 1963)
Baby Doll, dir. Elia Kazan (Warner Bros., 1956)
Best Years of Our Lives, dir. William Wyler (Goldwyn, 1946)
Big Parade, The, dir. King Vidor (MGM, 1925)
Big Sky, The, dir. Howard Hawks (RKO/Winchester, 1962)
Big Sleep, The, dir. Howard Hawks (Warner Bros., 1948)
Big Wednesday, dir. John Milius (Warner Bros./A-Team, 1978)
Body and Soul, dir. Robert Rossen (Enterprise, 1947)
Bonnie and Clyde, dir. Arthur Penn (Warner Bros./Seven Arts/Tatira/Hiller, 1967)
Bringing Up Baby, dir. Howard Hawks (RKO, 1938)
Cheyenne Autumn, dir. John Ford (Warner Bros./Ford–Smith, 1964)
Citizen Kane, dir. Orson Welles (RKO, 1941)
Close Encounters of the Third Kind, dir. Steven Spielberg (Spielberg/Columbia, 1977)
Cohens and the Kellys in Trouble, The, dir. George Stevens (Universal, 1933)
Crucible, The, dir. Nicholas Hytner (20th C–Fox, 1997)
Deer Hunter, The, dir. Michael Cimino (Universal/EMI, 1978)
Diary of Anne Frank, The, dir. George Stevens (20th C–Fox, 1959)
Dillinger, dir. John Milius (Movielab, 1973)
Drums along the Mohawk, dir. John Ford (20th C–Fox, 1939)
East of Eden, dir. Elia Kazan (Warner Bros./First National, 1955)
El Dorado, dir. Howard Hawks (Paramount/Laurel, 1967)
Face in the Crowd, A, dir. Elia Kazan (Warner Bros., 1957)
Freud, dir. John Huston (Universal International, 1962)
From Here to Eternity, dir. Fred Zinnemann (Columbia, 1953)
Gentleman's Agreement, dir. Elia Kazan (20th C–Fox, 1947)
Gentlemen Prefer Blondes, dir. Howard Hawks (20th C–Fox, 1953)
Giant, dir. George Stevens (Warner Bros., 1956)
Gone with the Wind, dir. Victor Fleming [George Cukor et al., uncredited], prod. David O. Selznick (MGM/Selznick Intl. Pictures, 1939)
Graduate, The, dir. Mike Nichols (United Artists/Embassy, 1967)

Grapes of Wrath, The, dir. John Ford (20th C–Fox, 1940)
Greatest Story Ever Told, The, dir. George Stevens (United Artists, 1965)
Greed, dir. Erich von Stroheim (Metro–Goldwyn/Louis B. Mayer, 1924)
Guess Who's Coming to Dinner?, dir. Stanley Kramer (Columbia, 1967)
Gunga Din, dir. George Stevens (RKO, 1939)
Hamlet, dir. Laurence Olivier (Rank/Two Cities, 1948)
Hardcore, dir. Paul Schrader (Columbia/A-Team, 1979)
High Noon, dir. Fred Zinnemann (Stanley Kramer, 1952)
High Plains Drifter, dir. Clint Eastwood (Universal/Malpaso, 1973)
His Girl Friday, dir. Howard Hawks (Columbia, 1940)
How Green Was My Valley, dir. John Ford (20th C–Fox, 1941)
Humoresque, dir. Jean Negulesco (Warner Bros., 1947)
Hustler, The, dir. Robert Rossen (20th C–Fox, 1961)
I Remember Mama, dir. George Stevens (RKO, 1948)
I Was a Male War Bride, dir. Howard Hawks (20th C–Fox, 1959)
In the Heat of the Night, dir. Norman Jewison (United Artists/Mirisch, 1967)
Informer, The, dir. John Ford (RKO, 1935)
Island in the Sun, dir. Robert Rossen (20th C–Fox, 1957)
It Happened One Night, dir. Frank Capra (Columbia/Capra, 1934)
It's a Wonderful Life, dir. Frank Capra (Liberty Films/RKO, 1946)
Jazz Singer, The, dir. Alan Crosland (Warner Bros., 1927)
Man for All Seasons, A, dir. Fred Zinnemann (Columbia/Highland, 1966)
Man on a Tightrope, dir. Elia Kazan (20th C–Fox, 1952)
Man Who Shot Liberty Valance, The, dir. John Ford (Ford Prods./Paramount, 1962)
Mean Streets, dir. Martin Scorsese (Taplin–Perry–Scorsese, 1973)
Meet John Doe, dir. Frank Capra (Capra/Warner Bros., 1941)
Mission to Moscow, dir. Michael Curtiz (Warner Bros., 1943)
Moby Dick, dir. John Huston (Moulin Pictures/Warner Bros., 1956)
Modern Times, dir. Charles Chaplin (Chaplin/United Artists, 1936)
Mr. Deeds Goes to Town, dir. Frank Capra (Columbia/Capra, 1936)
Mr. Smith Goes to Washington, dir. Frank Capra (Columbia, 1939)
My Darling Clementine, dir. John Ford (20th C–Fox, 1946)
North Star, The, dir. (Samuel Goldwyn, 1943)
On the Waterfront, dir. Elia Kazan (Columbia/Sam Spiegel, 1954)
Only Angels Have Wings, dir. Howard Hawks (Columbia, 1939)
Ox-Bow Incident, The, dir. William Wellman (20th C–Fox, 1942)
Panic in the Streets, dir. Elia Kazan (20th C–Fox, 1950)
Penny Serenade, dir. George Stevens (Columbia, 1941)
People of the Cumberlands, The, dir. Elia Kazan (Frontier, 1937)
Pinky, dir. Elia Kazan (20th C–Fox, 1949)
Place in the Sun, A, dir. George Stevens (Paramount/Stevens, 1951)
Plainsman, The, dir. Cecil B. DeMille (Paramount, 1937)
Posse, dir. Mario Van Peebles (Paramount/Bryna, 1993)
Purple Rose of Cairo, The, Woody Allen (Rollins–Joffe/Orion, 1985)

Quiet Man, The, dir. John Ford (Republic/Argosy, 1952)
Raging Bull, dir. Martin Scorsese (United Artists/Chartoff–Winkler, 1979)
Red River, dir. Howard Hawks (United Artists/Monterey, 1948)
Rio Bravo, dir. Howard Hawks (Armada, 1959)
Scarface: Shame of the Nation, dir. Howard Hawks (Caddo, 1932)
Search, The, dir. Fred Zinnemann (MGM/Praesens Film, 1948)
Searchers, The, dir. John Ford (C. V. Whitney Pictures, 1956)
Shane, dir. George Stevens (Paramount, 1953)
Song of Russia, dir. Gregory Ratoff (MGM, 1943)
Splendor in the Grass, dir. Elia Kazan (Warner Bros./NBI, 1961)
Stagecoach, dir. John Ford (Walter Wanger Prods./United Artists, 1939)
Star Wars, dir. George Lucas (Lucasfilm/20th C–Fox, 1977)
Streetcar Named Desire, A, dir. Elia Kazan (Charles K. Feldman/Warner Bros., 1951)
Swing Time, dir. George Stevens (RKO, 1936)
Taxi Driver, dir. Martin Scorcese (Bill–Phillips/Italo–Judeo, 1976)
Tiger Shark, dir. Howard Hawks (Warner Bros., 1932)
To Have and Have Not, dir. Howard Hawks (Warner Bros., 1944)
Treasure of Sierra Madre, The, dir. John Huston (Warner Bros., 1947)
Tree Grows in Brooklyn, A, dir. Elia Kazan (20th C–Fox, 1945)
Triumph of the Will (*Triumph des Willens*), dir. Leni Riefenstahl (Ufa, Germany, 1935)
Twentieth Century, dir. Howard Hawks (Columbia, 1934)
2001: A Space Odyssey, Stanley Kubrick (MGM/Kubrick, UK, 1968)
Ulzana's Raid, dir. Robert Aldrich (Universal/Carter de Haven/Robert Aldrich, 1972)
Unconquered, dir. Cecil B. DeMille (Paramount, 1947)
Vertigo, dir. Alfred Hitchcock (Hitchcock/Paramount, 1958)
Viva Zapata!, dir. Elia Kazan (20th C–Fox, 1952)
Who's Afraid of Virginia Woolf?, dir. Mike Nichols (Warner Bros., 1966)
Why We Fight series, dir. Frank Capra (U.S. War Dept., 1942–5)
Wild Bunch, The, dir. Sam Peckinpah (Warner Bros./Seven Arts, 1969)
Wild River, dir. Elia Kazan (20th C–Fox, 1960)
Wind and the Lion, The, dir. John Milius (Columbia/MGM, 1975)
Woman of the Year, dir. George Stevens (MGM, 1942)
You Can't Take It with You, dir. Frank Capra (Columbia, 1938)
Young Mr. Lincoln, dir. John Ford (20th C–Fox, 1939)

INDEX